IDEAS AND IDEALS IN THE
NORTH EUROPEAN RENAISSANCE

By the same author

The Art of Memory
Theatre of the World
Giordano Bruno and the Hermetic Tradition
The Rosicrucian Enlightenment
Astraea: The Imperial Theme in the Sixteenth Century
The Valois Tapestries
Shakespeare's Last Plays
The Occult Philosophy in the Elizabethan Age
Lull and Bruno. Collected Essays, Volume I
Renaissance and Reform: The Italian Contribution.
Collected Essays, Volume II

Frances A. Yates

IDEAS AND IDEALS IN THE NORTH EUROPEAN RENAISSANCE

COLLECTED ESSAYS

VOLUME III

ROUTLEDGE & KEGAN PAUL

LONDON, BOSTON, MELBOURNE AND HENLEY

This collection first published in 1984
by Routledge & Kegan Paul plc

14 Leicester Square, London WC2H 7PH

9 Park Street, Boston, Mass. 02108, USA,

464 St Kilda Road, Melbourne,
Victoria 3004, Australia, and

Broadway House, Newtown Road,
Henley-on-Thames, Oxon RG9 1EN

Set in Garamond by
Input Typesetting Ltd, London
and printed in Great Britain by
Hartnoll Print
Bodmin, Cornwall

Library of Congress Cataloging in Publication Data

Yates, Frances Amelia.

Ideas and ideals in the North European renaissance.
(Collected Essays; v. 3)
Includes bibliographical references and index.
1. Renaissance—Addresses, essays, lectures. 2. Reformation—Addresses, essays, lectures.
3. Renaissance—Book reviews. 4. Reformation—Book reviews.
I. Title. II. Series: Yates, Frances Amelia. Collected essays; v. 3.
CB361.Y37 1984   940.2'1   83–24743
British Library CIP data available

ISBN 0–7102–0184–2

CONTENTS

[v]

CONTENTS

[vi]

CONTENTS

EUROPE

CONTENTS

ILLUSTRATIONS

EDITORIAL NOTE

THIS THIRD and final volume of *Collected Essays* by Frances Yates has, like the second volume, been put together in fulfilment of her plans. The choice of materials for inclusion is, however, ours. To the previously printed essays which make up the bulk of the book, we have added at the end a selection, made by J. N. Hillgarth, of some autobiographical fragments intended by Dame Frances for working up into publishable form. We have also added a list of her published writings. We hope that we have thus made clear that our aim in putting together these volumes has been not only to make available in a convenient and compendious form the articles and reviews of Frances Yates, which might otherwise not be easy to consult, but also to give some idea of the intellectual formation and development of a remarkable and invigorating scholar.

In acknowledging responsibility for the selection of materials for this volume, we must say that we have also added titles to certain reviews. Titles of Dame Frances's contributions to *Encounter, New Statesman*, the *New York Review of Books*, the *Times Higher Education Supplement* and the *Times Literary Supplement* were composed by the respective sub-editors.

The journals named, and *The Book Collector*, the *English Historical Review, History, The Listener, Modern Language Review*, the *Review of English Studies*, Johns Hopkins University Press and Phaidon Press have generously given permission to reprint essays and reviews which were first published by them.

We are grateful also to the following for permission to illustrate objects in their ownership or charge: the Musée Granet, Palais de Malte, Aix-en-Provence, the Courtauld Institute Galleries, the Public Record Office, the Victoria and Albert Museum, the National Trust, Dunster Castle, and the Earl of Radnor, Longford Castle.

Professor Stephen Rees-Jones and Professor Marion L. Kuntz have kindly allowed us to reprint brief contributions by them in items 1 and 18 respectively. We owe special thanks to Angela Barlow, Anne Marie Meyer, Judith Wardman (who read the proofs and made the index), and D. P. Walker (for advice on selection).

London, August 1983   J. N. Hillgarth
                                                       J. B. Trapp

ENGLAND

Chapter One

THE ALLEGORICAL PORTRAITS OF
SIR JOHN LUTTRELL*

ONE OF THE most puzzling of sixteenth-century English portraits
is the picture at Dunster Castle, the seat of the Luttrell family, of
a naked man wading in an angry sea (Plate 1).[1] Behind him is a
sinking ship from which boatloads of people are escaping; the face
of a drowned corpse floats near him. He raises his right arm with
clenched fist into a world of allegory, sharply separated from the
scene of storm and desolation by the dark rim of the cloud within
which it is set. A female figure bearing an olive branch of peace
and surrounded by groups of other allegories bends down to
caress the arm of the determined character in the sea. The allegory
in the sky seems to form a picture in itself which is only very
clumsily linked by the incongruous gesture of the man in the sea
with the picture of shipwreck and storm of which he forms a part.

On the hero's wrists there are narrow bracelets. These contain
Latin inscriptions; on the right wrist, *Nec flexit lucrum 1550;* on
the left wrist, *Nec friget discrimen.* 'Neither swayed by love of
gain nor deterred by danger.'

More obvious are the inscriptions on the rock (Plate 3a) which
rises from the sea in the foreground. These are as follows:

MORE THEN THE ROCK AMYDYS THE RAGING SEAS
THE CONSTANT HERT NO DANGER DREDDYS NOR FEARYS.
.SIL.

* Published in *Essays in the History of Art presented to Rudolf Wittkower,* 1967.

[3]

Effigiem renouare tuam fortissime miles
Ingens me meritum fecit amorq[ue] tui.
Nam nisi curasse haeredem scribere fratrem
Hei tua contingerant praedia nulla mihi.
.1591. G.L.

1550
HE

The couplet in English at the top suggests the rock in the stormy seas as an emblem of the courage and determination of the man in the sea. The bottom inscription gives the date 1550 (also given on the right bracelet) and the monogram HE, composed of the letters H and E. The middle inscription in Latin, dated 1591, was added in that year by 'G.L.' or George Luttrell. A possible rendering of the Latin inscription of 1591 is as follows:

.SIL. [probably referring to 'Sir John Luttrell']²
Your great merit and my love for you cause me, brave soldier, to renew your portrait.
For had you not taken care to make your brother your heir, none of your possessions would have become mine.
.1591. G.L. [George Luttrell]

Sir John Luttrell was George Luttrell's uncle; he left all his landed property by will to his brother, George Luttrell's father.³ Hence there can be no doubt that George Luttrell's inscription refers to his uncle, Sir John Luttrell, through whose will the property has descended to him. And since he says that he is renewing or restoring the 'effigy' of this uncle, it is to be assumed that the subject of the picture, the man in the sea, is a portrait of Sir John Luttrell.

There is another version of this picture (Plate 2), now in the possession of the Courtauld Institute. It was bought for Viscount Lee at Christie's on 22 July 1932, at the sale of property from Badmondisfield Hall in Suffolk belonging to the Bromley family.⁴ Hence it reached the Courtauld Institute as one of Lee's pictures. The fact that a picture, usually described as a copy or replica of the Dunster picture, was in the possession of Lee and later of the Courtauld Institute has been generally known and is mentioned in catalogue entries concerning the Dunster picture. But no attempt was made to compare the two pictures until December 1960, when, at my request, the Courtauld picture was subjected to a technical examination by Professor Rees-Jones, and was also technically compared with the Dunster picture, kindly sent for examination by Colonel Walter Luttrell. It was thus possible to see the two pictures side by side in Professor Rees-Jones's studio, and possible for a technical examination of both to be made under the best conditions. It is through the kind co-operation of Colonel Luttrell and of Professor Anthony Blunt in arranging for the examination of the pictures that I am able to use for the first time in this article the evidence of the Courtauld picture in solving the problems of this strange allegorical portrait. Professor Rees-Jones's technical analysis of the two pictures is given in an Appendix[5] to this article, and is the basis of the following remarks.

The two pictures are on panels of approximately the same size but the technical evidence shows that they are not an original and a replica from the same workshop. They are not by the same hands. The Courtauld picture is the work of two painters. In the allegorical group in the Courtauld picture 'the paint . . . has been used with the greatest assurance to model forms such as the nude'. The figure of Sir John Luttrell, however, 'shows techniques similar to English or Flemish sixteenth-century portraits in general'. In short, the allegorical group in the Courtauld picture is by a mannerist painter of considerable expertise; the rest of the picture is by another hand.

The Dunster picture, on the contrary, is quite homogeneous, painted throughout by one hand. When the Peace allegory in the Dunster picture is compared with the Courtauld version of it, it becomes apparent that the Dunster version has omitted several details and has, in general, lost the firm moulding of the forms and the high quality of the painting in the Courtauld version. The shift of the figures to the right in the Dunster version has involved a distortion of the torso of Peace. The colours in the allegorical group in the Courtauld picture are 'brilliant . . . and in keeping with the mannerist style, whereas in the Dunster picture they are more subdued'. The conclusion to which the technical examination unmistakably points is that the Courtauld picture is the original and the Dunster picture a copy of it. The Courtauld picture is in bad condition, and the report suggests that 'It is not inconceivable that the onset of this deterioration at an early date led to the commission of the Dunster version in 1591, as the inscription suggests'. In short it is now evident that George Luttrell did not restore or 'renovate' the Dunster version of the picture. The 'only restoration to be seen [in the picture] is modern'. His renovation consisted in having a copy made of an already existing picture, painted in 1550, the picture now in the Courtauld Institute Galleries.

The inscriptions on the rock 'have been retouched in both paintings' but the Courtauld version of the rock (Plate 3b) shows only the English couplet at the top (which has been clumsily restored, introducing the mistake 'amlodys' for 'amydys') and '1550 HE' at the bottom. In the Dunster version (Plate 3a) the space between the two inscriptions was utilized by George Luttrell for his inscription of 1591.

From the revelations made by the technical examination and comparison of the two pictures, it follows that, whilst the inscription of 1591 on the Dunster picture gives evidence of the identity of the subject as Sir John Luttrell, any investigation of the possible origins and meaning of this very curious allegorical portrait should be based on the Courtauld version.

The general level of subject painting in England in the reign of Edward VI was archaic. Through what combination of circumstances arose the phenomenon that an allegory in French Renaissance style, executed by a mannerist-trained hand, should adorn the portrait of an Englishman painted in the year 1550? The search for an answer to this question involves an excursion into history, into the dark and troubled era of the reign of Edward VI, with its ill-starred war in Scotland, its conflict with Henri II of France over the town of Boulogne, ending in the peace treaty of Boulogne in 1550.

In 1547, Edward VI became King of England and Edward Seymour, Duke of Somerset, was appointed Protector during his minority.[6] Amongst the vigorous steps which the Protector took in this year was the expedition, led by himself, to Scotland. Its ostensible object was to force a marriage between Mary, Queen of Scots, and Edward VI, a project which had been mooted in the preceding reign. A great army marched to the north, a mass of excited, fanatical adventurers who were to wreak great destruction on the churches and abbeys of the north. Their iconoclastic mood is vividly reflected in the diary of William Patten.[7] A member of this army was Sir John Luttrell, of whom Patten speaks with approval as a brave captain.

The army was supported from the sea by a fleet of ships of which the admiral in command was Edward Fiennes, Lord Clinton. Clinton's navy made contact with the army at Berwick and thereafter moved up along the Scottish coast in close contact with the land forces.[8] On 10 September 1547, the English and Scottish armies met at Pinkie, or Musselburgh, on the Firth of Forth. In this battle, Luttrell distinguished himself as leader of a successful charge of three hundred men.[9] The victory of Pinkie-Musselburgh was, however, due to 'combined operations' between land and sea forces. Clinton's fleet was drawn in close to the shore during the battle, and the guns of his men-of-war came into action. The Scots found themselves pinned between the land forces and the ships and the result was a resounding victory for the Lord Protector and his men. This victory was the foundation of Admiral Clinton's reputation, for, as Fuller says:

> The masterpiece of his [Clinton's] service was in Musselburgh field, in the reign of Edward VI, and that battle against the Scots. Some will wonder what a fish should do on dry land, what use an admiral in a land fight. The English kept close to the shore, under the shelter of their ships, the ordnance from the ships at first did all.[10]

This metaphor of the 'fish on dry land' for the combined operations of the battle of Pinkie-Musselburgh is worth bearing in mind, since this was the battle in which Sir John Luttrell distinguished himself – on dry land, not with the fishes.

The Protector did not follow up his victory, for owing to difficulties at home and abroad he withdrew the main force of his army from Scotland, leaving only small bodies of men to garrison the places taken. Now began the misfortunes of Sir John Luttrell, who suffered long sieges with his garrisons, first on Inchcolm Island in the Firth of Forth and later at Broughty Craig.[11] He was placed in command at Inchcolm Island a week after the battle of Pinkie-Musselburgh. There was an abbey on the little island or 'rock' of Inchcolm, formerly inhabited by Augustinian canons, which now became Luttrell's headquarters. The idea of garrisoning this island was to control shipping in the Firth of Forth, but Luttrell and his men became a source of anxiety to the English commanders, since they were besieged on the island by enemy forces and it was difficult to reinforce or provision them. Instead of being able to control the navigation in the Firth, Sir John Luttrell was harried by Scottish ships and boats. Eventually he and his men were evacuated from the island by a vessel of the fleet, the *Mary Hamborough*, and had a very stormy voyage in her to Broughty Craig where another siege, and further adventures, most of them unfortunate, awaited them. Later on, Luttrell was captured and imprisoned. He was still in prison in Scotland in March 1550.[12]

Admiral Clinton, however, not long after the battle of Pinkie-Musselburgh, was moved from Scotland to other spheres. He was made governor of Boulogne.

Boulogne had been captured by Henry VIII in 1544 as part of an offensive war against Scotland and France in which he was then engaged. But when the Protector sent Clinton to Boulogne, this was more in the nature of a defensive policy. His rash campaign in Scotland had aroused much ill-feeling in France; the young Mary, Queen of Scots, was sent abroad to the French court to safeguard her against English designs for her capture. The Protector's revolutionary measures at home had aroused violent opposition and were throwing the country into a state of utter confusion; it was because of these many dangers at home and abroad that he had been obliged to withdraw his army from Scotland. Henri II of France saw that England's embarrassments might provide an opportunity for the recovery of Boulogne and he began to make extensive preparations for attacking the town.[13]

In September 1549, war with France broke out, and at about the same time England was further convulsed by the overthrow of Protector Somerset, which meant that the Boulogne garrison could expect little help. The French soon began to make heavy attacks on the town, which was closely invested. Clinton took his full share of the hardships, and held out during the winter of 1549-50, though without reinforcements and faced by growing difficulties and dangers. On 20 February 1550, a truce was concluded and peace terms began to be discussed. By a treaty made with Henry VIII in 1546, it had been agreed that England was to retain Boulogne for eight years, or until the debt to Henry VIII incurred by François I had been paid. In 1550, there were still four more of these eight years to run, but the French were determined to have the town at once, though they agreed to pay a sum of money for it. This sum was to wipe out all former debts and to end once and for all the English occupation of Boulogne.

On 24 March 1550, a treaty[14] was concluded between France and England, or rather between the kings of those countries, Henri II and Edward VI. The distinctive feature of the treaty was that Henri II agreed to pay four thousand crowns for Boulogne in two instalments. Half of this sum was to be paid immediately on the conclusion of the treaty, the remaining half in the following August. In return for this the English agreed to evacuate Boulogne within six weeks of the day of the signature of the treaty, and to give up all the munitions of war which they had in the town.

Provision was also made in the treaty for the evacuation or razing of the fortresses and places held by the English in Scotland. This treaty therefore marked the end of the Scottish war, the only result of which was – in spite of its initial success – that the English had to give up all that they had gained there and, in addition, to surrender Boulogne to the French.

The kings of France and England sent commissioners to Boulogne to conclude the treaty. One of these was Gaspard de Coligny, representing the Duc de Montmorency who had led the war in the Boulonnais on the French side. This Coligny was none other than the man later to become famous as a Huguenot leader; at this date, however, he was not yet either a Protestant or an admiral. The commissioners for the English side were John Russell, Earl of Bedford, Lord William Paget, Sir William Petre and Sir John Mason. [15] According to Grafton's *Chronicle*, Paget, Petre, and Mason crossed to Calais on 7 February and went on from there to meet the French commissioners at Boulogne, where 'a certayne house was newly erected for the sayd treatie to be had'. [16] This suggests one of those temporary buildings erected for the meetings of monarchs and decorated by artists, and though the Boulogne meeting was ungraced by royalty, Grafton's remark indicates that some effort may have been made to give it dignity. The English present might have reflected on the fall of their country's prestige since the days of Henry VIII and the Field of the Cloth of Gold. The great triangle – France, England, and the Emperor – in which England had played an important part in those days not so long ago was represented at Boulogne, for all these three were interested in the treaty (the Emperor Charles V at a distance[17]), but now England was a weak and defeated country surrendering Boulogne to the commissioners.

As always in such documents, the hard facts of the terms are masked in the treaty by a noble and inflated preamble. This is of importance, for it gives an idea of the kind of official imagery, or state allegories, in which this peace treaty was presented.

The kings of France and England, states the Treaty of Boulogne, are now to be joined in friendship, and peace is to be established between them throughout all ages to come. The evils and miseries of war will be banished eternally in this perpetual peace. *Pax,*

Amicitia, Confederatio, Unio, Liga, and *Summa Concordia* will forever link together these two illustrious kings and their heirs and successors. These allegories are later repeated, and the treaty is throughout described as a treaty of *Pax* and *Amicitia.* Then come the hard facts. France is to pay 2,000 gold crowns down, and another 2,000 in August. England is to evacuate Boulogne within six weeks and to leave in the town all the munitions of war. The fortresses in Scotland enumerated are to be yielded or destroyed.[18]

Boulogne was duly handed over on 25 April 1550, and the document which is the French receipt for the town exists in the Public Record Office.[19] It states that François de Montmorency and Gaspard de Coligny acknowledge having received the town of Boulogne and all the munitions of war in it from the hands of 'Messieurs Edouard Seigneur de Clincton, Richard Cotton, & Lyenard Bekoits,[20] & autres ayans Pouvoir specials du dit Seigneur Roy d'Angleterre'. Since Montmorency was not actually there (as the receipt states) and since Clinton as Governor of Boulogne would head the English commissioners in the transaction, it may be said that Coligny and Clinton were the chief actors in this drama.

Clinton probably left Boulogne, with the English garrison, on the day of its surrender and came over to England. There great honours and promotions awaited him, for it would seem that, although the surrender of Boulogne was actually a defeat, Clinton came out of it with honour because of his long and heroic defence of the town. On 4 May he was thanked by the Privy Council for his services, and taken by members of the Council into the presence of the King, who also thanked him and decreed that he should be made Lord High Admiral of England and one of the Privy Council.[21] The office of Lord High Admiral was a great one, the powers and prerogatives of which had recently been redefined.[22] Clinton was to hold it, with one short intermission, through the succeeding reigns of Mary and Elizabeth until his death in 1585. He first achieved it in this hour of his triumph in 1550. On 11 May the Privy Council decreed that, since Clinton's income was not sufficient to maintain his new office, he should be given land and estates 'forasmuch as his service at Bulloigne deserved notable consideration'.[23] Clinton was the hero of the hour.

The subject of the Treaty of Boulogne remained much in the public eye all through the summer of 1550, as anyone who cares to read through the contemporary documents will discover. In June, French ambassadors, one of whom was Coligny, came to London to receive the ratification by Edward VI of the treaty. They were met by a galley and two pinnaces at the mouth of the Thames which conducted their ship up the river to their lodgings. The next day they were escorted to an audience with the King by notable personages, amongst whom was the new Lord High Admiral, and on the following day the King took the oath of ratification. Entertainments were provided for the ambassadors, hunting parties, banquets, and a spectacle on the river, and on their departure they were given gifts of gold plate and jewels.[24]

Thus the year 1550, the date given on the portrait of Sir John Luttrell, was a year in which the Treaty of Boulogne was the major event. Eternal *Pax* and *Amicitia* linking the kings of France and England was the official theme, and the basic fact was the achievement of this Peace and Friendship by the payment of a large sum of money *in two instalments*. Moreover this Peace and Friendship was signalized by a French embassy to England for the ratification of the treaty. For a brief moment, the isolation from the Continent of the England of Edward VI was broken.

This might surely be the moment in which the phenomenon of a Peace allegory in Renaissance style painted by a mannerist hand in the England of Edward VI could be accounted for by the historical situation. With this thought in our minds, let us now turn to examine in more detail the Peace allegory in the portrait of Sir John Luttrell.

An admirable comparison for the central figure of Peace was pointed out by R. Wittkower in *British Art and the Mediterranean*,[25] where he illustrated a figure of Peace of the School of Fontainebleau (Plate 5a), now in the Museum of Aix-en-Provence, beside the Luttrell portrait (in the Dunster version). The graceful semi-nude figure of the School of Fontainebleau Peace bears in her left hand an olive branch; on her right a dove is perched. She wears a jewelled head-band, and a pearl drop hangs from her ear. Compare with this the semi-nude Peace of the Luttrell allegory, with her jewelled head-band and pearl ear-ring and bearing her olive branch. The comparison becomes even more striking when it is made with the Courtauld version of the allegory (Plate 4), with its more erect pose.

On either side of the Luttrell Peace are groups of other allegorical figures. The group on Peace's left contains a savage-looking horse into whose mouth a female figure is placing a bit. This bit, very distinctly painted in the Courtauld version, has been lost in the Dunster version. On Peace's right are two female figures, closely linked together by a loving embrace.

The group of the horse and the woman can be very easily explained as Venus curbing the wrath of Mars. The horse can often be the symbol of *Bellum*,[26] and this particularly fierce horse looks particularly warlike. The half-reclining Venus is curbing his rage by placing the bit in his mouth, at the same time softening with her gentle influence the martial helmet and breastplate on which she leans. The figures behind the Mars and Venus group seem to be Minerva (in the helmet) and the Three Graces symbolizing the return of peaceful cultural activities now that war is curbed.

the two ladies behind Peace's right shoulder are expressive of *Amicitia*. One places her right hand in loving friendship on the shoulder of the other, who looks back towards her. And this other has in her left hand a bag of money, whilst with her right hand she fumbles in a purse for more. *Two instalments.* The money which the King of France gave to the King of England for Boulogne was paid in two instalments. This detail of the two money-bags or purses, always noted as a puzzling feature of the allegory, is the detail which makes it absolutely certain that the Peace allegory here depicted refers to the Treaty of Boulogne. The theme of the allegory, as of the peace treaty, is *Pax* and *Amicitia*. The theme of *Pax* is stated in the central figure of Peace; *Amicitia* or eternal friendship between the kings of France and England is symbolized by the two female figures linked in friendship, one of whom is paying the other a sum of money in two instalments. This Peace is eternally banishing war between the two countries, symbolized by the bridling of the war horse by the gentle hand of Venus. *Pax* and *Amicitia* are the theme of the whole allegory, linking the two women engaged in the money transaction, expressed in the dominance of Venus over Mars, whilst Peace herself, as she lets her left hand fall on the arm of the hero in the sea, passes on to him the current of peace subduing war which is running between all the allegorical ladies.

The Peace allegory is personal to Sir John Luttrell only in the sense that the peace treaty of Boulogne meant for him the end of the campaigning in Scotland in which he had been engaged. All its details can be explained as in no sense personal to him (various attempts have been made to explain the money-bags in relation to

Luttrell). They can all be explained as an allegory of the Treaty of Boulogne, of the eternal peace and friendship established between the kings of France and England by the payment by Henri II to Edward VI of four thousand crowns in two instalments.

The Peace allegory in the Luttrell portrait is probably an echo of official imagery about the treaty current in 1550 when all the talk was of this peace, and when French ambassadors came to England to ratify it with the English King.

There was a tradition about the official imagery for peace treaties between France and England, and some study of the iconography of this tradition can throw further light on the allegory in the Luttrell picture.

The Treaty of Boulogne of 1550 was not the first treaty of the sixteenth century by which France and England had sworn to maintain an eternal peace. Such a treaty was made between Henry VIII and François I in 1527. There are two copies in the Public Record Office[27] of the ratification of this treaty by the French King, both of which are illuminated. One copy (Plate 6a) shows in its top margin a graceful little figure of *Pax Eterna*, with her branch, standing between the royal arms of France and England which she is linking together in amity. In the side margin are emblems of peace and love; a dove, a peacock (the bird of Juno, goddess of marriages) with tail outspread, two mating birds. In the lower margin, shepherds are dancing with a maiden to the tune of a piper; flocks and herds, trees laden with fruit, illustrate the blessings of peace. In the other copy of the same treaty (Plate 6b), another charming *Pax Eterna* stands between the two royal arms, and the capital F of 'Franciscus' (François I) is formed out of a crowned salamander. This creature was, of course, the badge or device of François I and appears in other Anglo-French treaties contracted by him.

Turning now again to the two ladies symbolizing the peace between France and England in the Luttrell allegory, we find certain details in them now explained from these earlier illuminated treaties. A peacock with outspread tail is shown behind France with the bags of money. The peacock with outspread tail in the margin of the 1527 treaty is there shown in a context of other emblems of marriage or peace between the two countries. This explains its appearance in the Luttrell allegory, where it does not mean that the lady beside it is Juno (she is not at all like a Juno). It appears as a marriage emblem, a love and amity emblem, symbolizing the loving marriage between France and England in a *Pax Eterna*, just as it does in the 1527 treaty.

France with the money-bags in the Luttrell allegory has a crescent moon in her hair (the Dunster copyist left out this detail[28] which is so conspicuous in the Courtauld version). This may be explained, by comparison with the device of a salamander symbolizing François I in the 1527 treaty, as a reference to a French royal device. The device of Henri II was, of course, a crescent moon. The crescent moon in the hair of France with the money-bags relates her to the present King of France, Henri II, who paid the money to the King of England. The peacock of Juno and the crescent of Diana may also be intended to introduce allusions to those goddesses into the Olympian allegory as a whole, but the two female figures with whom they are associated are neither a Juno nor a Diana. They represent the kings of France and England in amicable embrace. These two ladies engaged in their amicable money transaction are modern Renaissance allegories replacing the arms of the two kings or countries between which the *Pax Eterna* of the 1527 treaty stands. And how remarkably, too, *Pax Eterna* herself has been modernized, transformed from the still medieval and modestly clothed little Eternal Peaces of the 1527 treaty into a Renaissance nude! And the humble little rustic scene of happy shepherds enjoying the blessings of peace transforms into a Renaissance Mars and Venus allegory. But all the elements of a traditional Anglo-French treaty are present in the Luttrell picture though expressed in the new classicizing manner of the Renaissance.

The original of the Treaty of Boulogne, signed by Edward VI, exists in the Public Record Office;[29] also the ratification of the treaty by Henri II, with his signature.[30] If the precedent of 1527 had been followed, the latter document – the French ratification of the treaty – would have been illuminated with some figure of *Pax Eterna* and other allegories. But unfortunately the ratification of the Treaty of Boulogne is not illuminated, though it is adorned with a magnificent impression of the royal seal of France which depends from it.

Nevertheless, the allegory in the Luttrell portrait strongly suggests that an official allegorical representation, or representations, of this new treaty of *Pax Eterna*, expressed in the style of the French Renaissance, probably existed. One may fancy behind the Luttrell allegory the ghost of some long-vanished picture, brought by the French ambassadors for presentation to Edward

VI. The 'Peace' in the Museum of Aix-en-Provence (Plate 5a) is so extraordinarily close to the Peace of the Luttrell allegory as seen in the Courtauld version (much closer than to the Dunster version with which Rudolf Wittkower compared it) that one can imagine what such a presentation picture in the style of the School of Fontainebleau may have been like. And there seems good reason to suppose that the allegory in the Courtauld version of the Luttrell portrait is actually painted by a French or Italian artist, who had perhaps come to England with the embassy.[31]

Sir John Luttrell, when he induced a mannerist artist to reproduce on his portrait the official allegories of the Treaty of Boulogne, preserved for us an echo of the influence on art of the Anglo-French rapprochement of 1550 of which no other traces survive.

We have now to turn our attention to the main body of the picture, to this bearded man wading naked in the sea with his right arm upraised into the Peace allegory. We have the word of George Luttrell, in his inscription on the Dunster version, that this is intended to be a portrait of Sir John Luttrell. But why did this eccentric man choose to have himself represented in this extraordinary manner?

In the Victoria and Albert Museum there is a remarkable example (Plate 5b, c) of one of those jewels or pendants formed of a large or 'baroque' pearl which were fashionable in the latter half of the sixteenth century. They are usually of Italian workmanship, though some are Flemish-Italianate. The specimen in the Victoria and Albert Museum was bought in India by George Canning, when he was Viceroy in the early nineteenth century, hence the name by which it is always known, 'The Canning Jewel'. Its history before Canning acquired it in India is unknown. There is no documentary backing for the legend that it was a gift from a Medici prince to one of the Mogul emperors.[32]

The Canning Jewel represents a Triton, or merman, a figure with a bearded face whose body is formed by a single 'baroque' pearl, ending in a tail of coloured enamel. The head and arms are of white enamel, and an enamelled shield is held in the left hand. In his upraised right hand this pearly Triton holds a club in the form of a jawbone. On the wrist of the firmly clenched hand which holds the club he wears a narrow bracelet, and higher up on the right arm a wider bracelet, the function of which is to conceal the join of the enamel arm to the pearl body. The whole jewel is in the form of a pendant, with three large pearl drops depending from it.

The Triton of the jewel has affinities with those fierce sea gods, half horse and half fish, who wield fish-bone weapons in their conflicts, as depicted, for instance, in Mantegna's famous engraving of the *Battle of the Sea Gods*. Nevertheless there is also in the jewel a combination of Samson with classical marine mythology. The jawbone weapon recalls the jawbone of an ass with which Samson smote the Philistines.[33] The shield in the form of an animal head with widely stretched jaws may allude to another of Samson's exploits, the rending of the lion's jaws.[34] The two exploits – the smiting of the Philistines with the jawbone and the rending of the lion – are very commonly alluded to in representations of Samson,[35] but I know of no other example of Samson exploits associated with a Triton. This curious mingling of Biblical and classical to form a strong man of the sea seems peculiar to the Canning Jewel. It might suit a successful naval commander or admiral, but since the early history of the jewel before it left Europe is so totally obscure no suggestion about for whom it might have been made can be hazarded.

Comparison of the man in the sea of the Luttrell portrait with the Canning Jewel causes a shock of surprise. The Canning Jewel has a bearded portrait face; so has the man in the sea. The Triton of the Jewel wears a wrist bracelet very like those of the man in the sea, whose knotted scarf is worn at the point on the arm where the Triton wears an arm bracelet, to conceal the joint of his arm with the pearl. The Triton's body anatomy is rather indistinct, owing to the convolutions of the pearl; so is the body anatomy of the man in the sea, rising pearly white from the waves. The latter's arm poses, too, are rather unnatural – more like stiff enamel arms jointed to a pearl than arms studied from the human form. The Triton of the jewel has a weapon in his clenched right fist. This must surely be the explanation of the raised clenched fist of the man in the sea, that it held an invisible weapon.

The fierce Old Testament weapon which the Triton of the Canning Jewel wields in his strong right hand – Samson's weapon wherewith he smote the Philistines – would very well suit Luttrell, who had been one of the fanatically Protestant and image-smashing army which marched to Scotland under the Protector. However, owing to the indistinctness of the early history of the Canning Jewel, it is quite impossible to know whether Luttrell or his artist could have seen it in England in 1550. But something of the kind they surely must have seen, or known of, and the jewel explains the kind of allegorical character that Luttrell was aiming at for himself – a strong man of the sea. The man in the Luttrell portrait is not a wader in the sea; he is a creature of the sea with an invisible fish's tail, a Triton, naked with the allegorical nakedness of a water divinity.

Since Luttrell was a soldier, and not a sailor, a land captain and not a sea admiral, this marine role does not seem to suit him very well. The person whom it would have suited would have been Admiral Clinton, the hero of the land and sea battle of Pinkie-Musselburgh, the 'fish on dry land' of those combined operations, the governor of Boulogne and rewarded with the office of Lord High Admiral of England for his services in its defence – the great hero of the hour at the time of the Treaty of Boulogne. One wonders whether Luttrell, who evidently had a flair for picking up public official imagery and applying it to himself, picked up some current allegorical glorification of Clinton and applied it to himself.[36] After all, he had fought at Pinkie-Musselburgh, though on land not at sea, and his later operations on Inchcolm Island had been partly amphibious, involving minor naval engagements in the unsuccessful effort to keep the Firth of Forth open to English shipping.

At any rate, the striking similarities between the Canning Jewel and the Luttrell portrait give a new insight into that portrait as an allegory. We now understand that Luttrell presents himself as a fighting sea divinity, that he himself is an allegory, and one which he attempts to connect with the allegory in the sky through the raised right hand raised into the sphere of Peace. The hand has dropped its weapon and Peace's gesture is one of restraint, complementary to that of Venus as she bridles the horse of war and lays her restraining hand on the armour and the helmet. There are no Neptunes or water divinities in the allegory in the sky. This aspect of Olympus is represented by Luttrell himself. An attempt has been made to connect the Peace allegory with the allegorical portrait of Luttrell by representing him as a warlike water divinity restrained by the hand of Peace.

Or, in other words, the Scottish war is over and Luttrell's part in it is over. The *Pax* and *Amicitia* of the Treaty of Boulogne put a term to his warlike efforts. Though the juxtaposition of the curious figure in the sea with the civilized goddesses in the sky has a barbaric and ludicrous effect, one can see that an effort has been made to integrate mythologically those parts of the picture which seem at first sight quite disparate – the peace allegory in the sky and the allegorical portrait.

But artistically there is no integration. As the eye travels from the competently painted torso of Peace to the vague anatomy of the man in the sea it becomes ever more evident that these two parts of the picture were painted by different hands.

We now come to the last of the three elements which make up the parts of the picture – the storm in the sky, the foundering man-of-war, the terrified crew leaving the ship in boats, the drowned man floating in the sea. These scenes may be partly reminiscent of real experiences in the Scottish war, and partly an allegory of the storms and disasters of War now ended by Peace. The ship flies the flag of St George. She is therefore an English ship; her guns are clearly visible (Plate 7a, b). One of the most terrible of Luttrell's war experiences must have been the evacuation of himself and garrison from Inchcolm Island in the ship *Mary Hamborough* during a frightful storm. The ship was not wrecked, as here, but the scene perhaps recalls the evacuation and some tragedy of drowning which accompanied it.[37] (George Luttrell perhaps put some other meaning into the corpse in the sea, since the Dunster version of the picture elaborates it into a portrait.[38]) If this is the experience reflected by the storm and the shipwreck, these would yet still be an allegory – an allegory of those disasters of the later part of the Scottish war, those useless attempts to hold the places taken with insufficient garrisons – efforts now terminated by the Treaty of Boulogne with its stipulation that the fortresses held by the English in Scotland are to be delivered up or destroyed.

The storms of war are over. Peace dawns with the Treaty of Boulogne. The hero's hand is empty of its weapon. Sir John Luttrell celebrates his part in the campaign with this extraordinary portrait in which personal reminiscence mingles with public and official allegory to form a remarkable record of the mood of the year 1550 in England.

MORE THEN THE ROCK AMYDYS THE RAGING SEAS
THE CONSTANT HERT NO DANGER DREDDYS NOR FEARYS.

The eccentric, excitable, fanatical man has come through the storms of the dangerous years, and he celebrates his own rather small part in their events by a portrait in which he identifies himself with great state allegories.

The monogrammatist 'HE', who signs the Luttrell portrait on the rock, also signed, in the same year 1550, a portrait of Thomas Wyndham (Plate 8) now in the possession of the Earl of Radnor at Longford Castle.[39] On the barrels of the gun slung over his shoulder are the sitter's initials 'T.W.' and the inscription 'Aetatis sui XLII. MDL. HE'.

Wyndham and Luttrell were related, Wyndham being Luttrell's uncle.[40] And, like Luttrell, Wyndham had been through the Scottish campaign. In 1547, he was appointed vice-admiral, under Clinton, of the fleet which went to Scotland. He thus had some share in the glory of Pinkie-Musselburgh. He distinguished himself also at the subsequent siege of Haddington, and by a good deal of destruction of abbeys and other ecclesiastical property. He was still in Scotland in March 1550, negotiating for the release of Luttrell,[41] but returned to England later in the same year.

We have thus to picture these two, Luttrell and Wyndham, nephew and uncle, both just disbanded from the Scottish wars, both repairing to the 'HE' studio to have commemorative portraits of themselves painted, with results strangely different. The 'HE' portrait of Wyndham is a straight portrait and a good one. His exploits in the Scottish war are perhaps alluded to in the background scene, where the tents of a military camp seem to be stationed in the neighbourhood of some large church or abbey. But there is nothing allegorical in the solid presentation of this tough guy. How different from the marine fantasies of Luttrell and the allegories with which he linked them! The association between Wyndham and Luttrell continued after the peace and after the painting of their portraits, for they organized a privateering expedition to Morocco.[42] The expedition was ready to start in July 1551, but on the 10th of that month Luttrell died at Greenwich of the sweating sickness, which was very prevalent in that year. He was about thirty-one years of age. His portrait was thus his swan song. Wyndham continued with the project and duly sailed from Portsmouth on this new adventure, but died on one of his later voyages in 1553.

Amongst the portraits listed in the Lumley Inventory of 1590, a list of works of art said then to be in the possession of Lord Lumley, are the following:

Of Sir John Lutterel, who died of the sweat in K. Edw: 6
tyme.
Of Mr. Thomas Wyndeham drowned in the sea returninge
from Ginney.[43]

(These entries do not follow one another immediately, as given
here.) The Inventory gives no name of artist for either of these
pictures. The portrait of Wyndham can be traced from the Lumley
collection through subsequent owners to its present owner; it was
therefore the portrait of Wyndham signed 'HE'.[44] No such definite
history of the portrait of Luttrell mentioned in the Inventory has
been traced but it is assumed to be the allegorical portrait signed
'HE' in the version now in the Courtauld Galleries.[45]

In modern catalogue entries concerning the Dunster version
of the portrait of Luttrell – the only version hitherto seriously
considered – it is confidently stated that the picture is by 'Hans
Eworth'. This statement rests on the dubious arguments with
which Lionel Cust supported his assertion, in an article published
in 1912,[46] that the monogram 'HE' represents the initials of a
Flemish artist settled in England called Hans Eworth. Cust's
article has been enormously influential and his explanation of the
monogram has been accepted for more than half a century.

Cust noticed that three portraits listed in the Lumley Inventory
are there said to be by 'Haunce Eworth'. He discovered by
research among documents that a Flemish painter of this name,
or of something like this name under various spellings, was consecutively in England from about 1545 onwards. He thereupon
published his article of 1912 in which he asserted that all pictures
signed 'HE' are by Hans Eworth. It is strange that the uncritical
element in Cust's arguments was not noticed. Not one of the
three portraits assigned to 'Haunce Eworth' in the Lumley Inventory has been traced[47] (though one of them may be reflected in a
seventeenth-century copy). There is therefore no work of art
known to be by this artist from which his style can be known.
When 'the style of Hans Eworth' is spoken of, this means the style
of pictures signed 'HE' which Cust supposed to be by Eworth. He
assumes that because some portraits in the Lumley Inventory are
said to be by 'Haunce Eworth' therefore other portraits in the
list are also by this artist. The Inventory mentions portraits of
Wyndham and Luttrell but does not say that these portraits are
by Eworth; it gives no name of artist for them. It was Cust's
assumption that the Inventory means that these portraits are by

1 *Portrait of Sir John Luttrell.* National Trust, Dunster Castle

2 *Portrait of Sir John Luttrell* (before restoration). Courtauld Institute Galleries, London

3 (a) The rock in the Dunster version

3 (b) The rock in the Courtauld version

4 *The Peace allegory.* Courtauld version (before restoration)

5 (a) *Peace*. School of Fontainebleau. Musée Granet, Palais de Malte,
Aix-en-Provence

5 (b–c) The Canning Jewel. Victoria and Albert Museum, London

6 (b) Miniature in peace treaty between France and England, 1527. Public Record Office, E.30/1111

6 (a) Miniature in peace treaty between France and England, 1527. Public Record Office, E.30/1110

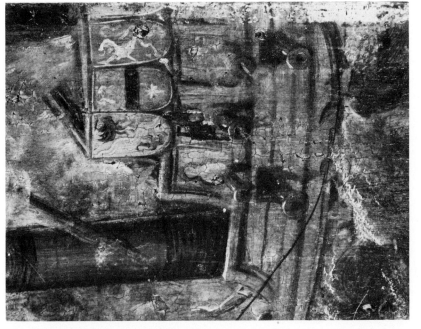

7 (b) Detail of the ship, Courtauld version
(before restoration)

7 (a) Detail of the ship, Courtauld version
(before restoration)

8 *Portrait of Captain Thomas Wyndham.* Collection of the Earl of Radnor,
Longford Castle

Eworth because in the same list it names other portraits which it does state to be by Eworth. This is surely a very extraordinary argument. Once Cust's article is critically examined, it begins to fall apart at many points and it becomes evident that the whole question of the portraits signed with the monogram 'HE' requires to be tackled in an entirely new way, with detailed examination of all the pictures. This work is now being undertaken,[48] and until the results are published no statement can be made about the artist, or the artists, or the firm which used the monogram.

This article has not been concerned with the 'HE' problem but only with the meaning and origin of the allegories in one of the pictures signed with the monogram, the portrait of Sir John Luttrell in the Courtauld version, of which it can be confidently stated that it is by more than one artist.

This picture is a curiosity; some may think it a monstrosity, but it is historically important. It catches something of the feeling of the hour in England in 1550, a dark hour, fraught with anxiety. It reflects the rapprochement with France over the Treaty of Boulogne and the coming of the French embassy. No other French embassy was to come to England for thirty years, until the time of the proposed marriage of Anjou with Queen Elizabeth in the 1580s. The vision in the sky in the Luttrell portrait is a vision of the outside world of Continental art which tries, awkwardly and unsuccessfully, to make contact with the sequestered world of the England of Edward VI.

What is also interesting in the picture is its revelation of the psychology of a man of the age of Protestant iconoclasm. The images have been smashed, but they come back in the form of the pagan imagery of the Renaissance. Amidst the storms of his turbulent life, Sir John Luttrell needs the kindly images of Peace and Friendship on which to call in the hour of shipwreck.

APPENDIX
Report on the Dunster Castle and Courtauld Institute Versions
of the Portrait of Sir John Luttrell
by S. REES-JONES

The two paintings, which will be referred to as D and C, are on panels of approximately the same dimensions. C measures 43″ × 33″, and D is ¾″ longer. The composition, however, suggests that C might have been cut on the left with the loss of the elbow of the figure with the two purses and part of the peacock. The possibility of some loss on the right cannot be excluded, judging by the look of the forearm and the bracelet.

There is further evidence of cutting in the dimensions of the outer panel members; the widths of the four members are:

at the top	7⅛″	8⅞″	9⅕″	7⅞″
at the bottom	7¼″	8⅞″	9⅛″	7¾″

The panel of C, in oak with dowelled joints, is typical of Flemish and Northern painting generally; D is in elm, a wood far less commonly used for panels.

This evidence suggests that the two works are not an original and a replica from the same workshop. They are certainly not by the same hand. The visual and X-ray evidence shows that D is homogeneous in execution and has nothing in common with C, which indeed might be the work of two painters. The X-ray photograph of the figure of Sir John Luttrell in C shows techniques similar to English or Flemish sixteenth-century portraits in general. In the allegorical group, on the other hand, the paint is thicker and has been used with the greatest assurance to model forms such as the nude, for example.

It thus becomes necessary to decide which of the two versions has the greater claim to be regarded as the original.

In support of the view that C is not a copy are the following points:

(1) The existence of a pentiment in the position of the dark band which separates the allegorical group from the sky.

(2) Several details occur in C and not in D; for example the crescent on the head of the figure with the purses, the flying figure, and the swirl of foaming water below the floating head. These details do not appear to have been lost in D through overpainting.

(3) There is a marked difference in tonality between the two

paintings which is not entirely to be accounted for by the state of the varnish. The sea is green in C and brown in D; D has a greenish-grey peacock which is a bright 'peacock' in C; the colours in the allegorical group are brilliant in C, and in keeping with the mannerist style, whereas in D they are more subdued.

The scale is the same in the two works, but since D includes the elbow of the figure with the purses there is a shift of the figures to the right. This shift (which was measured with full-size tracing) is curious in that it involves a distortion of the torso of Peace.

It is difficult to draw positive conclusions about the inscriptions on the rock because they have been retouched in both paintings. In D the retouching is simply a strengthening of some of the letters which had become thin. In C the many losses have been crudely made good and the entire inscription repainted. There is no trace of the Latin quatrain followed by '1591.G.L.' in C. It is not possible to decide on the technical evidence whether *renovare* implies restoration in the sense of picture conservation or whether the date 1591 gives the year in which the copy was made. The only restoration to be seen is modern.

The inscription on the left-arm bracelet in C is badly mutilated and has been restored to read NEC FECIT LUCRUM, which also appears on the right arm. There is, however, under the repaint NEC FREGIT DISCRIMEN as in D.

The Courtauld Institute version has suffered much loss of paint through flaking. It is not inconceivable that the onset of this deterioration at an early date led to the commission of the Dunster version in 1591, as the inscription suggests.

Chapter Two

THE SPIRIT OF CHIVALRY*

THE EUROPEAN cultural and political group ruled over by the Dukes of Burgundy occupied the heart of Europe, covering an area larger than modern France. In the fifteenth century, the Dukes of Burgundy were among the wealthiest of European rulers, rich from the productivity of their lands and from trade. They could afford to spend magnificently on art patronage, on festival production, and on a luxurious yet refined way of life which made their court a main carrier of the late medieval and chivalric type of culture.

It is the argument of Gordon Kipling's *The Triumph of Honour* that the main influences on the Elizabethan Renaissance came from Burgundy. When Henry VII wished to glorify the Tudor monarchy as a European power the example of a magnificent court which he followed was that of Burgundy. His Spanish-Burgundian alliance was cemented by the marriage of Arthur, Prince of Wales, with Catherine of Aragon. The elaborate cosmic-chivalric festivals for this marriage, which have been studied by Sydney Anglo, integrated the international and Burgundian cult of Arthur with the propaganda for Tudor monarchy, thus laying the foundation for major themes of the Elizabethan age.

The argument which Kipling works out of the strong Burgundian influence on the origins of the Elizabethan age is largely valid,

---

* Review of Gordon Kipling, *The Triumph of Honour: Burgundian Origins of the Elizabethan Renaissance*, Leiden, 1977, in *Times Literary Supplement*, 23 June 1978.

yet there are over-simplifications and crudities in his presentation which render the book not altogether satisfactory. Take, for example, the Hermit in the Woodstock romance in which Henry Lee enveloped the Accession Day tilts in honour of Elizabeth. The figure of the hermit, as Kipling points out, is constantly found in Burgundian chivalric romances. Therefore the Hermit of Woodstock is an example of Burgundian influence on the Elizabethan age. Yet it is unlikely that Elizabethan knights thought of themselves as mere imitators of Burgundian chivalry. Probably the main source for Lee's hermit theme was in Ramon Lull's textbook of chivalry, or rather in Caxton's preface to the English translation of that book in which he urges a revival of English chivalry, and renewed emphasis on the Order of the Garter with its cult of St George and its Arthurian associations. This was the heart of Elizabethan chivalry, though parallels with the Burgundian Order of the Golden Fleece were always present. The revival of chivalry was, throughout Europe, a national phenomenon related to the rise of the national monarchies. To class it all as 'Burgundian' is misleading.

Another over-simplification which runs through the book is Kipling's tendency to contrast Burgundian influence with the influence of Italian humanism, with Huizinga as the exponent of the former compared with Burckhardt as the chronicler of Italianate 'civilization of the Renaissance'. According to Kipling, the Middle Ages did not 'wane', as Huizinga argued, but continued as Burgundian influence on the Elizabethans, ranking with the Italian influence in importance for the understanding of the Elizabethan age. Again, there is something in this argument, but it might be advisable to evade both Huizinga and Burckhardt and start again, with more understanding of the importance of the chivalric revival in the Renaissance as a whole, and of the infinitely varied and subtle ways in which chivalric humanism blends and mingles with classical or Italianate humanism. Who can separate the 'Triumph' theme from Burgundian spectacle, and who can untwine the Burgundian from the Petrarchan influence in that theme? No Renaissance rulers were more absorbed in Burgundian magnificence and in draping themselves in its splendours (like the upstart Tudors of England) than were the upstart Medici of Florence. Poliziano's poem *La Giostra* is just as typical of Medicean interest in chivalric themes as the works of his friends and contemporaries, Ficino and Pico, are expressive of Florentine humanist and intellectual interests. The two strands combine and mingle constantly, as for example in the humanist passion for the construction of *imprese*, which are directly descended from heraldic devices. At the Italian humanist court of Urbino, the chivalric influences (including that of the Order of the Garter) combine with Renaissance moral philosophy to produce, in Castiglione's *Cortegiano*, one of the books most influential on the Elizabethans, the emergence of the gentleman from the knight. So one could go on with examples of these intertwinings, culminating in Rubens, the supremely Burgundian humanist.

That the Burgundian emphasis had a direct reference in the Elizabethan age to contemporary history was due largely to the Duke of Alva, the instrument of Philip II in suppressing the revolt of the Netherlands. Through the fanaticism of Alva and his master, Burgundianism took on a patriotic fervour as a protest against the destruction of the old Burgundy under Spanish rule. Thus a Protestant flavour entered into the cult of Burgundian values; the refugees from Spanish rule in the Netherlands strongly influenced Elizabethan art and spectacle. Prominent among these was Lucas de Heere, a chief propagandist in William of Orange's attempts to win Elizabethan England to support the Burgundian, as against the Spanish cause. Orange's propaganda in favour of Anjou as reviver of the old Burgundy is written in the language of Franco-Burgundian spectacle in the Valois tapestries, designed by Lucas de Heere.

It was during and after the terrible years of Alva's rule in the Netherlands that a kind of Burgundian Protestantism took a deep hold on Elizabethan chivalry, reflecting Elizabeth's role as defender of the Netherlands against Spanish oppression. Kipling has pages on this, and on Orange's revival of Burgundianism in the propaganda for Anjou. He does not raise a question which occurs to the reader of his comparison of the festivals for Catherine of Aragon with the imagery later used of Elizabeth I. How was it that the Virgin Queen was able to succeed to imagery used of Catherine of Aragon although she represented an opposite side in the religious situation? The mere asking of this question shows that Elizabethan chivalry belongs to the period after the fatal split in 'Burgundianism' due to the stresses and strains arising from the revolt of the Netherlands. It is perhaps true to say that Spenser's Red Cross knight is the English incarnation (or the 'Garter' incarnation) of Protestantized Burgundianism.

Kipling is undoubtedly right to stress the Burgundian influence on the Elizabethan Renaissance; his book is to be recommended for its careful and detailed examination of Tudor art and architecture, libraries, poetic theory and, above all, pageantry from his point of view. His theme that much which has hitherto been called Italian was also Burgundian is well illustrated in his examination of the poetic forms used by Thomas Wyatt, the Petrarchist, which were strongly influenced by the Netherlands Chambers of Rhetoric.

What I feel is lacking in his book is any deep attempt to define what is meant by 'Burgundian', as compared with, or separate from, Italian humanist influence. Perhaps this is a matter which has not yet been adequately investigated in contemporary Renaissance studies. The problem was clearly stated by Charles Mitchell in an introduction to illustrations from a fifteenth-century Italian Plutarch, published in 1961. Explaining why the Romans appear as knights in these pictures, Mitchell points out that the general European movement of chivalric revival was inspired, like humanism itself, by the effort to recapture the values of the classical past, for it was believed that the ancient Romans were the founders of chivalry. Hence the founding of new orders of chivalry and the revival of old ones were thoroughly Renaissance movements, accompanying the spread of Italian humanism and not contrasting with it as archaic survivals from a waning Middle Ages.

Chapter Three

FOXE AS PROPAGANDIST*

ATROCITY STORIES do not make pleasant reading and when the atrocity described in detail – execution by burning alive – is repeated again and again as one victim after another comes to the stake the cumulative effect is ghastly.

Bent on assembling a Protestant martyrology which should leave a mark on Protestant religious history as powerful as the tales of the early Christian martyrs, John Foxe spared his readers nothing. There is a painful similarity about accounts of death by burning; the process of gradual decomposition of the human body in the flames affords little variation, though sometimes the left arm may drop off first or on a windy day the last agony is protracted whilst the flames are blown away from the sufferer. In the dreadful case of Nicholas Ridley, a combination of windy weather with a badly made pyre kept him alive for three-quarters of an hour calling constantly for 'more fire'. Foxe made sure that the image of 'Bloody Mary' as perpetrator of these horrors should be indelibly stamped on the Protestant version of English history. For a devout Protestant reader in the Victorian age the stories of the martyrs belonged to a dark and distant past of wicked Papalism, infinitely remote from his contemporary world of progress. The modern reader may think the Marian martyrs relatively fortunate. Though brain-washing processes were attempted on

* Review of *Foxe's Book of Martyrs*, edited and abridged by G. A. Williamson, 1965, in *Encounter*, XXVII, 4 October 1966.

them, these were not very efficiently or scientifically organized; nor were they tortured and executed in secrecy. Each martyr was the central actor in a public drama and was allowed to address moving speeches to the onlookers. He could feel to the last at the centre of an eternal conflict between the conviction for which he was dying and its opponents, and know to the last that his impressive death was having an influence. Whether or not Latimer actually said these words as the faggot was being kindled at his feet – 'Be of good comfort, Mr Ridley, and play the man. We shall this day light such a candle by God's grace in England, as I trust shall never be put out' – this was the kind of thing that a Marian martyr was expected and allowed to say. No doubt learning from the mistakes of his unfortunate wife, Philip II later forbade public executions in his persecutions of Protestants in the Low Countries.

The lurid reputation of Foxe the martyrologist has obscured Foxe the historian. The martyr stories form only a relatively small part of an immensely long historical work, constantly added to in successive editions (the main edition was in 1570). Foxe himself did not call his book the 'Book of Martyrs'; he called it *Acts and Monuments* or *Ecclesiastical History*. Beginning about the year 1000 and ending with the accession of Queen Elizabeth I, Foxe's vast work presents a view of the meaning of history as a whole, worked out with a passion equal to that of Eusebius or Marx. Like all universal historians of a doctrinaire type, Foxe sees history as a conflict between opposed good and evil forces. In Foxist history, these forces are, not proletarians and capitalists, but Empire and Papacy, understanding Empire in the sense of Holy Roman Empire with its spiritual claims, with which are associated the imperial rights of sacred monarchs, like the Tudors, to reform the Church. When evil is dominant, there are martyrs, as in the reign of Mary when the wicked Papal power attempted a comeback. When good is dominant, as in the reign of Elizabeth, the sacred monarch terminates the reign of evil and brings back the true religion. Foxist history is propagandist history for the Tudor reform of the Church, not only warning against the Church of Rome through its scarifying stories of Romanist persecutions, but also through its whole interpretation of history in terms of Monarchy versus Papacy.

Books like these aim at making history; and Foxist history, like Marxist history, had an effect on the actual making of history.

Foxe's religious views, his passionate adherence to the more extreme attitudes of the Reformation, are tied in with his imperialist and monarchical convictions. He believed that the purity of the early Church was preserved when Christian emperors, from Constantine onwards, guided its councils, and that impurity and corruption set in when the Bishops of Rome, usurping the sacred imperial power, took the lead. His long history of the oppression of emperors by popes is illustrated with a series of woodcuts representing popes insulting emperors, as Hildebrand did at Canossa, or popes treading on the necks of emperors. This theme becomes related to English history through regarding English monarchs as representatives of the sacred imperial power, and he tells and shows in his illustrations the stories of a papal emissary poisoning King John or of Henry III being made to kiss the knee of the Pope's legate. Foxist history leads up inevitably to its climax in the break with Rome under the Tudors; a triumphant illustration shows Henry VIII trampling on the Pope as he throws off the Papal 'usurped power'. The triumph of the pure reformed Church is interrupted by the Papalist reaction under Mary, blackly underlined by the stories of the martyrs, but with the advent of Elizabeth history is consummated. Like a new Constantine she initiates a new golden age of pure religion, puts an end to the martyrdoms, and in her character of sacred imperial ruler she finally tramples on the Pope and rids England forever (Foxe hopes) of Papal interference.

Foxe's book is a perfect example of propagandist history, using a wealth of miscellaneous documentation always with single-eyed determination to weave all the strands into patterns which suit his argument. And his arguments fitted perfectly with those by which the Royal Supremacy over both Church and State – the keystone of the whole Tudor position – was justified. The arguments for the Supremacy were related to the position of emperors in the Councils of the Church, and the imperial title of English kings to complete sovereignty within their dominions had long been associated with the struggles of the English crown against Papal interference. Imperialist theory was of the greatest importance in England in buttressing the break with the Papacy. John Jewel's *Apology for the Church of England* (1560) is written from the same kind of Protestant-Imperialist position as Foxe's book and uses the same kind of historical example of popes oppressing emperors, followed up by claims of the sacred imperial rights of the English crown as justifying the reform of the Church by the monarch. It was as holder of the sacred imperial power that the monarch claimed the right to throw off Papal suzerainty and establish a national church. As one seventeenth-century writer puts it, 'the Britannic Church was withdrawn from the Roman patriarchate by the Imperial authority of Henry VIII.'

Seen in the context of the religious-imperial drapery with which the Royal Supremacy was invested, Foxe's unrolling of the scrolls of universal history on the themes of Papacy and Empire, with the former as the villain of the piece, is obviously a necessary and logical preliminary to his treatment of recent English history. The Pope's 'usurped power' was brought in again by Mary; hence the sufferings of the martyrs witnessing to the true Church. The pictures of martyrs burning at the stake with which the book is decorated are not more important than the pictures of emperors trodden on by popes until the latest Tudor inheritor of the imperial power finally kicks the Pope out of England. The two themes are interrelated. The martyrs are like the early Christians rescued by the Emperor Constantine; or rather they are the new Reformed early Christians rescued by the Sacred Empress, Elizabeth.

Those who have become impatient with Foxe's book as a vast confused mass of ill-digested material, the only readable parts of which are the spicy martyr stories, are those who have not found the thread through his labyrinth, which is the 'imperial theme'. With considerable skill, Foxe combined universal history of the Church on the model of Eusebius with the traditions of medieval imperialist theory to form a historical justification for the Tudor imperial and monarchical reform.

Though Foxe's use of Eusebius as a model is well known, the influence on him of medieval imperialist writers, not excluding Dante, has received far less emphasis. Foxe's quotations from Dante's *Monarchia* and from the *Divine Comedy* are one of the few evidences of the influence of Dante in sixteenth-century England. They are taken from a secondary source and they present Dante as one of a cloud of witnesses who have attacked the wickedness of the Papacy and have demanded a Reformation. Foxe sees Dante as an imperialist reformer, a believer in the traditions of sacred empire, who appeals to emperors to reform the Church. This is of course not untrue but to twist Dante into a Protestant imperialist reformer, a witness who can be called upon from afar to justify the Tudor reform, is of course a distortion, though one to which Foxe could have been led in the Protestant circles which he frequented in Basel during his exile in the reign of Mary.

Dante's *Monarchia* was first printed at Basel in 1559 by a Protestant printer as one of a collection of tracts on the rights and spiritual claims of the Empire. Protestant use of Dantesque imperialism against the Papacy was thus no new thing; when used by Foxe it introduces what one may almost call a Ghibelline atmosphere into his religious-imperial theme.

Foxist history is really entirely medieval in spirit, revolving around the twin pillars of Papacy and Empire, like the old chronicles. The fact that in the new Protestant interpretation, Empire is pitted against Papacy does not alter the fundamentally medieval character of Foxe's approach to the theory of history. He is quite untouched by the new critical schools of historical writing which had arisen in Florence and which broke completely with the old notions of Empire and its periodic golden ages. Foxe is no Machiavellian realist; he is an old-fashioned chronicler. Though he heaps together great masses of documents, these are not critically investigated but drawn into the great stream of Papacy and Empire patterns in their Protestant and English interpretation. His history of the kings of England is in straightforward chronicle tradition, as he draws English history into the over-riding pattern of the Protestant imperial theme.

He has to the full the chronicler's gift of vivid narrative which is shown most strikingly in his 'stories' of recent history, the stories of the martyrs, the material for which he drew from informants but wrote up in a dramatic and striking manner. His readers are unable to forget these terrible stories which go on, one after another, through the last part of the book. With careful attention to convincing detail and with innumerable touches calculated to arouse emotional sympathy, Foxe builds up story after story, until the reader, tried like a martyr almost beyond endurance, welcomes with sighs of relief the ending of the tyranny of the Papists with the advent of the imperial and Protestant Virgin Queen. Though the 'Book of Martyrs' is only a small part of the universal history of the *Acts and Monuments* it is the culmination of its whole theme, telling of the last and worst outburst of Antichrist in England. It was the combination of Foxe's power of building up a theory of universal history with his power of emotional appeal in these dreadful stories which made his book so utterly convincing in the tradition of English Protestantism.

It is impossible to exaggerate the influence of this book. Accepted from the start as the official history, telling every Englishman what he should know about the past of his country in relation to its present, it was placed in churches – chained Foxes can still be seen in some out-of-the-way village churches – to be read by the faithful, together with the Bible. To the Elizabethan reader it was not the diffuse, dull, over-lengthy compilation which it may seem to the modern reader. It was a red-hot presentation of sensational recent history. It told stories about the Queen and her strange family – her father and his many wives, her brother, her 'bloody' sister. It related the present state of England to the history of its former kings right back to King Lucius, the mythical first Christian king of England. And it presented the history of English monarchs in close connection with religious history, emphasizing the tremendous spiritual responsibility of kings. Every Elizabethan knew of or had read this book; Francis Drake is said to have taken it with him on his voyage round the world. It did its work, for there can be little doubt that Foxe contributed very materially to the success and stability of the Elizabethan settlement, that his themes became part of the warp and woof of contemporary thinking, and his history the prism through which many Elizabethans saw the history of their country.

Foxist history could serve to buttress the symbolism through which Elizabeth was presented in pageantry, art, and poetry throughout her reign. One of the chief and most deeply rooted of the Elizabeth symbols was that of the righteous virgin Astraea, who in the classical legend is said to return to earth when the golden age is established. Associated as it was with Roman imperialist propaganda, the symbol of the Virgin Astraea returning to earth with the establishment by Elizabeth of the imperial reform was particularly suited to the Virgin Queen in all her aspects, both as the Empress-Monarch and as the Monarch who was the head of a reformed Church. Though the symbol was used of Elizabeth very early in her reign, the Foxist official history which leads up to Elizabeth all through the ages as the Monarch of a new golden age, the female Constantine who ends the persecutions of the Church and establishes pure religion, gave a strong sanction to the symbol. It was the Protestant version of imperialist history, of which Foxe's book was the most powerful though not the only account, which made possible the creation of a national epic on Virgilian lines centred on the figure of the Imperial Virgin. *The*

Faerie Queene is a poetic statement of the Tudor religious position corresponding to the historical statement made by Foxe. Standing, perhaps, in a church, Spenser might have turned the pages of the *Acts and Monuments*. In that huge book he (and any Elizabethan) could have scanned the immense wealth of documentation through which Foxe supports his view of history, drawing into its service every writer who had maintained imperialist theory and every critic of the Papacy. Troubadours and philosophers, poets and humanists, all could be made to witness (often through very misleading quotation) to the wickedness of the Church of Rome and therefore by implication to the righteousness of the Just Virgin of the imperial reform. There among many other great names was the name of Dante, the distorted Dante of Protestant imperialism. The Spenserian antithesis between Una, the One of sacred empire, and Duessa, the false Whore, may owe something to the Protestant imperialist distortion of Dante to be found in Foxe, though not in him alone.

Long after Foxist history had played its momentous part in justifying the Tudor reform and in building up the Elizabeth symbolism, his book continued to sway generation after generation of English readers, with its terrible warnings of what might be the result of a return of Popery under some new 'bloody' ruler, with its impressive history of the universal Church in terms of Monarchy versus Papacy. This monumental universal history in the English language witnessed, like the Bible in English, to the validity of the English Protestant and monarchical reformation. Foxe and the Bible, the Bible and Foxe, these were the pillars of his belief for Bunyan and countless others. The history of our own times has shown us numerous examples of the power of propagandist history in establishing and maintaining a régime. Foxist history is a notable example of such operative history. Was it Foxe who made a Protestant succession to the throne an inevitable part of English history? Was Foxe still working even in the Protestant undertones of Victorian imperialism? Such questions have not yet been fully explored.

I profoundly disagree with J. F. Mozley, who has said of Foxe's book that its first readers were interested only in the martyr stories, 'not because it told of Constantine or Barbarossa or Hildebrand' or for its English translations of extracts from a mass of politico-religious literature. This comment misses the object of the work, underrates the appetite of the Elizabethan age for controversial religious literature, and the need of that age to take refuge in a powerful symbol to justify its break with the rest of Christendom – a symbol which Foxe and others provided in the idea of sacred empire. Nevertheless it seems that as time went on the 'Book of Martyrs' did become gradually divorced from its context in the universal history. Wesley made an abridgement, concentrating on the martyrs and explaining that he was omitting much 'trash which the honest and injudicious writer had put together'. The eviction of Foxe the historiographer by Foxe the martyrologist was thus already beginning. Nevertheless the main Victorian editions include everything and run into eight volumes. One should not feel too sure that Victorians of the type of the parents of Edmund Gosse were not still tracing the history of Antichrist in Foxist terms.

Of course, Catholic historians and propagandists had from the start entered the field against the imperialist arguments. Nicholas Sanders's *Rock of the Church* presents succinctly the opposite side of the medal. He refutes the imperialist theory of the rights of emperors in the Councils of the Church; execrates the setting up of a temporal prince above the lawful successor of St Peter as the very mark and badge of Antichrist; deplores with horror the display of the royal arms in English churches in the place of religious statues (the royal arms, marking the Supremacy, have been taken out of the churches, like the Foxes). The violence of Robert Parsons's attack on Foxe's book witnesses indirectly to its influence. The Catholic undercurrent of criticism was always present but it was probably not until the nineteenth century that the Protestant version of English history began to be seriously weakened under the influence of the Oxford movement and the Gothic revival. In this atmosphere, Foxe appeared as an old-fashioned tyrant. Heavy attacks on his veracity were made by Maitland and others, and his book, once so all important, disappeared and was forgotten. Reading Foxe today brings home how remote from contemporary literature are the presuppositions of Foxism, how completely he has been reversed. Compare the Thomas Becket of Foxe, traitor to his lawful monarch in supporting the interference of Antichrist, with the Becket of T. S. Eliot. Or compare our image of Thomas More with Foxe's More, an intolerant persecutor of the faithful, rightly punished for his cruelty by his own cruel death, exhibiting his frivolity by dying with a jest on his lips.

John Fisher Bishop of Rochester and Sir Thomas More, in King Henry's time, after they had brought Frith, Bayfield, and Bainham, and divers others to their death, what great reward won they thereby with Almighty God? Did not the sword of God's vengeance light upon their own necks shortly after, and they themselves made a public spectacle at the Tower Hill of bloody death, which before had no compassion of the lives of others?

Strange indeed are the whirligigs, not only of time, but of the presentations of times. Foxist history witnesses not only to the immense power of propagandist history but also to its transience, how it is cast aside and forgotten in the reaction.

It is only in comparatively recent times that attempts have been made to examine the importance of Foxe's book from a purely historical point of view, divested of the old partisanship. J. F. Mozley (*John Foxe and his Book*, 1940) made out a case for Foxe's reliability in the use of documents, against Maitland's criticisms that he invented martyrs and exaggerated the persecutions. By dismissing the universal history as unimportant, Mozley tends to continue the tradition of isolating the 'Book of Martyrs' from its context. In my article on 'Queen Elizabeth as Astraea' (*Journal of the Warburg and Courtauld Institutes*, 1947; revised and reprinted in my *Astraea*, 1975) I examined Foxist imperialist history in relation to the Elizabeth symbolism. The most important recent study is that by William Haller (*Foxe's Book of Martyrs and the Elect Nation*, 1963). Though the martyrologist is prominent in this book, Haller does not neglect the historiographer and examines carefully Foxe's use of Eusebius and other historical materials. He omits, however, to discuss Foxe and the medieval imperialist writers, and, though well aware that Foxe treats English history in relation to the spiritual responsibility of kings, he does not see the connection of this with the imperialist theory underlying the Royal Supremacy. Nevertheless, Haller's book marks a definite advance in serious historical treatment, and it appears to have been a review of it in which Philip Toynbee called for a new abridged edition of Foxe which inspired G. A. Williamson to undertake the editing and arrangement of a volume of selections.

No one but a 'dedicated scholar', thinks Mr Williamson, would read through the whole of Foxe's book and no publisher would risk reprinting it. Former abridgements were not made, he says, to save the reader's time but to make propaganda for the Protestant cause by concentrating on the martyrs. Yet this new abridgement, without having the excuse of fanatical belief in the Protestant cause – Mr Williamson seems pleasantly liberal in his views – also concentrates mainly on the martyrdom stories. What it presents is *Foxe's Book of Martyrs,* not the *Acts and Monuments.* Mr Williamson has omitted the whole of the first fifth of the book, accounts of events abroad, documents, letters, in short all the mass of material out of which the universal history was built up, and has made selections from the 'stories', which according to him form the meat of the book. When the martyrdom stories are taken out of their context in the universal history they become merely horror stories. Nor does Mr Williamson really attempt in his introduction to reconstruct for the reader the plan of the work as a whole. Though he mentions that Foxe, like Eusebius, is writing a universal history, he thinks that Foxe's faults as a writer stem from excessive adherence to Eusebius, and he deplores the 'blind optimism' of Eusebius and Foxe in believing that a golden age had arrived, in the one case with Constantine, in the other case with Elizabeth. This misses the whole point of Foxe's book as religious imperialist propaganda (which was also missed by Haller). One might as well regret the blind optimism of Virgil in believing in an Augustan golden age. Nor is this the only glimpse of lack of understanding of Foxe's work and its relation to its times which this introduction affords, suggesting that the writer was not well qualified to make an intelligent abridgement. I agree that this would be extremely difficult and that no abridgement can be entirely satisfactory. What is needed is a full reprint, probably of the 1570 edition, with detailed introduction and notes, a vast task needing both dedicated scholars and dedicated publishers. But until it is done an immense fund of most essential information about the Elizabethan age and how it used historical materials will remain inaccessible.

Nevertheless we must be thankful for what Mr Williamson has given us, and from his own rather limited point of view he has made quite a neat job of the abridgement. Regarding the meat of the book as narrative history, not theoretical history, he has put the stories together in consecutive narrative form. Beginning with Wiclif and the reigns of Edward III and Richard II, he passes to the Lollards and the reigns of Henry IV, Henry V, Henry VI, Edward IV, Richard III and Henry VII. Then comes the Reformation and the reigns of Henry VIII, Edward VI. Then the reversion to Rome and the reign of terror under Mary which takes up the greater part of the book. Mr Williamson has carefully retained Foxe's own language, making only some omissions and regularizations of spelling, and has provided a useful glossary in which the reader is instructed to look up, not only unfamiliar words, but familiar words used in an unusual sense. He has thus made available in convenient and readable form Foxe's History of England from Edward III to the accession of Elizabeth, with its specialized slant on religious history.

The abridgement has the advantage of including the whole of Foxe's treatment of Henry VIII and his family, which required delicate handling in relation to his theme. Henry's first marriage to his brother's widow was illegal, arranged by immoral Papists. Seized with qualms of conscience, the pious King sought a second marriage: Anne Boleyn has to be written up as sympathetic to the Protestant cause, since she both precipitated the Reformation and was the mother of Elizabeth. Foxe is a little evasive about her death but succeeds in a general way in leaving an impression on the reader that Henry's wives might have lost their heads through urging advance in a more Protestant direction on an irritable spouse. Henry is a slightly ambiguous figure, for though it was he who first broke with Antichrist and laid firm hold for the first time on the Two Swords (of both the spiritual and temporal power), his Reformation was not sufficiently advanced for Foxe's Puritan taste. The boy King, Edward VI, is fully one of the elect, marked out for an early death by his sanctity. When the dread doings of his eldest sister have been recounted, Foxe gives what Haller has called a not unsympathetic account of her personal tragedy, how she was neglected by the husband she loved, could not have the child she longed for, lost Calais. Foxe's personal impression of Mary has passed into history, yet sympathetic is hardly the word for it. Her misfortunes were the retribution always meted out by an angry Deity upon those who persecute the elect. Meanwhile her young sister was enduring sufferings which were but a preparation for her great destiny. Almost herself a Marian martyr but delivered in time by Providence out of the very jaws of Antichrist, the young Elizabeth moves impressively through Foxe's concluding pages, the dignity of her conduct under her sister's oppression enhanced by telling pathetic touches (the child who was forbidden to bring her flowers). This is one of the best pieces of writing in the book, and Foxe could write. The reader will be grateful to Mr Williamson for giving it to him entire. Imperial panegyric, with its underlying emotional rhythm, has not been unproductive of great literature, witness the *Aeneid*. Foxe leaves Elizabeth at the beginning of her golden age; her poets would continue the imperial theme.

Mr Williamson's abridgement will call attention to Foxe and to the power of his writing. Probably he is right that only a selection from the more obviously readable portions of the book would have found a publisher, and one cannot regret that at least some Foxe has been made available, for the earlier editions and abridgements are all out of print and hard to come by. Nevertheless his inadequate introduction is hardly a step in the right direction for fuller understanding of this tremendous work. And the very neatness of his solution of the problem of abridgement warns of its superficiality, for without the universal context the reader cannot recognize in this straight narrative the working out of the sacred imperial theme in terms of English monarchy.

Sacred monarchy was the most operative politico-religious idea of the sixteenth century, and it was John Foxe who provided a historical justification for the peculiar form of it which underlay the Tudor assumption of supreme authority in both Church and State.

Chapter Four

BROKEN IMAGES*

THE POPULATION of images in medieval England was doubtless more numerous than the scanty population of living human beings. Figured in windows, sculptured in statuary, carved and painted in countless scenes, the images were the close companions of medieval man. From them he learned what he knew of history and the Scriptures. With them he furnished his memory, setting his memory images on memory places. As he looked around his world, in which all the main buildings were ecclesiastical, he saw those innumerable figures of sacred history or of allegory, designed through their striking character to impress on his memory the teachings of the Church.

During a period beginning with Henry VIII's dissolution of the monasteries in 1535 and ending with the restoration of Charles II in 1660, this vast population of images was almost totally destroyed. The destruction raged in phases, sometimes more and sometimes less intense, and with some periods of attempted rescue and restoration, but the net result was that we of these later ages have never seen English medieval art as it was in its original setting, only broken remains of it, scraps of shattered glass, statues with their heads chipped off. We all know about iconoclasm as a historical fact, though we hardly realize how it happened nor can we

* Review of John Phillips, *The Reformation of Images: Destruction of Art in England 1535-1660*, Berkeley and Los Angeles, 1974, in *New York Review of Books*, 30 May 1974.

visualize the actual scenes of destruction. Still less do we realize what it meant internally, the breaking of the images within, the doing away of an ancient psychology of the imagination which had been taken for granted for centuries.

If we think about this phenomenon of the breaking of the images our reactions may depend on religious affiliations, lament for the Catholic past destroyed by Protestant Reformation, or approval of Protestant break with a superstitious past. Much more common than either of these attitudes today is probably the aesthetic reaction, the sense of dismay at the destruction of irreplaceable art treasures. The author of the book under review takes none of these lines. He does not take sides over the religious question, nor is he interested in the images as works of art. What Phillips attempts to do is to give a fairly factual account of the destruction and its phases, and to relate both the use of religious images and their destruction to changing attitudes toward psychologies of the imagination in their relation to theological issues.

In medieval theory, as laid down in particular by Thomas Aquinas, man's nature is so constituted that he cannot remember intellectual or spiritual concepts save through material images. To make him grasp an abstraction such as the vice of avarice, one must show him an image of a miser, perhaps holding a bag of money, an avaricious man. To indicate to him an abstraction such as the virtue of charity, one must show him an attractive human figure, a woman, exemplifying or exercising this virtue.

These are very simple examples of the principle of teaching man about the *intelligibilia* through the *sensibilia* which is at the root of medieval didactic art. To make man fear and avoid the sins which lead to hell, one shows him hateful images of sins and the great doom paintings or sculptures of the Last Judgement with their countless figures of the damned. Or to lead him toward paradise, one shows the glorious vision of the life of the blessed in heaven, the reward of virtue. The imagination is allowed to form material images, images from the world of sense, because it is only through such images that man can be taught, and made to remember, the higher intelligible truths.

This theory of the imagination as a lower power of the soul which is also the gateway to higher understanding underlies the whole panoply of didactic images by which medieval man was surrounded from the cradle to the grave. In practice, it was buttressed by the principles of the classical art of memory, that we remember better through images, and the more strikingly beautiful or horrible such images are the better we remember them. The appeal to memory was fundamental. The visual images were so constructed as to be memorable, and when reflected in memory they became the striking memory images.

This is, of course, an extreme simplification of the vast medieval effort to teach the whole scheme of theology and ethics through visual images of the actors in the scriptural story, of saints, of allegorical figures, and so on. Though the teaching through images was adapted for the unlearned, the schemes of images being the 'laymen's books', yet the images which the layman saw around him rested on a universally held psychology, the 'faculty psychology' according to which the imaginative faculty was a stage in the process of learning. And it rested on theology, the theology of the Incarnation through which the material world was sanctified as a gateway to the divine.

When the abuses in the medieval Church system were attacked at the Reformation, the return to the Scriptures as to the book from which religious truth is to be learned discredited the laymen's books of images and revealed the glaring discrepancy between some scriptural teaching about images and the practice of the Church. 'Thou shalt not make to thyself any graven image; thou shalt not bow down to them nor worship them.' The stern Hebraic injunction was a warning against idolatry, and it was precisely the charge of idolatry, that it encouraged the worship of images, which was one of the main charges brought against the Church by the reformers.

When does an image become an idol, the debased object of a basically heathen worship, rather than the allowed 'sensible' or material reflection of the intelligible world, or the allowed 'reminder' of spiritual truth? Can there be an inner idolatry, an imagination perverted by false use of imagery preventing the understanding of the Word, the written word of Scripture or the spoken word of the preacher, through which alone spiritual truths are conveyed? For the ardent reformer the Word took the place of the Image as the channel of religious instruction, and the multitudinous images of the Church of Rome became the mark of an idolatrous religion which must be destroyed.

This extreme position was not arrived at immediately in England, and it is the merit of Phillips's book that he tells the story of the phases of the attack on images while at the same time keeping in view the phases of the development of the theory underlying it. The break with Rome under Henry VIII brought with it a vast confiscation of Church property and initiated the great destruction process, much of which was obviously at this stage mere greed, the appropriation of the immensely valuable precious metals and stones which adorned the relics in the shrines, the theft of vestments, plate, and other wealth accumulated through the centuries.

Yet the Henrician type of reform did not exclude images as such, nor did the systematic smashing of images gather much momentum in his reign. In the Henrician type of reform, a distinction was drawn between the idolatrous worship of images and a legitimate use of images as 'laymen's books' to *remind* them of heavenly things. This distinction clearly recognizes the mnemonic character of the images, while warning against idolatrous abuse of them. In fact, efforts were made to classify existing images according to whether they were superstitiously worshipped, or 'abused', or merely taken as 'signs of remembrance', in which case they were to be regarded as 'unabused' and therefore harmless. This distinction between the harmless memory image and the idolatrously worshipped image was influential but proved difficult to apply in practice, and the extremists under Edward VI went in for the total destruction of images in England. Images were now seen as the visible signs of Antichrist and became the object of the fanatical hatred of the devout reformer.

Among the many significant and valuable quotations chosen by Phillips to illustrate the argument is one from Cranmer stating his belief that it was Antichrist, otherwise the Bishop of Rome, who introduced idolatry; first it was pretended that the images were to be used as remembrance, then they were worshipped. Here is the recognition of the memory principle behind images, while the danger of idolatrous corruption of images now leads to their total condemnation.

One curious result of the destruction of images was that mechanisms by which miraculous images were worked were revealed. A crucifix at the Abbey of Boxley in Kent had long been revered for its miraculous power of movement; the image would move its head, scowl with its eyes, reject or receive the prayers of pilgrims. When pulled down it was revealed that the venerated Rood of Grace contained 'certain engines of old wire', the manipulation of which caused the movements. The rood was brought to London and a sermon preached against it at Paul's Cross in 1538. When the preacher waxed warm and 'the Word began to work in the hearts of his hearers', the image was thrown to the crowd who tore it into a thousand fragments with great clamour.

Perhaps it was such discoveries as this made during the work of destruction that caused Latimer to call images 'juggling deceits'. Yet the old monks may have thought that they were doing a pious kind of mechanical magic, infusing the statues of their gods with life as described in the Hermetic writings. This aspect of the history of magic and mechanics has not yet received attention. There may well have been a revival of it at the Counter Reformation when the cult of miraculous images was stressed as a way of drawing the people back to the Church.

An argument against indiscriminate iconoclasm was that destruction of religious images might lead to civil upheaval and an attack on legitimate authority. It was pointed out that the nobility set forth their lineage and the remembrance of their notable deeds in images. Still more important, what of the royal authority, proclaimed in the royal arms? What of the royal seal, with St George on one side and the King's image on the other? One bishop argued that, just as the Church provides religious instruction for the illiterate by means of images, so the state and the nobility impress on men's minds their authority through seals and blazonry. This was indeed an important and a dangerous matter. Protector Somerset grouped images into three kinds. First, the King's arms and ensigns which are honourable 'and worshipped after the decent order and invention of human laws and ceremonies'; second, idolatrous images which are sacrificed to superstitiously; third, images of a commemorative nature which are used only as a 'remembrance'.

Somerset found it impossible to maintain the 'superstitious' or 'commemorative' distinction and finally recommended the destruction of all religious images, but the King's arms and the ensigns of civil authority grew in importance. While the religious images suffered persecution and destruction the royal image gained enormously in prestige. This process of increased emphasis on the royal image was a Renaissance phenomenon which also took place in Catholic countries, for example in France, but when the rising royal image was contrasted with the desolation of the religious images, as in the England of the Tudor reformation, the transfer of power from the one to the other was evident. It became a

familiar sight to see in the denuded churches the royal arms occupying the dominant position on the rood screen formerly accorded
to the crucifix.

The Tudor reform of the Church being an 'imperial' reform
undertaken by the monarch, sacred imperial imagery proliferated
around the Tudors, and particularly around Queen Elizabeth I,
hailed as 'Astraea', the Just Virgin of a renewed imperial golden
age. The involved, yet logically coherent, imagery built up around
the queen in portraits, pageantry, poetry throughout the Elizabethan age has been the subject of special study. Phillips brings
some discussion and description of the Elizabeth cult into his
book to contrast and compare with the theme of iconoclasm,
recapitulating what has been said about the cult of Elizabeth and
adding points which he has arrived at through his own studies:

> The cult of Elizabeth was a flexible symbol capable perhaps
> of being comprehended in many ways – for a church that
> needed an image of strength amidst the conflicts of the
> Elizabethan settlement; for a government unsure of its
> support; for a people accustomed to the externalisation of their
> devotions. The cult of the royal image was created in order
> to buttress public order at a time when the religious image had
> proved disruptive of that same order. Discovery of what
> constituted an abused image had never really been explored or
> clarified. The government's fear of disorder and unauthorised
> innovation deterred it from undertaking an investigation of
> this question, or from making a firm policy towards
> iconoclasts.

Thus the problem of when an image was for 'remembrance' only,
not superstitiously worshipped, was left open under Elizabeth,
like so many other difficult questions. Sporadic iconoclasm
continued and the churches were left in a ruined state, but the
Queen herself kept a crucifix in the royal chapel, and her private
attitude to such problems was ambiguous and made some of her
subjects uneasy. However, by a royal order of 1561 she returned
to the Edwardian policy of ordering the painting of scriptural texts
on the bare whitewashed walls of the now imageless churches.
Presumably through the advance of printing and the spreading of
printed Bibles, her subjects were now supposed to be able to read
such texts, and to memorize them.

Instead of the vanished and banished images, the 'laymen's

books', the literate layman can now, presumably, read and memorize a written text. Queen Elizabeth seems to have felt that the texts helped to give colour to the now bare interiors, for she wrote that the writing up of the Ten Commandments in a church was 'not only for edification, but also to give some comely ornament and demonstration that the same is a place of religion and prayer'. An extreme reformer might not have approved this lingering aesthetic motive in the Queen's order. And if we think in terms of memory of this church, from which the broken images have been carted away, its bare walls decorated only with written sentences, we have a strong factual and visual impression of the startling change from a memory populated with images stored in it 'for remembrance' to the new Ramist type of memory which memorized pages in a printed book.

The Tudor cult of the image of the monarch in a context of iconoclasm brings to mind, as Phillips points out, the iconoclastic movement in the Byzantine Empire, when, in A.D. 725, the Emperor Leo moved against images and began a policy of destroying them within the empire. The motive appears to have been fear of superstitious abuse of images, perhaps related to possible influence of dualist heresies on the emperor (though this is not certain). At any rate, religious images were banned by an emperor who regarded himself as a religious reformer. As in the Tudor reformation, the image of the emperor gained in potency and power against the background of the breaking of religious images. Tudor theologians were aware of this Byzantine parallel to their own situation. Bishop John Jewel compared the Tudor monarchs to the Byzantine emperors in their policy of iconoclasm as a protest against idolatry.

It is thus not accidental that some of the cult images of Queen Elizabeth I look like icons. Their stiffness and strangeness are not entirely due to the inadequacy of Elizabethan artists but may actually reflect an archaic type of emperor worship reviving in a situation which bore some superficial resemblance to the situation in Byzantium in the eighth and ninth centuries A.D.

The last and most severe and most systematically destructive outbreak of iconoclasm in England was inspired by the zeal of the Puritan Parliamentarians in the seventeenth century. Now there were no reservations about royal images. The living royal image, Charles I, was beheaded; and statues of kings fared no better at the hands of the new iconoclasts than did the religious images which now had to bear the brunt of a new campaign against them. Records of scenes at Canterbury in 1642 have been preserved. When the commissioners arrived to carry out the destruction they found so many images that it seemed to them that the cathedral had been built 'for no other end, but to be a stable for idols'. The images were cast down and broken wholesale. There was much stained glass still surviving which had escaped earlier destruction. The height of the building did not deter the chief commissioner, who climbed a great ladder and battered down vast windows, crucifixes, pictures. He pulled down with ropes a large stone image over the south gate, and congratulated himself that, as Christ had driven the merchants from the Temple, so he ejected from churches the idols which had defiled the worship of God.

Though we may shudder at the thought of that day's work in Canterbury, such scenes were not mere vandalism. Phillips suggests that the breaking of the images 'was an expression of a highly developed order of daring philosophical violence within the setting of profound social and political change'. The thought even occurs to compare the breaking of the images with Francis Bacon's aim of removing the inner 'idols', or preconceived ideas, from the philosophic imagination to make way for new conceptions.

Iconoclasm is a phenomenon which has to be taken seriously, its psychological roots examined, its historical meaning assessed. So far as I know, the attempt made by Phillips in this book to tell the story of iconoclasm in England in relation to the theory underlying the use of religious images and the theory of their destruction is a pioneer effort. It is therefore an important book on an important and strangely neglected subject. There is more in it than the points which I have selected for use in this essay; for example, an interesting chapter on Lollards and images. The illustrations are well chosen and add to the impression made by the book. There are some imperfections and confusions and some omissions. Not much is said about differing attitudes to images among different Protestant theologians. The theory of iconoclasm in its Byzantine phase is insufficiently analysed, and there is no mention of the iconoclastic outbursts in France and in the Low Countries in the sixteenth century, which ought certainly to be compared, both in theory and practice, with the English movement. Now that this subject has been opened up, we may expect that it will attract increasing attention.

Though Phillips is not concerned with poetic imagery, his book should be of importance to students of Elizabethan literature. It is strangely significant that the theory of the imagination and of the use of images which Spenser expounds in *The Faerie Queene* is based on the old faculty psychology. His poem unrolls a most complex system of images of virtue and vice in a context of chivalry and of the royal image of Elizabeth which, in many forms, dominates the poem. In one of its many aspects *The Faerie Queene* might be said to bring out into the world in terms of the monarch and her knights the theory of teaching and impressing on memory through images of a code of conduct, of approaching the *intelligibilia* through the *sensibilia*. And this had also been the theory of the imagination underlying the old broken images of the laymen's books.

Chapter Five

A GREAT MAGUS*

IN 1570, one of the most important books of the Elizabethan period was published in London. This was Henry Billingsley's English translation of Euclid, with a preface described on the title page as

> . . . a very fruitfull Preface made by Maister John Dee, specifying the chief Mathematicall sciences, what they are, and wherunto commodious; where also, are disclosed, certaine new secrets Mathematicall and Mechanicall, until these our daies greatly missed.

In this preface, Dee ranges over all the mathematical sciences then known and strongly urges their encouragement and improvement. As a manifesto for the advancement of science, Dee's mathematical preface has been said to be of greater importance than Francis Bacon's *Advancement of Learning*, published thirty-five years later, for Dee fully understood and emphasized the basic importance of mathematical studies for the advancement of science, whereas Bacon underestimated mathematics. Dee's mathematical preface had a great influence and was widely read until well on in

---

* Review of Peter J. French, *John Dee: The World of an Elizabethan Magus*, London, Boston and Henley, 1972; Furio Jesi, 'John Dee e il suo sapere', *Comunità*, CLXVI, 1972; and Wayne Shumaker, *The Occult Sciences in the Renaissance: A Study in Intellectual Patterns*, Berkeley and Los Angeles, 1972, in *New York Review of Books*, 25 January 1973.

the seventeenth century. Dee also exerted a strong personal influence through his many contacts with the school of mathematicians and scientists which made the later Elizabethan age a period of importance for scientific advance.

Another famous, or infamous, work by Dee is the *True and Faithful Relation of what passed for many years between Dr John Dee and some spirits*, published with a strongly disapproving preface by Meric Casaubon in 1659, half a century after Dee's death. This strange work, more briefly known as the *Spiritual Diaries*, describes the attempts made by Dee to summon angels with Cabalistic numerological conjurations, attempts made in association with Edward Kelley. It showed Dee in an extremely superstitious light, and stamped him with the reputation of a deluded fanatic, an object of scorn and derision, which lasted throughout the nineteenth century. This reputation eclipsed that of the author of the mathematical preface to Euclid and of the other genuine scientific works, which were completely forgotten.

Only in the present century have scholars begun the rehabilitation of Dee. Ignoring the *Spiritual Diaries*, they have rediscovered Dee the scientist, Dee the author of the mathematical preface. The pioneer in this respect was E. G. R. Taylor, who in a book published in 1930 examined Dee's geographical knowledge. Her work established the great practical services rendered by the 'conjuror', through his knowledge of scientific instruments and of geography, to the bold mariners of the Elizabethan age. In a later book (1954) she was concerned with the host of designers and makers of new and improved scientific instruments who flourished in the later sixteenth century in London, and again emphasized the importance of Dee as a leader in this movement. Meanwhile, in 1937, F. R. Johnson had drawn attention to Dee as an astronomer, and to his interest in the Copernican theory. More recently, in 1958, D. W. Waters in his study of Elizabethan navigation emphasized the importance of Dee's mathematical preface to the English Euclid in encouraging the development of mathematics and navigation.

How is Dee's reputation as an important mathematician and scientist to be reconciled with his reputation as a 'conjuror'? The two types of activity, which seem to us irreconcilable, must have belonged together in some way in Dee's outlook. The nineteenth century, which excluded Dee from serious consideration because of his 'conjuring', was wrong, as the historians of science have discovered. But to include him as a scientist while excluding the angel magic is also incomplete.

It is very clear in the mathematical preface to Euclid that Dee is following the outlines of that famous textbook of Renaissance occultism and magic, the *De occulta philosophia* of Henry Cornelius Agrippa. Agrippa divides the universe into the three worlds of the Cabalists: the natural or elemental world where the magus operates with natural magic; the middle celestial world where he operates with mathematical magic; and the supercelestial world where he operates with, among other procedures, numerological conjurations. This was how Dee thought, and Agrippa's book gives the clue to how one man could be a mathematician, interested in encouraging the use of applied mathematics and technology in the lower worlds inhabited by the Elizabethan artisans or 'mechanicians', and at the same time a 'conjuror' of forces in higher worlds. Dee's concentration on mathematics as the key to all the sciences included operating with number in applied mathematics and operating with number to conjure angels.

The researches of modern scholars have shown that Agrippa's book was the natural, though extreme, outcome of the whole movement which is loosely called Renaissance Neoplatonism. This movement contained a Hermetic or magical core, developed in the Italian Renaissance by Marsilio Ficino, to which Pico della Mirandola added Cabalist magic. The Renaissance Neoplatonist assumed that the whole universe is alive, that it is a vast system of correspondencies, linking the elemental world with the world of the stars and with worlds of spiritual beings beyond the stars. A textbook such as Agrippa's which describes techniques to be used in the elemental world, in the celestial world, and in the supercelestial world can be seen as the logical outcome of the world view of the Renaissance magus.

Those familiar with the work done in recent years on these sides of Renaissance thought have realized that Dee should be situated within this kind of thinking, that he was a remarkable example of the Renaissance magus, and that his scientific activities as well as his 'conjuring' fitted naturally into this outlook. What has been lacking is a full-length study of Dee that would situate him in time, in the milieu in Elizabethan England in which he moved, and within the history of thought and of the Hermetic tradition. Only so could the whole man come before us. This is what

Peter French has done in his book *John Dee: The World of an Elizabethan Magus.*

Many Renaissance scholars have been awaiting such a book as this, hoping for the great gap in our knowledge of the Elizabethan age to be filled by an adequate study of Dee. As the favourite philosopher of Queen Elizabeth I, as the protégé of Leicester admitted to inner court circles, as at the same time the popularizer of scientific knowledge for the Elizabethan artisan class, as the teacher of Philip Sidney, the leader of the Elizabethan poetic renaissance, as the owner of an astonishing library covering all aspects of Renaissance thought, Dee is the Prospero who touches the Elizabethan age at almost every point, whose version of the Hermetic tradition is a current that runs through that age.

Peter French has written a remarkable book which goes a long way toward filling the gap, though, being a modest and careful scholar, he emphasizes how much more there is to be done, how much has to be made up for centuries of neglect before a complete treatment of the subject can be achieved. He begins with the strange history of Dee's reputation, of how the name and fame of the philosopher-in-chief to the Elizabethan age degenerated into that of the foolish charlatan of nineteenth-century legend, which rested on the *Spiritual Diaries*. French points out, quoting the recent researches of P. M. Rattansi on the influence of Hermetic tradition on certain types of Puritan 'enthusiasts', that Meric Casaubon's publication of the *Spiritual Diaries* in 1659, with a damning preface, was a semi-political act which, by destroying Dee's reputation, aimed indirectly at discrediting Puritan 'enthusiasm'.

The Puritan divine John Webster published a defence of Dee against Casaubon in 1677, accusing Casaubon of purposely slandering Dee for personal reasons and stating that Dee was the 'greatest and ablest Philosopher, Mathematician, and Chymist' of his age. Thus Dee's reputation 'became a pawn in the religious conflicts of the Commonwealth'. The nineteenth century was totally ignorant of these facts when it accepted Casaubon as the sole guide to Dee. Nor is the modern scholar as yet clear about what can have been the historical stages through which the reputation of the Elizabethan magus passed that led to his being adopted by revolutionary Puritan enthusiasts under the Commonwealth.

After a useful account of Dee's early life, his pursuit of universal knowledge, his travels abroad and contacts with foreign scholars,

French discusses Dee's library, 'Elizabethan England's Greatest Library', of which he made a catalogue in 1583, manuscript copies of which survive. For many years I have been trying to get people to look at Dee's catalogue of his library, and I used it in my book *Theatre of the World* (1969) to illustrate the extraordinary range of Dee's studies in magic, science, history, literature, and indeed the whole encyclopedia of knowledge available in his time. By consulting the catalogue one can discover what was the range of books he was using for his preface to Euclid; for example, the discussion of Vitruvian architectural theory (which he rightly regarded as a branch of mathematics) in the preface can be illumi-nated from the catalogue, which shows that he possessed all the best modern Italian books on architecture.[1]

French carries further the analysis of the library, and through detailed study of the references to Dee and his library by contem-poraries he demonstrates that this remarkable library, perhaps unique in Europe for its range, which Dee had collected in his house at Mortlake, was at the service of English scholars and that they frequently used it. His house at Mortlake 'became a kind of academy that looked back to the earlier Platonic academies in Florence, emulated the More–Colet circle, and looked forward to the English Royal Society'.

In an intelligent account of the Hermetic philosophy, French relates this to Dee, bringing out the point emphasized in the title of his book that Dee was an 'Elizabethan magus'. He examines 'magic, science, and religion' as held together in Dee's outlook, using for this all Dee's known writings, not only the preface to Euclid but also the obscure figure described in the *Monas hieroglyphica*, which Dee regarded as the expression in hierogly-phic form of the core of his doctrine. It is impossible to mention all the points of great interest raised in this extremely rich study, though the following may be said to be the main heads of the argument.

There was an exoteric and an esoteric side to Dee's life and thought. On the outward-looking, practical, exoteric side, he appears as the propagator of mathematical science among the rising artisan class of Elizabethan London, to which the preface to Euclid is directed, with the object of encouraging invention and tech-nology among the 'mechanicians', to be used for the betterment of their estate. There is already here the utilitarian motive in the plea for science, which Francis Bacon is usually supposed to have been the first to emphasize. This side of Dee's interests made him the friend and adviser of navigators, gunners, instrument makers, and 'mechanicians' generally. On the other hand, his teaching had an esoteric core, concealed in the mysteries of the *Monas hieroglyphica*. Here lay its appeal to the inner circle of poets and courtiers, headed by the Queen herself, who expressly asked Dee to explain the *Monas* to her.

French makes a brave attempt to tackle the *Monas* and the angel magic to which it is no doubt in some way related. Published in 1564, with a dedication to the Emperor Maximilian II, Dee's *Monas hieroglyphica* describes a sign composed of the signs for the seven planets and of the zodiac sign Aries, in which he believed he had found a unifying statement that included the whole universe. The commentary on the *Monas* combines alchemical, mathematical, and Cabalistic modes of thought, and was probably expressive for Dee of ascent through all the three worlds described by Agrippa – the elemental, the celestial, the supercelestial – to the First Cause or the One. Dee always regarded his *Monas hieroglyphica* as his supreme achievement. For this man of extraordinary genius who lived within the categories and magical presuppositions of the Renaissance world of Hermetic Neoplatonism, it was presumably an expression in what Francis Bacon or Leibniz might have called 'real characters' – signs believed to be in actual contact with reality – of some profoundly unifying experience.

Like Giordano Bruno, whose career touches his at several points, Dee believed that his initiation into Hermetic mysteries laid upon him the responsibility of becoming a religious leader, with a mission for establishing a universal religion of love which should do away with all religious differences, wars of religion, and persecutions. Unlike Bruno, whose 'Egyptian' magical religion implied a kind of deism, Dee believed himself to be profoundly Christian, in contact with good spirits or good angels. However misguided he may have been in his belief in the revelations of his angels, there can be no doubt that Dee was absolutely sincere in his professions of deep piety, and that the religious motive was indeed the mainspring of his life.

French conducts the reader through the complexities of Dee's mind in a style both critical and clear, and he is firmly historical in placing this strange figure within the context of his age. One of the most remarkable aspects of his book is the number of people in it, the very large number of references to Dee by contemporaries, which he has skilfully assembled to bring out the fact that Dee had some kind of contact with practically everyone of note. The combination of factual presentation of Dee's movements among his contemporaries with subtle presentation of his ideas and suggestions about their possible influence is particularly interesting in the chapter 'John Dee and the Sidney Circle'.

We know from Thomas Moffett that Dee was Sidney's teacher, but it has not been realized to what extent the whole circle of Sidney's relatives and friends was familiar with Dee. French shows that the most important and most intimate sphere of Dee's influence was that of the Sidney circle. We know that Sidney was interested in 'the mathematicals' and in 'chymistry', both Dee subjects, and French asks what other aspects of Dee's outlook might have influenced the young poet who was to be the leader of the Elizabethan poetic renaissance. Here he raises the important question of Hermetic theory of the imagination as basic to the outlook of a Hermetic magus, mentioning those theories of magical animation of mental images in the occult arts of memory to which I have drawn attention in my book *The Art of Memory*.

French re-examines Sidney's *Apology for Poetry*, looking for traces of Hermetic theory and using passages from Dee's preface to Euclid that have certainly never been used before in connection with Sidney. He wants to establish that Renaissance theories of music, affecting theories of poetry, could have reached Sidney through Dee, and that the creative imagination of the poet is allied to the magical activity of the magus, stimulating the creation of vital poetic images. French is here trying to grapple with the core of the problem of the mental image, its relation to art and poetry, and the relation of Hermetic theories of magical imagination to the stimulation of the creative imagination. The chapter is a little confused; he is trying to do too much and perhaps does not entirely succeed in making his points. But no student of Sidney or of the Elizabethan poetic renaissance should neglect this chapter, which raises the central problems of the 'creative imagination' (that jargon-ridden phrase but here not used as jargon) in the context of the study of Dee and his influence.

Finally, in the chapter 'John Dee as an Antiquarian', French discusses Dee as a Tudor historiographer and antiquary, friend of Camden and Stow, an authority on the Arthurian legends, and influential in building up the propaganda for British imperialism around Queen Elizabeth. He 'helped to reinvest the Arthurian legends with their old appeal', which had important implications for Spenser and for the whole Elizabethan political-religious aspiration. Thus even for the Elizabeth cult Dee was indispensable, and this adds the final touch to the picture of the Elizabethan magus as permeating every side of the Elizabethan age, helping to create that age in almost every aspect of its activity, not excluding the creation of the image of the queen who was its symbol.

This scholarly book, based on impressive original research (in the valuable bibliography French cites over seventy manuscript sources which he has consulted), should put an end, once and for all, to the fantastic neglect from which Dee has suffered and to the equally fantastic nonsense which still continues to be written about him. It emphasizes the deeply religious core of Dee's thinking, and how the difficult problem of his angel magic should not be approached through cheap sneers at the 'conjuror' but through attempts to understand the Renaissance world view of which it formed a part. The only criticism of the book which I have to make is that it is incomplete, but this is anticipated by French's modesty. 'After working on Dee for several years,' he says, 'I do not think that a single individual is capable of examining adequately his importance in all areas of Renaissance thought'. He points out that he has not attempted to examine Dee's influence on the Continent during the phase of his life which began with his departure from England in 1583. 'I have merely attempted to make a beginning,' he says, 'and to present a picture of Dee that may induce others to study him and his thought'.

The way is now certainly open for the long-overdue reassessment of the Elizabethan age in the light of better knowledge of the Renaissance Hermetic-Cabalist tradition and of its Elizabethan representative, John Dee.

Dee has also been attracting attention in Italy during the current year. Furio Jesi in his article 'John Dee e il suo sapere' has had recourse to the manuscript catalogue of the library and notes the wide range of scientific interests which it reveals. He emphasizes Dee's dependence on the *De occulta philosophia* of Agrippa and is fully aware that Dee's scientific studies belonged to the kind of outlook outlined by Agrippa. Jesi is not well-informed concerning the preface to Euclid, and does not know of Dee's encouragement of 'mechanicians'. He has, however, made rather a careful study of the *Monas hieroglyphica* and is under the impression that Dee was only in contact with the aristocratic world of the court, and

with the Queen, standing aloof from the ordinary world of men.
As we know, this is only half the truth, and leaves out the exoteric
side of Dee's teaching.

Jesi emphasizes Dee's cult of Queen Elizabeth I and his build-
up of imperial prospects for her. He points out that in the *Monas
hieroglyphica* Dee appeals to rulers, asking them to follow the
way of mystical 'adepts' and not of 'tyrants' and suggests that Dee
might have envisaged the wide rule which he planned for Queen
Elizabeth as the rule of an 'adept' in his philosophy. Like other
suggestions in this article, the point is intelligently raised though
not supported by wide knowledge of the present state of Dee
studies. Jesi notes the importance of Dee's religious position,
which allowed him to be 'Anglican in England and Catholic in
Prague', arguing that this apparent indifferentism belongs naturally to the attitude of esoteric Christians of the sixteenth century,
for whom Cabala, associated with Neoplatonism, provided a
mystical approach to religious problems which enabled them to
keep clear of the ferocity of the wars of religion. Though less
firmly based in historical knowledge than French's analysis of
Dee's religious position, this Italian article corroborates French's
approach.

Jesi is interesting on Dee and the English poets, the discussion
of which he limits to two dramatic texts, Shakespeare's *Tempest*
and Ben Jonson's *The Alchemist*. While avoiding crude statements
– that Prospero, the magus, *is* Dee, or that Abel Drugger, in *The
Alchemist*, is a satire on Dee – he argues that, while Prospero
belongs to the kind of outlook exemplified in England by Dee,
Ben Jonson is hostile to it and may make direct mocking references
to the *Monas hieroglyphica*. This fits in with Jonson's later hostile
references to Robert Fludd, who succeeded Dee as the representative of the Hermetic-Cabalist tradition in England, and I would
agree that much might be learned through careful study of Ben
Jonson's antagonism.

Wayne Shumaker's *The Occult Sciences in the Renaissance* is
divided into five sections, 'Astrology', 'Witchcraft', 'White
Magic', 'Alchemy', and 'Hermes Trismegistus'. 'Every literary
person', he states, 'knows, or thinks he knows, at least a little
about astrology, witchcraft, magic, and alchemy, or about one or
more of them, if not, perhaps, about Hermes Trismegistus.'

After describing the recovery in the Renaissance of the *Corpus
Hermeticum*, the collection of writings ascribed to the fictitious

'Hermes Trismegistus', Shumaker gives some account of these works which he thinks represent a philosophical mysticism, entirely free from magic or astrology. Though he mentions that there are numerous other writings ascribed to Hermes Trismegistus which are certainly magical, alchemical, or astrological, he says that these have nothing to do with 'Hermes himself', stating that modern scholars, like A.-J. Festugière, have not thought them relevant to the philosophical *Hermetica*.

Shumaker is describing, and adopting, the old-fashioned attitude to these writings which sought to keep the philosophical *Hermetica* quite apart from implications of magic or astrology. Walter Scott took this line in his introduction to his edition of the *Hermetica* (1924–6). It was completely disproved by Festugière in his foundation work *La révélation d'Hermès Trismégiste* (1950–4), the first volume of which is devoted to the magical, alchemical, and astrological texts with the object of showing that these cannot be separated from the writings of the *Corpus Hermeticum* and the *Asclepius* because the latter texts, though they are expressive of philosophical and religious meditation, are steeped in the gnostic atmosphere of their period, which implied a religious use of magic and an astrological setting for religious experiences. The Hermetic initiate rises up through the spheres of the planets in his regenerative experience.

Shumaker's method of reverting to Scott's type of interpretation while not mentioning that this is against Festugière, whom he cites, seems a strangely unscholarly mode of procedure. I might add, though this is not so important, that he involves me in a similar way, mentioning indebtedness to my works in his preface but not mentioning in his 'Hermes Trismegistus' chapter – which the unwary reader might think was based on the first chapter of my *Giordano Bruno and the Hermetic Tradition* – that his interpretation is quite unlike mine, which follows Festugière.

I may seem to have dwelt overlong on this point, but it really throws out Shumaker's whole approach to the occult sciences in the Renaissance, which arose out of the rediscovery of the Hermetic texts and out of Marsilio Ficino's interpretation of the magical passages in the *Asclepius*, as has been established by D. P. Walker. In his pages on Ficino's magic, which draw heavily on Walker's *Spiritual and Demonic Magic* (1958), Shumaker omits Walker's scholarly demonstration of the sources of Ficino's magic, thus distorting the whole argument.

There may be some matter in Shumaker's book of use to students, for example the long analysis of the contents of Cornelius Agrippa's *De occulta philosophia*, though this gives no help in explaining allusions. For example, Agrippa's mention of 'the four furies' will be inexplicable to a student who does not know about the four Platonic *furores*, or grades of enthusiasm. I dismiss the base thought that perhaps Shumaker does not know about them either, though there is a lack of grasp throughout his book of the fundamental connections between Renaissance Neoplatonism and the Renaissance interpretation of the *Hermetica* which make it impossible to isolate 'white magic' or 'Hermes Trismegistus', as he tries to do. As for Bruno and Campanella, they are summarized as 'implicitly covered under witchcraft', a truly amazing remark!

The illustrations reproduced from Robert Fludd's works are not integrated with the text and make no sense in isolation. Bibliographical material is scrappily arranged. The few pages at the end on Hermetic influence on English literature are singularly inadequate. In short this book confuses more than it clarifies, and cannot be recommended as a reliable guide to occult sciences in the Renaissance.

It is only negatively that Shumaker's book comes into the subject of this article. John Dee's name does not appear in the index, but on hunting about in the notes I finally located the remark, 'the English John Dee, a rather silly man', followed a page or two later by a reference to Meric Casaubon's edition of the *Spiritual Diaries*. These are the only two references to Dee in the book. Shumaker has reverted to the nineteenth century, to the deluded man of Casaubon's tendentious preface, to total ignorance of all Dee's other works and activities. This is a wonderful specimen to add to the long history of Dee's reputation and will no doubt be cited in future books as what must surely be the last attempt at keeping Dee out.

Chapter Six

BACON'S MAGIC*

It is now more than ten years since Paolo Rossi's book on Bacon was published in Italy. Those who have known this book have been aware that it made, for the first time, the right historical approach to Bacon. Now that it is at last available in translation, it makes an important contribution to Bacon studies in the English-speaking world, even though since its first publication in 1957 there have been movements in the history of thought which will make some of its themes seem less revolutionary and surprising than they did when the book first appeared.

Rossi was trained in the Italian historical-philosophical school, led by Eugenio Garin, in which the Renaissance magical tradition, with its glorification of man as magus, was seen as important in the pre-history of the scientific revolution. In this book, he applies this tradition to Francis Bacon. He shows that many of Bacon's major themes can be found in Cornelius Agrippa's textbook of Renaissance magic. In his *De occulta philosophia*, Agrippa outlines the Renaissance Hermetic tradition, incorporating the ideas and attitudes of Marsilio Ficino and of Pico della Mirandola, and takes Renaissance magic further in the direction of bold presentation of magical science as power, and of man, the magus, as dominator over nature and as operator. The domination of nature was to be,

* Review of Paolo Rossi, *Francis Bacon: From Magic to Science*, translated from the Italian by Sacha Rabinovitch, London, Boston and Henley, 1968, in *New York Review of Books*, 29 February 1968.

of course, the major Baconian objective, and the theme of the use
of science for the betterment of man's estate, so characteristic of
Bacon, is also to be found, in the form of magical science, in
Agrippa. These discoveries will cause little surprise today now
that knowledge of the importance of the Renaissance Hermetic
tradition is widespread. The book on Agrippa by Charles G.
Nauert, which I reviewed in these pages in March 1966 (see below,
pp. 262–7), carries the Agrippa–Bacon comparison further,
though Nauert did not know of Rossi's book and arrived indepen-
dently at similar conclusions.

Though some of Rossi's themes are thus no longer novel, his
analyses of Bacon's reactions against the Renaissance magical tradition to which he was at the same time indebted have not been
explored elsewhere in such depth. Rossi presents Bacon as in
reaction against the Renaissance magus ideal largely on moral
grounds. He deplores the self-centredness and spiritual pride of
those who use their knowledge and powers for self-glorification.
The works of God in nature must be approached with profound
humility; scientific knowledge should not be kept secret while its
possessor glorifies himself with pretensions of omniscience and
power. The work of those who seek into the truths of nature
must be shared with others; only through collaboration of many
workers can advances be made, and these advances are to be
made in the interests of mankind at large, and not for individual
aggrandizement.

These Baconian themes, which foreshadow co-operative
scientific effort in institutions such as the Royal Society, are well
known. What Rossi shows, through his attempt throughout the
book to place Bacon in a historical context, is that Bacon was here
reacting against the magus ideal. Though his programme of man
as operator and dominator of nature derives from the magus ideal,
he reacts from it in the direction of the need for humility, open-
ness, and for pooling one's efforts in collaboration, as necessary
for scientific advance. Through these sound and reasonable arguments, Bacon makes an impression of modernity, of having
crossed the frontiers, leaving behind him that atmosphere which
we have to make a tremendous mental effort to enter – the atmosphere surrounding a Renaissance magus – and entering the
modern, soberer world of sensible scientific collaboration which
we can understand without difficulty.

Yet Bacon is himself steeped in the Renaissance tradition. In *The*

Advancement of Learning he discusses subjects which belong fully in the sphere of the magus, such as 'fascination'. Moreover, as Rossi points out, the 'simple forms' to which he wishes to reduce nature are based on alchemical principles. He does not discard astrology, but wants a reformed astrology. In fact his programme does not, whatever he may say, discard the Renaissance tradition but is a reform of it, fundamentally a moral movement in which the proud and pretentious magus transforms into the humble scientist.

Seen in this light, as both continuing Renaissance traditions and opposing them, Bacon becomes once more a key figure in the history of thought, not for the old nineteenth-century reasons and wrong assessments, such as his emphasis on experiment, but as a figure in whom we can study those subtle transformations through which Renaissance themes become, in the seventeenth century, modernized, as it were, and are given a more reasonable aspect. Bacon is not an impossible Renaissance magus; he is quite possible as a member of the future Royal Society. The times have moved, the atmosphere has changed, yet it is basically the Renaissance Hermetic tradition which is modulated or transformed into a seventeenth-century outlook through the mind of Francis Bacon.

As Rossi shows, Bacon thought of the proud Renaissance philosophers, imposing their systems on the universe from the isolation of their haughty self-communings, as having brought about a second Fall of Man through their pride and presumption in impressing their own image on the divine creation, instead of studying it with humility. The reform needed is a moral process, a humble approach to nature through observation and experiment. By this process, eventually, the innocent communion with nature which Adam had before the Fall will be restored. Bacon's 'Great Instauration' of the sciences was intended to lead to this millennium, perhaps in a fairly short time – for Bacon believed that a full understanding of nature might be achieved fairly quickly, once errors and fallacies were put aside and the true method established. Here too, in his Adam mysticism, Bacon has affinities with Agrippa, who believed that through the procedures of learned magic the magus could achieve a communion with nature like that of Adam before the Fall. But here again the Baconian atmosphere is different, and his reasonable arguments in favour of scientific co-operation and his stress on the importance of technological development for the betterment of man's estate have a modern ring. They can be, and often are, read without noticing the passages which reveal the underlying cosmic mysticism, so that Bacon as a thinker makes a different impression from that of his predecessors.

These differences are subtle, and it is the great merit of Rossi's book that he draws attention to the fine points that arise when Bacon is seen against the background of the Renaissance philosophies which he is discarding with disapproval while he is, at the same time, emergent from them. Through this historical approach the whole problem of Bacon becomes much richer and more complex than in those over-simplified clichés about him which are passed around in general histories of culture.

Rossi's book is a beginning rather than an end, and many of the stimulating ideas which he adumbrates demand further exploration. It is possible, for example, that some of Bacon's mistakes might have arisen from his anxiety to dissociate himself from the magus tradition and, at the same time, his wish to make a powerful plea for scientific advance by putting it on a more morally acceptable basis. For example, it has been thought surprising that Bacon should have rejected the Copernican hypothesis. Might one reason for this be that it was associated in his mind with the proud assumptions of a Renaissance animist philosopher, and with, in particular, the philosophy of Giordano Bruno – who is mentioned by name by Bacon, together with Patrizi, Campanella and Gilbert, as an example of a philosopher of the 'second Fall' – who had associated heliocentricity with his magical and Hermetic outlook? Again, Bacon's disapproval of Gilbert on the magnet has caused surprise as coming from the advocate of scientific research. What Bacon disapproved of was Gilbert's imposition of his magnetic philosophy on the cosmos, after the manner of a magus; there are indeed passages in the *De magnete* which are very close to Bruno.

Finally – and this is perhaps a point of considerable potential importance – the question might be asked whether Bacon's underrating of mathematics might be traced to a wish to dissociate himself from the Renaissance tradition in which number held a place of primary importance. In particular, the surviving influence and reputation of John Dee in Bacon's time should be taken into account. Dee was a magus and a spiritualist as well as a mathematician, and in his preface to Euclid of 1570 had set out a programme for scientific advance which was actually of greater scientific importance than the programme of *The Advancement of*

Learning because it was based on an appeal for the revival and encouragement of mathematical studies. Rossi's method of Baconian study should be extended to the study of Bacon against the background of both the Dee mathematical tradition and of the contemporary philosophy of Robert Fludd, which seems, and indeed is, the antithesis of that of Bacon: for Fludd's may be the example of a philosophy which imposes its own patterns on the universe of which Bacon is chiefly thinking. It is interesting that Fludd enthusiastically welcomed Harvey's discovery of the circulation of the blood, published two years after Bacon's death. For Fludd, the discovery was a confirmation of parallelism between macrocosm and microcosm – the basis of his own Hermetic philosophy – showing a connection between circular movement in the heaven of the macrocosm and in the body of man, the microcosm. A recent study of Harvey by Walter Pagel has emphasized Fludd's welcoming attitude to his thought, and has suggested that the circle analogy may even have been a factor in leading Harvey to his discovery.

At any rate it may perhaps be said that the approach to Harvey's problem through the contemplation of the circle as a possible 'model' may bring us closer to what we now know about the basis of scientific discovery in hypothesis than does Bacon's insistence on experiment. Yet, if Bacon may sometimes have gone wrong in his reactions against mathematical magicians and their mystical diagrams, these reactions in themselves were modern and progressive, and were beginning to create the more rational atmosphere of a new era.

Rossi devotes a long chapter to analysis of Bacon's use of mythology. This again is novel in a book on Bacon's philosophy, for in works on Bacon as a thinker it has been customary to treat his work on myths as irrelevant, belonging to his literary side and not to his philosophy. Rossi shows how constant and basic to his thought was Bacon's preoccupation with myth, not only in *The Wisdom of the Ancients* but in many other works. Developing the tradition which interpreted myths as hidden statements of the truths of natural philosophy, Rossi shows how Bacon invested his own philosophy with mythical forms, perhaps to hide its potentially dangerous anti-Aristotelian bias from his opponents, though, as Rossi subtly argues, the problem is a much more profound one than that of mere concealment. It involves the problem of whether mythical form of statement comes closer to reality than does discursive reasoning. Rossi's analysis of what appears to be

Bacon's change of opinion about this in different works is extremely interesting. He is, I am sure, right in thinking that it was a
central problem for Bacon. Here again a new kind of comparison
with Renaissance philosophers would be valuable, for example
with Bruno's use of myths in his arts of memory as memory
images which he believes to be in direct contact with cosmic
reality. How far does this magical element survive in Bacon's
treatment of myth, and, if modified, in which way is it modified?
This again ties up with Bacon's advocacy of 'real characters', the
use of signs having a direct contact with reality, which he regards
as one of the basic necessities for the advancement of science. This
idea has an obvious connection with magic signs, but, again,
Bacon's treatment of it is detached and rational.

This brings us to Bacon's belief in the importance of the art of
memory – a reformed art of memory, not used with pretentious-
ness and pride (perhaps he was thinking of Bruno's and Fludd's
magic arts of memory), but humbly, as an instrument of scientific
classification and method. Rossi was the first, in the original Italian
edition of his book, to draw attention to the importance of the
art of memory for Bacon, and to Bacon's treatment of it as a step
in its evolution in the direction of scientific method. Rossi has
carried these researches further in his *Clavis universalis* (1960). It
may be that it is on these lines – in the search for a 'real' notation,
for a universal language using 'real characters', and for a method
incorporating Lullism, Ramism, and the art of memory – that
Bacon's greatest importance will be seen to lie in the scholarship
of the future, as it traces these strands from the Renaissance to
Leibniz. Rossi's chapters on these themes in his *Francesco Bacone*
were a pioneer effort in this direction. I think that much in these
chapters might now be put more clearly.

It is unfortunate that Rossi was not able to use Walter J. Ong's
work on Ramus (published in 1958) and therefore has missed the
point of the Ramist method as an art of memory without images.
This point is very important for Bacon's attitude to Ramus; for
when it is grasped, it can be seen how non-Ramist Bacon is in his
retention of images in his art of memory, and in his search for
'real' images or characters to use in scientific method. On the
problem of the mental image and changing attitudes to it – an
absolutely central one for the history of our civilization – Bacon
again stands between two worlds. On the one hand he knows,
still at first hand, so to speak, of the Renaissance imaginative

magic; on the other, he begins to detach himself from it. When events like these, occurring within the psyche, are better understood, we may come at last to a better understanding of the great turning points in history, such as the modulation of Renaissance into seventeenth century.

I would like to put on record here my own debt to Rossi's work, which makes everything else on Bacon look pale and insipid, and how glad I am that it is now available in a good English translation.

Chapter Seven

BACON AND THE MENACE OF
ENGLISH LIT.*

FRANCIS BACON's reputation has suffered strange vicissitudes. From being the admired father of the experimental method, dear to nineteenth-century progressives, he has been assigned a position of very limited importance by some, though not all, modern historians of science. These extreme oscillations are themselves an indication of the intrinsic power of this great figure, and those favouring the extreme of contempt have not succeeded in accounting for the undoubted fact that the early members of the Royal Society looked to Bacon as the inspiration of their efforts. Brian Vickers takes another way to the solution of this apparent anomaly. From his study of Bacon's prose style which was geared to the rhetorical purpose of persuasion, he concludes that Bacon's enormous influence 'is not to be explained by the actual detailed content of his scientific programme . . . but rather by the terms in which it was formulated and the imaginative eloquence with which these were transmitted.' That is to say, the real significance of Bacon lay in the persuasive power of the language in which he urged the advancement of knowledge.

Though this is not exactly a new discovery, Vickers brings to bear on Bacon's prose style a detailed examination based on 'the most enlightened modern discussions of stylistic analysis'. He

---

* Review of Brian Vickers, *Francis Bacon and Renaissance Prose*, Cambridge, 1968; and Joan Webber, *The Eloquent 'I': Style and Self in Seventeenth-Century Prose*, Madison, Wisconsin, 1968, in *New York Review of Books*, 27 March 1969.

believes that the analysis of style is a literary, not a scientific, discipline, and he draws up in his first chapter the principles on which he would base the study of a writer's style. There is much portentous statement of the obvious in this chapter, but one would not quarrel with the definition of the main features of Bacon's style as the insistence on a carefully designed structure, the importance attached to aphorisms, the use of symmetrical syntax, and, above all, of imagery. If this chapter encourages specialists in English literature to concentrate less frantically on 'structure' and to turn some, at least, of their attention to imagery, it will have done good work.

Bacon, says Vickers, thought in images, like a man of the Renaissance; every thought is immediately clothed in an illustration or an analogy which seems born with the thought and is inseparable from it; his images even seem to run ahead of his thought, and to determine it. Vickers rightly suggests that this is a mode of apprehension which should be called poetical, based on a fundamentally religious and poetical view of the world. In a valuable survey of the history of attitudes toward Bacon's style, which oscillate between admiration and contempt like the attitudes toward Bacon as a scientist, Vickers draws up from oblivion Shelley's illuminating statement that 'Lord Bacon was a poet.'

'Philosophers', said Giordano Bruno, 'are in some way painters and poets; poets are painters and philosophers; painters are philosophers and poets.' The intense imaginative vision of Renaissance man, which made fusions like this possible, was fed by the science of imagery. Elaborate textbooks expounded the moral and 'physical' (or philosophical and scientific) meanings of the figures of classical mythology which the painters painted and the poets described. Such apparently pedestrian analysis of the great mythological figures did not diminish their power to integrate the vast imaginations of men like Bruno and Bacon. For Bacon, as we know from his *Wisdom of the Ancients*, his own most deeply held philosophical convictions were hidden in, or integrated with, the myths. And there was a strong infusion of magical power in such figures – intensive cultivation of the imagination always has an element of magic in it, and Renaissance magic was an imaginative art – constantly infiltrating into poetic and artistic creation. Bacon is a man of the Renaissance in whose prose style the Renaissance magic of imagery is still alive, imparting to it the 'fascination' which he cultivated and the power of rhetorical persuasion raised to a magical degree. Vickers's carefully constructed net of stylistic analysis, though it does bring up the right fishes, has killed them in the process.

And this killing process seems to have been deliberate, the result of his deliberately restricting the book to the concept of the 'literary'. 'The literary student', says Vickers, 'is forced to retreat' when faced with the discovery that analogies, for Bacon, are really correspondencies revealing the unity of nature. Even from the strictly literary point of view, such retreat is unwise, for it obscures the living bond between word and thing which gives density and power to Bacon's style. And the intensive concentration on images in the literary style is related to that search for 'real characters', for a notation which should make direct contact with reality, which was perhaps Bacon's most notable contribution to science, leading, as it did, to the search for universal languages, and thence, eventually, to Leibniz.

The Eloquent 'I' is also concerned with seventeenth-century prose style. Though purists will be antagonized by the deplorable title and by the author's bullying manner, this book does attempt to tackle the problem of style at a deep level. Joan Webber selects eight authors whom she takes as characteristically 'Anglican' or 'Puritan' and tries to define their differing attitudes to themselves as writers, and hence to their prose style. The 'Anglicans' are Donne, Burton, Sir Thomas Browne, Traherne; the 'Puritans' are Bunyan, Lilburne, Milton; and Richard Baxter is an 'Anglican Puritan'. The attempt made to relate differences in style to deep levels of the personality where the 'I' faces God and the cosmos through different religious traditions results in some valuable observations.

Joan Webber finds that the seventeenth-century 'Anglican' is deeply concerned with man as a microcosm of the universe and hence with cultivating a 'cosmic personality'. She has no difficulty in finding striking passages in support of this thesis in Donne's *Devotions upon Emergent Occasions*, in Browne's *Religio Medici*, and in Traherne's *Centuries*. The Anglican 'I', she argues, is wrapped in this contemplative cosmic awareness, which it expresses through elaborate imagery. The Puritan, on the contrary, sees himself not as here and now related to the eternal and the divine, but as journeying through time to eternity. This gives a practical urgency to his awareness of himself and a certain combativeness to his prose style. Milton's prose controversies are, of course, taken as typical of the Puritan 'I' as a writer, while the chapter on Donne and Bunyan attempts, through contrasting the totally different styles of these writers, to elucidate the basic differences which the book aims to bring out.

This book has a certain value as an attempt at tackling a very important problem, the inner, deep-seated changes in the psyche during the early seventeenth century, the vital period for the emergence of modern European and American man. Its best observation is the emphasis on 'Puritan' shift, from 'Anglican' cosmic consciousness to a 'progressive' attitude toward the religious life, and hence to the emergence of a different kind of 'I'. The book's drawbacks are the arbitrary classification of the writers studied and a good deal of ignorance of the backgrounds of thought on which they drew. It seems curious, for example, to write a chapter on Burton's *Anatomy of Melancholy* without once mentioning the Renaissance revaluation of the melancholy humour (which could well have been worked out according to the 'I' theme) and the chapter on Sir Thomas Browne is also very unsatisfactory. The book's rigid classifications do not work for such a mind as Browne's whose whole effort was toward the avoidance of rigidity.

The general reflections which arise in my mind after reading these two books are about the enormous influence on contemporary academic thought and writing of the concept of 'English literature'. Theses and books have to be designed to meet the requirements of boards of studies in English or for the consumption of students taking English courses or degrees. Brian Vickers's book is impeccable from the English literature point of view; it is designed to draw attention to Bacon as a 'great prose writer' through careful examination of the rhetorical devices that he used. But when he draws near to the things that interested Bacon, and that made him want to write persuasive prose, Vickers as a 'literary student' must 'draw back'. Though Joan Webber is less afraid of being unliterary and tackles larger issues, she too is conditioned by literature, for her book has to be about the emergence of different prose styles, or rather about style as the expression of the 'I'. This ever-present preoccupation distorts even her good ideas and observations and frequently leads her into painful insensitivity, particularly noticeable in the chapter on Traherne. This vitally important period, the early seventeenth century, has an abundant literature devoted to its literature, the authors of which are often interested in non-literary topics. But they have to approach these topics mainly through the study of the literary texts, which are then supported by some 'background' reading in the history of religion, philosophy, or science.

It seems to me that this results in a perpetual situation of putting the cart before the horse. The actual deep-seated movements of the period, which influenced the psychic and psychological changes underlying the emergence of the seventeenth century from the Renaissance, are little understood. Surely one should begin with these before coming to their expression in literature. Literary students suffer from insufficient knowledge of these movements. Histories of religious affiliations in England, with their sharp differentiations between Protestant and Catholic, or between Puritan and Anglican, will not account for some of the phenomena glimpsed behind the literary texts.

For example, why should seventeenth-century 'Anglican' prose writers dwell on 'cosmic consciousness', on man as microcosm? Should we not ask where in the period this philosophy was expressed as philosophy, and not as literature? There is no mention in Joan Webber's book of the great exponent of macrocosm and microcosm in seventeenth-century England, Robert Fludd; he did not write in English, does not figure as a literary person; therefore English literature passes him by. The type of cosmic consciousness expressed by the Anglican writers was not a medieval survival but a new Renaissance development of medieval tradition. Francis Bacon knew this when he complained that the ancient opinion that man is a microcosm 'hath been fantastically strained by Paracelsus and the alchemists.' Writers like Donne or Browne were Renaissance writers, aware of Renaissance trends from which the literary student must not draw back.

It is, I think, impossible to understand Traherne's writing without some knowledge of the Hermetic tradition by which he was obviously influenced, particularly in his religious and mystical aim of reflecting the universe within. He is also probably aware of Renaissance adaptations of the art of memory for this purpose. The 'inner iconoclasm', through which Puritan Ramists attempted to destroy as idolatrous the formation of inner images, should be a basic consideration in any attempt to define the Puritan mentality.

The Puritan–Anglican antithesis itself is in need of new historical evaluation. Too little is known of what Friedrich Heer has called *Die dritte Kraft*, the third, or middle, way of reconciliation or toleration pursued in this period of mystical secret societies, by *politiques*, and by liberal and inquiring individuals, through which some of the most profound and fruitful tendencies of the age seem to pass undisturbed from one confessional camp to another.

Philip Sidney is a key figure here; he wore a Puritan label but probably had other mysterious affiliations and certainly overlaps in his style with what Miss Webber would call 'Puritan'. A concept like Utopia is labelled Puritan by Miss Webber, because of the Utopian planning of the Puritan mind under the Commonwealth. Yet the first Utopia was written by a Catholic, Thomas More; others are by the heretical Catholic, Campanella, and by the 'Rosicrucian', Valentin Andreae, not to mention Francis Bacon (to whom Miss Webber omits to apply her rules of thumb). In plotting the course of the history of Utopia one crosses and recrosses the conventional religious frontiers. And indeed the crossing of such frontiers was actually the aim of Utopians.

Literature is important; the history of literary style is important. My argument is only that seventeenth-century English literature reflects deep-seated movements of the human spirit, and that a renewed, or quite new, study of these movements is needed before we can understand the literature. The critical school, to which Brian Vickers perhaps partially belongs, will of course maintain that literary texts should be studied in a vacuum. But if any kind of historical interpretation is brought in, the history should precede the interpretation, the horse should come before the cart.

I would also like to enter a protest against the use of literary jargon, of which the authors of both books under review are guilty, though their kinds of jargon are different. I will illustrate this by an anecdote from Richard Baxter's autobiography – one of a list of several stories about his providential escapes from danger – which Miss Webber uses as a basis for stylistic analysis, taking it as an example of Baxter's insistence on literal detail. She quotes the anecdote as follows:

Another time, as I sat in my Study, the Weight of my greatest Folio Books brake down three or four of the highest Shelves, when I sat Close under them, and they fell down on every side of me, save one upon the Army; whereas the Place, the Weight, and greatness of the Books was such, and my head just under them, that it was a Wonder they had not beaten out my Brains, one of the Shelves right over my head having

the six Volumes of *Dr. Walton's Oriental Bible,* and all
Austin's Works, and the *Bibliotheca Patrum,* and *Marlorate,*
&c.

This story impressed me and I looked up at the shelves in my
own study rather nervously. It also puzzled me. Why did this
scholarly divine possess a book on 'the Army' and why did he
refer to it in this inaccurate way when he is so much more
particular about the other large tomes which featured in this
disaster? Also, what did actually happen? My impression was that
the book on the army was the only one which did not fall, while
the oriental Bible, Augustine, and the Fathers crashed all around
him. But Miss Webber's interpretation is different; she comments
facetiously on 'the fact that Baxter was struck by a book on the
army, but not by the Fathers of the Church. God's Providence is
altogether excessive.' She uses this story as a peg upon which to
hang a specimen of English Literature jargon.

> One may usefully compare the 'metaphysical' effort, in a
> writer like Donne, to force an abstraction into a confining
> and very specific figure of speech: the conflict between the
> two, when the figure is successful, creates that dazzling union
> of humor, passion, and intensity that is called metaphysical
> wit. Here the effort is to graft a rigid concept of history upon
> a very literal, detailed rendering of individual experience in
> order to prove the working of God's providence upon
> Richard Baxter.

This does not help about the book on the army so I looked up
the reference in Baxter, where I found that what he actually says
is that the books fell down 'on every side of me, save one upon
the Arm'. So that was it. All the books fell and missed him save
one which gave him a bang on the arm. Why dilate on Baxter's
attention to literal detail then destroy his story by misquoting its
literal detail? And then obliterate the mangled story in clouds of
jargon?

Good old Richard Baxter, the Puritan! I went on reading his
book and found its dignified lucidity an immense relief. 'His Soul',
he says, 'ever lay open to the Evidence: His Eye was first upon
the Matter to find that out: he then considered Words as the fit
Portraictures of Things and . . . was ever careful to give expres-

sions their strict and just interpretations, and to be clear about the fixed sense of doubtful terms.'

If one cannot be a poet who fuses words and things, perhaps one should try for precision, like Baxter. Jargon is neither poetic nor precise. Sometimes one wishes that the old Puritan sense of the ethical importance of accuracy and plain speaking could be revived to protect English prose style.

Chapter Eight

AN ALCHEMICAL LEAR*

AMONG THE 'RENAISSANCES' of the Renaissance one of the most important was the renaissance of alchemy. Like the occultist movement in general, the alchemical movement involved a return to ancient sources, in this case an intense interest in, and revival of, medieval writers on alchemy. The fascination of, for example, the obscure works of the medieval alchemist George Ripley for the intelligentsia of the sixteenth and early seventeenth centuries can be seen as a form of *prisca theologia*, a return to Hermetic sources. 'Hermes Trismegistus', the secret patron of Renaissance Neoplatonism, was associated with the 'Egyptian' science of alchemy, as the supposed author of alchemical texts.

The part played by alchemy in the Hermeticism of the Italian Renaissance is not yet clear, but in the sixteenth and early seventeenth centuries in northern Europe alchemy may be said to have been a dominant form of the occultist tradition. Charles Nicholl's book tackles the difficult subject of the alchemical renaissance, the intense interest in alchemical practice and the great spate of learned and obscure works on alchemical theory, which poured from the presses of Europe, particularly around the turn of the century. It is characteristic of this new alchemy that it grounded itself on the works of medieval alchemists like George Ripley or Roger Bacon. By a process which in other contexts would be called 'humanistic',

---

* Review of Charles Nicholl, *The Chemical Theatre*, London, Boston and Henley, 1981, in *New York Review of Books*, 19 November 1981.

this return to ancient sources resulted in something new, the new alchemy.

Though he interestingly brings out this archaizing aspect of the new alchemy, Nicholl is aware of other influences that were affecting alchemy, the influences of other magical and occult systems with which the alchemical renaissance was associated. He emphasizes John Dee's *Monas hieroglyphica* with its manifold meanings, alchemical, Cabalistic, mathematical, as a potent expression of the new alchemy, but he does not explore these other aspects, singling out only the alchemical side of the complex movement for special study and analysis.

His goal is the influence of the alchemical renaissance on English poetry. He discusses, rather hurriedly, alchemy in Donne and Ben Jonson, without bringing out that *The Alchemist* is a very well-informed satire on the whole movement, and one which touches on its Cabalistic and mathematical sides. But his chief objective is *King Lear*, which he treats as an alchemical allegory.

One of the best parts of the book is the survey of alchemical literature published in England in the last years of the sixteenth century and first years of the seventeenth, the years when *Lear* was forming. Nicholl's analysis of the publications of these years includes some little-known writers, for example, Thomas Tymme, author of a lost translation of John Dee's *Monas hieroglyphica*. Nicholl argues that *Lear* is suffused with the influence of 'spiritual alchemy', the application of the terminology of alchemical processes and imagery to inner psychological processes of transformation and renewal. He gives a detailed analysis of Lear's spiritual history in alchemical terms, illustrated by alchemical images. He presents Lear as destroyed in the storm, which represents the destruction of matter in the *nigredo*, and as restored and regenerated by Cordelia, who represents the Philosopher's Stone.

This 'alchemical reading' of Lear as essentially on the theme of regeneration makes the tragedy less dark. Lear is destroyed only to be born again through the agency of Cordelia. One might feel attracted to this idea in a general way without necessarily accepting the too rigidly argued identification of Cordelia with the Stone. In all his alchemical reading of the story of Lear and his daughters, Nicholl ignores the fact that the story was taken by Shakespeare from pseudo-historical sources and from Spenser's poetic presentation of the 'British King' in *The Faerie Queene*. One is reminded of Michael Maier, the Rosicrucian, who in his *Arcana arcanissima* argues that all myths are really about the Stone.

Nicholl's thesis is supported by some remarkable comparisons of language in the play with poetic passages in contemporary alchemical literature. These possible Shakespearean parallels should be carefully investigated. Nicholl's reading of *Lear* would make of the play a stage in the process of Shakespeare's evolution toward occult themes of which I have argued the presence in my *Shakespeare's Last Plays* (1975). He thinks that the alchemical side of the movement is dominant in *Lear*, while the last plays are more generally magical and mystical. He hesitates to call the movement as found in Shakespeare 'Rosicrucian', because of the date of the Rosicrucian manifestos, too late to have influenced Shakespeare. However, the Rosicrucian type of alchemy, combined with 'Magia' and 'Cabala', is present in the outlook of Shakespeare's contemporary John Dee, who is perhaps a chief architect of the alchemical-Cabalist-mathematical movement of which the Rosicrucian manifestos are an expression.

This book will fill a gap for students of the Elizabethan age in its detailed analysis of the literature on Renaissance alchemy available in England. The interpretation of *Lear* strictly in terms of alchemical processes strikes one as forced, and too rigidly argued. Nevertheless, in a general way, Nicholl's alchemical quotations bring home the fact that he is tapping neglected sources of poetic-alchemical imagery, and they suggest that, for contemporary audiences, the imagery of *Lear* would have had alchemical resonances which afterward became inaudible.

A point which Nicholl does not make is that *Lear* as a tragedy of kingship falls within an area associated with 'Hermes Trismegistus', who was called 'Thrice Great' because of his triple role as priest, philosopher and king. Francis Bacon reminded James I of his triple Hermetic destiny in the flattery of the King in the dedication of *The Advancement of Learning* (1605). 'Because there is met in your Majesty a rare conjunction, as well of divine and sacred literature, as of profane and human; so as your Majesty standeth invested of that triplicity, which in great veneration was ascribed to the ancient Hermes.' The date usually conjectured for Shakespeare's writing of *Lear* is 1605. Let me hasten to state that I do not regard this coincidence in dating as evidence that Bacon wrote *King Lear* but only as a straw in the wind blown toward Nicholl's Lear as an alchemical king.

Chapter Nine

REVIVALIST*

THE 'LIVING MONUMENT' of Miss Bradbrook's title is explained by her as

> the English chronicle history which belonged to Shakespeare's days at the Theatre and remains its living monument; at the end of his life he returned to material recollected from his earlier acting days and refashioned it in his final romances.

She duly emphasizes the fact that at the end of the century

> . . . the English history play suffered a sudden and almost total eclipse. It had been the main means of transferring to the Elizabethan stage that providential linking of past and present which enlarged the dramatic experience into something like a social ritual . . .

Shakespeare's history plays had worked up to a climax in *Henry V*, so closely involved in the enthusiasms aroused by the Earl of Essex. The English history play collapsed, but Miss Bradbrook sees the genre continuing during Shakespeare's middle period, the period of the great tragedies, in the form of the mythical 'British history', based on Geoffrey of Monmouth, with its tale of the

* Review of M. C. Bradbrook, *The Living Monument: Shakespeare and the Theatre of his Time*, Cambridge, 1976, in *New Statesman*, 17 December 1976.

descent of British kings from Brut, the Trojan – the history outlined by Spenser as leading to the providential appearance of Queen Elizabeth I as the culmination of prophecy. But something terrible had happened to the British history. The 'Brutan' plays, *Macbeth* and *Lear*, are tragedies, and *Lear* is one of the direst tragedies in the whole of literature.

Coming to Shakespeare's last plays, the period of his 'late romances', Miss Bradbrook asserts their importance and devotes a large proportion of her book to their examination. Instead of seeing Shakespeare's later Jacobean period as an aftermath to the great histories, comedies and tragedies, she sees it as a living return to his earlier inspiration. She is fascinated by a historical figure in this period, Henry, Prince of Wales, who died tragically and unexpectedly in 1612, but not before he had made himself felt as an energetic character, a potential leader of outstanding promise, in marked contrast to his father. There is a good deal about Prince Henry in Miss Bradbrook's book – and about his sister Princess Elizabeth – and she allows the Prince a position of definite influence on the literature of the period. *The Tempest* was produced, together with other Shakespeare plays, as part of the festivals for the Princess and her husband. Miss Bradbrook stresses the importance of these celebrations as marking the end of the Shakespearean era in the theatre.

The Living Monument is of much interest to me, since in my book *Shakespeare's Last Plays* (1975) I argued that the last plays reflect an 'Elizabethan revival' centred on Prince Henry and his sister, and that through this revival or renovation of 'Elizabethanism', within the Jacobean period, Shakespeare recaptured his former hopes and translated them into the romances. It is strange that Miss Bradbrook does not make more use of *Cymbeline* as a play which caps her argument: this last play is definitely a 'Brutan' play and one which has emerged from history into romance in the Prince Henry period.

In the course of her discussion of the Shakespearean opus Miss Bradbrook makes many references to the work of other critics, to such an extent that her book becomes almost a survey of current critical literature. Perhaps her most penetrating pages are those in which she analyses, as a critic in the literary tradition, the profundities of *Macbeth* and *Lear*. Yet many and various are the strands worked into her account of the Shakespearean drama. She is interested in reactions between dramatist and audience and discusses the plays as sociology. As a theatre historian, she follows theatre history in relation to the plays, with special reference to the influence of masque on the late Shakespeare and to contemporary pageantry and the reflection of its imagery in the drama.

There is one type of Elizabethan pageantry which Miss Bradbrook rather neglects, despite its relevance to her themes. The central pageants of the Elizabethan age were the annual Accession Day tilts in which the cult of the Queen was expressed in a setting of chivalrous romance. These tilts were highly theatrical: the tilters appeared in fancy costumes, and the performances contained elements foreshadowing the masque, even in the Elizabethan period. The presentation of the Queen as a Vestal Virgin, which Shakespeare reflects in the famous lines in *A Midsummer Night's Dream*, was produced as a mythological tableau at a tilt. The development of chivalrous exercises into masques is clear in the masques for Prince Henry as a Fairy Prince, successor to the Fairy Queen of the tilts. The close association of fantastic chivalrous exercises with theatrical developments was a European phenomenon, as for example in the dramatic festivals at the French court. All this side of Elizabethan and Jacobean pageantry would connect with Miss Bradbrook's theory of continuity between Elizabethan and Jacobean phenomena, and with her interest in interaction between theatre and masque.

And there is no doubt that the chivalric spectacle was a fundamental influence on Shakespeare. It was the official celebration of the cult of the monarchy, the theme with which he was so deeply concerned. The English history plays running at the Globe, which Miss Bradbrook has characterized as the use of history as a social ritual, were contemporary with the courtly social ritual of the tilt. The public theatre and the tiltyard were both playing-places for the acting out of the great drama of the age, historical, national and religious.

One critic whom Miss Bradbrook does not mention is G. Wilson Knight, whose book *The Imperial Theme* draws out of his sensitive understanding of the poetry the idea that there is an imperial theme running always in Shakespeare's mind, in the sense of a universal religious meaning which he seeks in the world and in history. My studies of the imperial imagery used of Elizabeth endeavoured to show that the universal religious theme was present in that imagery, through the adoption of traditional images of sacred empire, such as the image of Astraea, the Just Virgin of the golden age, to express the religious-imperial role ascribed to her. The Elizabethan images of universal empire contained within them those associations which Wilson Knight elicits from his study of the 'imperial theme' in Shakespeare's poetry. The imagery invoked universal precepts; and in a period in which universal ideas were terribly threatened by the divisions of Christendom, such imagery was charged with great poignancy.

Referring to my study of Queen Elizabeth as Astraea, Miss Bradbrook makes the strange remark that this image belonged to pageants and pageant-like plays, but 'could not be used in the drama of the public stages because it was essentially a static image'. This seems rather to miss the point of the religious-imperial imagery and its impact on the Shakespearean conception of monarchy as a religious and universal theme, with implications stretching far beyond that of the national chronicle. It was the failure of some immeasurably vast concept which made the tragedy of *Lear* so unbearable, a tragedy of Greek proportions involving the whole universe of nature and of man.

What was the nature of the theatre in which these stupendous chronicles were first enacted? A useful feature of Miss Bradbrook's study is the list of the London theatres of the period and map showing their theatrical scene; however, she rightly stresses that it was with Burbage's original theatre of 1576, and its descendant, the Globe, that Shakespeare was identified. What was the original Theatre like? Miss Bradbrook refuses to admit a classical influence on the design of the Theatre-Globe; but her own chronicle might suggest that the setting for this historical drama should contain at least some allusion to a Trojan-Roman origin for the British theatre.

However, it would be pointless to go over again here my arguments for the Globe as an adaptation of the ancient theatre, a Theatre of the World, reflecting the cosmos in the proportions of its geometrical plan.

Chapter Ten

ENGLISH ACTORS IN PARIS DURING
THE LIFETIME OF SHAKESPEARE*

THE IMMENSE popularity of the drama in England during the reign
of Queen Elizabeth and after naturally created a large demand for
actors, and numerous companies sprang into existence. But it
often happens that a sudden demand for persons trained to a
certain calling will result soon afterwards in a glut. People hear
of large openings and opportunities in a particular direction and
rush to take advantage of them; the first-comers do well, but the
profession soon becomes overcrowded. So it was among professional actors in Elizabethan England; the supply soon exceeded the
demand, and many of the less fortunate or less able practitioners of
the art found it difficult to make a living. In these circumstances
it was natural enough that some of them should turn their attention
to foreign fields of enterprise. The dramatic art was far less developed in most of the countries on the Continent than in England
at that time, and companies of English actors travelling abroad
were received with admiration and generally well remunerated.
Among the Alleyn Papers there is a letter, which has often been
quoted, from one Richard Jones, an actor, to Edward Alleyn
asking for a loan of three pounds. He is about to 'go over beyond
the seas with Mr. Browne and the company', and requires the
money in order to release 'a sut of clothes and a cloke' from pawn.
He must have the clothes, 'for if I go over, and have no clothes,
I shall not be esteemed of', and he has no money to pay for them

* Published in *Review of English Studies*, I, 1925.

himself; but 'by God's help', he continues, 'the first mony that I gett I will send it over unto you, for hear I get nothinge: some tymes I have a shillinge a day, and some tymes nothinge, so that I leve in great poverty hear.' The case of Richard Jones is probably typical of most of the English players who took to travelling abroad in the late sixteenth and early seventeenth centuries.

The English companies are known to have travelled fairly extensively in Germany, Austria, the Netherlands, Sweden, and Denmark. The researches of Albert Cohn and others amongst the municipal records of German towns have thrown a good deal of light upon the movements of the English comedians in Germany and Austria. But less attention has been paid to the two visits of English actors to Paris during the lifetime of Shakespeare for which evidence exists. They are referred to in passing by Lintilhac and Rigal; Armand Baschet has a long footnote on the subject in his book on the Italian comedians in France;[1] J.-J. Jusserand devotes several pages to it.[2] Finally, on the English side, Sir Edmund Chambers has summed up all the material hitherto available at the end of his chapter on 'International Companies'.[3]

This material is extremely scanty. It consists of two short references found among the papers of the Hôtel de Bourgogne and of a few meagre entries in the Journal of Jean Héroard. I propose to deal here, first with the above-mentioned entries in the Hôtel de Bourgogne register and in Héroard's Journal, which together comprise all that has hitherto been known concerning the English actors in Paris at that date; and then to add a few new details which help to throw a little more light on the subject.

In the 'Inventaire des titres et papiers de l'Hôtel de Bourgogne', published by Eudore Soulié, there occurs the following entry:

1598. 25 mai – Bail fait par les maîtres de ladite confrérie a
'Jehan Sehais, comédien anglois, de la grande salle et théâtre
dudit hôtel de Bourgogne, pour le temps, aux réservations, et
moyennant les prix, charges, clauses et conditions portées
par icelui' passé par devant Huart et Claude Nourel, notaires.[4]

The Confrérie referred to is, of course, the 'Confrérie de la Passion', sole owners of the Hôtel de Bourgogne. Jehan Sehais is evidently a French misspelling of an English name. Sir Edmund Chambers conjectures that we have here 'one John Shaa or Shaw, conceivably related to Robert Shaw of the Admiral's men, who witnessed an advance by Henslowe to Dekker on 24 November

1599.' We only know one other fact about Sehais or Shaw and his company – namely, that shortly afterwards they were prosecuted by the Confrères for having broken the terms of their contract.

It is quite possible that they may not fully have understood this contract. The organization of the theatre in Paris at that date must have been a surprise to English actors. London, with its numerous theatres and theatrical companies, had certainly reached a more advanced stage of dramatic development than the French capital at the same epoch. In Paris the 'Confrères de la Passion' not only owned the only theatre in the town – the Hôtel de Bourgogne – but they held a monopoly of acting, ratified by the 'Parlement', which authorized them to prosecute and fine any persons, not members of the Confrérie, who should attempt to give dramatic performances in Paris. They formed, in fact, a very close and jealous trade union, determined at all costs to prevent competition.

But in spite of the monopoly and protection which they enjoyed, their position at the end of the sixteenth century was not a prosperous one. As their title, 'Confrères de la Passion', indicates, they were a survival from the Middle Ages, and they represented an art which was dying out. They clung to the medieval genres, mysteries, moralities, farces, etc., and these had fallen into disrepute. An outcry had been raised against the ribaldry which had crept more and more into the representation of the mysteries, and in 1548 a decree of the Parlement forbade the Confrères to act any but 'mystères profanes'. They were thus deprived at one blow of the most important part of their programme. Not only was authority ranged against the old genres, but the new literary school which was growing up attacked them on aesthetic grounds. Admirers of Garnier had only scorn for the crudities of farce and morality. Thus it came to pass that the Confrères had ceased to flourish, in spite of the protection they enjoyed, because they were an anachronism.

As a result of this failure to retain the public attention the Confrères at length decided that it would be more profitable to let their theatre and their monopoly to other companies. Eugène Rigal thinks that they did not definitely abandon their theatre to professional actors until near the end of the sixteenth century. In this case, Jehan Sehais and his English comedians were among the first outsiders to hire the Hôtel de Bourgogne.

But, as was hinted above, matters did not run smoothly for long between the new players and their employers. The next entry relating to the English comedians in the 'Inventaire' is dated only ten days later. It runs as follows:

1598. 4 juin – Sentence du Châtelet donnée au profit de ladite confrérie à l'encontre desdits comédiens anglois, tant pour raison du susdit bail que pour le droit d'un écu par jour, jouant par lesdits Anglois ailleurs qu'audit hôtel.

So the English players, either ignorantly or wilfully, had flouted the monopoly of the Confrères and dared to perform elsewhere than at the Hôtel de Bourgogne. What, one wonders, induced them to take this action? Did they find it impossible to make both ends meet at the Hôtel de Bourgogne? Rigal tells of some of the difficulties undergone by companies who hired this theatre.[5] The takings were probably not great, and were still further diminished by the number of people who had a right to enter gratis. A part of the hall had to be reserved for the use of the Confrères and their friends; members of the king's household might enter free of charge, and lackeys following their masters also slipped in without payment. So that after the fee due to the Confrères had been deducted there cannot have been a very wide margin of profit left for the players themselves. Probably the English comedians were driven to giving extra performances in another quarter in order to supplement their meagre earnings at the Hôtel.

We do not know whether Jehan Sehais or Shaw and his English company continued at the Hôtel de Bourgogne after this disagreeable encounter with the law. The entire absence, as far as can be ascertained, of any mention of them in contemporary records would seem to indicate that their stay was not long enough to make an impression on Parisian audiences. On the other hand, the next let recorded in the 'Inventaire' is not until 28 April 1599, and it seems improbable that the Confrères would have allowed their theatre to remain empty for ten months.

The only other reference to English comedians in Paris at this period which has hitherto been mentioned by literary historians occurs six years later in the Journal of Jean Héroard.[6] Héroard was appointed by Henri IV in 1601 to be first physician to the Dauphin, afterwards Louis XIII. He was responsible for the child's health, and supervised all the details of his daily life. He grew very fond of his charge; the little Louis saw far more of him than of his own father and mother, and seems to have returned the good physician's affection. Héroard's Journal is a minute and painstaking account, written down day by day, of the Dauphin's every action. The following is the first of the interesting entries referring to English comedians:

Septembre 1604, à Fontainebleau.
Le 18, samedi. – A trois heures et demie goûté; mené en la grande salle neuve ouïr une tragédie représentée par des Anglois; il les écoute avec froideur, gravité et patience jusques à ce qu'il fallut couper la tête à un des personnages . . .

Héroard does not tell us how this incident in the play affected the child, whether he was interested or frightened. He goes on briskly to the next event, and we learn that Louis was taken into the garden after the play and went to watch the hunt.

But the following entries show that the English actors made no small impression on the little prince, then aged about four. Ten days later Héroard makes the following observation:

Le 28, mardi. –
Il se fait habiller en masque, son tablier sur sa tête et une écharpe de gaze blanche, imite les comédiens anglois qui étoient à la Cour et qu'il avoit vu jouer.

This game proved fascinating, for the next day we read:

Le 29, marcredi. –
Il dit qu'il veut jouer la comédie; 'Monsieur, dis-je, comment direz-vous?' Il répond: *Tiph, toph,* en grossissant sa voix. A six heures et demie, soupé; il va en sa chambre, se fait habiller pour masquer et dit: *Allons voir maman, nous sommes des comédiens.*

And again on Sunday, 3 October:

Il dit: *Habillons-nous en comédiens,* on lui met son tablier coiffé sur la tête; il se prend à parler, disant: *Tiph, toph, milord,* et marchant à grands pas.

Imitation is the sincerest form of flattery; the English comedians[7] evidently excited the interest and admiration of one of their audience at least. And, as Jusserand remarks, the child's powers of observation were well developed; for we know that the loud voice and great strides – strutting and bellowing, as Hamlet unkindly puts it – were characteristic of English declamation at that time.

What was this tragedy played before Henri IV and his little son at Fontainebleau during Shakespeare's lifetime? One or two attempts have been made to solve this question. Eudore Soulié summarizes the data relating to English comedians in the inventory of the Hôtel de Bourgogne and in Héroard's Journal and suggests that it would be interesting to discover 'le personnel de ces troupes et les pièces de leur répertoire'.[8] In the following year Henry Charles Coote, the antiquarian and lawyer, attempted a reply.[9] Ignoring the larger questions raised by Soulié, he confines himself to guessing what play it was that the Dauphin saw acted by the English comedians.

Coote suggests that the child's 'Tiph, toph, milord', represents the English phrase 'Tap for tap, my lord', spoken by Falstaff in *Henry IV, Part II,* Act II, scene i. The complete phrase is: 'This is the right fencing grace, my lord; tap for tap, and so part fair.'

Coote seems to have forgotten the other piece of information which Héroard gives us about the play, namely, that 'il fallut couper la tête à un des personnages.' Evidently the play which the Dauphin saw contained fairly striking references to an execution. The only mention of an execution in *Henry IV, Part II,* occurs at the end of Act IV, scene ii. The Archbishop of York, Lord Hastings, and Lord Mowbray have been arrested on the battlefield, and Lancaster orders them to be led away immediately to the 'block of death, Treason's true bed and yielder-up of breath'. The incident is not of central importance, and a child of four who did not understand English would probably not find it striking. Moreover, Héroard distinctly says '*one* of the characters', and here there are three prisoners who are to be put to death.

The most recent suggestion is that of Sir Edmund Chambers, who says 'the theme may have been the execution of John Tiptoft, Earl of Worcester, at the restoration of Henry VI in 1470.' He also mentions in a note that the phrase 'tiff toff' occurs as a stage direction in the play *Lingua,* and is explained by Collier as hiccups; by Fleay as stage blows.

I venture to put forward another suggestion for what it is worth. The very slight indications which we have to go upon make it impossible to do more than guess at the identity of the play. There is a well-known scene, turning upon an execution, in *Richard III,* Act III, scene iv. Gloucester is determined to put

Hastings to death, but before declaring his intention openly he plays with his victim. He asks him what punishment traitors deserve, and displays his misshapen arm, declaring that enemies have bewitched his body. Hastings, alarmed at his threatening expression, falters out:

If they have done this deed, my noble lord –

Then Gloucester's full rage and vengeance burst forth. He shouts at him the famous words:

If! thou protector of this damned strumpet,
Talk'st thou to me of 'ifs'? – Thou art a traitor –
Off with his head!

It is an immense outburst, and it may well have been at this point that the little Louis began to sit up and take interest. 'If, off.' There is tremendous emphasis on those two words, and perhaps 'Tiph, toph' is a child's rendering of the sounds. It is true that 'my lord' does not occur in Gloucester's speech; but Hastings has just used the title twice. Also it is very probable that 'milord' was the only English word known to the Dauphin and his attendants. They would hear the English ambassador and notable English visitors addressed by this title; it would therefore be quite natural for him to tack the expression on to his 'Tiph, toph.' Probably he imagined that these words meant 'Cut off his head.' Perhaps he pointed to Mme de Monglat or to his dear Héroard as he strutted about the room, intending 'Tiph, toph' as an order for their execution.

But all this is mere conjecture, and must remain so unless any further documentary evidence on the subject is brought to light. I had hoped to find some mention of this performance at Fontainebleau in the despatches of the English ambassador then at Paris; but Sir Thomas Parry makes no reference to any performance by English actors in his despatches for that year. However, among the Foreign State Papers at the Public Record Office I came across two letters which do add a little to our scanty knowledge of this subject.

Before proceeding to quote these letters, which have not hitherto been published, it would be as well to make clear the circumstances in which they were written. As I mentioned before, Sir Thomas Parry was English ambassador in Paris at this time, having succeeded Sir Ralph Winwood in 1602. Parry had as his secretary a very able young man who was afterwards to become a famous diplomatist. The young man's name was then simply 'Mr' Dudley Carleton, but a brilliant career lay before him. He was afterwards ambassador at Venice and the Hague, and became Chief Secretary of State under Charles I. As secretary at the English Embassy in Paris he was then serving an apprenticeship to the diplomatic career.

Early in March 1602 Parry sent his secretary on a mission to Metz. The French King and court were visiting that town, and Carleton went thither to represent the ambassador at the court and to transact some business with Villeroy relating to a certain 'rembursement of her majesty's monie' – which errand did not meet with much success, as we learn from his letters to Parry. Before leaving Paris, Carleton had evidently requested his friends at the Embassy to let him know of anything which might occur during his absence. The relations of the secretary with his chief were not of the smoothest, as transpires from Carleton's letters home, and he was no doubt anxious to keep himself well informed as to the trend of affairs at the Embassy during his absence.

These letters, written from Paris to Carleton at Metz, are preserved in the Record Office; and those two of them which are of interest to us here describe an incident in which the English comedians figure. The more important of the two, from our point of view, is written by an Englishman called John Loveden; the other is from a French gentleman of the name of Saint Sauveur. Both these men were attached to the English Embassy. Saint Sauveur is spoken of as a 'secretary'. Loveden, judging by the style of his address to Dudley Carleton and by his rather ill-spelt letter, was perhaps a man of inferior position. But he also must have been some kind of secretary because several of the ambassador's later despatches are in his handwriting.

The following is Loveden's letter:

My good Mylord Carleton, We have not as yet heard any newes out of England. And for my parte I know nothinge heere worthie of relacon for that I fear my letters wilbe rather troublesome than any waies answerable to expectacon, yet my promise and your desire hathe constrained me to be unmannerlie and to writte havinge not occasion. I can certifie you of nothinge but that my lorde is in good healthe and the rest of the gent. in the house whoe remember their hartie

comendacons. I am very unwillinge to trouble you with a
folyshe mutinie our Welsche men made heere on Tuesday
last, whoe in remembrance of that day as the Custome is weare
a licke in their hatte. And these men heere in token of their
rejoicynge went to a Taverne to be merry admittinge some of
our Englyshe players into their companie, of which faulte
some speache litle before your departure passed betweene us.
Which players havinge not longe kept their rounde in the
Taverne were well charged, and one of them amongest the rest
runneth out of the house with a legge of mouton in his hand,
gnawinge it as he passed the streate. At which howe muche
the people weere offended you may judge. He went not farre
but one of the Towne reprehended him for it, which this
drunckard take[th] in ille parte and heere uppon drewe out
his dagger and broke the poore man's heade. Wheereuppon
the people, very much offended, gathered themselves togither
at St. Germaines gate, neere unto which this fellowe was,
wheere they had good stoare of stones which they threwe at
all the Englyshe men as thicke as yf they had ben Hotte; but
some of our companie havinge rapiers drawed them and ranne
in amongst them and made all the Frenshe retire within the
gate. Some of our house knowinge nothinge cominge neere
unto the place weere in danger but none of them very muche
hurte some twoe or three their faces and heades broken with
stones but I marvaile howe they escaped soe well. I thinke the
proverbe is true a druncken man will never take hurte. My
lorde hearinge of it hath warned them to forbeare the companie
of these companions. I doubt I have been over bolde and
therefore with very hartie comendacons I doe end.

Paris this 14th of Marche, 1603.

Yr. very lovinge friend to comand

JOHN LOVEDEN.[10]

So there were English players in Paris in March 1603 – that is
to say, five years after the company we know of at the Hôtel de
Bourgogne and one year before the performance at which the
Dauphin was present. Evidently the actors of whom Loveden
speaks had been in the town some time, because this was not the
first occasion on which the 'Welsche men' had consorted with
them. This is clear from the phrase 'of which faulte some speache
litle before your departure passed betweene us'. The 'faulte'
referred to is the unfortunate habit of the 'Welsche men' who

persisted in 'admittinge . . . Englyshe players into their companie'. Loveden and Carleton must have talked this over together. The Welshmen were evidently attached to the Embassy in some capacity or other, and it would certainly be advisable to avoid as far as possible any street altercations between Parisians and members of the English staff. The society of the English players was dangerous from this point of view, as the travelling companies evidently took with them their London habit of brawling in taverns. After this dreadful scene at St Germain's gate, Sir Thomas Parry put his foot down, as we learn from Loveden: 'My lorde hearinge of it hath warned them to forbeare the companie of these companions'. It is disappointing that Loveden gives no names. Can the gnawer of the leg of mutton have been our old friend Jehan Sehais?

Saint Sauveur, writing four days later, refers to the same incident, though in a very different style. John Loveden contented himself with a plain narration of facts. Saint Sauveur aims at scholarly elegance and wraps up the story of the riot in a wealth of classical allusion. He treats the affair as a humorous incident and adopts a tone of refined badinage. From our point of view, the Loveden manner with its straightforward narration of facts and inclusion of picturesque detail is to be preferred. Saint Sauveur's account is rather obscure. The following is an extract from his letter:

Je vous diray que le Jour St. David les panachaches [sic] de queüe de poreau selon leur sainte coustume se voulurent faire paroystre. Mais je ne scay par quelle fatalle destinée leur oroscope se trouva encernée du dieu Mars qui courrouce contre eux pour je ne scay quelle occasion les abandonna au pere Denis: qui apres les avoir menes tous (?) en son selier au Monst[11] les laissa à la Merci des Centaures qui ne se contenterent de les bien esbaudir mais encores leur offerent leurs glaives.[12]

It is only with the aid of Loveden's account that we can endeavour to translate this parable. The 'panachés de queüe de poreau' are, of course, the 'Welsche men', and the references to Mars and Dionysus only confirm what we already know – namely, that they were involved in a drunken brawl which began in a tavern, or, as Saint Sauveur prefers, in the wine-cellar of Dionysus (le père Denis). But it is not at all clear who are meant by the

Centaurs. The fact that they encouraged (*esbaudir*) the Welshmen in their behaviour leads one to suspect that the players are intended. We are also told that the Centaurs offered them (i.e. the Welshmen) their swords. The only reference to swords in Loveden's letter is the phrase 'some of our companie havinge rapiers drawed them and ranne in amongst them and made all the Frenshe retire within the gate'. By 'our companie', Loveden may mean here the English as opposed to the French, and this would of course include the players. Saint Sauveur adds practically nothing to our knowledge of this affair. One could wish that the learned secretary had been rather more explicit and less allegorical.

Further research among the State Papers at the Record Office brought to light another fact which is of interest here. Sir Thomas Parry, in his despatch of 11 August 1604, adds the following postscript after his signature:

> The king hath at this present signed a warrant under his hande, to one Browne an English Comedian, for ye transporting of doggs Beares and Apes etc. for his specyal pleasures, a sure argument of his martial intentions.[13]

And again, on 3 October of the same year, he writes to Cranbourne:

> I heare with repayre unto your Lordship one Brown, to whom this king hath committed ye chardge to provide hym sum beares and doggs etc. for his recreation. Certayn of my goode frends here about ye Court desyred me to help them to sum Inglish mastifs, whom I would gladly gratify, the said Brown hath promysed to provide them for one if he may have lyve to pass. I pray your Lordship lett hym have your favourable meanes for licens to transport them.[14]

The dates of these two letters are interesting. It will be remembered that the performance at Fontainebleau which Héroard records took place on 18 September 1604. Parry's two references to 'one Browne an English Comedian' occur in August and October, that is to say, the month before and the month after the date given by Héroard. If this Browne was a member of the company which performed on that day, his presence in Paris in August and October would indicate that the English actors must have remained in Paris at least three months on this occasion, and if this was so they probably gave other performances.

It would be tempting to assert that we have here to do with that Robert Browne who was perhaps the best-known and the most successful of all the Elizabethan actors who travelled abroad. But, unfortunately, it seems almost certain that he and his company were performing at the Harvest Fair at Frankfurt am Main in 1604, and therefore they could not have been in Paris. There is, however, a good deal of uncertainty as to Browne's actual movements in these years, as the following quotation from Sir Edmund Chambers shows:

> Robert Browne, for some years after the opening of his fourth tour at Frankfort in the spring of 1601, does not appear to have attached himself to any particular Court. He is found at Frankfort, with Robert Jones, in September 1602, at Augsburg in the following November and December, at Nuremberg in February 1603, and at Frankfort for the Easter fair of the same year. With him were then, but it would seem only temporarily, Thomas Blackwood and John Thare, late of Worcester's men, who had doubtless just come out from England, when Elizabeth's illness and death closed the London theatres. He is probably the 'alte Komödiant,' whose identity seems to have been thought sufficiently described by that term at Frankfort in the autumn of 1604.[15]

It is also perhaps worth while pointing out that when in the service of the Landgrave of Hesse-Cassel in 1595, Browne was sent over to England to fetch a consignment of bows and arrows. This seems rather a striking parallel to the errand which 'one Browne an English Comedian' performed for Henri IV.

There were several other Brownes in the profession, notably Edward Browne, William Browne, and John Browne. A Robert Browne was showing puppets at Coventry and Norwich in 1638 and 1639.[16] This Parisian Browne may have been one of the above. Curiously enough, Loveden, in another letter to Carleton, dated 26 March 1603, speaks of a certain 'Robbin Browne', whom he calls 'my very good friend'. He further mentions that this Robbin is 'sonne to Mr. Browne clerk of the greene cloth', and that he has 'latelie come out of Italie and this day departeth towards Rouen'. But I am afraid we cannot connect this 'Robbin' with our English comedian. It is unlikely that Loveden, who shows such scorn of the players in his other letter, would ever have called one of them his very good friend.

This concludes all that we have hitherto been able to discover about this interesting subject. It is curious to think that on the eve of the birth of French classical drama, Elizabethan plays were represented in Paris by Elizabethan actors. The very year which saw the English actors performing at Fontainebleau witnessed also the birth of Jean Mairet, author of the first French drama on the classical model.

Chapter Eleven

SYMBOLIC PERSONS IN THE MASQUES OF BEN JONSON*

THAT THE Renaissance compendia of mythology were as widely read in England in the sixteenth and seventeenth centuries as they were on the Continent is now a well-known fact. Natale Conti, Vincenzo Cartari, Lilio Gregorio Gyraldi, and Cesare Ripa are to be reckoned with as potential 'sources' for Elizabethan and later writers. Particularly is this true, of course, for the masque-writers who had to be concerned with the correct visual representation of their allegorical and mythological figures and who turned for the information they required to the illustrated handbooks of Cartari and Ripa. Professor Gilbert has arranged the 'symbolic persons' of Jonson's masques in alphabetical order, and under each entry he gives – where these are available – Jonson's own hints as to how, and with what attributes, the 'person' concerned appeared on the stage. He has no difficulty in proving still further Jonson's dependence on the manuals for the presentation of his masques. Where Jonson gives no definite indications, Professor Gilbert uses the handbooks – mainly Ripa – to reconstruct the probable appearance of the character in question. He also uses the evidence of the designs by Inigo Jones for the masques. And he sometimes adds descriptions of symbolic figures by other contemporary English poets to compare with Jonson's presentation of

---

* Review of Allan M. H. Gilbert, *The Symbolic Persons in the Masques of Ben Jonson*, Durham, North Carolina, and Cambridge, 1949, in *Review of English Studies*, New Series II, 1951.

them. The book thus becomes in itself a 'mythological manual' through which the student who looks up Aglaia, Agrypnia or Vigilance, Amphitrite, Apollo, Architecture, or Avarice (to take a few entries at random from the 'A' section) can discover the form in which such persons might probably have been visualized by Jonson and his contemporaries. It contains seventy-one reproductions from Ripa, Cartari, and other sources.

The bibliography of 'Works accessible to Jonson' (pp. 260-75) would have been more valuable if some consistent attempt had been made to list the contemporary editions of classical authors which Jonson might have used. For example, under Catullus it would have been useful to have mentioned the fact that Jonson himself quotes Constantius Landus's commentary on Catullus (*Works*, ed. Herford and Simpson, VII, 226, note *d*), which shows that he was using the Paris edition of 1604 in which the commentary by Landus, a pupil and friend of Alciati, appears (see the article by D. J. Gordon, 'Hymenæi: Ben Jonson's Masque of Union', *Journal of the Warburg and Courtauld Institutes*, VIII, 1945, 129). This omission is hardly redeemed by the Appendix of 'Authors, in addition to those listed in the bibliography, mentioned or quoted in the Masques and Entertainments' in which the name Landus appears without being connected with Catullus. Equally unilluminating is an entry such as 'Hottomanus' in this Appendix (p. 283), which makes no use of recent research (Gordon, *art. cit.*, 130, 141-2) which has shown that the work referred to is Antoine Hotman's *De veteri ritu nuptiarum*, 1585.

But Professor Gilbert has not set out to give us a complete survey of the sources of Jonson's second-hand learning. He has concentrated on his use of the mythological handbooks and on the forms of the symbolic persons which he has drawn from them. In the Introduction he discusses the meanings which may underlie Jonson's use of these forms, quoting the poet's own statements that his purpose in the masques was not only to please but to teach, and that 'remou'd mysteries' underlie these glorious shows. In Professor Gilbert's view Jonson's 'teaching' is aimed primarily at the royalties themselves for whom the masques were written and around whom their symbolism revolved. This view of the masques as an extended 'Mirror for Princes' with the symbolic figures acting before the monarch's eye the precepts used in the training of a 'Philosopher King' is illuminating and valuable. But, to a mind steeped in ideal theories of kingship, although the prince has indeed to be taught virtue, yet from his office as prince virtue flows of itself. One cannot think that a masque-writer who set himself up to instruct princes in virtue would find much favour with James I unless his 'remou'd mysteries' contained also some version of 'divine' kingship in its religious and cosmic aspect.

An important attempt has been made (by D. J. Gordon, 'The Masque of Blacknesse and the Masque of Beautie', *Journal of the Warburg and Courtauld Institutes*, VI, 1943) to relate the idealization of James I in the *Masque of Beautie*, with its central symbol of the throne of Beauty dominated by the figure of Harmony, to the cosmic harmony as interpreted in the current Neoplatonic philosophy. Professor Gilbert in his notes on 'Harmonia' (p. 118) seems by implication to reject this interpretation, or at least he does not discuss it. Possibly the arrangement of the book, which necessarily breaks up the inner coherence of the individual masques by marshalling the symbolic persons in alphabetical order, precluded the treatment of such a theme under the individual headings. Indeed, it must be confessed that, however valuable such an arrangement may be from the point of view of the student who wishes to use Jonson's masques as a handbook to mythology in the English Renaissance, it has certain grave disadvantages. The symbolism of a work of art – whether visual, or literary, or a combination of the two like the masque – obviously cannot be fully relished, either as to its artistic form or as to its inner content, by detaching individual figures from the whole picture of which they form a part. The artist may, as in Jonson's case, be drawing his symbols from identifiable second-hand sources, but he is using them in original combinations, in fresh historical or religious contexts, through which new life flows into them, subtly transforming both content and form. It is only by studying the symbols in relation to the artist's intention in his work of art as a whole that one can appreciate the new values which he is giving to them. Several of the hieroglyphs carried by the Ethiopian ladies in the *Masque of Blacknesse* are taken from Horapollo, probably via the *Hieroglyphica* of Giovanni Pierio Valeriano. What is interesting, however, is not the fact of the borrowing from a handbook of hieroglyphics, but the problem of how Jonson is using these symbols in relation to the dark theme of the masque. Professor Gilbert seems to admit this by listing them all under 'Blacknesse' (these hieroglyphs have nothing whatever to do with 'blackness' in Horapollo or Valeriano) but he shelves the problem.

Nevertheless, Professor Gilbert's method brings out points of comparison and throws light on general tendencies. For example, the tendency to heap up attributes on to the symbolic figures, in excess even of those allowed by Ripa, comes out again and again. This heavy over-elaboration must have been a feature of the Jonsonian masque. Interesting comparative material is brought together by the entries 'Apollo', 'Amphion', 'Harmonia' and 'Orpheus' on the question of the use of the modern viol as an alternative to the ancient lyre as the attribute of musical figures. The relation of the modern viol to the ancient lyre is most elaborately discussed in Blaise de Vigenère's commentary on the 'Amphion' of Philostratus (Blaise de Vigenère, *Les Images ou Tableaux de platte peinture des deux Philostrates* . . ., Paris, 1614, pp. 79 ff. in the 1629 ed.), a discussion which probably reflects theories in Baïf's Academy of Poetry and Music. Philostratus was one of Jonson's favourite authors, and though the Vigenère commentary was published too late for him to have used it in the earlier masques, it should, I think, be consulted in relation to Jonson, for it reflects the mythological learning of those French circles out of which the *ballet de cour*, so close a relation of the English masque, was born.

Chapter Twelve

ENGRAVING IN ENGLAND IN THE SIXTEENTH AND SEVENTEENTH CENTURIES*

THIS MAGNIFICENT work will take its place in all libraries beside A. M. Hind's volumes on engraving in England in the Tudor period and in the reign of James I as their indispensable continuation. The reign of Charles I, as mirrored by the English engravers, now joins the series; this third volume follows the same editorial plan as the earlier ones and keeps up the impeccably high standard of editing. Every historian of the period, every student of its literature or of its art, will want to own this book. And less specialized readers as they turn the pages of the 214 plates will gain a visual impression of the times, of its major trends and interests, such as is to be found nowhere else.

As in the earlier volumes, the material is grouped with the engraver responsible for it, beginning with an introductory note on the engraver concerned, which is followed by the array of his portraits and of his subject pieces. In this way an impression is gained of the personality and work of each engraver and interesting points emerge. We see, for example, how the specialization of William Marshall on emblems influences all his work, even when he is not illustrating Quarles. Or how Robert Vaughan, who may

---

* Review of *Engraving in England in the Sixteenth and Seventeenth Centuries. A descriptive Catalogue with Introductions. Part III: The Reign of Charles I*. Compiled from the Notes of the late A. M. Hind by Margery Corbett and Michael Norton, Cambridge, 1964, in *The Book Collector*, XIII, 4, Winter 1964.

have been a connection of the Hermetic Vaughans, specialized on alchemical illustrations.

It is naturally a matter for some regret that the standard of portrait engraving in the period was not higher, for though we see here practically every well-known personage, and many less known and unknown ones, we sometimes wish that we could see them through the eyes of better artists. Milton's dissatisfaction with the engraver's version of his countenance –

> A portrait limned sure, by an unskilled hand
> Thou'dst say, if thou behold'st his native face –

may well have been felt by a good many of the other subjects.

As the editors point out, the extraordinary wealth of emblematic and symbolic illustration in the work of these engravers is one of its most striking characteristics, and to those interested in the history of ideas through iconographical study, this book holds out enormous possibilities of finding new and fruitful lines of investigation. Foreseeing the importance of the volume from this point of view, the editors have provided an admirable subject index with special reference to emblematic material.

What has impressed me particularly in looking through the plates is the prominence in so many of them of the tetragrammaton, the four Hebrew letters of the Name of God, sometimes in a glory with angels, sometimes in a geometrical framework. The subject index with its entry 'Tetragrammaton, *passim*' confirms the ubiquity of this representation of the Deity. It occurs not only in a purely religious context, as on the title-page of James I's translation of the Psalms or as the ultimate object of emblematic pilgrimages of the soul, but also on the title-pages of scientific or technical works. One wonders whether there may have been an influence on some of these engravers of de Bry's illustrations to the works of Robert Fludd (particularly to be seen, perhaps, in 'The Divine Cosmographer', Plate 77c). But nowhere is this symbol more prominent and striking than on the title-pages of the works of Francis Bacon. It thus seems to radiate, not only over purely religious illustration but also over the Baconian philosophy, and over science and technology. This phenomenon requires explanation. Is it possible that an inquiry into the history of the use of the tetragrammaton as a main symbol for the Deity might lead one into the heart of the seventeenth century? No such inquiry has, so far as I know, ever been made.

One notices, too, the survival or transformation of earlier dominant symbols. Once again, the title-pages of Bacon's works are interesting, for the two columns of the *instauratio magna*, with the ship passing between them, are surely an adaptation of the famous device of Charles V of the two columns signifying the columns of Hercules marking the limits of the empire of the ancients, but which his new empire extending into new worlds unknown to the ancients has surpassed. The device was adapted to Queen Elizabeth I and was extremely well known in the Tudor period. On the Baconian title-pages, it is adapted to the Baconian philosophy which is to pass beyond the limits set by the ancients into new worlds of thought.

Another less certain but possible survival or transformation of an earlier famous symbol may be the three crowns so prominent in the *Eikon Basilike*, the emblematic presentation of the death of Charles I. The crowns are his earthly crown which he abandons, the thorny crown of his martyrdom, and the celestial crown awaiting him in the skies. One is reminded of the famous device of Henri III of France, the two crowns of his earthly kingdoms and the third crown awaiting him in heaven. Since Henri was also, in a manner, a king martyred by the religious dissensions among his subjects, such an echo of his device in the new tragedy of royalty might have been not unsuitable.

The fascinating lines of inquiry opened up by this book are unending and it is certain to stimulate much new research.

FRANCE

Chapter Thirteen

UNDERGROUND ROUTES*

THE REVOLUTION in the attitude to Renaissance thought which has taken place in recent years rests largely on a new understanding of Renaissance Neoplatonism. In the nineteenth century Neoplatonism meant a movement arising from the rediscovery of the works of Plato and the ancient Neoplatonists, centred in the Medici circle in Florence. There was nothing wrong with this as a fact; what was wrong with the old view of Renaissance Neoplatonism was the assumption that Ficino and his friends read the texts in much the same way as nineteenth-century classical scholars were doing. This assumption led to the impression that Renaissance Neoplatonism meant a vaguely mystical and Christianized revival of Platonic idealism, which had pleasing results in many ways, as in its influence on art and poetry, but which was weak as a philosophy and certainly not in a line of development leading to important seventeenth-century movements.

This view was altered by the discovery that Renaissance Neoplatonists approached the writings of Plato and his followers in a way of their own. At about the same time that the Platonic and Neoplatonic texts were rediscovered, there had also come to light various magical and mystical writings believed to have been written by sages with prestigious names – Orpheus, Zoroaster,

* Review of D. P. Walker, *The Ancient Theology: Studies in Christian Platonism from the Fifteenth to the Eighteenth Century*, 1972, in *New York Review of Books*, 4 October 1973.

Hermes Trismegistus – in times long before the birth of Plato, probably contemporary with Moses. The most important of these ancient theologians was Hermes Trismegistus, supposedly an Egyptian priest and supposedly the author of a body of writings known as the *Hermetica*. The Renaissance Neoplatonist read these writings believed to be by Hermes with profound respect, as those of the teacher of Plato, and also, by another series of misunderstandings, as those of an inspired prophet of Christianity. Thus Renaissance Neoplatonism had a Hermetic core and was the source of that Hermetic movement which is now seen to be of such fundamental importance for the history of thought.

Though several scholars, particularly Eugenio Garin and Paul Oskar Kristeller, had been aware of the importance of studying the Hermetic movement and its sources, it was D. P. Walker who first put these subjects on a firm basis in an extremely learned book, *Spiritual and Demonic Magic from Ficino to Campanella*, published in 1958, and in some fundamental articles, published a few years earlier in the *Journal of the Warburg and Courtauld Institutes*. It was Walker who sorted out the complexities of *prisca theologia*, which he now prefers to call 'ancient theology', and it was he who established by a masterly exercise in precise scholarship that Ficino used the Hermetic magic. These pioneer writings have been somewhat hidden in inaccessible publications, though *Spiritual and Demonic Magic* is available in a Kraus reprint. In *The Ancient Theology*, Walker has now republished in a revised and expanded form his basic articles 'Orpheus the Theologian' and 'The *prisca theologia* in France'. By the 'ancient theologians' he means Hermes Trismegistus, Zoroaster, Orpheus, and so on, believed to be the ancient sages to whom profound religious truth was accessible and whose teachings were believed to be inextricably involved with those of Neoplatonism.

The most important of the 'ancient theologians' was Hermes Trismegistus, the supposed author of the writings known as the *Hermetica*. Written in Greek by unknown authors in about the second or third centuries A.D., these texts reflect various influences circulating in the late antique period, such as popularized versions of Greek philosophy, probably also Persian and Hebrew influences. It is by no means impossible that there may be some Egyptian influence in the *Hermetica*; the Egyptian temples were still functioning when they were written. Some scholars deny the Egyptian influence, as does A.-J. Festugière, the great French scholar whose French translation of these texts is the only authoritative modern translation. Other scholars think that the *Hermetica* contain traces of Egyptian influence.

What can be said in a general way is that the *Hermetica* belong to the atmosphere and background of thought of late antiquity, the time when Christianity was spreading in the midst of a world which was a melting-pot of many religions and philosophies. The same is true of the *Chaldean Oracles* and the *Orphica*, texts belonging to about the same period and which the Renaissance scholar believed to have been actually written by Zoroaster and Orpheus, just as he believed that the *Hermetica* were written by the mythical ancient Egyptian priest 'Hermes Trismegistus'.

Walker's articles not only cover precise discussion of the late antique milieu of the supposed writings of the 'ancient theologians' but also draw upon his extraordinarily wide and deep knowledge of their use by Renaissance writers and scholars. They are thus fundamental for all those interested in trying to unravel the hidden meanings of Renaissance literature or art, for 'the whole structure of the Ancient Theology rests on the belief that the Ancient Theologians wrote with deliberate obscurity, veiling the truth . . .' And the articles republished in *The Ancient Theology* are also fundamental for historians of religion in the Renaissance period.

Walker shows that the ancient theology encouraged a liberal and tolerant attitude in religious controversy. 'Most of the writers we have examined were more concerned with finding similarities than differences between various philosophies and religions . . . these liberal tendencies were reflected in practical, religio-political life.' The advocates of the ancient theology held eirenic, reunionist opinions and tended to belong to the middle or tolerant party, known in France as the *politiques*.

A remarkable example of the skilful scholarship with which Walker disentangles the Hermetic elements in well-known writers is the chapter on the ancient theology in Philip Sidney's *Arcadia*, first published as an article in 1954. In the sequence of the argument of *The Ancient Theology* as a whole, this reprinted article stands out as the first attempt to relate Sidney as a religious thinker to the Hermetic currents of the Renaissance. It proves with unanswerable logic, and through wide knowledge of the contemporary sources available to Sidney, that Pamela, the Arcadian heroine who refutes the atheism of her wicked aunt, bases her arguments on the ancient theology. Admirers of Sidney, though madly keen to identify the lady to whom he addressed his sonnets, have been less interested in trying to discover what he believed.

The unemphatic style of Walker's study must not deflect the reader from realizing its extreme importance. The detection of Sidney's Hermetic theology rests on scholarly techniques as impressive, in their way, as Walker's detection of Ficino's Hermetic magic. As well as these chapters based on already published work, *The Ancient Theology* contains four entirely new studies, all of great interest and importance.

Edward Herbert of Cherbury has a firmly established position in the history of thought as the father of English deism and as a thinker in whose ideas Descartes is known to have been interested. By a careful analysis of Herbert's posthumously published book, Walker shows that Herbert's deism had a Hermetic basis, a fact hitherto unsuspected which gives a different slant to the whole problem of the early history of deism. It had not been noticed that Herbert's thinking in his *De religione gentilium* bears a striking resemblance to those astral religious philosophies propagated by Giordano Bruno and Tommaso Campanella, the two Italian magi who were missionaries for a Hermetic religion of the world. This included a kind of astral magic in the cult of the divine in the cosmos, and a kind of deism which they hoped could become a basis for appeasing the religious differences which were leading to destructive wars.

Walker's analysis of the *De religione gentilium* leads him to think that Herbert's eirenic and *politique* religious attitude had a similar foundation. Like Bruno and Campanella, who had hopes of somehow reconciling their astral religion, their Hermetic and magical philosophy of universal harmony, with the Church in a manner that would 'unite the whole of mankind and heal all religious differences', so, thinks Walker, Herbert's astral deism included similar aims. 'I think that to these two cases [Bruno and Campanella] we can add Herbert, though with very important reservations: he was not a Magus . . . But in a tentative form, he was promulgating the same religion as the two Magi, and with the same eirenic intentions.' This is a startling fact for rational historians of deism to digest.

Walker asks how such influences could have reached Herbert, mentioning various possibilities, to which should be added the fact that an intensive revival of Hermetic thinking had been taking place in Germany in the early seventeenth century, in the circle of the Elector Palatine and his wife, a movement with which Herbert had almost certainly been in touch, as many indications in his autobiography suggest. Walker's study of Hermetic influences in both Philip Sidney and Herbert of Cherbury will help to connect the Elizabethan with the seventeenth-century phases of the movement.

Another field on which Walker's original research throws a new light is that of the French Jesuit missions to China in the seventeenth century. By analysis of many contemporary sources, Walker shows that in their conversion of the Chinese the Jesuits made enormous use of ancient theology, particularly of the supposed writings of Hermes Trismegistus, whose teachings, they argued, were consistent with ancient Chinese religious thought. In fact, ancient Chinese mystics, like Fohi, the supposed author of the mysterious *I-Ching* or *Book of Changes*, were presented as practically identical with Zoroaster or Hermes Trismegistus, as ancient theologians who understood the true nature of things.

Leibniz was interested in the Jesuit use of the *I-Ching*, which seemed to him analogous to his own recently invented binary system, to convert the Chinese to Hermes Trismegistus, whence they were inevitably led to Christianity through the time-honoured traditions which taught that Hermes was a prophet of Christianity. So strong was the impact of Chinese ancient theology that it was actually used to support the slightly damaged authenticity of Hermes, Zoroaster, and the rest. Chinese ancient theology, by its conformity with Western Hermetic tradition, was thought to have proved the truth of the latter.

Though the Jesuits made use of the element of comparative religion in the ancient theology in their converting methods, they were not liberal in the sense of seeking means of reconciliation between opposing branches of Christianity through appeal to Hermetic tradition, as the *politiques* did. The Jesuit missionaries warmly welcomed the revocation of the Edict of Nantes which made France '*toute Catholique*'.

Perhaps the most exciting chapter in the book is the last one on the Chevalier Ramsay, Scottish mystic and Freemason, whose addiction to ancient theology was playfully alluded to by his wife when she addressed her letters to '*mon cher Zoroastre*'. Ramsay's very popular novel, *The Travels of Cyrus*, first published in 1727, proves that, 'even at this late date the Ancient Theology is still a living force.' Cyrus in his travels makes a point of visiting all the countries of the ancient theologians, talking with disciples of Zoroaster in Persia and of Hermes Trismegistus in Egypt. In Ramsay, the ancient theology is combined with a very liberal and mystical Catholicism (he was a friend of Fénelon) and with Freemasonry. And, true to thè Hermetic traditions which turned men's minds toward religious interest in the cosmos, and thence to scientific exploration of its mysteries, Ramsay includes in *The Travels of Cyrus* long discussions of Cartesian mechanics and of Newton's aether hypothesis.

I must leave the reader to examine for himself Walker's profoundly interesting discussion of Ramsay on the aether hypothesis, which Walker connects historically with Ficino's *spiritus* theory, the vehicle of his magic. Walker concludes:

> I think he [Ramsay] did see Newton as standing in a line of Ancient Theologians, as the culmination of a long tradition of pious cosmology . . . We now know, thanks to the work of Messrs. Rattansi and McGuire, that this was how Newton saw himself.

It is impossible to do justice in a short review to the wealth of new discovery and new research contained in this book (I have omitted all mention of an important chapter on Savonarola), but I hope that enough has been said to indicate its extreme importance. The work of a scholar of absolute reliability and integrity, it makes available a wealth of material for those interested in the new history of thought, and uncovers the real roots of continuity between the Renaissance and the seventeenth century. From Ficino to Newton, the route lies underground, in the Hermetic tradition.

Chapter Fourteen

THE OLD NEW HISTORY*

AMONG THOSE gaps in knowledge to which Francis Bacon draws attention is the absence of any 'just story of learning'. What are the antiquities and originals of knowledge? What have been the flourishings, oppositions, decays, depressions, oblivions, removes, 'and all other events concerning learning throughout the ages of the world'? History, says Bacon, has not yet concerned itself with these matters, with the rise and fall of what we would call civilizations. Later he speaks of 'imperfect' and 'perfect' histories. Imperfect are memorials or 'naked' accounts of events; imperfect, too, are antiquities, or monuments and other fragments of the past scrupulously collected. There could be, however, a 'just and perfect' history, though in defining this he becomes unclear.

The Advancement of Learning was published at the beginning of a new century, in 1605. Its author seems unaware that in France in the century just ended there had been a great historiographical movement profoundly concerned with the rise and fall of civilizations throughout the ages of the world, which sought to use every kind of historical discipline in the effort to evolve '*l'idée d'une histoire accomplie*', or a new, universal, all-inclusive, 'perfect' kind of history.

George Huppert's book explores the writing of history in

---

* Review of George Huppert, *The Idea of Perfect History*, Urbana, Illinois, 1970, published in *New York Review of Books*, 22 October 1970.

sixteenth-century France, a neglected field in the history of historiography. Huppert is not the first to point out this gap, as he acknowledges. There is a chapter on 'The French Prelude to Modern Historiography' in J. G. A. Pocock's book *The Ancient Constitution and the Feudal Law* (1957), and George Nadel has pointed to the 'untilled field' between the overcultivated areas represented by Machiavelli and Voltaire.

The French writers now brought to the notice of historians of history were largely trained jurists, drawn from the influential magistrate class. They represent in France the importance of the legal tradition in the development of interest in history; Andrea Alciati had carried to France from Italy the latest legal-historical techniques. The historians were monarchists, whether Catholic or Huguenot in their religious views: they were interested in theories of monarchy and largely belonged to the liberal, tolerant, *politique* group which sought to override religious differences through loyalty to a liberal conception of monarchy. Huppert argues that the recognition of their work has been delayed because it was suppressed and temporarily forgotten in the rigidity of the reaction against liberalism, called 'disorder', in the repressive and absolutist climate of seventeenth-century France. Yet their writings survived and surreptitiously fed the streams leading to Bayle, Voltaire, and the historiography of enlightenment.

This is a convincing thesis and fits in with what one knows of other aspects of the culture of sixteenth-century France and of other traditions stemming from that wonderful age that were broken and obscured by the religious wars in which the century finally went down in chaos, and still further forgotten in the determination of the new century to obliterate the confusions of the past by imposing a superficial order.

Outstanding among the representatives of the French historical school discussed by Huppert is Estienne Pasquier, whose *Recherches de la France*, which he began to publish in 1560, was not completed until many years later – a truly monumental life-work of erudition. Pasquier insisted on quoting original documents and giving references for his statements; some of his friends felt this as a blemish on the literary elegance of a historical work. But Pasquier belonged to a new and coming school of history, which sought by antiquarian research to reach a more accurate idea of the past than that provided in the rhetorical tradition of history writing.

In his treatment of French history Pasquier made a surprising new departure. He did not begin it with the old legends about the descent of the French kings from the mythical Francus, a Trojan escaped from burning Troy to become the founder of the French royal line. The first in this line was supposed to be Pharamond, a personage as mythical as Francus.

The *Recherches* was the first treatise on French history which began without any mention of Francus, Pharamond and their like, and the omission must have caused general astonishment. Pasquier began his history of France with the Gauls, who are not mentioned in the old legends. He went to what he took to be primary sources, the descriptions of the Gauls and their institutions given by Caesar and other classical historians. Caesar found the Gauls in Gaul (not Francus or Pharamond), whose manners and institutions he describes. Pasquier uses Caesar's history as a primary source which can be relied upon as giving accurate information about the ancestors of the French people. And he rests his French patriotism, not on the legendary descent of French kings from Rome through a non-existent Trojan ancestor, but on the character and intelligence of the Gauls and the excellence of their institutions as described in the classical sources.

Thus institutional history, the development of French customs or the French *parlement* from Gallic roots, becomes important for Pasquier (parallels with later research in England into the Anglo-Saxon origins of Parliament of course come to mind). Pasquier sets the tone for what will be one of the most important aspects of the French school of history writing, its interest in the history of peoples, of cultures and civilizations, of the passage through time of national groups, each with a contribution to make to the history of civilization.

With the formidable figure of Jean Bodin we have a member of the French historical school who has already attracted much attention as an original historical thinker. Bodin's *Methodus*, a method for studying history published in 1566, is probably the most important book on historiography of its century. Bodin divides history into three branches, divine, natural, and human, which correspond to three kinds of knowledge, faith, science, and prudence. In the realm of human history, prudence may be acquired by studying the history of different cultures, comparing them with one another in order to find rules of social behaviour which are valid in recurring situations.

This may remind one of Machiavelli's use of history for political guidance, but with the important difference that Bodin, like all this French group, concentrates on peoples, cultures, civilizations, as the stuff of history. He aimed at compiling a universal history with a view to eliciting general principles governing historical change. In his *République* he sought to establish by a comparative study of laws of all nations a law which should apply universally. He studies history as the behaviour of men in groups, thus departing from the normal types of political history. He believed that his method would explain the rise and fall of states.

Louis Le Roy in his *De la vicissitude des choses* (1575) also treats history as group history and emphasizes the cultural rhythms in history.[1] His *De la vicissitude* is a history of civilizations, of the rise and fall of learning and sciences, of arts and technologies, as different societies have risen to prominence and declined in the passing of the ages.

He begins his history with Egypt whence, so he believes, all learning, science and skills had their origin. He then passes through other cultures, noting always the vicissitudes – that a period of advance in knowledge is always succeeded by a relapse into barbarism, light periods alternate with dark periods. Yet each wave of advance carries knowledge a little further and its gains are not entirely lost in the inevitable recession. The present, thinks Le Roy, is an age of advance in which the culture of the ancients has been recovered and technical inventions, printing and the mariner's compass, have greatly enlarged man's knowledge and power. Bodin, too, regards the sixteenth century in France as a period of great advance in the history of mankind.

Nicholas Vignier compiled a vast work which he called a *Bibliothèque historiale* (1588). It is a world history constructed on a rigid and doubtful chronological basis, but Vignier's originality consists in his collections of references, the 'libraries' of source material which he provides, grouped under the dates of his chronology. And he endeavours to assess the reliability of such sources, to provide something like a critically chosen bibliography for the historical student. Vignier was official historiographer to Henri III, and his work is a notable indication of the progress which interest in history and historical methods made toward the end of the century.

La Popelinière's *Histoire des histoires* (1599) and its accompanying treatises on *L'Idée de l'histoire accomplie* and *Dessin de l'histoire nouvelle des françois* indicate to what extent these historical movements were felt, by those taking part in them, to be essentially new movements, attempting to approach history in new ways and to write history of a new kind, a search for an 'Idea of Perfect History'. La Popelinière insists that history must be universal, that it must include all peoples and nations from the most ancient to modern times, and that it must cover not only political events but the history of the culture and learning of the peoples. Universal history may, however, be broken down into smaller parts which can be studied separately. For example, the history of the French people, their descent from the Gauls, their culture and institutions are a part of universal history. La Popelinière's demands for perfect history are so reminiscent of remarks in *The Advancement of Learning* that one wonders whether Francis Bacon had perhaps after all heard of how French historians were trying to fill the gaps in history which he deplored.

Huppert's study of these and other works of the period fully justifies the claim that French historiography of the sixteenth century must henceforth have a place in the history of history writing. The large number of books on history published in the period testifies to the interest of the public. Even the disturbed nature of the times helped in allowing freedom of thought. There was no central authority firmly enough established to exercise a censorship on how history should be written, as there was in sixteenth-century England and would be later in France in the seventeenth century. The last Valois king, Henri III, was interested in the new history and encouraged it, according to La Popelinière.

From Huppert's treatment of the historians as a group, certain general characteristics stand out. The criticism of the Trojan legend in the traditions of French monarchy seems common to all the group, not only those I have already mentioned. The celebrated *Franco-Gallia* by François Hotman, the Huguenot jurist, is also concerned with substituting critical history of the Gallic origins of the French people for the legendary tales of Francus. Earlier in the century the build-up of the French monarchy as a rising nationalist-imperialist power had laid a new stress on the Trojan descent which linked the French monarchy with imperial Rome and its symbolism. The story of Francus was proclaimed anew in uncritical histories in the time of François I, and was used throughout the century, at royal entries and other shows, as part of the normal propaganda for the French monarch.

There was a closely parallel situation in England, where Brut, the legendary Trojan ancestor of the British Tudor royal line, was prominent in royalist propaganda. In England, too, a critical historian, Polydore Vergil, had undermined Geoffrey of Monmouth and his tale of the Trojan Brut. Yet in both England and France the Trojan legends continued to be used in the propaganda although educated people now knew that they were not literally true. Brut takes his place as an ancestor in Spenser's glorification of Elizabeth in *The Faerie Queene*, and Francus is the hero of Ronsard's *La Franciade*, an unfinished epic in honour of Charles IX. Ronsard's preface to *La Franciade* (1572) explains how it was possible to know and accept the fact that modern criticism had unmasked Trojan ancestors as unsound history while at the same time continuing to use them as propaganda figures. The descent of the French kings from Francus is, says Ronsard, poetically and spiritually true, though it is clear that he does not subscribe wholeheartedly to the literal truth of the legend.

Such subtleties belong naturally to the Renaissance outlook, with its proclivity for seeing varying levels of interpretation in myth, and it is not so surprising as Huppert thinks that Vignier as historiographer to Henri III should criticize the Trojan legend. That subtle monarch would probably have shared the Ronsardian attitude toward Francus.

There was a mythic side to the critical historians' build-up of the Gauls as the real historical ancestors of the French people, as against the unreality of the Trojan ancestors of French kings. The Cabalist, Guillaume Postel, had propagated, at about the time that the new historical school was growing up, mystical notions about French origins, in which a certain 'Gomer Gaulois', supposed grandson of Noah, was associated with the Gauls, and with the wisdom of the Druids, their religious teachers and the propagators of their excellent laws and institutions. Pasquier dwells at length on the wisdom and sanctity of the Druids in his treatment of Gallic origins in the *Recherches*; Bodin also has a profound respect for Druidic law, which he calls religious, and he seems more than half to believe in Gomer Gaulois.

Nevertheless, though it had its own mythic elements, the Gallic school of French history developed the view of history as the story of civilizations, their rises and falls, their changing courses. As the Gauls and their institutions developed into the modern French, as exact historical techniques were applied to the examination of this process, as sources were more and more carefully chosen and tested, a kind of French history emerged which La Popelinière at the end of the century rightly hailed as 'new'.

The most striking characteristic of the French school is its concern with universal history, with the search for a history which should cover, not only the emergence of modern France from Gaul, but the rises and falls of all the cultures known in the history of man. Though Huppert is much concerned with the future of the French ideas, with their probable influence on later historical schools, he does not ask any question about their origins – why this interest in histories of civilizations throughout the ages of world history should have arisen in France in the sixteenth century.

Huppert has missed perhaps the most revealing and informative of the universal histories of the French historians, the one which can throw light on them all. I mean *La Galliade ou la Révolution des Arts et Sciences* by Guy Lefèvre de la Boderie, published in 1578. Perhaps Huppert missed this because it is in the form of a long epic poem and he may think that all history should be in prose. But *La Galliade* is absolutely central to his theme.

The hero of the epic is Gomer Gaulois, and La Boderie's use of this hero takes the form of a universal history running through all civilizations. Art, letters, light, and learning, stemming originally from Gomer, the Gauls, and their teachers the Druids, take a course through world history, having manifestations in all the great civilizations, to return at last to France, their original Gallic home, in the great outburst of cultural splendour taking place in sixteenth-century France.

La Galliade is steeped in Cabalist and Hermetic mysticism, in that cult of ancient wisdoms or ancient theologies which underlies Renaissance Neoplatonism. La Boderie personifies the ancient wisdoms whose migrations he studies as 'the sisters Poetry and Music'. The present reappearance of these sisters in France is the latest phase in their age-long travels in the course of which they have dwelt in ancient Gaul, Egypt, Judaea, Greece, Rome, Italy. As these various civilizations are visited by the sisters, long lists are given of the groups of learned men, artists, musicians, scientists, propagators of every aspect of culture and civilization who have lived in the various epochs. It is a technique very similar to that of Le Roy in *De la vicissitude*, where he gives long lists of celebrated individuals who have flourished in the various civilizations.

Yet with La Boderie the universal history of civilizations does not have at all that 'secular' appearance which Huppert believed to be characteristic of the French school. It is immersed in the atmosphere of Renaissance Neoplatonism with its cult of *prisci theologi*, or ancient theologians. Druid, Egyptian, Hebrew, Greek, Roman, Italian Renaissance cultures are seen by La Boderie as manifestations of ancient wisdom which shows itself in periodic cultural reappearances – the revolutions of the arts and sciences – as the sisters Poetry and Music travel through the ages.

It is clear that the inspiration here is in the concept of *prisca theologia*, propagated by Ficino in the Italian Renaissance, the concept of the wisdom of Egypt as connected with Hebrew wisdom, with Plato and Greek wisdom, and culminating in Christian wisdom. The *prisca theologia* was much studied in France in the sixteenth century in both philosophical and ecclesiastical circles, as D. P. Walker has shown.[2] It was easy to assimilate other occult wisdoms to the tradition, and the Druids are frequently mentioned as belonging to it. What seems to have happened in La Boderie's poem is that the Druids, representing ancient Gallic wisdom, are put first in sequence, and also – and this is the important point – the wisdoms are interpreted in terms of civilizations, as the motive forces behind all the arts and sciences, laws and cultures which have periodically shown themselves in different national guises throughout the ages of world history.

La Boderie's poem cannot be dismissed as the fantasy of an eccentric individual. It belongs to the atmosphere of the period for it seems to have been designed as a kind of pre-history of Baïf's Academy of Poetry and Music, founded in 1570 under royal patronage and representative of all that was most advanced in contemporary French culture. All the poets and musicians of Baïf's Academy are mentioned by La Boderie, and his poem is a major source for the Academy. Another major source for it is the section on French poetry in Estienne Pasquier's *Recherches de la France*. The historian should not be studied in isolation from the poet; Pasquier and La Boderie may represent complementary aspects of the study of ancient Gaul by patriotic Frenchmen of the sixteenth century.

If we turn again to Le Roy's *De la vicissitude* it becomes perfectly clear that his enthusiastic admiration for the religion and wisdom of Egypt, his studies of subsequent civilizations, belong to the atmosphere of the history of ancient wisdom, now interpreted so as to include the history of civilizations.

Huppert regards Le Roy's *De la vicissitude* as

> . . . in reality a philosophic manifesto, the prototype of the
> encyclopaedic works of Bayle, Voltaire, Diderot. The break
> with theological history is complete. Embracing the whole
> world, delighting in non-Christian and exotic cultures, Le
> Roy ransacks the erudition of his time to provide illustrations
> for his philosophy of history.

He may be right about the forward-looking aspects of Le Roy's
work, but he certainly has no understanding of the mind of a
Renaissance Neoplatonist in contact with the contemporary
French forms of religious syncretism.

Histories of historiography and history writing are becoming
fashionable as people ask what is the history of our present sense
of history. The preoccupation with history is as characteristic
of our times as the preoccupation with science and technology.
Historians of history may be subject to the danger which has beset
historians of science, I mean the danger of reading the history
forward to some modern concept of history, or modern scientific
position, extracting from the people of former times what seem
to be the forward-looking elements in their thought and neglecting
their context in the thought as a whole.

Huppert does not escape this danger. In his eagerness to prove
a 'secular' and therefore enlightened outlook on history in his
French historians he ignores other sides of the writers' minds. If
the 'French prelude to historiography' is of great importance as a
hitherto neglected link with the historiography of the seventeenth
and eighteenth centuries – and I have no doubt that it is – the
importance of seeing it as a whole, of linking it with its past as
well as its future, becomes all the more pressing. Huppert has
made a beginning, but before we can fully understand this fascinating movement, we need other books on the thought of these
sixteenth-century French historians which do not omit their roots
in the French Renaissance.

Chapter Fifteen

THE FEAR OF THE OCCULT*

WHEN FONTENELLE was composing his *éloge* of Isaac Newton for delivery in the Académie Royale des Sciences, he was able to consult notes by John Conduitt from which he would have learned that one of Newton's motives in beginning his work in mathematics was to investigate whether judicial astrology had any claim to validity. In writing his *éloge*, Fontenelle omitted any reference to this fact, an omission which, as Brian Copenhaver points out, was normal in the Age of Enlightenment. Astrology for Fontenelle was unworthy of even passing reference. 'The occultist tradition and all its claims about the powers of magic, alchemy, divination, witchcraft, and the secret arts, no longer demanded a serious response from serious thinkers.' How did it come about that such subjects had disappeared from the mainstream of European mental equipment, banished from the surface to pursue in future only a discredited existence underground? Copenhaver writes:

By the time the first edition of the *Encyclopaedia Britannica* appeared in 1771 the transformation was complete. The first *Britannica* gave only one hundred and thirty-two lines, less than a full page, to articles on astrology, alchemy, Cabala, demons, divination, the word 'occult', and witchcraft.

* Review of Brian P. Copenhaver, *Symphorien Champier and the Reception of the Occultist Tradition in Renaissance France*, The Hague, Berlin, New York, 1978, published in *New York Review of Books*, 22 November 1979.

Astronomy occupied sixty-seven pages, and chemistry one hundred and fifteen.

An irresistible historical transformation had taken place. Modern science, beginning its victorious career, had blotted out the immediate past. In such overwhelming movements, the facts which one generation consciously omits are genuinely forgotten by its successors. Later generations forgot Newton's interest in alchemy until confronted with his unpublished papers. But the Fontenelle attitude dies hard, even when faced with documentary evidence that Newton attached equal, or greater, importance to his alchemical studies than to his work in mathematics.

Efforts have been made in recent years to penetrate the curtain which shrouded the influential figures of the past in nineteenth- and early twentieth-century histories of thought. When I was a young person (I will not say a young student, for I did not study these subjects in any university) the books which I read on Marsilio Ficino described him as a Neoplatonic philosopher, which of course he was, but they did not mention that he was a Neoplatonic magician. Ficino's theories on magic, and his use of talismans, have been a discovery of recent years. D. P. Walker's examination of Ficino's astral medicine proved its dependence on the *Asclepius*, the magical treatise attributed to 'Hermes Trismegistus'.[1] Similarly, when I read thirty years ago about Giordano Bruno, the books of that time presented him as an enlightened Renaissance philosopher, defender of Copernicanism against reactionaries. Yet it turns out that Bruno quoted at length from the *Asclepius* on magical reform, and that his defence of heliocentricity was itself influenced, perhaps inspired, by 'Hermes Trismegistus' on the sun. This rereading or reinterpretation of noted figures in the history of thought is a process which has only recently been begun. It needs to be extended in detailed studies of many other figures, preparatory to a general reassessment of the processes through which phases in the history of thought were obscured by the Fontenelle type of forgetfulness.

In the history and scholarship of today, the magical and the occult are not forgotten, or debarred from serious study. On the contrary there has been an enormous increase of interest in these subjects. The advanced studies of today tend to treat them under sociology or anthropology and in generalized approaches. Brian Copenhaver maintains that

though it may eventually become possible to write the history
of occultist thinking from the point of view of a sociology
of knowledge, we are not yet in a position to do so. We need
first to have a better idea of what past states of knowledge
were and what they claimed to be. For this it is necessary to
have a clearer idea of what important individuals thought and
claimed to think about occultism.

And it is this which Copenhaver has tried to do for Symphorien
Champier.

Champier was born near Lyon about 1474; for most of his life he
was associated with that city, though he trained at the University
of Paris, at Montpellier for medicine, and travelled to Italy in the
suite of his patron. In Champier's time, Lyon was seething with
the Renaissance influences coming in from Italy. Champier was
very receptive to the life and thought of his times, and was a
most prolific author: his many books constitute a mine of source
material for the early French Renaissance. He is accused of
unoriginality; his books tend to be a tissue of quotations, but this
may actually increase his value as a mirror of the times. He was
primarily a practising doctor; many of his books and pamphlets
are on medicine. Though a firm Galenist, he was yet not unrecep-
tive to some new tendencies in medicine. In religion he was an
ardently conservative Catholic, horrified by the spread of heresy
and by the violence of the mob of Vaudois heretics who pillaged
his house in the great 'rebeine' of 1529. As a very patriotic Frenchman he upheld French institutions like the University of Paris
and the monarchy. As an enthusiastic spectator of the invasions
of Italy he would have seen those brilliant troops of French
knights, with their heraldic devices which so much struck the
Italians. Champier was present at the field of Marignano, at which
he was knighted, not it would seem for any feat of arms but
because he had translated Ramon Lull's book on the Order of
Chivalry.
    Symphorien Champier steps out of the marvellous French
Middle Ages which produced so many clever Parisian-trained
minds, such devotion to the sacred French monarchy. What could
such a man as this have had to do with the new magic and
occultism introduced in Italy by Marsilio Ficino and Pico della
Mirandola? As the title of Copenhaver's book states, Champier
was vitally concerned with 'the reception of the occultist tradition

in Renaissance France'. In two books written early in his career, the *Nef des Princes* (1502) and the *Nef des Dames* (1503), Champier was among the first to propagate Ficino's Platonism in France. The *De quadruplici vita* (1507) and the *De triplici disciplina* (1509) contain 'Champier's peculiar mixture of medicine, philosophy, theology, and occultism', and are profoundly influenced by Ficino.

In an article published twenty-five years ago and reprinted in his book *The Ancient Theology*, D. P. Walker contrasted the reception of occultist and magical thinking in France with its reception in Italy. In Italy, the new magic was embedded in the Neoplatonism so enthusiastically welcomed by Ficino and Pico. In France, though Neoplatonism was also the fashionable philosophy, the core of Hermetic and Cabalist magic in the movement was regarded with greater caution, and efforts were made to receive the philosophy while being wary of the magic. Walker attributes the greater caution towards magic of the French Neoplatonists to the strength of Parisian scholasticism. Champier is an excellent example of the cautious French Neoplatonist and Hermeticist. Stalwart defender of all things French, including Parisian scholasticism, he was also profoundly attracted by Neoplatonism and by the holy 'Hermes Trismegistus', the true source, according to this way of thinking, of Plato's thought, and as ancient as Moses.

Champier published a new edition of the *Hermetica* which included a dialogue on the sun which had not been known to Ficino. He was fascinated by the holy Hermes and his mysterious works, and sought to clear him of dangerous magic by arguing that the magic in the *Asclepius* was not taught by Hermes himself but had been introduced into the Hermetic treatise by Apuleius of Madaura when he translated it into Latin. The account in the *Asclepius* of how the Egyptians infused life into the statues of their gods had been the basic source of Ficino's magic. Champier avoids it by his assumption that the deeply magical passage in the *Asclepius* was not by the holy Hermes himself but had been falsely introduced by the wicked translator of the treatise. In this way Champier tried to avoid the Hermetic magic while retaining the admired magico-mystical philosophy of Hermes.

Champier's fear of magic was associated with his fear of heresy. In fact the *Dyalogus* against the magical arts may have been directed as much against the Vaudois heretics as against the learned magicians of the Italian Renaissance. There was always a strong undercurrent of fear in the occultists, fear of the forces they might be invoking, anxiety to keep on the safe side in dealing with them. Ficino was full of fear and anxiety; Champier's cautiousness is an attempt to avoid the dangers of the subject which fascinated him.

The nearest approach to magic in Champier's outlook was made through his medicine. The correct Galenist doctor was awake to contemporary influences through his firm belief in interaction between body and soul. As Copenhaver points out, Ficino's astral medicine, aimed at affecting both body and soul through the imagination, was the side of Ficino's occultism that most affected Champier. The physician of Lyon is one of the ancestors of the long line of influences on medicine, deriving ultimately from the occultist side of Renaissance Neoplatonism, which reaches from Ficino through Champier and others, and on through the history of medicine up to Mesmer and Charcot. The intensive exercise of the power of the imagination, cultivated in Renaissance Neoplatonism, when applied to medicine, led in due time in the direction of psychiatry.

Champier was only one among many Neoplatonists of the French Renaissance. One of the most important of the group was Jacques Lefèvre d'Etaples, an extremely interesting figure about whom we have as yet no major study. As Copenhaver emphasizes, Champier was deeply influenced by Lefèvre, his great contemporary. Lefèvre, like Champier, was concerned with spreading in France interest in Ficino's Neoplatonism, closely associated with profound respect for 'Hermes Trismegistus' as a deeply religious thinker, believed to be earlier than Plato and a prophet of Christianity. Lefèvre published another edition of the *Hermetica*, including the *Asclepius*, with a commentary by himself on the latter in which he warned against the magic introduced by the translator. (There existed no original of the work from which to check these statements about the magic introduced by the translator.) This cautious rejection of the magic enabled deeply religious thinkers like Lefèvre and many French ecclesiastics to become enthusiastic about a Hermes Trismegistus cleared of magic. But, there exists, in two copies, a manuscript by Lefèvre in which he appears to be involved in a deeply magical outlook, raising the suspicion that he was fascinated by the magic which he publicly deplored. May one perhaps wonder whether the same may be true of Champier? The strong pressures of public opinion, and the deep-seated fears evidently felt by those who, like Champier and Lefèvre, try to keep their Hermetic-Cabalist interests 'safe', must be taken into account in trying to assess their public statements on these subjects. Copenhaver has made a useful attempt, in an article which he does not use in the book, at unravelling the strong Cabalist influence on Lefèvre.

Lefèvre, unlike the orthodox Champier, had leanings towards reform. One of the many threads in the tangled skein of religious history in the Renaissance is the connection of the occultist movement with movement towards reform. Pico della Mirandola intended his syncretist movement, which drew so much of its strength from Hermetic-Cabalist Neoplatonism, as a step towards universal religious reform and religious union. This aim was never forgotten by Renaissance occultists and syncretists, and persists strongly even in the work of Henry Cornelius Agrippa, one of the most outspoken of the magicians. Indeed one is tempted to wonder whether radical reform and radical, or extreme, occultism did not sometimes go together.

We need many more detailed studies of individual thinkers such as Copenhaver's of Champier before the history of the whole movement can be assessed. Although not an exciting figure in himself, Champier lived in the exciting time of the early French Renaissance, and amid varying types of reception of the occultist tradition. Rabelais, for example, almost certainly knew Champier, and was far more lenient towards evangelical reform than the Galenist doctor. What would have been the attitude of Doctor Rabelais towards Champier's dabbling in Ficinian medicine?

Champier's close relations with the orthodox clergy of Lyon would surely have made his work known to Pontus de Tyard, Bishop of Châlons, poet of the French Pléiade, and theorist of 'the effects of poetry and music', the idea which inspired the poets and musicians of Baïf's Academy of Poetry and Music. The degree of magic behind the incantatory psalms and songs of Baïf's Academy is difficult to assess, but the movement could certainly be related to the Ficinian therapy in which the use of music was advised. David charming away Saul's melancholy with his harp was the obvious image for musical-medical humanism.

With Marin Mersenne, deeply interested in the theories of Baïf's

Academy and a main source for them, we move into the seven-teenth century. Mersenne's *Harmonie universelle* is crucial for the adaptation in the seventeenth century of sixteenth-century theories of harmony with their close relationship to the musical-magical cosmology. What degree of occultism or magic was dropped in the process of this adaptation? This is extremely difficult to assess, but what is clear is Mersenne's anxiety, his painful efforts to keep his passionate interest in universal harmony, and its associated ideas, clear from imputations of magic. Nervous marginal notes warn the reader against *anima mundi*, the key concept in the cosmology which favoured magic.

Mersenne's anxieties reached a climax in his controversy with Robert Fludd. The representative of French caution in dealing with Neoplatonism and its associated magics naturally viewed with alarm the incautious Fludd, inheritor of the ideas of John Dee whose lack of caution led him into (almost) open angel-conjuring. Fludd represented an uninhibited occultist tradition which Mersenne, if only to protect his own orthodoxy, was eager to condemn.

For the understanding of such later developments, Champier in his mid-sixteenth-century Lyon circle is important, and it is good that there is now a book devoted to him. Copenhaver has distilled the somewhat dry works of the Lyon doctor, discussed their place in the history of medicine, and assessed Champier's reception, or rather his critical half-reception, of the Renaissance occult tradition.

He has made an attempt to cover all the sources used by Cham-pier, including not only the Renaissance sources but also occultism in the Greek and Latin classics, in early Christianity, in Islam, in the Middle Ages. He examines point by point Champier's critique of occultism, discusses Champier on the world soul, on natural magic, on demonology, and other related topics. Finally, he reprints Champier's *Dyalogus . . . in magicarum artium destruc-tionem*, a major statement of his critical position.

Copenhaver's book should be in the library of all those interested in the elusive subject of Renaissance magic. The large problems raised by his discussion of the meaning of the word magic are not solved by him but it is always useful to raise the question. And his query about when the magical world view ceased to command attention, ceased even to need attacking but silently disappeared from the general consciousness, is also still unsolved. It was not

Copernicus who most upset it, but Darwin, who dislocated Genesis and substituted the apes for the ancient philosophers as witnesses of the dawn of human history.

Studies of French Neoplatonism such as Champier's bring out the fear and reserve which many people felt about the dangers of Renaissance occultism. Though the witchcraft scares of the sixteenth and early seventeenth centuries are usually presented as popular movements, it is, I believe, probable that fears of the learned magic entered to some extent into the popular scares. Surely it is significant that the *Démonomanie* of Jean Bodin, one of the writers most influential in fomenting the witch craze, opens with an attack on Pico and Agrippa for what Bodin held to be their wicked use of Cabala for magic. That the Renaissance occultism of Pico and his successors was directed toward religious reform laid it open to frantic propaganda against heresy, with which sorcery was so often associated in the minds of the orthodox. Under these pressures of alarmed public opinion, the Renaissance magus turned to ever greater secrecy, while his image turned into the Faust image. Giordano Bruno, who abandoned all caution and openly preached a religious reformation based on the magical religion of the Egyptians, as described in the terrible *Asclepius*, very naturally ended his career at the stake.

One very important aspect of this problem is the question of how far these pressures and fears affected the way in which the great thinkers of the early modern period presented their work. Why did Newton publish his mathematics and optics while concealing his interest in alchemy and in the proportions of Solomon's Temple? Does this concealment of part of their outlook also affect other famous figures, for example Descartes? It is clear from Baillet's life of Descartes that the philosopher was very much afraid of being taken for a Rosicrucian on his return from Germany. It has been argued in a recent book that the automata and other mechanical inventions that Descartes saw in the gardens of the Elector Palatine at Heidelberg[2] suggested to him the outlines of his mechanical philosophy. Such inventions as these were normally classed in the occult tradition as 'real artificial magic', an expression not used by Descartes or the Cartesians in connection with the mechanical philosophy. Another way of looking at this problem might be to ask whether the contemporary outcries against witches, sorcerers, Rosicrucians and so on helped to release science from the magical associations, discarded and avoided through fear of the scares.

It is perhaps worth while to ask such questions in the light of Copenhaver's book, for Champier's dilemma of both accepting and rejecting the occult tradition may represent an early form of the problem.

Chapter Sixteen

ORACLE TO THE COCK OF FRANCE*

NOSTRADAMUS IS a name which belongs to popular culture, to the world of the almanac and sensational forecasting. The main events of European history are supposed to have been prophesied in his riddling verses: the execution of Charles I, the French Revolution, the career of Napoleon, the rise of Hitler (Goebbels used the prophecies in his propaganda). I understand that even Nixon and the tapes were foreseen by Nostradamus! These extraordinary successes make all the more alarming the supposed prophecies as yet unfulfilled.

Though this strange prophet has been famous in sub-culture for 400 years, in itself an interesting phenomenon, there has been no modern critical edition of the *Prophéties* and no sustained attempt at putting this substantial body of French verse into historical context. The edition of the *Prophecies and Enigmas of Nostradamus* by Liberté LeVert has now filled this gap. It contains all the quatrains in the 1555 first edition and others from the second and third series. They are printed exactly as in the original French, together with a new literal English translation. The critical commentary sweeps away all the nonsense that has grown up around the prophecies in their passage through the centuries.

The reader will derive a good deal of enjoyment from this lively

---

* Review of *The Prophecies and Enigmas of Nostradamus*, translated and edited by Liberté E. LeVert, Glen Rock, New Jersey, 1980, in *Times Literary Supplement*, 14 March 1980.

commentary, which unravels the allusions as referring mainly to the events of Nostradamus's own times, not to ages yet unborn. The retirement of a great personage to a small place is not a prophecy of Napoleon on Elba but reflects the retirement of the Emperor Charles V, which had occurred not long before the publication of the prophecies. When Nostradamus speaks of 'Bretaigne' he means Brittany: hence political convulsions in 'Bretaigne' are not prophecies of the execution of Charles I and other sensational events in British history but are about happenings in Brittany in the sixteenth century. 'Hister' is the river Danube, not a boss shot at 'Hitler'. The prophecies are almost entirely concerned with sixteenth-century history, with particular reference to the French monarchy and its relations with other contemporary powers. When Nostradamus actually makes a prophecy of something which is to occur in the future, he is nearly always wrong, his most tremendous blunder being the presage of a glorious career for Henri II made shortly before that monarch's unexpected death in a joust.

The double task of providing for the first time a reliable text and translation of Nostradamus's poetry and of sweeping away the trashy interpretations with which centuries of low-grade exploitation have covered it, has at last unveiled the real Nostradamus and his work. As LeVert says, we have not hitherto known either.

Michel de Nostradame (1503–66) was born at Saint Rémy, near Marseilles. On both sides of his family he was descended from converted Jews. He always proclaimed his adhesion to the Catholic Church, though he did not entirely escape Inquisitorial inquiry. He was grounded in Latin at the papal school in Avignon, then trained as a doctor at Montpellier, specializing in the plague. Rabelais was a medical student at Montpellier at the same time as Nostradamus; there is no evidence that these two unusual students knew one another. Nostradamus's education was evidently rather rich and varied (he always said that he learned to prophesy from his family) and there is no doubt that he was a learned man – he worked for a time with the great scholar J. C. Scaliger.

In 1555, Nostradamus published at Lyon the first series of *Les prophéties*, which attracted the attention of the French court. He was summoned to Paris; Catherine de Médicis was deeply interested in the occult; Nostradamus, who was an astrologer (not a very good one, according to LeVert), seemed a likely person to find favour at court, and to be useful both as astrologer and doctor. He lived on the fringe of court favour though he was not fully accepted until too late. The misfortune of the untimely death of Henri II probably delayed his career.

From the standpoint of his accurately edited text of the *Prophéties* and newly directed examination of it, LeVert arrives at some important discoveries. He reveals Nostradamus, first of all, to have had a good knowledge of versification. Though his verse prophecies relate to the almanac world, they are by no means popular doggerel; as refined by a learned hand they become minor French poetry of the sixteenth century. LeVert analyses the versification closely and uses it to help with the riddles. Noting that Nostradamus observes the caesura strictly he finds this a guide in deciphering. For example, a worrying character called 'Voldrap' disappears when it is noticed that 'vol' comes at the end of the first half of a line and 'drap' at the beginning of the second half; 'Voldrap' was born of a printer's disregard of the caesura.

Second, LeVert offers a new interpretation of the prophecies in terms of the world in which Nostradamus lived. There were quite enough sensational events in the sixteenth century for a prophet to brood over without filling in with colourful allusions to Oliver Cromwell, Napoleon, or Hitler. LeVert knows his way about in the sixteenth century extremely well, though he wears his historical erudition lightly and wittily. He does not force interpretations but simply leaves blanks where he cannot understand. He is amusingly aware of the cautious obscurity in which prophets from the Delphic oracle onwards have veiled their meanings. Through the dark sayings of the prophecies he traces events in the French invasions of Italy; the sack of Rome by the imperialists; adventures of well-known personages of the French court; the spread of new heresies from Germany and Switzerland; and the policies, victories, and defeats of the leading power centres of the age – the German Emperor, Charles V; the French King, François I, and his successors; the Republic of Venice; and, of course, the Papacy. Fully alive to political allegory, he gives close attention to the Eagle (the Emperor), the Cock (the King of France), and the Lion (Venice), in their constantly recurring appearances. With shocking disrespect he refers to these noble creatures as 'the usual military zoo'!

It seems evident (though LeVert does not go into this) that Nostradamus's favourite creature is the Cock of the French monarchy. The crucial prophecy is the one about Henri II which should have made Nostradamus's fortune had it not been for that unlucky joust.

> Au chef du monde le grande Chyren [Henri II] sera,
> Plus oultre après aymé; craint, redoubté
> Son bruit & loz les cieulx surpassera,
> Et du seul titre victeur fort contenté.

(At the head of the world shall be the great Chyren. 'Plus ultra' [is left] behind. [Great Chyren shall be] loved, feared, dreaded, [Chyren's] fame and renown shall rise above the skies, And with the single title, 'Victor' [he shall be] well content.)

As unriddled by LeVert this means that the French King Henri II ('Chyren' is an anagram of 'Henric') will be universal monarch, leaving far behind the German Emperor, Charles V, with his famous motto *Plus Ultra*. Everyone at the time would have understood this as contrasting the French monarch with the German Emperor and claiming for the former the right to world rule, which the German Emperor claimed. The imperial device with its proud motto was very well known in France and was replied to by the device of Henri II, a crescent moon with the motto *Donec totum impleat orbem* (Until the moon [of French monarchy] fills the world).

Nostradamus is moving in the great world of 'imperial themes', the themes of universal empire for French monarchy or German Empire, aspirations which lay at the root of the struggles of the age. Both the imperial figures claimed the aura of Roman Empire and the Trojan descent (to which the prophecies often allude). Naturally, Nostradamus weighted his prophecy on the French side.

In what light did Nostradamus see himself? How did he wish to present himself to his readers? The opening quatrains of the series make an impressive claim to divine inspiration. 'Seated alone at night in serious study' he sees a flame appearing. 'Wand in hand', he performs magical rites and, in fear and trembling, 'sees the divine splendour'. In the following quatrains he sees what sound like visions of a universal monarchy and a weakened Papacy, but very obscurely worded. The prophet takes care not to be too explicit. LeVert thinks that Nostradamus does not really believe in all this, but is aiming only at a conventional invocation of the muse. Yet these things were taken very seriously in the sixteenth century. The poet Ronsard made claims to inspiration by divine *furor* and made prophetic statements about the times. He respected Nostradamus as a prophet.

What Ronsard says about Nostradamus (not quoted by LeVert) is revealing as to how a contemporary poet regarded him. For him Nostradamus is a prophet sent from God to warn France of danger, but these warnings have not been heeded. Ronsard asks whether Nostradamus's enthusiasm is inspired directly by the Eternal God, or by some good or bad demon or angel. But he has no doubt that the words of this sombre and melancholy prophet are inspired. He has read into the prophecies meanings which might relate to the wild prophecies of universal religious rule for French monarchy that were the theme of the strange Christian Cabalist Guillaume Postel, though Nostradamus was a much more hard-headed character than Postel. Yet it seems that contemporaries, like Ronsard, might read Nostradamus's prophecies as prophetic in the Hebraic sense, and relating to the religious destinies of France.

There is another side of Nostradamus which raises interesting questions. He was a writer who took a popular form, the almanac type of prognostication, and re-expressed it in terms of classical or humanistic versions of prophetic themes. As LeVert says, he is a kind of humanist, with some knowledge of classical texts on prophecy such as Marsilio Ficino was reviving. He is in a sense a humanist, related to the 'élitist' Renaissance culture of Ronsard and the Pléiade. Yet he comes out of the popular almanac tradition, and it was in that tradition that his name survived. Nostradamus became a name used by popular almanac writers, but Nostradamus the minor Renaissance poet was forgotten. He is a curious example of how a popular form could be taken up for a while into an educated milieu, afterwards falling back again into sub-culture. Nostradamus's fellow medical student at Montpellier, Rabelais, shows a somewhat similar use of popular culture, in his case the French farce tradition, to convey weighty themes. One might say that Rabelais's name, too, survives as a farcical *bon viveur* rather than as the enthusiastic evangelical whom modern research has revealed.

The light-hearted style in which LeVert presents his edition of Nostradamus does not obscure the fact that he has done a serious and original piece of research in excavating this author and his work.

Chapter Seventeen

VICISSITUDES*

IN THE late sixteenth century a French scholar surveyed his own times with feelings of mingled hope and despair. He had seen the Renaissance revival of learning take hold with tremendous force in France. Technological advance, the use of printing, had made the resulting proliferation of new knowledge and new ideas universally available at a rate and in a volume undreamed of in the previous history of mankind. Knowledge was not only immensely increased; it was immediately communicated in the form of the printed book to the bewildered public. Another technological advance, the invention of the mariner's compass, had brought far regions near, had found new lands beyond the seas unknown to the ancients. Third, the improvements in fire-arms had transformed the art of war. In this world of infinitely increased potentialities for good or evil there was no peace. The old loyalties which bound together the old order of society were breaking down; religion was weakened by dissension, and the century of the Renaissance in France had been the century of the wars of religion. Wherever one looked, east or west, north or south, there was conflict and unrest. Man's new opportunities had included opportunities for the expansion of his lubricity and a new disease had appeared, syphilis. In the great cycles of history civilizations had arisen, to flourish for a while and then to vanish, destroyed by

---

* Review of Werner L. Gundersheimer, *The Life and Works of Louis Le Roy*, Geneva, 1966, in *New York Review of Books*, 24 August 1967.

the seeds of disintegration lurking within their triumphs. Was the present age the last of these cycles, and was it doomed to go down into a final ruin?

The man who asked these distressingly familiar questions was Louis Le Roy, in a book called *De la vicissitude ou variété des choses en l'univers*. First published in 1575, it went through many editions and was widely influential, particularly in England. It filled a need in providing a philosophy of history for men who lived in bewildering times. Le Roy was the Spengler or the Toynbee of the sixteenth century and merits the careful attention of historians of history. It is therefore fortunate that Werner L. Gundersheimer has written a good book on him.

Le Roy had himself played an important part in the diffusion of knowledge in sixteenth-century France, as is well brought out in Gundersheimer's book. He was born in 1510, of poor parents. What little is known of his life is characterized by a total and unremitting commitment to learning and scholarship combined with extreme penury. Why Le Roy never succeeded in getting himself subsidized by a patron remains a mystery, for his work was of a kind which should have appealed to French Renaissance royalty and aristocracy. This work included the translation into French of some of the major works of Plato, with commentaries, and of the *Politics* of Aristotle. Le Roy's translations and commentaries were an important factor in spreading knowledge of the Renaissance revival of Plato and the Neoplatonists in France. Since he used in his commentaries the works of modern Italian philosophers, particularly those of Ficino and Pico della Mirandola, he is a key figure for the popularization of Florentine Neoplatonism in France. His translations contributed to the perfection and improvement of the French language and helped to provide a philosophical background for the literary and poetic movements of the century which are associated with Ronsard and the other poets of the Pléiade. Le Roy's publications were also influential in England; it has been suggested that his translation and commentary on Plato's *Symposium* may have been used by Spenser. His *Politiques d'Aristote* was much read in England, was translated into English in 1598, and may have influenced English seventeenth-century political theory.

In politics, Le Roy was a liberal monarchist, and wrote many pamphlets in which he deplored religious intolerance and strife and appealed for a return to order. He belonged to that important liberal and tolerant line of thinking which was supported by many of the greatest names in sixteenth-century France (not excluding the much maligned Catherine de Médicis). Too little is known of this outside the circle of French specialists. To the general reader, the history of sixteenth-century France is perhaps still a confused mass of savage religious wars and massacres, enlivened by court scandals about the amours of *'la reine Margot'* or the *'mignons'* of Henri III. A friend once remarked to me that sixteenth-century French history was still at the 'technicolor' stage, and although matters have improved since then, the steady growth during the century of enlightened political and religious thinking (stimulated by reaction from the horrors of the wars) is probably not generally known. In that movement, Le Roy holds an honourable place. Like his similarly minded contemporaries, he believed that the French monarchy, liberally interpreted, represented the principle of order which must be maintained and preserved amid the growing chaos. This conception was not wholly nationalist in spirit but a revival of the idea of the French monarchy as one of the great props of European order which had a very long history behind it.

Though Le Roy was gradually moving toward his philosophy of history in his commentaries and pamphlets it was not until nearly the end of his industrious and poverty-stricken life that he published the *De la vicissitude* (he died in 1577, two years after the appearance of the first edition). This book was also much read in England; it was translated by Robert Ashley and imitated by John Norden. From primitive origins onward, Le Roy traces the cultural achievements of the major civilizations known to him, including Egypt, Babylon, ancient Greece and Rome, the Mohammedan world. The beginnings of 'the present age' he places in the fourteenth century and presents, rather strangely, the Scythian conqueror, Tamburlaine, as its initiator (Marlowe may have drawn ideas for a play from this), passing immediately from Tamburlaine to Petrarch and the Italian Renaissance. The vicissitudes of history proceed in cycles, rising with increases of culture supported by force – or what Le Roy calls, using a well-known topos, the combination of 'letters and arms' – and declining with the decline of culture and vigour.

Gundersheimer has interestingly analysed some of the strands from which Le Roy's tapestry of history is woven. Obviously, the vicissitudes are a legacy from the classical cycles of alternating decline and *renovatio*, but interpreted realistically as dependent on cultural achievements and with no mention of mythical 'golden ages'. Yet Le Roy is no pagan but a believer in Divine Providence. Though there is no mention of Eden and the Fall in his discussion of primitive origins, some traces of the linear progression of providential history, which always moves forward to its fore-ordained end, is apparent in his belief that one era can pass on to the next some of its advances because not all of its achievements are wiped out in the vicissitude of darkness. Yet in his insistence on cultural advance, and particularly on scientific and technical advance, as marking the crests of the vicissitudes, Le Roy is neither medieval nor humanist but is moving towards a seventeenth-century type of progressive outlook. He can almost be regarded as a precursor of Francis Bacon, though Bacon is, in a way, less a realist than Le Roy, for his great instauration of the sciences was to lead on to a restored Eden, after the manner of mythical history. Undoubtedly the great realist influence on Le Roy's view of history was Machiavelli, whose theme of *virtù* – or the capacity, intelligence, and force which maintain a civilization – is recognizable in Le Roy's interpretation of 'letters and arms'. Like Machiavelli, Le Roy attempts to face history in a realistic way and to learn from it.

De la vicissitude des choses is not a great book. Its composite medieval, humanist, and modernist structure is not fused into a satisfying whole, and it is marred by much tediousness, such as the long lists of famous men who flourished in the various eras. Nevertheless it was a book which served its times because it attempted to face the fears of its times. Gundersheimer calls Le Roy a pessimistic optimist, or an optimistic pessimist. Though fascinated by the 'broadening stream of culture', the immense gains in man's knowledge and power which he had witnessed during his lifetime, he was also appalled by the menace of universal war and the possibility that a vicissitude of darkness might be at hand. Yet if there were new dangers there were also new hopes:

> We can truly affirm that the world is today entirely manifest, all of mankind known, all mortals able to communicate their goods among themselves and help each other in their mutual indigence, as inhabitants of one community and world commonwealth.

But can we be sure that all the 'power, wisdom, disciplines, books, industry, work, and knowledge' of the world of today may not 'plunge headlong again, and perish as they have done in the past'?

Le Roy's view of history was double; it was not only cyclic but also providential and this enabled him to hope. All is not lost in the vicissitudes, and events depend 'principally upon divine providence' which is above the mutations of history. Le Roy's God urges upon him the duty of labouring to transmit and augment the treasures of civilization:

> He wishes that we may carefully preserve the arts and sciences, with the other things necessary for life, and that we transmit them to posterity by means of learned and elegant writings on good subjects, giving clarity to the obscure, faith to the doubtful, order to the confused, elegance to the unpolished, grace to those bereft of it, novelty to the old, authority to the new.

Le Roy's own past life was of a piece with the advice offered here. He had toiled incessantly to contribute to the stream of culture with his numerous ill-rewarded publications. The man's constant poverty lends a kind of impressiveness and dignity to his life and work. We can be sure that, had he lived in the present age, the bomb would not have deterred him from his labours, for he was accustomed to facing bleak truths about the vicissitudes of history without losing the providential hope.

THE MYSTERY OF JEAN BODIN*

THE BOOK here presented in translation was once a secret, dissemi-
nated in manuscript copies among a few chosen spirits, and
referred to with bated breath, if mentioned at all, though it may
have been a power in the background, or the underground. It is
in fact the *Heptaplomeres*, written by Jean Bodin in the late
sixteenth century. The Latin text was not printed until 1857. A
partial French translation appeared in 1914. There has been no
English translation until now, when the *Heptaplomeres* in full is
at last revealed to the English-speaking world.

Jean Bodin (1530–96), a French lawyer, possibly of Jewish
descent on his mother's side, was confronted like all his generation
with the problem of the wars of religion. His early life is obscure,
but he would seem to have moved from Catholicism to an interest
in Reform, and to have found a compromise in the party of the
politiques, believers in religious toleration. In 1571 he became
associated with François de Valois, youngest son of Catherine de
Médicis, the leader or figurehead of the *politique* party. Bodin
became completely identified with François and the *politiques*. He
was with the French prince in England during his unsuccessful
courtship of Queen Elizabeth I; he followed François to Antwerp

---

* Review of Jean Bodin, *Colloquium of the Seven about Secrets of the Sublime (Colloquium
Heptaplomeres de rerum sublimium arcanis abditis)*, translated with an Introduction,
Annotations and critical Readings by Marion Leathers Daniels Kuntz, Princeton, 1975,
in *New York Review of Books*, 14 October 1976; with reply by Professor Kuntz.

and was a prominent member of his entourage during his brief reign as Duke of Brabant, an abortive attempt to found a state in which religious toleration would be practised.

The collapse of that régime in 1584 ruined the hopes of the *politiques* and broke Bodin's career. In the dark years of the end of the century he was in eclipse, and somewhat sullied his earlier liberal reputation by declaring after the death of Henri III for Mayenne and the Catholic League, though he joined Navarre, now Henri IV, as soon as he began to be successful and had abjured Protestantism.

Bodin was one of the most learned men of his age, author of important books on history and on political theory. He believed in monarchy as the best form of government and as the best for France; his legal definitions of sovereignty in his *Methodus* (1566) and *République* (1576) were very influential. His sense of order is also apparent in his survey of universal nature, the *Universae naturae theatrum* (1596), arranged under headings which recall those of Renaissance memory-theatres. Historians of thought are aware of Bodin's many-sided mind, but the work of his which has come into prominence today, owing to the contemporary interest in witchcraft, is his *De la démonomanie des sorciers* (1580). For this liberal man of encyclopedic culture believed intensely in the reality of magic, and of the witches' sabbath, and by his extreme intolerance of supposed witches was highly influential in fomenting the terrible witch craze.

In the *Heptaplomeres*, Bodin gives his secret views on religion, and as Marion Kuntz rightly remarks in her introduction, it connects with all his other works, including the *Démonomanie*. As a key to the state of mind through which a learned magistrate could feel it his duty to burn supposed witches, and to write with passion against their supposed alliance with demons, the *Heptaplomeres* is an important document for what has been called one of the most mysterious episodes in the history of Europe – the witch craze of the late sixteenth and early seventeenth centuries. And this work is important for the history of religion, for it is a remarkable survey of comparative religion.

The Seven who hold these colloquies about Secrets of the Sublime are Coronaeus, a Roman Catholic; Fredericus, a Lutheran; Curtius, a Calvinist; Toralba, who represents natural religion; Senamus, who accepts all sects; Salomon, a Jew; Octavius, a Moslem. There are no atheists; the tone is in fact profoundly religious. Each speaker expresses his own view with complete frankness, yet there is no quarrelling. The meetings end with the singing of psalms in perfect amity.

Each of the Seven is given such a fair hearing that the reader, unaccustomed to hearing his own side and its opposite as well, may wonder whom he is to follow, and this is no doubt intentional. You may follow whom you will provided that you are tolerant of the others and join with them in psalms and hymns. Who of the Seven was Bodin's own favourite? There have been various opinions about this. The late Pierre Mesnard believed that it is the Catholic, who convoked the assembly and, in a manner, presides over it. Others have argued for Toralba and natural religion. A case could be made for the Moslem, who, unlike the Christians, does not persecute (Octavius is in fact a convert to Islam from Christianity).

Readers of this translation may decide that it is Salomon, the Jew, who seems to have the most authority. When all the others have made their points, we wait to hear what Salomon will say, and he comes out very clearly and strongly, very certain of his profound knowledge of the Law and of its mystical interpretation in the Cabala. However much the others may disagree with him they defer to him and to his ability to clarify the greatest difficulties from the secret shrines of the Hebrews.

As one reads and rereads the book, one becomes more and more aware that its guiding theme is the Law, the sacred Law given by Jehovah to the Jews through Moses, recorded in the Hebrew Scriptures, and from which both Christianity and its various sects, and Islam, are derived. The point of contact between them all is the Law, expounded in its purity by Salomon, together with Cabalistic interpretation of its mysteries.

In the introduction to her translation, Marion Kuntz rightly stresses the importance of Cabala in Bodin's work, though she makes no systematic attempt, either in her introduction or in her notes, at tracing his sources for what he calls Cabala. François Secret has said that, although Bodin knew Hebrew, he might have derived most of what he says about Cabala in the *Heptaplomeres* from secondary sources. This all-important question must await further investigation. In the meantime it can be said that Bodin discusses at some length the question of forced conversion, the problem of the *marrano* compelled to conform outwardly to a religion in which he does not believe. This may indicate that the rumour of his descent from a refugee from the expulsion of the Jews from Spain in 1492 may have some truth in it, and that his obsession with toleration and with what he calls Cabala may have deep personal roots. Salomon rejects what he suspects as efforts by Christian Cabalists to convert him, and states firmly that he expects a Messiah to come in the future.

Whatever his sources, Salomon is respected by the others as a Cabalist. This comes out particularly clearly in Bodin's third book. Toralba states that divine matters are hidden in a certain occult discipline called Cabala. It is expected that Salomon will speak on this but he is silent. They break up after singing a hymn to the accompaniment of lyres and flutes, but return later to discuss the theme of truth hidden in allegories and fables. Salomon explains that Cabala means tradition, and that it is a method for finding hidden meanings in the Scriptures which is understood only by the learned. As an example of Cabalist allegorical interpretation he takes the story of Adam and Eve. Adam sinned, but not because he tasted the forbidden fruit offered to him by his wife, as people imagine in their childish error. The story is an allegory of a victory of the sensual part of man over the intellectual part. Similarly, the talking serpent is an allegory which only those versed in Cabala can understand. Some of the allegories quoted by Bodin he could have found in the writings of Philo Judaeus, and not taken directly from the *Zohar*.

It would seem that Cabala, or Bodin's conception of the Jewish mystical tradition, is really the sublime secret of the *Heptaplomeres*, which enables all the Seven to meet on a mystical level. No ecumenical solution of the religious differences is sought or arrived at. The conclusion states that the speakers remained in their various opinions, talked no more of religion, but nourished their piety in a profound harmony and integrity of life.

The cosmology which is the setting for this remarkable essay in comparative religion is a magical one, operated by angels and demons as agents of the Eternal God. 'God's majesty', says Salomon, 'seems more awesome because of the service of angels and demons than if he cared for all things in and of Himself, as He is able to do.' Though angels and demons belong to the normal framework of the Judaeo-Christian tradition, this intense sense of their omnipresence and power suggests a Cabalist mentality, and it is this vivid belief in good and bad spirits which makes Bodin so obsessed with the danger of bad magic. For magicians can have a 'wicked alliance with demons' and can cause untold harm. Fredericus, the Lutheran, is particularly aware of bad magic and describes a witches' sabbath. It is here that Bodin's *Heptaplomeres* connects with his *Démonomanie* and its indictment of witchcraft.

As D. P. Walker has pointed out, much of Bodin's polemic against magic in the *Démonomanie* is directed against Pico della Mirandola and Henry Cornelius Agrippa, that is to say, it is against Renaissance magic. Pico's advice in his Magical and Cabalist Conclusions about 'marrying earth and heaven' by magical procedures, about use of Cabalist letter-formations in magic, is quoted with horror as the wicked teachings of a magician. Pico's statement that the hymns of Orpheus have as much power for magic as the psalms of David for Cabala is an abominable attempt to equate pagan incantations for attracting the demon, Pan, with the pure use of the psalms by a pious Cabalist. In fact, Pico is presented as teaching the use of Cabala for magic, a most wicked degradation of the true religious meaning and use of Cabala.

And if Pico is a wicked magician, Agrippa is much worse. Bodin's fulminations against the *De occulta philosophia*, Agrippa's handbook of Renaissance 'Magic and Cabala', are alarming. It is an utterly damnable work, and the black dog which was seen to leave Agrippa's house at his death and to jump into the Rhône was the demon who had inspired his master's evil practices. The wrong use of Cabala by such sorcerers is compared with the true Cabala, which is a spiritual discipline and a method of Scriptural exegesis used by good and holy men. It draws out deep meanings through allegorical interpretation of the text and leads the devout into holy secrets.

The same contrast between bad magic and good Cabala is implied in the *Heptaplomeres*. In the second book, dreadful cases of magic are collected, the witches' sabbath is described, and Agrippa's dog jumps into the Rhône. In the third book, Salomon expounds the true and holy Cabala, its method of allegorical exegesis, using at times the same words as are used in the *Démonomanie* on these themes. Comparison of the *Démonomanie* with the *Heptaplomeres* brings out that Bodin's condemnation of Pico and Agrippa was the disapproval of a Cabalist of bad and unlawful uses of Cabala. Though Bodin nowhere actually states in the *Démonomanie* that it was Pico and Agrippa and their disciples who let out the demons and were responsible for the awful increase in the number of those agents of the demons, the witches, this may be implied.

Bodin has no difficulty in proving that the Law of God condemns sorcery and witchcraft. Texts on this from the Old Testament are assembled in the preface to the *Démonomanie*. Thus we can begin to see that Bodin, the magistrate, prosecuting witches, fits with Bodin, the devout believer in the Law of God. He is proclaiming the Law in the demonic world by controlling demons, just as he proclaims it in the religious world as the root of all true religion.

Bodin does not sweep away all Renaissance themes. His pages on universal harmony in the *Heptaplomeres* have a true Renaissance ring; in fact his reaction from certain aspects of the Renaissance has much of the Renaissance in it. But he bans Renaissance magic. He may represent something like a crisis in the European tradition, a shift from Renaissance occultism that was made in the name of a purer occultism, of Cabala returned to its Hebraic sources. He is a kind of puritan as he dismisses Orphic singing as diabolical and demands a pure Cabalism, cured of Renaissance contamination. Is it possible that the European witch craze might be, in one of its aspects, a symptom of this shift?

The *Démonomanie* was first published in 1580; the writing of the unpublished *Heptaplomeres* is usually dated 1593, but Marion Kuntz claims to have found the date 1588 on a manuscript. At any rate the two works belong in the same phase of the late sixteenth century, and they are undoubtedly closely connected. Their writer was a theorist of French monarchy and in a position to be familiar with court circles, and this is curious. For at this time those great artistic manifestations of the Renaissance magical tradition, the French court spectacles, were produced. The sirens and satyrs of the *Ballet comique de la Reine* (1581) would presumably have been classed as demons by Bodin; they were in fact used in the Catholic League's propaganda against Henri III as a sorcerer. And a famous contemporary of Bodin, Giordano Bruno, published at Paris in 1582 a book containing incantations of the type which Bodin thought most diabolical. Bodin's magical universe is, in theory, quite close to Bruno's. There are passages in the *Heptaplomeres* which remind us of Bruno, for example Bodin's insistence that the stars are living animals, moving because they are alive. Yet Bodin is obviously not, like Bruno, a magus. No doubt he would have strongly approved the burning of such a dangerous magician.

It is strange to think that these two men impinged on the Elizabethan world at about the same time. Bodin was in England in 1581 accompanying François d'Anjou and having conversations with Queen Elizabeth I (Marion Kuntz refers to an unpublished thesis by Kenneth McRae which contains evidence about Bodin and the Queen). A year later, Bruno came to England.

An Englishman who might have been influenced by Bodin – and this has been suggested – is Francis Bacon. This is perfectly possible since Bacon in his early youth, in 1576, stayed at the English Embassy in Paris at the time when Bodin was prominent among the *politique* supporters of François d'Anjou. Or Bacon could have met Bodin in England. Nor is it necessary to suppose an actual meeting for Bacon to have become aware of Bodin's encyclopedic historical, political and scientific erudition. And there are aspects of Bacon's outlook, his disapproval on moral grounds of the Renaissance magus, his Hebraic mysticism, which might chime in with that of Bodin, though with variations.

Bodin's attitude to natural philosophy and science is as closely connected with the Law of God and with Cabala as is his demonology. For the laws of nature are, he believes, hidden in the divine law and can be drawn from the Scriptures through Cabalistic interpretation. Hence his *Universae naturae theatrum* is an exposition of the law of nature as revealed both in nature and in the Scriptures, which secretly contain that law within them. These ideas are also present in the *Heptaplomeres*, in which Toralba expounds a way to God through nature, and both he and Salomon speak of the revelation of nature in the Scriptures. Toralba explains that the ten headings of the Decalogue correspond to the ten spheres of the universe, and that therefore the study of the Law is also study of the world. The hidden treasures of nature are concealed, says Salomon, in the Law of God, and the Decalogue is an epitome of natural law. Thus, for Bodin, science is in fact natural law, and natural law is the same as, or concealed in, the Divine Law taught in the Hebrew Scriptures, and it can be drawn out, or revealed, from the Scriptures through Cabalistic exegesis.

Bodin on the Law of God and the law of nature brings us to a subject of great importance, namely to 'Needham's Question'.

One of the most impressive scholarly achievements of our time is Joseph Needham's amazing history of Chinese science. The question which this great scholar asks is why did modern science develop in the West, but not in China, which in the Middle Ages was scientifically ahead of the West? Seeking for an answer he suggests that it might be because Chinese culture lacked the idea of a celestial law-giver, the idea so strongly imprinted on the Judaeo-Christian tradition, and which, developing as the laws of nature, formed the basis of the seventeenth-century advance. He thinks that the turning-point, at which the West pulled ahead of China, came between Copernicus (1473–1543) and Kepler (1571–1630), who was one of the first to express laws of nature in mathematical terms. It is at exactly that point between Copernicus and Kepler that Bodin stands.

Did he stand alone, or was he affected by some vast movement of his times, a movement involving tremendous vindication of Judaic Law and intense spiritual training in Jewish Cabala? The great work of Gershom Scholem has revealed the history of Cabala after the expulsion of the Jews from Spain in 1492, and how a movement of intense expectation of a Messiah developed among the dispersed Jews. The connections of this immensely powerful movement with the general history of culture have only just begun to be explored. I suggest that Jean Bodin's *Heptaplomeres*, at the end of which the Expulsion is significantly mentioned, is a work which should be examined from this point of view.

Marion Kuntz has based her translation of *Heptaplomeres* on the Latin text published by Noack in 1857, a text which Roger Chauviré, an excellent Bodin scholar, criticized as unreliable. An Edinburgh scholar has spent many years collating manuscripts in preparation for a translation based on the best texts, an enterprise which she abandoned on hearing of the Kuntz project. It might be argued that Marion Kuntz has not followed sound principles in taking the Noack text as her foundation, though she has collated Noack with two manuscripts. Her translation, when compared with the Noack text, reveals a good many inaccuracies. The Noack text has been reprinted (Stuttgart, 1966) and is thus available for use by scholars with her translation.

Her annotation is sadly inadequate. She has used standard works of reference such as the *Encyclopaedia Britannica* and the *Catholic Encyclopedia* to elucidate obvious points, but for the difficult or inaccessible works and authors she gives no help, simply leaving blanks. It is true that for a satisfactory annotation of the *Heptaplomeres* a team of experts in many fields would be required. The

Kuntz annotation is only a stop-gap; the work remains to be done.

In her introduction she surveys what is known of Bodin's life. She admires his religious attitudes but evades his darker side, the role played by the *Démonomanie* in reimposing the stereotype of the witch, which Johann Wier had questioned. In fact she makes no mention of the great witch craze or of the essential part played by Bodin's work in encouraging it, an extraordinary omission.

She has not noticed the condemnation of Pico della Mirandola and Renaissance magic in the *Démonomanie* and so naturally misses the reflection of this in the *Heptaplomeres*. She assumes that Bodin is an uncritical follower of Pico della Mirandola, that he is practically a Renaissance Neoplatonist, a believer in *prisca theologia*, belonging within the Hermetic-Cabalist tradition as formulated in the Renaissance. The truth would appear to me to be that, although there are Renaissance and Neoplatonic elements in the *Heptaplomeres*, there is a great shift from Pico's position in Bodin's outlook. Salomon does not admire *prisci theologi*; they were sorcerers. Renaissance magic is banned. There is, I think, a basic misunderstanding of Bodin's position in describing the *Heptaplomeres* as 'truly a Renaissance book'.

Following a rumour of some connection between speeches on different religions by Guillaume Postel, when at Venice, and the speeches in the *Heptaplomeres*, Marion Kuntz tries to connect Bodin's thought closely with that of Postel. It is true that both Bodin and Postel believed in French monarchy, were influenced by Cabala, and showed interest in Islam, but their attitudes were different. Postel was, like Pico, a Christian Cabalist, and had vast missionary aims; Bodin appears not to have been a Christian and was against Christian Cabala (this has been noticed by François Secret). Postel, however eccentric, was a better oriental scholar than Bodin. On all these counts, it would seem that Postel belongs to a different line from that of Bodin, though of course it is not impossible that Bodin might have adapted Postel material to his own purposes.

Jean Bodin is something of a mystery and will remain so until far more work has been done on the many problems surrounding him. Marion Kuntz has drawn attention to him, and this may stimulate a long-overdue movement of new research on this important figure. The style of her translation combines an enthusiasm which carries the reader along with a certain dignity. She has not cheapened the *Heptaplomeres*. And she brings out the personalities of the speakers, particularly that of Salomon, whose impressive presence dominates the work.

LETTERS

BODIN'S DEMONS

To the Editors:
I am pleased that *The New York Review* chose to review my book *The Colloquium of the Seven about Secrets of the Sublime*, a translation with introduction and annotations of Jean Bodin's *Colloquium Heptaplomeres de rerum sublimium arcanis abditis*. I am honored that one of the great Renaissance scholars of our time, Frances Yates, wrote the detailed review and indicated the value of the *Colloquium* as an area of research. I am also very pleased with Dr Yates's approval of my translation and certain points in my introduction.

Therefore, with great respect for the scholarship of the reviewer and in the best interests of scholarly debate, I challenge several of the assumptions in Dr Yates's review.

Dr Yates's deep interest in and thorough knowledge of Renaissance magic has led her to place more emphasis on demons and magic than is warranted by the text of the *Colloquium*. She constantly refers to Bodin's *Démonomanie* and seems to find it necessary to impose the ideas of the *Démonomanie* upon the *Colloquium*. Certainly there are lively discussions in the latter work about demons, magic, and the spirit world, but these conversations in the early part of the work lead the discussants to the central problem of events which seem to happen outside the laws of nature. Toralba, the natural philosopher of the dialogue, indicates that these events do not happen from necessity or the necessary power of demons for this would snatch away free will from God (*Colloquium*, p. 27).

The discussion of demons and magic is only a springboard to a lengthy analysis of free will and necessity. At the conclusion of Book II Toralba advises his friends that the origin of demons, their place, and condition seem far removed from positive proofs, but that hidden scientific knowledge had proceeded from the Chaldeans in a certain occult discipline called Cabala. The point here is that the orientation of the *Colloquium* is not demonic. Rather the conversations about angels and demons provide a *locus ex quo* for unfolding the major theme of universal harmony, which finds much of its source in the Cabala.

Demons and magic are introduced most often to prove certain points that the speakers want to make; for example Simon Magus and Apollonius of Tyana are said to be better magicians than Jesus. This scandalous remark surfaces among the lengthy discussions in Books V and VI concerning Jesus's Messiahship and what hinders each greatest magician making himself a god, if miracles make gods.

Dr Yates errs in her belief that Bodin, the legalist, the prosecutor of witches in the *Démonomanie*, is complementary to the upholder of the *Law* in the *Colloquium*. While Salomon the Jew does proclaim the Divine Law and its primacy, Toralba argues equally cogently that: 'If the law of nature and natural religion which has been implanted in men's souls is sufficient for attaining salvation, I do not see why the Mosaic rites and ceremonies are necessary' (*Colloquium*, p. 186).

And here is precisely where Dr Yates's reading of the *Colloquium* is most in error. She uses the statement of one speaker to prove a point she wants to make. For example, she thinks there is a 'great shift from Pico's position in Bodin's outlook' because she believes that Salomon does not admire *prisci theologi*, that Renaissance magic is banned. This is fallacious argument because what one speaker believes, four, five, or even six others may disbelieve. The only belief that all seven share is that there is a God. Dr Yates thinks that I failed to recognize Bodin's criticism of Pico in the *Démonomanie*. This is not the case; rather it is a different Bodin speaking in the *Colloquium*, for in the *Colloquium* he calls Pico the most learned philosopher of the century (*Colloquium*, p. 283).

One of the most amazing paradoxes of the *Colloquium* and indeed one of its greatest mysteries (there are many, many more!) is the relationship of Guillaume Postel to the *Colloquium*. I detailed aspects of Postel's thought which appear in the *Colloquium* and are more typical of Postel than Bodin. I agree with Frances Yates that Postel belongs to a different line from Bodin, but in no way does this alter the fact that Bodin used Postel in the work clandestinely circulated under the title *Colloquium Heptaplomeres*; the internal and external evidence will be revealed in my book on Postel which will be appearing shortly. The manuscript tradition of the *Colloquium* also supports my thesis.

In speaking of manuscripts I must point out that I do not 'claim to have seen a manuscript with the date 1588 on it'. I saw a manuscript, have a complete copy of said manuscript, and noted the manuscript number in my introduction (p. xxxviii). If Dr Yates had wanted to verify my citation, she could have written to M. Piquard, Director of the Bibliothèque Mazarine.

Frances Yates assumes that Roger Chauviré was correct in his negative assessment of Noack's Latin text (1857). That mistake has been repeated too often. Chauviré was wrong about the date because he did not bother to look at the manuscript. He was wrong in stating that Noack's text was unreliable. Noack had a poor typesetter, but his edition is based upon the Senckenberg codex, which reflects the readings of Bibliothèque nationale, MS. lat. 6564, 6565, 6566, as well as the British Library MS. 9002 in the Sloane collection, of which Chauviré was unaware or which he failed to consider. I have collated all the best sixteenth- and seventeenth-century manuscripts of the *Colloquium*; I recorded in my book the readings of Bibl. nat., MS. lat. 6564 (Memmianus) and Vatican Library, MS. Reginensis 1313, and on occasions Mazarine MS. 3529, when I preferred their readings to those of Noack. I have established the stemma of the *Colloquium* manuscripts, and a lengthy study of the manuscripts will appear in the coming year. My manuscript studies support my method of using Noack's text, the only complete text of the *Colloquium*, and of correcting it when necessary by use of Bibl. nat. lat. 6564 and Reg. 1313.

One final point must be made. Dr Yates faults my annotations as 'sadly inadequate', stating that I used standard reference works to elucidate obvious points. I annotated 2,480 references in the *Colloquium*, eighteen of which are from the scholarly eleventh edition of the *Encyclopaedia Britannica* and forty-two from the *Catholic Encyclopedia*. Where better to locate Priscillians, Noetians, Ubiquitarians, Eutychians, Sabellians, etc.? The other 2,420 annotations are from primary sources for the most part. I am certain that if a team of scholars in various disciplines had pooled their resources the annotations would reflect their expertise. But lo, I am only one woman, and since the *Colloquium* had been neglected for more than three hundred and fifty years, it seemed necessary for one to do something about it.

However, in the true spirit of the *Colloquium*, Dr Yates should be allowed her 'demonic' reading, and I shall maintain that universal harmony and toleration are the heart of the matter. I feel certain there will be many other interpretations. The *Colloquium* is that kind of work. The closing sentences of the *Colloquium* (p. 471) seem apropos: 'Henceforth, they nourished their piety in remarkable harmony and their integrity of life in common pursuits and intimacy. However, afterwards they held no other conversation about religions, although each one defended his own religion with the supreme sanctity of his life.'

Marion L. Kuntz

Regents' Professor of Classics
Chairman, Department of Foreign Languages
Georgia State University
Atlanta, Georgia

3 March 1977

Frances Yates *replies*:

I want to thank Professor Kuntz for the courteous tone of her reply to my review of her book and to emphasize to her the more positive aspects of the review rather than the remarks which she has felt to be overly critical. For instance, I say: 'In the *Heptaplomeres*, Bodin gives his secret views on religion, and as Marion Kuntz rightly remarks in her introduction, it connects with all his other works, including the *Démonomanie*.'

Bodin's intense belief in demons and fierce persecution of witches is notorious. The awareness of this aspect of his mind is no invention of mine but has been the preoccupation of all Bodin scholars, except those who try to forget it in concentrating on his political thought. Professor Kuntz is not one of the obscurantists, as the above quotation from her introduction shows, but she disagrees, in her letter, with my interpretation of the references to demonology and witchcraft in the *Heptaplomeres*.

In his article 'Jean Bodin's Demon and his Conversion to Judaism' (*Jean Bodin*, Proceedings of the International Conference on Bodin, Munich, 1973), Christopher Baxter was, I believe, the first to make the suggestion that the connection between all Bodin's works may be his insistence on the Mosaic Law, which would also account for his severe disapproval of witchcraft and sorcery. It is a pity that Baxter's projected translation of the *Démonomanie* has not been published. A translation of the *Universae naturae theatrum*, fundamental for Bodin's science and full of demons, is also much needed. We already have translations of *Methodus* and *République*, and now of *Heptaplomeres*. The addition of *Démonomanie* and *Theatrum* to Bodin in English would help, by bringing the works together, to place this strange man in relation to his French Renaissance contemporaries.

Concerning the Bodin manuscripts and concerning Professor Kuntz's work on Bodin and Postel, it would be pointless to argue until we have the further information promised in her forthcoming studies, to which I look forward with the greatest interest. In the meantime I assure her that I do indeed appreciate the magnitude of the task which she undertook in producing single-handedly a translation and critical edition of this formidable work. As I remarked at the end of my review, her publication of an English *Colloquium Heptaplomeres* is bound to attract general attention to the work.

Chapter Nineteen

THE LAST LAUGH*[1]

OF ALL writers of the first rank, Rabelais is perhaps the least read. The reasons for this are obvious. First of all the language, the torrent of words poured forth to suggest the talk, movements, ideas of the characters in his amazing novel – a language untranslatable and often unintelligible even to French Renaissance experts. Submerged in this garrulity, the reader first gains the impression of being introduced to a master of burlesque, to a gallery of intensely comic figures whose adventures are above all intended to excite laughter. 'Pleasant' and 'facetious' were adjectives commonly applied to the adventures of the giants Gargantua and Pantagruel and their friends, as recounted by François Rabelais; and pleasantry and facetiousness implied in the French sixteenth century a strong admixture of the grossness of the farce tradition.

Yet this joker turns out to be a consummate humanist scholar, having at his command a vast range of classical reading, Greek and Latin. He is also a skilled theologian, a philosopher well versed in Renaissance Neoplatonism, and his scientific interests include medicine, architecture, mechanics – to mention only a few of the aspects of the Rabelaisian encyclopedia. This Laughing Philosopher, this Democritus (as he was called), presents the student of the Renaissance with one of his hardest problems. He throws us his comic saga as a bone, the marrow of which we are

* Review of Mikhail Bakhtin, *Rabelais and his World*, translated by Helene Iswolsky, Boston, 1968, in *New York Review of Books*, 9 October 1969.

to try to extract. He tells us that his comic figures are like those boxes, made in the form of a drunken Silenus, within which Plato says that precious things are hidden, likening them to the rough and ridiculous exterior of Socrates which hid his divine wisdom. Yet in the same breath in which we are told to seek for a hidden 'marrow', or to open the Silenus boxes, we are also told that there is no hidden meaning, no allegory behind the lives and adventures of the Rabelaisian troop of comic characters.

The baffled reader is inclined to give up trying to understand a writer who is obviously too profound to be taken as a mere farceur but who gives so little help for his deciphering. Hence Rabelais remains unread, though the adjective 'Rabelaisian' has a wide currency, used generally of wit or humour, and usually implying gross humour. Perhaps Rabelais himself might be well satisfied that only the exteriors of his Silenus figures are still known and that his secret (if he had one) is still hidden.

Rabelais was born about 1490. Very little is known of his early years save that his native town was Chinon, situated in the midst of the wine-growing districts of the Loire valley. His father owned a vineyard and he must often have heard the 'propos des buveurs' as they sampled the exhilarating vintages of Touraine. By about 1520, Rabelais had entered the Franciscan order and had become an inmate of the convent of Fonteney-le-Conte. All that we know of his life in the convent is that he was a keen student of books in both languages, that is, Greek as well as Latin.

At this time Greek studies were still an exciting novelty. We know of Rabelais's early interest in Greek from the letters of the great scholar Guillaume Budé. The authorities of the convent, alarmed at the unsettling effect of the new learning, confiscated Rabelais's books. He left his convent for another, and then left that one also. In 1530 he was studying medicine at Montpellier, having shaken off the monastic life. In 1532 he was at Lyon, engaged in literary work, and in 1533 and 1535 the first editions of *Gargantua* and *Pantagruel* came out, to be followed, after a long gap, by a third and fourth volume of the novel.

The early years of Rabelais's life, the formative years before the publication of his famous work, were a momentous turning-point in the history of Western civilization. The tools of Latin and Greek philological scholarship, polished by the Italian humanists in their recoveries and re-editions of classical texts, were now being used on religious texts, on new editions of the Fathers, on the Scriptures, culminating in Erasmus's Greek New Testament of 1516, which marked a new return to the Gospels and to the Pauline epistles, opened up by the new humanist scholarship. These tremendous innovations in theological studies, revolutionizing the medieval traditions, came at a time when many seeking souls were profoundly dissatisfied with the deadness and corruption of the Church and were thinking about reform. The writings of Erasmus, written in a most vivid and readable Latin style, were speeding about in Europe. One in particular, the *Encomium Moriae* or *Praise of Folly*, written while Erasmus was living in the house of Thomas More in London and published in 1511, made an immense impression. The demand for this little book was insatiable; it both stimulated and suited the ferment of the times.

The *Praise of Folly* satirizes the old learning, the old medieval world, the monks and friars, the pilgrimages and processions, the cult of saints, in a style of biting humour. Erasmus was a great humorist, subtly ironical and elusive. In the *Praise of Folly*, Folly herself comes to life as a personage. There is probably a mystical influence on Erasmus's Folly. Did not St Paul say that the wisdom of the Gospel is foolishness in the eyes of men? While perhaps hinting at such evangelical innocence, Erasmus's Folly can also recall the comic figures of farce, the Fool with his bauble. The words 'Evangelical Reform' do not conjure up in our minds the idea of some immensely comic yet immeasurably profound personification. We think rather of hymns and prayer meetings, occasions which do not generally echo with gigantic laughter.

Rabelais was studying Greek in his convents, restlessly leaving his convents, during the years of the Erasmian movement and the early Lutheran Reformation movement. Like Erasmus, and unlike Luther, Rabelais never left the Church; in his later life he moved in influential French Catholic circles. But these vast questions of religious unrest and the need for reform pressed on the lives and minds of all thinking people in those times. Many scholars have sought to find Rabelais's answers or thoughts about them in his comic novel with its huge laughter-provoking figures.

Abel Lefranc, the Rabelais scholar who was active in the twenties of the present century, believed that Rabelais was an atheist and that he was hiding this dangerous opinion in his novel. He worked out this view in some detail, and it was at that time one of the attractions of Rabelais that he was thought to have been so bold as to disbelieve in God at such an early date. Since Lefranc's time there has been a great expenditure of scholarly effort on the history of religion, including the history of religion in early sixteenth-century France. Lucien Fèbvre studied the problem of unbelief in the sixteenth century and decided that there were no atheists in that century. In his book *La religion de Rabelais* (1942), he demolished Lefranc's proofs of Rabelais's atheism. Fèbvre's argument is that Rabelais derives from Erasmus; that he is not more bold than Erasmus in his treatment of religious controversy; that his boldness is of the same kind as that of Erasmus though presented in the form of a humorous novel; that his religion was that of Erasmus, an evangelical Christianity, impatient of scholasticism and monasticism. These views have since been developed in greater detail by other scholars, particularly M. A. Screech, who in his *L'évangélisme de Rabelais* (1959) proves Rabelais's close knowledge of Biblical texts and commentaries, particularly those of Erasmus, and argues that Rabelais's religion was influenced by Luther but above all by the Erasmian type of evangelism.

The image which Erasmus presents to the world and to history, that of the studious and ascetic scholar, may seem quite the opposite of the popular Rabelaisian image, yet the similarities between the Erasmian attitude to the times and that of Rabelais are profound. Erasmus began the witty and popular discussions of current religious problems which Rabelais continued in a form apparently still more popular but in reality just as learned. Erasmus and Rabelais glory in the new learning and pour scorn on medieval backwardness. Erasmus and Rabelais, both in their different ways, are drunk with enthusiasm for the new Greek studies which, exciting as they were for every aspect of human thought and activity, were of revolutionary excitement for religion. Silenus figures might contain the new wine of a Gospel which it was dangerous to proclaim.

One of the few pieces of documentary evidence which we have from Rabelais himself about his inmost thoughts and sympathies is the letter which he wrote to Erasmus in 1532. Rabelais had heard that Erasmus was thinking of publishing a Latin edition of the *Jewish Antiquities* of Josephus and was seeking a Greek manuscript of the text. Rabelais obtained one for him from Georges d'Armagnac, Bishop of Rodez, and wrote to announce its arrival. In this letter Rabelais addresses the great scholar in language almost of passion, calling him 'my spiritual father and mother' and stating that all that he has, all that he is, he owes alone to Erasmus and his writings, to this beloved father, the protector of letters and the defender of truth. This debt would certainly include the Erasmian evangelism. And Erasmus, like Rabelais, incurred the reproach of grossness in some of his wit and of irreverence in his treatment of sacred subjects. Being, however, so obviously Christian, and not given to mystifications as to the 'marrow', the 'substantifique moelle', of his meaning, Erasmus is never likely to become a favourite with atheists.

Yet there are occasions in the Rabelaisian corpus in which mystification is laid aside, when jokes and laughter cease, and the evangelical attitude is expressed with unfeigned seriousness. One such occasion comes in the famous description of the Abbaye de Thélème. This abbey was built and endowed by the amiable giant, Gargantua, for that cheerful character, Friar John, who wished to found a new kind of order. Monks and nuns were to be excluded from the abbey and only well-dressed and good-looking persons admitted. Though the sexes dwelt together in it, there was no disorder, and the motto of the abbey, 'Fay Ce Que Vouldras', or 'Do what you will', meant indeed that the inmates were at perfect liberty and could come and go at will, but being civilized and well-bred persons they possessed a natural instinct which inclined them to virtue and saved them from vice.

This instinct they called their honour. The inmates of the abbey were to be splendidly and richly dressed; each had an apartment magnificently furnished, with a chapel attached to it for private devotions. Their time was enlivened by sumptuous entertainments, jousts and balls and other diversions; and the abbey contained an important library, rich in many Greek, Latin, Hebrew, French, Italian, and Spanish volumes, grouped in sections. Its courtier-inmates were to be versed in the learning of the Renaissance as well as in all the refinements of the new affluence. The abbey was situated on the banks of the Loire; its architecture is carefully described and its plan shows knowledge of Renaissance architectural theory. It was evidently to be a 'château of the Loire', an ideal product of the dawning age of French Renaissance culture. And the inscription on the main gate of the abbey invited the wise, the gay, the courteous to enter, and particularly scholars who propound 'novel interpretations of the Holy Writ'. From this abbey, as from a fort and refuge, they are to attack false teaching and destroy the foes of God and of his Holy Word:

[157]

> The Holy Word of God
> Shall never be downtrod
> Here in this holy place.

The Abbaye de Thélème is a French Renaissance courtly utopia, strongly tinged with Erasmian evangelism, forecasting both the brilliance of sixteenth-century French scholarship and the brilliance of the French Renaissance court.

Yet such formulations can reach or express only a part of the rich and profound genius of Rabelais. His Erasmianism reaches new dimensions of experience, sometimes hidden, after the humanist fashion, in myth. During the marvellously realistic storm (partly imitated from Erasmus's description of a storm in one of his colloquies) which overtakes Pantagruel and his motley crew of passengers in the Fourth Book, the prayer of the giant is that of a pious evangelical: 'O Lord my God, save us, for we perish. Yet not as we would wish it, but Thy holy will be done.' And in the wonderful account of the death of Pan (based on Plutarch), which follows later in the same book, Pantagruel makes this impressive statement:

> For my part, I consider the Pan in question to have been the mighty saviour of the faithful, who was shamefully put to death in Judaea by the envy and iniquity of the doctors, pontiffs, priests and monks of the Mosaic law. I really think this interpretation is in no wise shocking, for, after all, God may perfectly well be called in the Greek tongue, *Pan*, the supreme shepherd.

This interpretation of Pan as both Christ the 'All', and also as the 'all' of nature, may contain the essence of Rabelais's religious attitude, which is perhaps not entirely covered by Erasmian evangelism, fundamental though that ingredient is. The insistence on God as 'the all' in the Pan episode might imply knowledge of the religion of the Hermetic treatises, in which this definition is commonly used. These treatises had been published in France by Lefèvre d'Etaples in 1505 and exercised a great influence on French religious thought in the early years of the century. It is, I would suggest, probable that Hermetic influences should be added to the Erasmian influence as formative for Rabelais, though this aspect of his thought has not yet been investigated with the thoroughness accorded to the Erasmian side. A recently published book by G. Mallary Masters, *Rabelaisian Dialectic and the Platonic-Hermetic Tradition* (Albany, N.Y., 1969), interprets Rabelais's novel as 'Platonic-Hermetic' allegory, making very large use of the Fifth Book, Rabelais's authorship of which is disputed, and giving a personal interpretation of the meaning of 'Platonic-Hermetic'. Though there is much of interest in the book, it is not the kind of study that I have in mind. I am thinking of a cautious historical approach to the problem of the possible influence on Rabelais of the *Hermetica* (a distinct body of writings). The model for such an approach would be D. P. Walker's fundamental article on the *prisca theologia* in France.

In the Third Book of the novel, Pantagruel says that the soul in heaven contemplates an infinite intellectual sphere of which the centre is in every part of the universe but its circumference nowhere, adding 'c'est Dieu selon la doctrine de Hermes Trismegisstus'. This definition of God does indeed come from a thirteenth-century Hermetic treatise and Rabelais could have met with it (as A. J. Krailsheimer points out in his book *Rabelais and the Franciscans*, 1963) as quoted by Bonaventura, whose works he would have studied in his Franciscan convent. That he chooses it as a definition of God, as did Nicolas of Cusa and Giordano Bruno, is interesting, and suggests that 'Hermes Trismegistus' would have been an important authority for him.

The forces of the Renaissance – religious, philosophic, scientific, artistic – are condensed in potent form in Rabelais's novel, ready to explode in sixteenth-century France. And all this wealth is poured into a popular mould, into the popular forms which Rabelais chose as his vehicles. He took his giants, and their names, from a popular adventure story which sold well at the fairs. Jean Plattard has described (in his *Vie de François Rabelais*, 1928) the carnivals, festivals, farces which were a part of the student life at Montpellier and in which Rabelais would have been involved when he was a medical student at the university. The plot of a farce which he saw acted at Montpellier is described in the Third Book. His time at Montpellier, when he was enjoying his new freedom and excited by his new studies, was probably the time when the sap of creation was rising within him, perhaps the time when the use of popular forms in his work occurred to him.

Yet Rabelais's farcical themes are not popular in content; they require knowledge and sophistication for their appreciation. Take for instance the theme of the Third Book in which Panurge consults many different types of soothsayers on the problem of whether or not he should marry. This is in itself a farcical theme, particularly Panurge's fear of being cuckolded, which makes him hesitate to marry. Yet this theme has also a serious connection with Rabelais's views on marriage (which M. A. Screech has discussed in his study *The Rabelaisian Marriage*, 1958). And the wit of the long-drawn-out farce of Panurge's hesitations among the soothsayers requires knowledge of Neoplatonic forms of divination for its understanding, and knowledge of Renaissance texts on these subjects. The humorous appearance of 'Herr Trippa' as one of the experts consulted by Panurge would lose much of its force if the reader failed to pick up the allusion to Henry Cornelius Agrippa, the German author of the *De occulta philosophia*.

Montpellier was certainly a turning-point in Rabelais's life. Perhaps his medical interests are reflected in his concentration on the body as a living organism. In the Third Book there is a long passage on the human body as a microcosm of the universe, fashioned by the Creator as a host for the soul. Its wonderful organization is described with awe and reverence: how food is carried into the maw of the belly, where it is digested and the best of it turned into blood, leaving behind the excrement, which is expelled through special conduits. The members of the body behold with exquisite joy and gladness this transmutation into blood, a joy greater than that of the alchemists at transmutation into gold. It is clear that it is with scientific enthusiasm that Rabelais here and in other passages examines bodily functions, and as a Renaissance doctor he would have been taught to see the body as Nature, and therefore good. It is perhaps in this light that one should see the Rabelaisian giants with their enormous powers of food and drink intake, of digestion, and of excretion. They present in comic form the Renaissance preoccupation with man in all his aspects, physical as well as intellectual. The physical and bodily powers of the giants are matched by their vast powers of intellectual intake; they have huge libraries as well as huge meals.

It is a moment of triumphant optimism of the early French Renaissance to which Rabelais's 'joyous' novel gives expression, the optimism of the new evangel, of an optimist gnosis as to the nature of the universe and man's powerful position in it. A laughing philosophy was suited to this moment and this mood.

Rabelais's view of the nature of laughter is expressed in the verses prefixed to *Gargantua*:

> Mieulx est de ris, que de larmes escrire:
> Pour ce que rire est le propre de l'homme

– which is a quotation of Aristotle's statement that one of the marks distinguishing man from the animals is his power of laughter.

The book on Rabelais by the Russian critic Mikhail Bakhtin, now published in an English translation, appears to have been written many years ago. The Introduction states that in the early 1930s the author 'tragically disappeared from the scholarly horizon' for more than two decades, that his book on Dostoevsky was republished in 1963, and soon afterward, in 1965, the monograph on Rabelais, which had been written in 1940, was made available. It should therefore be taken into account that this is an old book, and that the author has not been in a position to keep abreast of the progress of Renaissance studies in general, and of Rabelais studies in particular, during the last quarter of a century.

Bakhtin belongs to the 'Formalist' school of Russian criticism and is noted for linguistic analysis, though in the study of Rabelais he 'is no longer confined to verbal language but investigates and compares different sign systems such as verbal, pictorial, and gestural'. This 'science of signs', and its application to Rabelais, is not, as Bakhtin uses it, abstracted from history and from interpretation of the meaning of the signs. On the contrary, Bakhtin very definitely makes a historical approach to Rabelais and on this he bases an interpretation of what he calls his sign systems. It is with this historical and interpretative part of his work that my criticism is concerned.

It is, he states, the tradition of the 'festival laughter of the marketplace', manifested in popular festival and carnival and continuing from the Middle Ages into the Renaissance, which inspires Rabelais, and which he picks up or reflects. The book attempts a history of carnival and of what the author calls festival laughter or the laughter of the people in the marketplace. This is the Rabelaisian kind of laughter, according to Bakhtin, and it is dominant in all his sign systems. 'In this way Rabelais's art proves to be oriented towards the folk culture of the marketplace of the Middle Ages and the Renaissance'. Not only does this approach provide the historical key, according to Bakhtin, to Rabelais's signs and images; it also gives the key to their meaning. For the festival laughter of the people in the marketplace is concerned, according to Bakhtin, with the body and with bodily functions, and its laughter is aimed at depreciating or degrading all 'higher' or more abstract conceptions through this earthiness or body-concentration. It is also in this way and with this meaning, says Bakhtin, that Rabelais uses his festival-marketplace bodily signs and images – images of eating, drinking, urinating, defecation, sexual intercourse, and so on – to degrade or depreciate or 'uncrown' all lofty or abstract notions in the name of a naturalism or materialism deriving from the medieval and Renaissance laughter-tradition of the marketplace.

These conclusions are supported by a process of bowdlerization, by the omission or censorship of all evidence against them. For example, the abbey of Thélème must be excluded because

> Thélème is characteristic neither of Rabelais's philosophy nor of his system of images, nor of his style. Though this episode does present a popular utopian element, it is fundamentally linked with the aristocratic movements of the Renaissance. This is not a popular-festive mood but a court and humanist utopia . . . In this respect Thélème is not in line with Rabelais's imagery and style.

And the interpretation of the Rabelaisian 'body' images as intended to depreciate, degrade, 'uncrown' the intellectual, abstract, or 'higher' (Bakhtin uses this word) preoccupations of man has to be supported by omission of all discussion of Rabelais's scholarship or religion.

It would be easier to understand this book if the author were totally anti-historical, bent solely on the 'science of signs' in the abstract. But he believes in the historical approach, thinks he is making one himself, and approves of Lucien Febvre for his 'fully justified' method of reconstructing Rabelais's intellectual milieu. He thinks that his own historical interpretation of Rabelais, combined with his scientific analysis of the images, has at last produced the right answers to the Rabelais problem.

Anyone who knows anything about the Renaissance, and about Rabelais, will know that the Bakhtin method has come up with totally wrong answers. It may be questioned whether it is not altogether a waste of time to apply such a method to a Renaissance text, with its subtle and elusive use of image, myth, and symbol.

Yet there is a certain freshness and force about this Russian effort to assimilate Rabelais which is impressive and should surely be welcomed.

Chapter Twenty

FRENCH ROYAL FUNERALS IN THE RENAISSANCE*

WHEN HENRY V of England died in France his effigy, made of boiled leather, was carried on the top of the coffin to the coast. A few weeks later comes the first fully recorded use of an effigy at a French royal funeral, that of Charles VI in 1422. Ralph E. Giesey thinks that this was actually the first use of an effigy at a French monarch's funeral, and, since Charles VI's funeral was imitated from that of Henry V, he regards the custom as an importation from England. This view, based on his analysis of the meaning of the word *représentation*, hitherto thought to be synonymous with *effigie*, in references to French funerals prior to the fifteenth century, is not convincing. From 1422 onwards the effigy of the dead monarch is a well-documented feature of French royal funerals until the practice was abandoned at the death of Louis XIII. During the sixteenth century, the effigy gained astonishingly in importance and strange new rituals became associated with it. The effigy of François I, fashioned by François Clouet from the death mask, had ceremonial meals served to it for eleven days, and these elaborate effigy-rituals were carried on at the funerals of Henri II, Charles IX (there is, of course, a gap for Henri III), and Henri IV. Dr Giesey argues that the chief meaning of the effigy in the sixteenth century was that it served as the channel for the continuance of the undying royal dignity during

---

* Review of Ralph E. Giesey, *The Royal Funeral Ceremony in Renaissance France*, Geneva, 1960, in *English Historical Review*, LXXVI, 1961.

the interregnum between the death of a king and the coronation of his successor. He bases this on a careful examination of how the effigy became separated from the body, and of how the new king's absence from the funeral rites indicated that the effigy, with which the royal insignia were placed, still held the royal power. These are novel and important observations, and Dr Giesey's deduction from them, that the royal dignity was in a manner magically stored in the effigy, is impressive. He regards this effigy-practice as belonging to medieval political theory which emphasized the kingly office as distinct from the person of the king, and sees in its discontinuance in the seventeenth century a reflection of the absolutist theory which concentrated kingship on the person of the king. An absolute king is sovereign from the moment his predecessor dies; his assumption of full kingly office does not have to wait until his coronation. Therefore an effigy of the dead king is not needed to carry the sacred royal dignity across the interval between the death of one king and the coronation of his successor, as in former times. Thus Dr Giesey would relate the abandonment of the use of the effigy to the shift to the new theory. This last point is argued with a wealth of detail, and it is interesting, though one wonders whether factors such as the change in taste and the rise of classical principles of decorum might not have something to do with the disappearance in the seventeenth century of the frighteningly realistic effigy and its queer rituals. The sixteenth-century theorists draw parallels between the French use of the royal effigy and Roman imperial practice, though Dr Giesey thinks that there is little real connection and that such allusions are but a surface classicizing of the basic medieval theory. Here he underestimates the force of the sacred imperial idea in relation to the French monarchy in the sixteenth century, which would give such allusions a living meaning. He gives no reason for the enormously increased prestige of the effigy, with its new and unchristian cult of the ceremonial meals, in the sixteenth century, as compared with the much simpler and more truly medieval usage of the fifteenth century. This reason may well be that the Roman imperial parallels, even when spurious (Jean du Tillet's belief that there was a funeral effigy of the Christian emperor Constantine was based, as Dr Giesey points out, on a misreading of Eusebius, nor were the effigies of the pagan emperors actually fed with ceremonial meals), related the sixteenth-century effigy to the developing imperialism of the French monarchy. Or, to put it in other words, the Renaissance ruler-cult gave greater potency to the ruler's effigy. This, incidentally, would provide a better background for the magical storing of the royal dignity in such an intensely personal image as the life-like effigy than the unadulterated medieval theory of the kingly office. By insisting so strongly on the purely medieval foundation of his Renaissance funerals, Dr Giesey seems to miss out a stage in the history of kingship, the intermediate stage between the Middle Ages and seventeenth-century absolutism. An immense amount of original research has gone to the making of Dr Giesey's book, which is a mine of detailed information on all aspects of his subject, and he is a pioneer in pointing out the relevance of the Renaissance funeral to wider historical issues. The question of the history and meaning of the royal funeral effigy, which he has tackled with so much courage, of course needs to be integrated with that of the effigy in general, and it bristles with problems and difficulties. Such criticisms of his work as we have ventured to proffer here should be taken as proof of its thought-provoking quality, and not in any negative sense.

Chapter Twenty-one

POLITICS AND RELIGION IN SIXTEENTH- AND SEVENTEENTH-CENTURY FRANCE*

THIS BOOK is concerned with the political and religious hopes centred on Henri IV of France in the late sixteenth and early seventeenth centuries. Using a mass of evidence, from both unpublished sources and from little-known published writings, Corrado Vivanti builds up an image of Henri IV as seen by contemporaries which is very different from that of the able but gay monarch with which historians usually present us.

The author traces the rising hopes in Henri of Navarre as saviour at the end of the religious wars, and dwells on the significance of his conversion as a fatal blow to the Catholic League raising possibilities of some general solution of the religious question. He next discusses the traditional role of the French monarchy in Europe and analyses the symbolism through which Henri IV was presented as a Gallic Hercules with a world mission. The projects for a new Council of the Church are examined, a Council in which it was hoped that the moderating Gallican influences over-ridden at the Council of Trent would prevail, under the auspices of Henri IV. Next come chapters on two eirenists in the circle of Henri IV whose lives were spent in the cause of religious reunion, Jean Hotman and Jean de Serres. Though Jean Hotman is modera-tely well known, he has never been studied so fully as in the chapter on him here, which brings out his importance as a religious

* Review of Corrado Vivanti, *Lotta politica e pace religiosa in Francia fra Cinque e Seicento*, Turin, 1963, in *History*, L, 1965.

reunionist belonging to the Henri IV group. Jean de Serres is a very little-known figure, now brought to life in a long study in which, again, the interest is centred on his importance as an eirenist. Hotman and De Serres, as presented in this book, stand out as the two most important figures working for religious reunion from the Protestant side, and with the blessing of their master the King of France.

Vivanti next examines the history of his own times by J.-A. de Thou as a history written from the point of view of the pacificatory movement centred on Henri IV, and as a humanist history, written with the political intention of propagating and supporting this movement. This chapter is the best study as yet in existence on this important and influential historian. And, as the following chapter emphasizes, the pacificatory aspirations embodied in the movement around Henri IV lead on into the later seventeenth century when, in the 'Europe of the Learned', the religious peace so much desired by the eirenists in pursuit of a 'Christian Republic' transforms into the stabilization of the times which enabled intellectuals to pursue their tasks undisturbed. Incidentally, these two chapters together help to explain the immense influence in Europe of de Thou's history, as a kind of historical manifesto.

In my opinion, this is a very important book. It breaks entirely new ground, for there is no book in existence covering the subject with which it deals. It is packed with material drawn from firsthand examination of sources; this brief notice cannot begin to do justice to its wealth of content. The historian of political and religious ideas in England in the sixteenth and early seventeenth centuries cannot afford to neglect it, for the French movement with which it deals had many echoes in England.

I would strongly urge that there should be an English translation of this book.

Chapter Twenty-two

SOME NEW LIGHT ON 'L'ÉCOSSAISE'
OF ANTOINE DE MONTCHRÉTIEN*

IN SPITE of the researches of modern scholars a good deal of obscurity still surrounds the work and the lives of that group of men who were the pioneers of classical tragedy in France. In particular the career of Antoine de Montchrétien contains elements of mystery which have never been satisfactorily cleared up. Since so little is known of the man and of his work, the following small discoveries in connection with *L'Écossaise*, Montchrétien's most celebrated play, may be of interest to students of that mysterious poet and economist.

Able critics have dealt with the literary and aesthetic aspects of *L'Écossaise*, pointing out its importance as one of the finest examples of the sixteenth-century type of classical tragedy and its value as lyric poetry. Attention has also been drawn to the interesting fact that the subject of the play, the execution of Mary, Queen of Scots, was drawn from modern, almost contemporary, history, instead of dealing with the usual classical or Biblical themes, and this is the point which it is the purpose of the present article to develop.

It was not a new idea to use contemporary events as the subject of a play; to quote only two examples, Pierre Matthieu dramatized the assassination of the Guises in 1589, and in 1612 Claude Billard put the murder of Henri IV on the stage. In fact the dramatization of contemporary events seems to have been used as a kind of

---

* Published in *Modern Language Review*, XXII, 1927.

political journalism in the late sixteenth and early seventeenth centuries. Montchrétien's play on the death of Mary Stuart, although immeasurably superior in execution to the general run of these political plays, is not unlike them in subject and design and the question arises whether or not *L'Écossaise* was intended by the author to carry a political implication. There are in effect two references among English diplomatic records of the period, which have, I believe, hitherto escaped the notice of students of Montchrétien, and which would seem to prove beyond all doubt that this play was considered by some contemporaries to have a dangerous political significance.

In Sir Ralph Winwood's *Memorials*, there is a letter from Winwood at Paris to Cecil, dated 17 March 1601, O.S., in which the following passage occurs:

> Since the beginning of Lent, certaine base Comedians have publicklie plaied in this Towne the Tragedy of the late Queen of Scottes. The King being then at Vernueil, I had no other recourse but to the Chancellor; who upon my complaint was very sensible of that so lewde an Indiscretion, and in my hearing gave an especiall Charge to the Lieutenant Civill, (to whose Duty the Provisions for such Disorder doth appertaine,) to have a care, both that this Folly should be punished, and that the like hereafter should not be committed. Since, Monsieur de Villeroy (upon the Notice which I gave him) doth promise that he will give order both for the Punishment of that which is past, and for future Remedy.[1]

It might be argued that as the author is not here mentioned by name and as the title is given in English, we have no certain proof that Winwood is indeed speaking of Montchrétien's play on the death of the Queen of Scots. There may, of course, have been other plays on the same subject extant. But the precise way in which this information of Winwood's fits in with a letter found by L. Auvray, which has hitherto constituted the only known mention of a performance of *L'Écossaise*, proves, in my opinion at least, that the English ambassador is indeed referring to Montchrétien's play and to no other. I beg leave to quote in full the letter found by M. Auvray among the correspondence of Pompone de Bellièvre in order that it may be compared with Winwood's:

Lettre de M. de Beauharnais, lieutenant général à Orléans, au chancelier Pompone de Bellièvre.

Monseigneur,

Pour obéir à voz commandemens, je me suis tres soigneusement enquis quelz estoient ces comédiens qui avoient joué en cete ville, depuis deux mois ou environ, une tragédie sur la mort de la feue royne d'Ecosse, et n'ay peu aprandre autre chose, sinon que le chef de leur compaignie se nomme La Vallée, et qu'ilz sont partis de cete ville depuis ung mois ou six sepmaines, sans que j'aye peu scavoir où ilz sont allez. Mais j'ay tant faict, que j'ay recouvré ung livre de tragédies, la première desquelles, nommée 'l'Ecossoise' aultrement 'le Désastre,' est celle mesme qu'ilz ont représentée, ainsi qu'il m'a esté asseuré par gens d'honneur qui y ont assisté. Je vous envoye, Monseigneur, ce livre, tres marry que je ne puis obéir entièrement à ce que vous m'avez commandé, et supplie Dieu le Créateur vous donner, Monseigneur, heureuse yssue de tous vos desirs et vous conserver en longue vie pour le repos de ce royaulme. A Orléans, ce xxi juin 1603.

Vostre très humble serviteur,
Beauharnois,
lieutenant général à Orléans.[2]

The details given by Beauharnais establish beyond all doubt that he is certainly referring to Montchrétien's play; *L'Écossoise ou le Desastre* is its exact title in the first edition, and in that edition it is the first play in the book. And if we now compare Beauharnais's letter with Winwood's, I think we shall be convinced that they are both writing about the same play.

The significant points of the comparison can be summarized thus: in March 1602, Winwood complained to the Chancellor about a public performance of the 'Tragedy of the late Queen of Scottes'. The Chancellor proclaimed himself 'very sensible of that so lewde an Indiscretion' and gave orders to prevent its occurring again. In June 1603, the Chancellor (the same man, Pompone de Bellièvre, was still in office) wrote to Orléans to inquire who had been acting in that town 'une tragédie sur la mort de la feue royne d'Ecosse' – an exact translation, be it noticed, of the expression Winwood uses to describe the play. Evidently the Chancellor was keeping the promise he made to Winwood and was doing his best to prevent the performance of a play which gave offence to the

English ambassador and was considered unbecoming by the French authorities themselves.

But the incident was not even yet closed, as the following extract from a hitherto unpublished despatch among the State Papers at the Public Record Office shows. The English ambassador (Parry) at Paris writes to Cecil on 13 February 1605 as follows:

> The Comedians, ye heretofore sd, bn. prohibited to represent on stage ye Tragedy of ye death of ye k. mother, adventured this weeke to act it agayne publickly. But ye k. counsel advised of it, caused them ye next morning to be apprehended and imprisoned, where they yeat remayn: besides ye booke is suppressed, and the author and ye printer inquired after to tast of ye same cupp. The k. shewed hymself very highly offended, and hath commanded very rigourous punishment to be done on them al.[3]

There is little doubt, I think, that we have here to do with Montchrétien's play again. Parry especially states that the subject has been mentioned before: 'The Comedians, ye heretofore sd, bn. prohibited etc.' Also it is known that La Vallée, whom Beauharnais mentions as the leader of the troupe which performed *L'Écossaise* at Orléans, and his company were at the Hôtel de Bourgogne in 1605,[4] the year in which Parry writes. It was therefore almost certainly at the Hôtel de Bourgogne that the performance of which Parry speaks took place.

The most interesting aspect of these two new documents – Winwood's letter of 1602 and Parry's of 1605 – is the proof which they afford of two public performances in Paris of *L'Écossaise* by professional comedians. This, with the performance at Orléans recorded by Beauharnais, brings the total number of public performances of this play of which we now have proof up to three. The old view that the sixteenth-century type of classical play, of which Garnier and Montchrétien are the chief exponents, was not meant by its authors to be acted on the public stage has been gradually exploded by the evidence of actual public performances of such plays which Gustave Lanson has collected.[5] The evidence of Winwood and Parry adds two further small items to M. Lanson's list. *L'Écossaise* must have had a considerable vogue with the public since the comedians continued to present it in face of such risks.

Secondly these documents are of interest since they are a small addition to the very fragmentary material from which the biography of Montchrétien has to be constructed.

'Ye booke is suppressed', Parry tells us. It is strange to hear this because it was in 1604 that the new and emended edition of Montchrétien's tragedies appeared at Rouen. Perhaps these happenings account for the depressed tone of the preface of the new edition, addressed to the Prince de Condé. 'S'il m'estoit possible de les dégager [i.e. les tragédies] totalement du public,' says Montchrétien, 'ce me seroit un grand contentement et par mon propre consentement elles seroient desormais plustost supprimées que reimprimées.'

'The author and ye printer inquired after', continues Parry. Is it not possible that this affair may have been at the bottom of Montchrétien's hasty departure into England which biographers, following the *Mercure François*, have hitherto attributed solely to his having killed the son of the Sieur de Grichy-Moinnes in a duel?

It must be confessed that these documents tend to increase rather than diminish the mystery of Montchrétien's life. How can one reconcile these records of complaints of *L'Écossaise* made by English representatives in France with the legend that Montchrétien dedicated this very play to James I, and through James's intercession with Henri IV on his behalf, obtained permission to return to France? The following is the passage from the *Mercure François* on which this tale is based:

> Il [Montchrétien] a esté des bons poetes tragiques de son
> temps; il fit imprimer plusieurs tragedies qu'il avoit
> composées, lesquelles furent bien receues: entr' autres il desdia
> l'Ecossoise au Roy de la Grande Bretagne, ce qui lui sauva
> la vie; car s'estant trouvé en un rencontre accusé d'avoir tué
> le fils du sieur de Grichy moynnes pres Bayeux, en feignant
> de luy demander la vie, il s'en alla en Angleterre, crainte d'estre
> pendu, jusques à ce que sa M. de la grande Bretagne obtint
> du feu roy Henry 4 sa grace.[6]

It is, perhaps, not inconsistent with what we know or can guess of Montchrétien's character that he should have taken the bold step of dedicating to the English monarch the very play which had given offence to the English authorities. He may have taken the bull by the horns and turned failure into success by these impudent methods. But it is also very possible that the author of the passage in the *Mercure*, who is writing some fifteen years after the events, may have been misinformed, or may be giving an intentionally misleading account of the connection between *L'Écossaise* and the British government.[7] At any rate he confirms the fact that there was some such connection, even though the details he gives seem difficult to reconcile with the information we have derived from the ambassadors' despatches. It is possible that further search among English correspondence of the period might throw more light on this problem.

Why did the English ambassadors disapprove of a play which seems to us now a most mild and harmless elegy on the death of the ill-fated Queen? What can have been the political significance of *L'Écossaise* in the eyes of contemporaries? Let us now turn to the play itself, and dismissing from our minds all aesthetic considerations, let us endeavour to discern what are the political views which it reveals or fails to reveal.

Practically every critic who has ever had anything to say about *L'Écossaise* has been struck by the remarkable fact that the last three acts seem to have no logical connection with the first two. The play falls into two distinct halves. The heroine of the first half is Queen Elizabeth. She is represented as being most unwilling to give the order for Mary's execution. She shrinks from an act which seems to her cruel and unwomanly and brings forward every argument she can think of in Mary's defence. But her counsellors lay before her the reasons which render the execution of the Queen of Scots imperative – namely, that she is known to have been plotting with the Spaniards and other enemies of England. These plots have had for their object nothing less than the assassination of Elizabeth and the seizure of the throne for Mary. Nothing but Mary's execution will put a stop to these continually renewed conspiracies, which are a menace not merely to Elizabeth but also to England. In the name of her subjects, the representatives of Parliament implore Elizabeth to put an end to the life of the treasonable Queen. Overwhelmed by this reasoning Elizabeth consents to Mary's death, and then, touched again by pity, rescinds the order. Montchrétien leaves her at that point and does not show Elizabeth actually giving the order for Mary's death. Elizabeth, then, is represented as having been unwillingly forced to the deed for the good of her subjects. In short the first two acts are a presentation of what one may call broadly the English-Huguenot view of the subject.

In the last three acts we hear no more of Elizabeth and her

counsellors. Mary, the noble and innocent victim of a cruel sentence, holds the centre of the stage. She is shown going to meet her death with nobility and fortitude, and the poet appears to be doing all he can to engage the sympathies of the reader on Mary's side. Great stress is laid on the enormity of putting a lady of royal blood to death in this manner and the choruses expatiate on the sacred immunity from violence which should surround the persons of kings. In these last acts Montchrétien seems to have gone over completely to the French-Catholic position.

It is therefore somewhat difficult to decide what the politics and religion (the two were inseparably bound together at that period) of our author really were, since he states the two opposite positions consecutively without making any attempt to reconcile them. He gives more space to Mary, and his heart seems to be much more in her defence than in that of Elizabeth. Therefore some biographers have concluded that he was a Catholic when he wrote *L'Écossaise*, although he would appear to have gone over to the Protestant side later in life.

It is my belief, however, that Montchrétien's two-sided presentation of the subject is less original than at first appears. I suggest that Pierre Matthieu's *Histoire des derniers troubles de France* (1597) should be added to the list of sources of *L'Écossaise* compiled by Lanson in his article on the subject.[8] Matthieu's *Histoire des derniers troubles* was widely read by contemporaries, as the number of editions it went through proves, and at the end of the second book there is a fairly long 'Digression sur la mort de la Royne d'Escosse', the argument of which can be briefly condensed as follows.

France mourned at the death of the Queen of Scots, whereas in England it was a cause of rejoicing. After making this statement Matthieu proceeds to examine the arguments which support these two contrary opinions and he casts his examination in the form of a dialogue between a Frenchman and an Englishman, the former supporting Mary whilst the latter is the champion of Elizabeth. The keystone of the Englishman's argument is that since Mary had been conspiring against the safety of the realm, reasons of state made her execution imperative. He describes at length Elizabeth's reluctance to consent to the deed, and the pressure put upon her by her counsellors and by the 'Estats d'Angleterre' (compare Montchrétien's 'chœur des Estats'). 'Le Chancelier, au nom des trois ordres d'Angleterre, la supplia de laisser le cours à la Justice.' This is also the plea of the 'chœur des Estats' in *L'Écossaise*:

Ains que tu permettras que la iuste sentence
Donnee en plain Conseil en ta sainte presence
Contre ceste Princesse, aye son libre cours.⁹

'Puckering Procureur general, luy remonstra que la longue prison,
ny la continuation de la bien veillance de sa Maiesté n'avoit peu
fleschir une ame tant ingrate et obstinee, qu'elle n'eust souvent
entreprins contre sa vie, et la tranquilité de sa Couronne. . .'
Compare this with:

Quoy que de sa prison l'ennuyeuse longueur
Peust un iuste courroux allumer en son cœur;
Par mon doux traitement elle devoit l'esteindre,
Se plaignant en son mal de ne s'en pouuoir plaindre:
Mais l'on m'a rapporté qu'en ce dernier effort,
Elle brigue mon Sceptre, et minute ma mort.
Seroit-ce donc l'amour, Ame ingrate et legere,
Que me iuroit sans fin ta bouche mensongere?¹⁰

Matthieu's 'Chancelier' and 'Puckering Procureur general' correspond to Montchrétien's 'Conseiller' who argues with Elizabeth
in the first act of *L'Écossaise*; in the second act 'Conseiller' disappears and his argument is continued by the 'chœur des Estats'.
Montchrétien exactly follows Matthieu's order in this; for we read
in the *Histoire des derniers troubles* that when the Chancelier and
Puckering had exposed their arguments: 'Elle [i.e. Elizabeth] non
contente de ses remonstrances envoya encores un Milord à
Messieurs du Parlement, les supplier d'esprouver tout pour sauver
la vie à ceste Roine . . . lesquels encores qu'ils regrettassent le
desastre de ceste Princesse, trouverent que la Roine feroit bien de
s'asseurer.' Notice the word 'desastre' in this passage, used by
Montchrétien as a sub-title to his play.

What would you have had the Queen do? asks Matthieu's
Englishman, amongst all these 'contraires agitations'. She was
warned by M. de Believre,¹¹ he continues, that Mary's death
would raise an avenging host of relations and allies. Compare
Montchrétien:

Les Roys qui font mourir ceux qui leur sont contraires,
Pensant les amoindrir, croissent leurs aduersaires . . . ¹²

But the Englishman thinks this an idle objection. 'Pour eviter un grand danger il se faut hasarder au danger.' In short, I believe I am right in saying that every argument used by Montchrétien in the first two acts can be traced to this passage in the *Histoire des derniers troubles*.

Matthieu's Frenchman bases his argument on the premise that a sovereign prince is above all human laws and answerable only to God. Elizabeth and her Parliament had therefore absolutely no right to pass a sentence on the Queen of Scots. 'Quant aux souverains qui ne recognoissent superieur que Dieu, je ne lis point que jamais ils ayent passé par les arrests d'un Parlement, ny au jugement de leurs voisins.' There is no form of punishment which can ever be applied to a sovereign, and to inflict on a queen the indignity of a public execution was a most unheard-of sacrilege. Compare Montchrétien:

> On fait si peu de cas du sacré sang Royal
> Que la hache s'en trempe et le bras desloyal
> L'espand ne plus ne moins que le sang mercenaire;
> On donne aux maiestez le supplice vulgaire . . .[13]

In short, to Matthieu's Frenchman, as to Montchrétien in the last three acts, Mary is the innocent victim of a cruel and unjustifiable sentence.

I hope I have said enough to prove that this passage of Matthieu's must have suggested the plan of *L'Écossaise* to Montchrétien.[14] The discrepancy which we have noted between the first two and the last three acts of the play is thus explained; Montchrétien has simply presented the Englishman's argument in the first two and the Frenchman's in the last three acts. Like Matthieu, he gives far more space and weight to the French argument without ever definitely condemning the English position. Matthieu's closing paragraph may even have suggested to the poet the larger philosophical significance of Mary's fate, as a type of the transitory nature of fame and beauty and the shortness of human life. 'Voila une vie bien tragicque, et un vray tableau de la vanité des grandeurs du monde', says Matthieu, and concludes his 'digression' with the exclamation 'Allez faire estat des felicitez du monde!' The historian's prose style, pompous and stilted though it is, is capable of achieving a certain dignity at times.

It is, perhaps, not irrelevant to add here that some years later Pierre Matthieu, like Montchrétien, also got into trouble with the English ambassador. The incident is related in the State Papers at the Public Record Office.[15] In 1610 a libellous book on King James I appeared in France. The English ambassador in Paris was instructed to endeavour to trace the author; and King James himself suggested that Matthieu might possibly be the culprit because the style of the libel resembled that of the historian and also because 'he [Matthieu] hath been ghirding at this State before.' It transpired, however, that one Rebout was the real author of the libel. Matthieu had a serious conversation with the ambassador, in the course of which it was explained to him that 'for the partialities which we had observed he had shewed against the State of England, in his Storie, his pen, which was formerly accused by us, was the more suspected upon the coming forth of this lewed booke', and was then dismissed with a warning. Matthieu had written various other historical works, so the rather vague expression 'his Storie' may or may not refer to the *Histoire des derniers troubles*. But it is a rather curious coincidence that the author of what we believe to be the source of *L'Écossaise* should also have come into conflict with the English authorities.

This discussion as to the source of *L'Écossaise* has led us somewhat from our original inquiry, which was to discover what it was that the English ambassadors objected to in the play. One might have thought that a poem which glorified the memory of James's mother whilst palliating the part played in the affair by Elizabeth would have met with their approval. But no doubt the truth of the matter is that the disapprobation of the English ambassadors did not rest upon fine distinctions of this kind, but upon a general principle which was gradually being formulated in England, the basis of which was that any representation on the stage of a 'modern Christian king' was, in itself, unseemly.[16] In their horror at hearing that the characters of Queen Elizabeth and Queen Mary were being presented on a public stage, they would not stop to consider the matter or the argument of the play.

But a French contemporary did ponder the argument of *L'Écossaise* and seems to have seen in it a dangerous attempt at arousing again the old popular passion for the Guise family, a stirring up, as it were, of the embers of the League.

I base the above statement upon my interpretation of *Le Triomphe de la Ligue*, a play by R. J. Nerée, published in 1607, which I believe the author intended as an answer to *L'Écossaise*. In order to support this claim I shall be obliged to give a short résumé of the argument of the play.

Its central theme is the painful story – then still very fresh in the minds of Frenchmen – of the religious wars of the preceding century, the bitter struggle between Catholics and Huguenots. The first act begins with a long monologue deploring the unhappy state of France, spoken by a personage entitled 'Constance garde-loix' who afterwards turns out to represent the Reformed Religion. Then 'Giesu' (Guise), 'Numiade' (Du Maine, i.e. Mayenne), and 'Jeusoie' (Joyeuse) appear upon the scene. The Guises are here represented as ambitious self-seekers who have fomented civil wars and ruined France to further their private ends – namely the seizure of the crown of France for their own family. François II and Charles IX were their tools, but the third brother, Henri III, has proved less tractable. To crush him they have formed, with the help of Spain, the Catholic League; they have deluded the people into supporting this with empty promises. Henry of Navarre is the hero who contrasts with these villains, although he never appears in person. The Guises regard him as their most dangerous enemy, first, because he is the legitimate heir to the throne which they had hoped to seize for themselves, and secondly because his valour and personal charm have made him extremely popular. The author of this play is himself a Protestant; but he bears no grudge against Catholics who will accept Henry of Navarre as king, that is to say Catholics who are not Leaguers. He belongs, in short, to that body of *politique* opinion which found its chief expression in the *Satire Ménippée* and which did so much to place Henri IV firmly on the throne of France.

This general presentation of the situation occupies the first three acts. In the last two we learn, through the mouths of various messengers, of the successive blows which fell upon the House of Guise and the League. First of all – and this is the most significant part of the play from our point of view – a Jesuit, just returned from England, imparts to Guise the news of the death of the Queen of Scots. The Duke is enraged at this affront to his family, and realizes at once what a set-back this will be to his ambitious schemes. The next piece of bad news Guise receives is the intelligence of Henry of Navarre's victory at the battle of Coutras. And then comes a third great blow, the news of the ruin of the Spanish Armada, for the fortunes of the League are bound up with those of Spain. One feels that the object of the author is to demonstrate the intimate connection between events in France and events in England; between the League, the tool used by Spain to destroy France, and Mary, Queen of Scots, the centre of Spanish intrigue against England; between the Duke of Guise, who hoped to oust the legitimate kings of France, and Mary of Scotland – whose maiden name was Mary of Guise – whom her supporters hoped to place upon the throne of England.

The last scene of the fifth act is devoted to the description of Guise's assassination which, of course, is excused on the grounds that the Duke was plotting to murder the King and seize the crown.

It is easy to see how the argument of this play refutes Montchré-tien. By putting the death of Mary into its historical context, Nerée demonstrates that the Frenchman who sympathizes with that unhappy Queen, must, if he is logical, be still an adherent of the League and a traitor to His Majesty King Henri IV. The plots in England against Elizabeth, of which Mary was the centre, had the same Spanish origin as the plots in France against the legitimate French sovereigns. This is made quite clear, and great stress is laid on the fact that the execution of the Queen of Scots was a blow to Guise and to the League.

The proof that Nerée really did intend this play to be an answer to Montchrétien's is the fact that the speeches of 'Visteie' (i.e. 'Jesuite') are verbally reminiscent of *L'Écossaise*. In order to support this claim I shall be obliged to quote at some length. It will be remembered that in the final chorus of *L'Écossaise*,[17] Montchrétien enumerates the charms of Mary – her eyes, her forehead, her hair, etc. – and concludes that everything in life must be transitory indeed since such beauties have already faded into nothingness. Bearing this passage in mind it is interesting to read the following oration made by the Jesuit in Act IV, scene i of *Le Triomphe de la Ligue*:

> ô grandeurs qu'on adore,
> Patronnés vous ici, veu ce front dont l'aurore
> Empruntoit la splendeur, ces yeux riants et doux
> Ains ses brillants souleils, qui d'Apollon jaloux
> Ternissoient les rayons, cest amoureux Chef mesmes
> Que s'est veu honorer de deux grands diademes,
> Leur beau lustre ecclipser par la meurtrière main
> D'un infame bourreau, ô supplice inhumain!
> Puis allez vous fier aux blandices du monde,
> Aux trompeuses faveurs, malheureux qui s'y fonde . . .

The whole passage is an obvious and not unskilful imitation of Montchrétien's style.

The Jesuit also tells us that Mary prayed for the League with her last breath:

> Aidez au moins la Ligue, et prenez la défense
> Du parti commencé dès que j'estois en France.

And it must be admitted that Montchrétien had put a similar sentiment, though couched in much vaguer terms, into the mouth of the Queen of Scots. In the long 'farewell' speech in *L'Écossaise*, Mary thus apostrophizes her relations the Guises:

> Adieu braues Lorrains, qui de Lauriers couuers,
> Faites que vostre Race en tous lieux estimée,
> Vante encor' à bon droit les palmes d'Idumée.[18]

It will be noticed that Nerée replies to the argument of the last three acts of *L'Écossaise* and evidently considers that they, and not the first two, contain Montchrétien's real opinion. He also strongly attacks the statement that it was a sin to put to death a person of royal blood. In the chorus which immediately precedes the scene between Guise and the Jesuit, Nerée puts forward his views on this subject in no uncertain terms. The power of kings is indeed, he says, divinely ordained, and in that sense they are sacred. But if they provoke God to anger they forfeit all immunity from punishment. Let all wicked princes come now and behold the terrible fate that has recently overtaken a queen!

> Voiez, voiez ceste fois,
> Froids de peur, rouges de honte,
> *La Roine des Escossois*
> Qu'*un desastre* estrange dompte:
> Apprenez par ses douleurs,
> Qu'en ces bas lieux ou nous sommes,
> Vous n'estes rien que des hommes
> Subiects a mesmes malheurs.

The words which I have italicized are surely a final proof that Nerée had Montchrétien in mind. They are, I believe, an allusion to the titles of the latter's play, which in the first edition was called *L'Éscossoise ou le Desastre*, and in the second, *La Tragedie de la Reine D'Escosse*.

It has also occurred to me that the dedication of the *Triomphe de la Ligue* to 'Samuel Korecky, Comte de Korec' – obviously a made-up name – may also be aimed at Montchrétien, whose high-sounding title of 'Seigneur de Vasteville' was of rather doubtful authenticity, or so his enemies hinted.

It would be interesting to identify the author of *Le Triomphe de la Ligue*. Beauchamps[19] attributes it, curiously enough, to that same Pierre Matthieu who wrote the *Histoire des derniers troubles*. But Beauchamps has confused *Le Triomphe de la Ligue* with Matthieu's play *La Guisiade*. Paul Lacroix suggests Nicholas Rapin, one of the principal authors of the *Satire Ménippée*. He says: 'Le style [du *Triomphe de la Ligue*] a beaucoup d'analogie avec celui de Rapin, qui fut mandé à la cour l'année même de la publication de cette pièce . . .' [20] If this hypothesis should be correct, the play would take on an additional importance as an official reply to *L'Écossaise*, sanctioned – possibly even ordered – by Henri IV himself.

It would appear, then, that Montchrétien's play, since it called forth the ire of Winwood and Parry and elicited a reply from Nerée, must have been something of a storm centre in the early years of the seventeenth century. And yet one feels that it was primarily as a poet and as a man of sentiment, rather than as a politician, that he was first attracted to the story of the beautiful and ill-fated Queen of Scots. Montchrétien always seems to have had a genius for getting into difficulties, and I leave it to others to follow up the clue to some of his difficulties which the facts related above would seem to suggest.

EUROPE

Chapter Twenty-three

PRINT CULTURE: THE RENAISSANCE*

IN THE AGES of what has been termed 'scribal culture', all reading matter was written by hand. The chief function of the learned man, or scholar, was the transmission of available knowledge through scribal labours. The scribal culture stretched from the dawn of history to the middle of the fifteenth century A.D. when the printing presses introduced a miraculous and magical way of dispensing with the scribe. The age of print culture began and has been continuing up to the present, that is for about five centuries – a pathetically short space of historical time compared to the untold scribal ages which preceded it.

This obvious fact is so enormous that its sheer size tends to make us forget it. The advent of printing meant that many copies of texts and diagrams could be made simultaneously; it meant that scholars could use libraries of printed books instead of having to travel to read rare manuscripts. In her remarkable book *The Printing Press as an Agent of Change*, Elizabeth Eisenstein argues that printing should not be listed with gunpowder and the compass as one of several inventions which came into use in the Renaissance. It was the one invention which made possible the whole subsequent astonishingly rapid evolution of European culture, which

---

* Review essay on Elizabeth L. Eisenstein, *The Printing Press as an Agent of Change: Communications and Cultural Transformations in Early Modern Europe*, Cambridge, 1979; and Allen G. Debus, *Man and Nature in the Renaissance*, Cambridge, 1978, in *Encounter*, LII, 4, April 1979.

spread the scientific advance which fostered the rapid interchange of ideas. Rather fifty years of Europe than a cycle of Cathay, as Tennyson remarked in his prophetic utterances.

The ages of scribal culture were also the ages of memorizing. It was intensely important to hold in memory the knowledge so difficult to refer to in scarce manuscripts, to store in memory the material of culture. As is now well known, the classical art of memory, using striking images remembered on memory-places, was widely used, and its techniques affected basic mental processes, and even the design of manuscripts or the arrangement of buildings. When I look back on my own work over the past decades I am always oppressed by the thought of how little I have done, how I have only touched the outskirts or fringes of subjects which I have attempted, how many are the paths branching out from these subjects which are still untrodden.

I think of those dramatic masks, expressive masks of comedy or tragedy, to be seen here and there in ancient frescos. Are these intended to be used in memory systems, based on these frescos – expressive dramatic masks providing striking images to fix points in a memory system? The long descriptions of pictured rooms in buildings described in narrative poetry, both classical and post-classical, are almost certainly related to the principles of the classical mnemonic. I have touched in my book on *The Art of Memory* on how the Gothic interpretation of artificial memory underlies much medieval art, and must be studied in relation to the great *summae* expressed in images on places in the medieval church, on how the advice for making images memorable affects the figures of virtues and vices. Those who have deeply studied the virtue-vice systems, for example the late Rosemond Tuve, have thrown much light on them but have omitted the important point that in their exaggerated expressiveness these images are following the classical advice for making images memorable.

The more I think of it, the more obvious it seems to me that memory is the chief object aimed at in the putting into images of the medieval encyclopedia. The whole subject awaits a general and extensive treatment, and one which might fascinatingly combine art, imagination, and memory, and the transformation of a classical theme into Gothic expression. One of the books which I would like to write, and may still write if I have time, would be on Dante and the Art of Memory, using *summae* of similitudes by Dominican preachers. The varied images of Prudence which run through the *Inferno* underline the theme that it is a part of Prudence to remember Hell.

Memory systems and memory principles continue into the age of print but their roots were in the scribal age and they gradually became no longer a prime necessity. Memory patterns continue to be discernible in the print culture, for example in the lay-outs of Ramist logic which are often copied from the patterns in Lullist manuscripts (Lullism was a form of the art of memory). The impact of the artificial memory and its techniques on the print culture, which began to dispense with it, is pointed out by Eisenstein in many perceptive remarks. She mentions that printing was sometimes significantly called 'the artificial writing'. The artificial writing of print took over the functions of the artificial memory. The print culture released the scribe from the bondage of copying. It also released memory from the heavy artificial burdens upon it. A culture which the need for memorization renders static is replaced by a culture liberated by print to put all its powers into original thinking and advance. Though Eisenstein's thesis of the enormous importance of the switch to print as a factor in the development of European culture in the centuries after the fifteenth century may seem a stating of the obvious, yet the force and detail with which she has driven the truth home are impressive.

The use of printing does not account for the choice of the themes which the print culture developed. These were already there. As Eisenstein points out, there had been many classical Renaissances before the Petrarchan and Italian Renaissance of the fifteenth century, but the Italian Renaissance achieved permanence through being fixed by the print culture. Printing does not account for European culture or solve the problems of its history. It is only the improved technological tool which made possible its vast development, which made available a hugely increased range of knowledge.

The new print culture printed everything, Hermetic philosophy as well as Aristotelian, alchemical treatises as well as mathematical treatises. Eisenstein is chiefly interested in the development of seventeenth-century physical science which she argues was strongly assisted by printing and its techniques of organization. Allen Debus in *Man and Nature in the Renaissance* gives a more general picture of the science of 'Renaissance man' by including alchemy-chemistry, and here again (though he is not concerned with this) the print culture comes into play. Would the alchemical Renaissance have developed as powerfully as it did without the energy of printers in printing huge volumes of alchemical texts? Would the spread of learned magic have been so far-reaching without the spread of the literature of magic? Ficino drew his magic images of the planets and of the decans from manuscript sources. Giordano Bruno quotes his magic images from the printed work of Cornelius Agrippa.

It was the whole of the European tradition, literary and cultural, theological and philosophical, scientific and magical, which poured in ever-increasing volume from the rapidly increasing and expanding print-shops. Out of this great volume, and its accompanying thought-movements, arose the predominantly print culture of modern Europe. Eisenstein's thesis owes something, as she acknowledges, to the McLuhan fashion, but she develops this in a much more reasonable and convincing way.

In contemplating the extraordinary record laid out in print in the era which followed Gutenberg and the establishment of printing presses, we are impressed by the fact – an obvious fact which Eisenstein has made us see – of its all-inclusiveness. The exciting newly-established print culture increased the imagery available to poets and artists, familiarized the world with the great literatures of the past, served mathematics and science through the printing of scientific texts. It also favoured the development of Neoplatonic and Hermetic mysticism. The occult, the mystical, the numerological Pythagorean movement grew in volume, and the 'genuinely' scientific or mathematical approaches to nature grew with it. There is certainly an interrelation, or mutual influences of some kind, between the two.

In some of my books, particularly *Giordano Bruno and the Hermetic Tradition*, I have endeavoured to make some study of this problem. I would like, however, to take this opportunity of stating clearly and firmly that there is no 'Yates thesis' about this. The expression is erroneous and puts a wrong colouring on my work. As I am never tired of repeating, in prefaces and elsewhere, I am only a historian, and I have urged that historians of thought and culture should include within their purview the vast literature vaguely called 'occult' which proliferated to such an extraordinary degree, particularly in the late sixteenth and early seventeenth centuries. The 'occult' literature should not be ostracized from 'genuine' historical studies but should be tackled as a historical problem, demanding accurate and careful historical work for its elucidation. This is not a 'thesis', or a doctrinaire statement of any kind. It is simply a call for work, urging the research scholars of the present and the future to undertake the mapping and critical examination of a vast body of neglected material.

Yates is painfully aware that she has not done nearly enough work (and that her time for new work is running out). I have vaguely called the movements with which I have been concerned 'Hermetic-Cabalist' and in my books I have concentrated mainly on the Hermetic side, though I did devote a chapter in *Bruno* to Pico della Mirandola and the Cabala. More and more I begin to see that the Cabalist side, and its yoking together with the Hermetic, is essential. Dee's *monas* sign was Hermetic and magical, Pythagorean and numerological, but it was also Cabalist, concerned with the profound mysteries of the Hebrew alphabet. Until we try to wrestle seriously with 'Christian Cabala', we are not fully facing the whole problem. In my next book I make an attempt at this. It will not be a 'Yates thesis' but only another Yates attempt at laborious digging, or a sign-posting of fields in the hope that others will dig more deeply.

A question which is continually nagging at me now is the question of the censorship. Amongst the many suggestive observations made by Eisenstein is her remark that we have no clear history of the censorship as it developed in the sixteenth and seventeenth centuries, of which books were put on the index and when, of changes in emphasis in censoring, and their dates, of what were the main lines of thought objected to by the Council of Trent, of how these objections were acted upon by the censors and in what order. Lack of clarity about this subject, or of adequate scholarly treatment of it, may account, or partially account, for our uncertainty about the end of the Renaissance, or about what stopped the Renaissance, or, if it did not entirely end, through what altered or distorted forms it continued. The thought occurs that if we were sometimes to begin, not with the rise of the Renaissance but with its decline, and work backwards from there, we might learn much. The lack of adequate history of the censorship, which Eisenstein has noted, makes it difficult to follow through what stages the movement of repression passed. The Italian scholar, Antonio Rotondò, has indicated some aspects of the movement against Platonism, and Neoplatonism, and their attendant occultisms, which was certainly a part of ecclesiastical post-Tridentine policy. He notes that Platonism in association with Cabala was considered particularly dangerous. I have seen in censored copies of works by Francesco Giorgi, in words written in ink on the title-page by the censor, the warning that the work is to be read with caution because it contains errors of 'Platonists and Cabalists'. This may be an important clue; that is to say, Cabalist Neoplatonism or Neoplatonic Cabalism may have been a particularly explosive charge the suppression of which entailed loss of Renaissance force, or the distortion or deflection of that force into other channels. When found in association with Paracelsan alchemy (itself influenced by Hermeticism and Cabala), Christian Cabala may have turned into 'Rosicrucianism'.

A good many years ago I drew attention in a lecture (afterwards published) to the importance of Francesco Giorgi's *De harmonia mundi* as a Renaissance text, objected to and criticized by Marin Mersenne, though it obviously influenced Mersenne's own *Harmonie universelle*. I suggested that it might be revealing to make a detailed comparison of the two works in order to try to define why Giorgi is still 'Renaissance' while Mersenne has moved into the beginnings of the 'Scientific Revolution'. So far as I am aware this detailed comparison has not yet been made. I now suggest that a fuller exploration of the Christian Cabalist movement is necessary for the understanding of Mersenne's attitude to Giorgi, which may have had something to do with the shift away from Cabalist studies in orthodox circles. We know too little about this shift and its stages, which must surely have affected the Renaissance atmosphere which owed so much to Pico della Mirandola's combination of Christian Cabala with Ficino's Neoplatonism. What happened, for example, to Cardinal Egidius of Viterbo's movement for Catholic reform, based on Christian Cabalist arguments which became unorthodox?

My own view is that the outcry against magic and witchcraft, which grew to such alarming proportions in the late sixteenth and early seventeenth centuries, profoundly affected the late history of Renaissance Neoplatonism and its associated occultisms. The frantic propaganda in Germany in the early years of the Thirty Years War against Rosicrucians, the fever of which spread to France, must be taken into account as the background against which Mersenne so cautiously avoids implication with the Rosicrucians, and their 'horrible pacts' with the devil as depicted in contemporary Jesuit propaganda. In my next book I make the daring statement that, under the pressure of such attacks and hysterical fears, the Renaissance magus turned into Faust. This atmosphere must be reckoned with in attempts to discern what became of the Renaissance. Such attempts may sometimes involve trying to peer through the fog of the witch craze.

In *Man and Nature in the Renaissance*, Allen Debus has produced an admirably balanced account of how Hermeticism, and Neoplatonic mysticism generally, affected the Scientific Revolution. The great advantage, or the great novelty, of Debus's book is that it is cast in the form of a history-of-science textbook, yet includes with its account of the exact sciences in the period (particularly mathematics-astronomy and medicine-chemistry) a survey of the occult, or mystical, or Hermetic approaches to nature as inextricably bound up with the whole movement of thought, which included both the magical and mystical and the 'genuinely' scientific. Thus, as the cover-flap states, this book is 'an ideal textbook for students taking courses in the history of science and the general history of western civilization'. Published by the Cambridge University Press in its History of Science series (and also available in paperback) nothing could be more respectable, yet, in its quiet way, this book represents a minor revolution. It overcomes one of the main difficulties which have stood in the way of the encouragement by reputable scholars of the study of the 'Hermetic' and the 'occult' in the Renaissance. I have always felt that the chief obstacle may have been a 'teaching' obstacle. How can the 'occult' subjects be integrated into a Renaissance course for students? Debus provides the answer by providing this perfectly sensible textbook.

Reading its lucid pages I find myself constantly meeting with subjects with which I have long been concerned, and with personalities who figure in my own works. After headed paragraphs ('Observation and Experiment', or 'Mathematics and Natural Phenomena') designed to provide the student with the kind of prepared food to which he is accustomed, we come to 'Mysticism and Science', and here we read that 'A fourth ingredient in the formation of science . . . was the new Renaissance interest in the mystical approach to nature.' The *monas* or the One is being chopped up into student-food, but at least the student's diet has been enriched by an essential ingredient. This is followed by a discussion of the work of Robert Fludd (to whose huge works Debus has devoted a lifetime of study), and who is here said to offer 'an excellent example of an Hermetic-chemical approach to mathematics'. And some pages later the student meets John Dee and his hieroglyphic *monas*, and is introduced to the 'Christian neo-Platonic and Hermetic philosophy of Paracelsus'.

Thus this student's handbook on Renaissance astronomy, mathematics, medicine, anatomy, chemistry, botany, husbandry, and the developing sciences generally, is firmly correlated to the mystical, the occult, the Hermetic, in the Renaissance outlook. It is skilfully done, and undoubtedly right in its general outlines. It should mean that the new historical approach to the occult sciences has arrived, and will continue.

Chapter Twenty-four

A MAGICAL CRITIC*

ROBERT KLEIN was a Rumanian Jew, born in 1918. As was to be expected from this time and place of birth, his life was not an easy one. Before the outbreak of the Second World War he studied philosophy in Prague, science in Bucharest. After the outbreak he first did military service, then compulsory labour for Jews; after the liberation of Rumania, he engaged as a volunteer in the war in Hungary and Czechoslovakia. In 1947 he won a French government scholarship to study in Paris which was afterwards withdrawn. From 1948 to 1962 he supported himself in Paris by odd jobs, which included dish-washing, while working for a diploma in aesthetics with a thesis on Giordano Bruno. He was employed as secretary and research assistant by Augustin Renaudet and Marcel Bataillon. In 1962 he became attached to the Centre National de la Recherche Scientifique and worked with André Chastel on various projects. He was professor of history of art at the University of Montreal for the academic year 1965–6.

In 1966 he went to Florence as fellow of Harvard's Berenson foundation at the Villa I Tatti. His many brilliant published essays and reviews had aroused interest in his work and he seemed set for a successful career as an art historian. His attractive personality had won him many friends, who were overwhelmed with dismay at the news of his suicide in April 1967.

---

* Review of Robert Klein, *Form and Meaning: Essays on the Renaissance and Modern Art*, New York, 1979, in *New York Review of Books*, 21 February 1980.

A collection of his writings was published in 1970 with the title *La Forme et l'intelligible*. The French volume was itself a selection from the mass of Klein's essays. *Form and Meaning* is an English translation of a selection from the French volume, which should still be consulted for the omitted material, particularly the concluding essay on ethics which has dropped off in the English volume.

Klein was above all a Renaissance scholar, though with continuations into the modern period. His field is not easy to define; art historian, historian of culture, he was both of these. Among the subjects studied in this book are Renaissance perspective, utopia and utopian planning, Lomazzo and mannerist art theory, the *impresa*. The title of the book, which is that of one of the longest essays, suggests that a leading theme is Form and Meaning, applied mainly to the form of a work of art and its meaning. The essay on iconography, based on Panofsky's work, is obviously concerned with this problem. The concluding essays on modern art contrast this with Renaissance theory and practice.

As reviewer of this book, I am in something of a quandary. Among the most important essays in the book are those on perspective, which are well known to specialists. About these I am not qualified to speak and so shall refrain from discussion, beyond indicating that Klein's perspective studies are now available in English in this volume. About modern art, I know nothing; on this topic, too, I shall wisely refrain from ignorant prattle. But some of Klein's interests cross with mine, particularly his concern with the image and its meaning, which I have studied in relation to the history of the use of imagery in the art of memory, and which can throw light on the history of imagery in art. The change from Aristotelian psychology, dominant in the Middle Ages, in which the imagination ranked low in the hierarchy of the faculties, to Renaissance Neoplatonism in which imagination became the supreme vehicle for the grasp of truth, profoundly affected imagery and its meaning. Such problems, which I studied in relation to the memory image, are the kind of problem with which Klein was concerned. His interest in magic, and in magic as affecting the image, is also central to my work. And that he saw in Giordano Bruno's works on memory clues to this problem is again very much in accord with lines which I have attempted to pursue.

I do not think that he can have seen my books on Bruno and

on the art of memory, published not long before his death. He visited the Warburg Institute and I met him, I do not remember in what year [it was 1959. Eds], but I had then no knowledge or understanding of his work. This now seems to me strangely unfortunate, and I try to present in this review some impression of the many-sided brilliance of this scholar.

The first essay in the book is a subtle discussion of the *impresa*, and of the possible connection between theory of *impresa*-construction and theory of art. The book is not illustrated; there were a few illustrations in the French volume but none of *imprese*. It may be a little difficult for readers unfamiliar with the subject to grasp, without a picture, what an *impresa* is. It is a statement in visual form of the purpose or aim of its inventor, accompanied by a motto which expresses in words what the little picture expresses visually. A well-known example is the dolphin and anchor with the motto *festina lente*, the device of Aldus, the Venetian printer, printed in the books published by the famous Aldine press. The swift movements of the dolphin controlled by the stability of the anchor state in visual form the meaning of the motto 'Make haste slowly'.

Another famous *impresa* was that of the Emperor Charles V, two columns with the motto *Plus oultre*, or 'Further yet', alluding to his vast empire extending beyond the confines of the ancient world (bounded by the Straits of Gibraltar, known as the pillars of Hercules) into the New World. The idea seems fairly simple, not to say childish, an idea similar to that underlying chivalric coats-of-arms and their obscure mottoes. In fact, one of the Renaissance theorists suggested that the *impresa* was a development out of the heraldic device arrived at by the Italians, who were impressed by the heraldry displayed by the French knights in the French invasions of Italy.

For the Renaissance mind, the *impresa* held profound meanings. Collections of famous *imprese* were published, with treatises on the subject. These include strict rules on how a good *impresa* is to be constructed, and they explore the philosophies underlying these images. The *impresa* is related to the emblem, though the rules distinguish carefully between the two forms; its diffusion and the seriousness attending its construction illustrate the Renaissance attitude to the image.

Klein's analysis of the *impresa* treatises attempts to show how their theories concerning the *impresa*, which is, after all, an art form, have a bearing on Renaissance theory of art in general. He finds that the psychology underlying *impresa* theory is basically Aristotelian but with the addition of Neoplatonic influence. These writers conceive of the image in a mystical sense, as itself containing ultimate truth (in the manner defined by E. H. Gombrich in his celebrated essay 'Icones Symbolicae', first published in the *Journal of the Warburg and Courtauld Institutes*, XI, 1948 and now available in Gombrich's collection, *Symbolic Images*, 1972). The treatises also use Aristotelian definitions. I believe that this problem could be further pursued through sources which Klein does not use, namely the memory treatises, in which the classical mnemonic, using places and images, is philosophized according to Aristotelian psychological theory, as, for example, in the treatises of Romberch, Dolce, Rossellius, and others. The change to a Neoplatonic theory of the image can be traced, in some cases overlapping with Aristotelian theory, in the later memory treatises. Above all the change can be fully realized in Giulio Camillo's memory theatre, a fully Neoplatonic memory construction in which medieval theory of the memory image is replaced by Neoplatonic theory.

I think that Klein's study of the treatises on *imprese*, and his suggested link with art theory, can best be understood through comparison with the memory treatises, also linked with philosophical discussion and with artistic practice. The memory treatise, I would suggest, is the ancestor of the *impresa* treatise, which is a development of the philosophizing about the image transposed into a Neoplatonic world. The *impresa* is in fact classed as a memory image by some of the writers on memory.

The great exemplar of the Renaissance Neoplatonic transformation of the medieval art of memory is the memory theatre of Giulio Camillo. In my *Art of Memory* I give a rather full description of Camillo's memory theatre reconstructed from the description of it in *L'Idea del theatro di Giulio Camillo* (1550). Based on the classical rule that memory systems must use places and images, Camillo's theatre is a memory building divided into seven sets of places labelled with the names of the seven planets. These are described by Camillo as 'seven governors', an expression taken, as Camillo explicitly states, from the *Pimander*, one of those mysterious treatises, deeply revered as supposedly by 'Hermes Trismegistus', which had an enormous diffusion in Ficino's Latin translation. These 'seven governors', though called by the names of the seven planets, are not to be classed as 'astrology' in the normal sense. They are rather the planets as archetypal images, to be used as ladders on which ascent and descent is to be made by the seeker after gnosis or illumination. Camillo's theatre is a Hermetic memory system, based, as Camillo frequently states, on the philosophies of Marsilio Ficino and Pico della Mirandola. On these philosophies, the Hermetic-Cabalist core of Renaissance Neoplatonism, Camillo constructs his theatre, a plan of the psyche stocked with an elaborate system of images.

This introduction of Camillo's theatre may seem to be leading us away from Robert Klein. On the contrary it is leading us straight back to him, for, through one of those remarkable insights which the student of the Renaissance finds in Klein's work, Camillo's theatre becomes a very important guide to mannerist art theory.

One of Klein's essays, actually the one on form and meaning which gives the title to the book, is on Giovan Paolo Lomazzo, the well-known theorist of mannerist art. Klein was interested in Lomazzo, devoting several years of study to his works. One of these has the title *L'Idea del tempio della pittura* (1590). Klein pointed out (in an essay not included in the volume of English translations) that Lomazzo explicitly states that his Idea of the Temple of Painting is based on Camillo's *L'Idea del theatro*.

Lomazzo presents his *Tempio* as a more limited and inferior form of the vast conception of Camillo, that 'divine man' as he was called, who had included the whole universe in his *Theatro*. Lomazzo's more modest aim is to include the whole of art in his *Tempio*.

Like Camillo's theatre, Lomazzo's temple is divided into seven sections representing 'seven governors', that is to say the seven planets as archetypal forms, or 'shadows of ideas' as Giordano Bruno calls them, forms intermediary between forms in the lower world and the 'ideas' in the divine world. The expression 'seven governors' used in this sense comes ultimately, as Camillo states, from the Hermetic *Pimander*. Lomazzo no doubt knew the Hermetic source, as well as the use of the term by Camillo, and also by Cornelius Agrippa. Into this basically Hermetic-Platonic system, Lomazzo introduces seven great artists whom he associates with the seven governors. With the Saturnian governor, he places Michelangelo; with Apollo-Sol, Leonardo da Vinci; with Venus, Raphael; with Luna, Titian; and other artists with the remaining planetary governors.

One cannot quite realize the full force of Klein's discovery of Lomazzo's dependence on Camillo's theatre without looking at the plan of Camillo's system (drawn out in my *Art of Memory*). Lomazzo's placing of the artists with the seven governors implies the whole series of Saturnian, Venereal, and so on, images which are ranged in Camillo's theatre behind the planetary governors. Thus associated with Michelangelo would be Saturnian-style images; with Raphael, Venus-style images, and so on. I have used the word 'style' of these variations, but the word which Lomazzo uses is '*maniera*'. There is a Saturnian *maniera*, exemplified by the power and sternness of the great Saturnian artist, Michelangelo; there is a Venus *maniera*, typified by the softness and beauty of the exquisite Raphael, and so on. Pondering on these things one begins to wonder whether there is here an important clue to mannerist art theory. Was the mannerist artist one whose powers of expression were linked to astral *maniere*, not in the sense of astrology or astrological determinism but in the sense of this astral psychology, of the varying styles or *maniere* imprinted on the soul in its descent through the spheres?

In his suggestive pages on 'Magic and Art', Klein pursues these problems further. He notes during the Renaissance period a 'slow ascendancy of magical themes in the intellectualist theory of art'. This tendency was not restricted to the later years, but, as he says, it 'attended Neoplatonism', that is to say it belonged to the movement initiated by Ficino and Pico, the movement of Renaissance Neoplatonism which, as we know, had a core of Hermetic and Cabalist magic. Klein finds that in its application to art, it is clearly and openly theorized in the mannerist movement, and particularly by Lomazzo, both in his *Tempio della pittura* (1590) and in his *Trattato dell'arte della pittura* (1584). Klein showed – and this again was a discovery of his – that both these works are heavily influenced by Cornelius Agrippa, with many quotations, acknowledged and unacknowledged, from the *De occulta philosophia*. He concludes that in his magical conception of art, Lomazzo found 'confirmation, support, even guidance, in Agrippa'.

The magical conception of art includes the application of the astral psychology to the formation of magical, or talismanic, images in art, designed to influence the beholder through a kind of sympathetic magic. Klein acutely points out that Giordano Bruno in his *De vinculis in genere* sets out a comprehensive theory of 'links', and that this theory 'welded together in the strongest possible manner form and the meaning it bears. It was a general aesthetic of fascination, carried to its extreme, which, taken literally, would exclude the very possibility of a theory of art.'

The talismanic, magical view of art was, I believe, present from the start of the influence of Neoplatonism, in Ficino's magical theories applied to talismans, applied by Camillo to memory images in his theatre, expounded by Agrippa in his *De occulta philosophia* (which is compounded out of Ficino and Pico), and finally brought out into the open by Lomazzo in his so-called mannerist theory of art. This word 'mannerist', with its suggestion of affection, has lost its magical connection with astral *maniere*.

Klein is quite exceptional in pointing to Bruno's works on magic images as guides to 'mannerism'. This investigation could be carried much further, as no doubt Klein intended to do. In one of his books, the one on the composition of images, Bruno gives lists of images grouped under astral *maniere*. Bruno does not use this word, but he is doing what Camillo does in the theatre, though with more pronounced magical intention to fascinate. In a list of magical Venus images, Bruno describes one which sounds vaguely reminiscent of Botticelli's Venus. This is due to common dependence on the classical source, but to meet Venus rising from the sea and crowned with flowers in a list of images intended to fascinate the beholder and to induce in him a Venus *maniera* is interesting, because this is in fact what Botticelli's picture does.

Klein's style is difficult; sometimes he seems to contradict himself; but he is trying to say difficult things. Another example of his acute but involved discussion of magic is the essay on the concept of '*spirito peregrino*' in Dante which leads from an analysis of the trance, in which the spirit 'peregrinates' from the body, to a theory of magical psychology of the love-conceit.

The chapter on 'Utopian Urban Planning' is rich in detailed knowledge of utopian theory and its expression in architectural plans:

   . . . the elementary forms out of which ideal-city plans are
made serve to transform the draftsman into a magus. It is
difficult to suppress the thought that the well-ordered
labyrinth of Christianopolis had for Andreae the effect –
however unconscious – of an exorcism, and that when
Campanella transposed his abortive republic into the plastic

vision of the City of the Sun, he sensed in himself the
beneficent effect which the plan of that city was supposed to
work upon its inhabitants.

Klein does not mention the magical city in *Picatrix* which regulated
the life of its inhabitants through drawing down favourable astral
influences. There is no doubt that magic of this kind underlies
Campanella's plan for his City of the Sun (and the related Christianopolis of Andreae). The use of such city plans as memory
systems is relevant to the understanding of their meaning. We
know that Campanella's City was to be used in this way, and is
related to Giordano Bruno's more complex memory schemes.
The utopia chapter well illustrates Klein's double gift for detailed
learning and scholarship combined with the understanding of
underlying mental attitudes, or of the meaning within the form.

Much of Klein's writing consisted of reviews and criticism, in
which he excelled. Examples of his gifts in this direction in the
collected volume are his logical analysis of the principles of iconographical interpretation, based on the work of Panofsky, whom he
greatly admired as an art historian; and his essay on 'Burckhardt's
Civilization of the Renaissance Today'.

The enormous influence of Burckhardt's book throughout the
later nineteenth century and up to our own day is impressive
testimony of the brilliance of the writing and of Burckhardt's
power of presentation of many aspects of Renaissance culture to
form a comprehensive whole. He was a pioneer in his attempt to
use many types of material – for example festivals and their
imagery – in building up his interpretation of a period.

While paying full respect to Burckhardt's brilliance and originality, Klein also analyses the aspects of his work which are now
out of date. Burckhardt treats the Italian Renaissance as a complete
break with the Middle Ages, whereas we now know that there was
no such definite break. He assumes that the Italian Renaissance
contrasted with northern medieval backwardness, whereas we now
know that northern elements formed an integral part of the Italian
culture, and that it can be argued that contemporary Flemish or
Burgundian cultures were equally advanced and, in fact, strongly
influenced the Italian towns. And Klein notes how little attention
Burckhardt pays to history of ideas, mentioning, for example,
Florentine Neoplatonism only in passing, and without understanding that yearning for return to ancient sources which perme-

ates the Renaissance outlook. Klein's own work is in striking contrast to the Burckhardtian approach, with his concern for inner motives and attitudes informing outward changes. Klein's essay is useful to recommend to students on how to read Burckhardt today.

Klein's analyses in the final chapters of the breakdown of the Renaissance tradition and the rise of modern art raise questions which to many readers may be the most important aspect of his studies but which I have excluded from this review. Headings such as 'Notes on the End of the Image', 'The Eclipse of the Work of Art', 'Modern Painting and Phenomenology' may give some idea of the scope of these chapters. The last chapter on 'A Season in Hell' does not appear to refer to modern art but only to Rimbaud, though one wonders whether the End of the Image may have had anything to do with the ultimate despair.

It is with deep regret for the untimely disappearance of a brilliant mind that one lays down this subtle and complicated book.

Chapter Twenty-five

PARADOX AND PARADISE*

MODERN ADVANCE in the study of Renaissance historiography has concentrated mainly on Italy; the application of its results to English Renaissance historiography and literature has been curiously long delayed. This is strange, since the tracing of rhetorical themes in the English Renaissance has grown in recent years into a formidable output of studies. In this enthusiasm for rhetoric it seems to have been forgotten that history as developed in the Italian Renaissance was itself a branch of rhetoric allied to moral philosophy; that arising out of the emphasis on history there arose new schools of historical thought which transformed the old assumptions; that of all the Renaissance themes adopted in England in the sixteenth century the new emphasis on history was one of the most prominent. In England the old style of chronicle history still held the field throughout the century, though humanist influences came flowing in. Hall and Holinshed are chroniclers; a humanist educator, like Ascham, advises study of ancient historians for their style, and Thomas Elyot in *The Governour* and Walter Raleigh in his *History of the World* quote Cicero on the moral value of history. Humanist emphasis on exemplarism – on history as moral philosophy teaching right conduct by taking

---

* Review of Herschel Baker, *The Race of Time*, Toronto, 1967; Rosalie L. Colie, *Paradoxia Epidemica: The Renaissance Tradition of Paradox*, Princeton, 1966; and A. Bartlett Giamatti, *The Earthly Paradise and the Renaissance Epic*, Princeton, 1966, in *New York Review of Books*, 23 February 1967.

historical personages as examples of virtues and vices (this was of course also a medieval tradition) – was taken for granted, and humanist imitation of ancient historians flourished. How far the more advanced types of critical historical thinking really penetrated English theory or practice in the period is a moot question.

In his lectures at Toronto, now published as *The Race of Time*, Herschel Baker attacks the subject of English Renaissance historiography through studying three main themes, illustrated from a very wide range of reading. Among the many historians discussed or quoted are Holinshed, Speed, Camden, Selden, Thomas More, Cotton, Hakewill, Raleigh, Francis Bacon, and Milton. First he emphasizes that the Renaissance historian was concerned to find the 'truth' of history, whence it followed, since truths differed from opinions, that history tended to be strongly propagandist. Next he proves that the exemplarist view of history was dominant. Finally he discusses the 'Form of History' and finds that there was a growing dissatisfaction with traditional historical methods and a search for new approaches. He has skilfully organized his rich material to make these three points, and the points themselves are well chosen and fundamental.

The 'truth' of history which had to be set forth under the Tudor dynasty was the truth of the providential rise to power of the Tudors. All English chronicles must move towards this end; if they deviated from it, the censorship stepped in. We hardly yet realize the power of the censorship in Tudor England; as applied to history writing, it was devastating; Baker mentions the case of Fulke Greville, who aspired to write a history of the reign of Elizabeth but was denied access to the records by Cecil. The great official propagandist history was John Foxe's *Acts and Monuments*, basically a chronicle history adapted from Eusebius's history of the Church to the Tudor Protestant Reformation. Foxe's book was chained in churches as compulsory reading for loyal church-goers. All history, ancient or modern, could be suspect of 'taxing the present state', as Ben Jonson put it. It might be illuminating to compare the English historical output with that in contemporary France, where the unsettled and chaotic situation actually allowed of far more freedom of expression; there was no counterpart in England to that mass of fairly outspoken memoirs which make the sources for French history of the period almost embarrassingly profuse.

Yet it was precisely that chaotic situation which they saw across the water that did much to reconcile Englishmen of many differing shades of religious opinion to the stability and order of their Tudor monarchy, made them willing to write propagandist history in its favour, not excluding those myths of its Trojan descent which Polydore Vergil had exploded as factually unsound. The compulsory propagandist history was not necessarily insincere; after all that other more famous Virgil presumably really believed in Augustus as a valuable stabilizing figure and was not insincere in weaving round him the Trojan myth on which the Tudor myth was modelled, though from the historiographical point of view the question arises as to how far the supremacy of the monarchical idea and the subservience of history to it delayed the advent in England of more modernist and critical approaches to history.

In his second section, Baker draws together a mass of evidence of the dominant moralizing and exemplarist view of history. Though the material is again interestingly presented, one misses here some more definite recognition of historical exemplarism as itself a branch of humanist rhetoric, or more precise indication of the ancient historians which were taken as models, and of the mingling of humanist influences with the native chronicle tradition.

In the last section on the 'Form of History' the growing search for new historical methods is indicated by many quotations, some of them from little-known writers, a new emphasis on documentary research is stressed, and a gradual change towards more critical attitudes to history writing becomes apparent. Baker mentions Bruni and the Italians, but seems to think their influence relatively unimportant; he underestimates the significance of the spread of Machiavellian realism and perhaps of the influence of Guicciardini's tragic view of history. More might have been said of Thomas Blundeville as the first Englishman to put forward a theory of history writing. Nevertheless this section is most interesting, showing that a great golden age of imaginative, if uncritical, history gradually passed away.

A general criticism of the book might be that by studying more or less the same range of writers of the sixteenth and early seventeenth centuries under three heads, it breaks each of them up into three parts and blurs the outline of their individual significance. Yet this is but the reverse side of its quality in laying emphasis on the right points. The book as a whole is a useful move towards opening up the neglected field of English Renaissance historiography in a scientific way. And it is significant that it is written by an expert in English literature who has constantly in mind the application of his themes to poets and playwrights. It is to be hoped that the book will initiate more systematic study of history as propaganda, history as rhetoric, history as poetry, in relation to the great literary figures.

In a clever little book, *The Happy Beast*, published more than thirty years ago, George Boas discussed paradoxes, 'little essays against the prevailing opinion of mankind' which were popular in the Renaissance: that it is better to be ignorant than wise, that war is better than peace, better to live in a cottage than a palace, to be in prison than at liberty. In a Renaissance smart set a lady might suddenly 'try the wit' of a courtier by demanding an amusing speech in praise of flies, quartan fever, or baldness, and the wisest and gravest, like Erasmus, would break into paradoxical praise of folly. The paradoxical encomium was a branch of classical rhetoric well acclimatized in England. Puttenham called it 'the wondrer' because of its surprising effect. Interest in Renaissance paradox has been gathering momentum and has now reached a crest in Rosalie Colie's book.

There is room for a book on this subject, which should be based on careful definitions of what constitutes paradox in its various aspects and of how the Renaissance used this rather elusive mode. These requirements are not fulfilled in *Paradoxia Epidemica*. The rhetorical paradox is assimilated to the logical paradox by an impossible argument, inducing confusions which run all through the book, nor is any attempt made to define and delimit Renaissance paradox, to distinguish what is genuinely paradoxical from other modes of expression or thought. This confusion is, however, intentional, since Miss Colie seems to believe that paradox, as she interprets it, does cover practically everything in the period. Had she been more precise in her definitions and more moderate in her claims she might have made a good case for paradoxy as an important ingredient in the Renaissance outlook, but she wildly overdoes it. That favourite Platonic image of the boxes made in the likeness of ugly Silenuses which when opened were found to contain holy things, as the comic exterior of Socrates hid his divine teaching, implies for her a 'strict correspondence of opposites' and is therefore a paradox and one connected with the rhetorical paradox since it includes the element of surprise. It is not a paradox but an image or metaphor relating to the fundamental Renaissance concept that truth is hidden under many disguises, as in the theory of mythology where the fables are the husk or bark under which truth is hidden. Or again, Utopia, says Miss Colie, is a paradox because it is nowhere and to be nowhere is an ontological paradox, a fantastic overstraining in the effort to stretch everything on the Procrustean bed of paradox.

The book is divided into rhetorical and psychological paradoxes; paradoxes in divine ontology; ontological paradoxes; epistemological paradoxes. Under these heads are treated, among other subjects and writers, Rabelais, Petrarch, Sidney, Donne, Marvell, Milton, Burton, Spenser, Herbert, Shakespeare, Pascal, still-life painting, and suicide. Milton deals in paradoxes of time and eternity, foreknowledge and free will; *The Faerie Queene* is about being and becoming and is therefore based on an ontological paradox; Montaigne's self-examination represents an epistemological paradox of self-reference. No coherent picture emerges from this ambitious programme, which is confused by the basic failure to define the subject, strains to include much that is not relevant, and omits much that would have been relevant.

The Renaissance 'epidemic' of paradox died down, thinks Miss Colie, when the scientific revolution took over. Paradox became degraded as one result 'of a revolution in thought which valued clarity and exactness above the tricky duplicities of comprehension induced by paradox'. In support of this she quotes from Galileo's *Dialogue Concerning the Two World Systems* passages in speeches by Simplicius against maintaining paradoxes and deriding the 'liar' paradox as a sophism. She has forgotten that Simplicius is the Aristotelian pedant who is arguing against the paradox of heliocentricity. His fatuities are not evidence of Galileo's own views, as she takes them to be, but quite the reverse. On this curious misunderstanding she builds several pages of argument about the decline of Renaissance paradoxy with the coming of the scientific revolution!

The best parts of the book are the studies of the English paradoxical poets; here Miss Colie's wide reading and experience as a stimulating exponent of English literature show to great advantage. Her analysis of the love conceit brings out its paradoxical aspects and she suggests a possible answer to problems such as the simultaneous maintaining of Petrachrist and Anti-Petrarchist opinions, as by Sidney. Her examination of Donne's poetry on the two levels of love paradoxes and divine paradoxes will be read with interest, and she has much to say on Shakespeare and paradox. There are suggestive and imaginative insights in the book, which, though not an authoritative study of Renaissance paradox, certainly arouses thought on the subject.

The Earthly Paradise is an example of the approach to the Renaissance through tracing the history of what E. R. Curtius called a topos. It begins with classical gardens and golden ages, traces the absorption of these themes into Christianity, their conflation with the Garden of Eden or Earthly Paradise, and studies the garden theme in Dante, Ariosto, Tasso, Spenser, and Milton. The book is a sound piece of scholarship, with very good bibliographies, and may be rather warmly recommended as useful for students. Usefulness of this kind is indeed the modest aim of the author, and though the tracing of topoi can lead in some hands to dullness, this is not the case with Giamatti's handling of his paradises. He is a subtle psychologist, extremely sensitive to poetry – with the great advantage of being equally at home in Latin, Italian, and English poetry – and his garden sequences present what amounts to quite an original approach to Spenser and Milton.

'My Spenser', says Giamatti, 'is really a very conventional one.' He sees the poet as taking the method of allegory from his medieval sources but mingling it with influences from the epics of the Italian Renaissance. This is indeed an elementary idea, because Spenser himself states that he is following Ariosto and Tasso. Why then does Giamatti's deceptively simple approach come as something of a surprise? Because we tend to think of allegory as essentially medieval, without studying its Renaissance transformations, and because no one reads Ariosto and Tasso.

The theme, or one of the themes, which Giamatti studies through his garden images is that of illusion as both the instrument and the result of evil. Astolfo, master of good magic, tries to educate the simple knight Ruggiero into seeing the difference between illusion and reality as he plays for his soul in the false garden paradise of Alcina, malignant manipulator of illusion. Ariosto's Alcina is succeeded by Tasso's Armida who makes the artificial seem real in the garden of delights where she seduces Rinaldo to abandon his magic shield (like Ruggiero before him) and forget his mission to recover the City. Tasso succeeds brilliantly in presenting a double vision, the garden on its own terms as the home of delights and the garden as false by the standards of the City. When Giamatti passes from his fascinating explorations of the Italian enchanted gardens to Acrasia's Bower of Bliss in *The Faerie Queene*, he carries us with him to full realization of how essential it is not to jump straight from medieval allegory into Spenser; here is the same theme of illusion as the source and result of evil explored with a new and quite unmedieval subtlety.

Giamatti suggests that Milton turned from the Renaissance enchanted gardens and returned to the true Christian Earthly Paradise which Dante had depicted, yet that in Milton's Paradise the tempter is a Renaissance master of illusion. The remarkable analysis of Satan's illusionist techniques and of the corruption of the garden into a landscape of despair owes something to examination of these themes by other scholars, but Giamatti has contributed a new understanding of the Miltonic garden by taking us first on his voyage of discovery through the beauty and duplicity of the Italian false paradises.

This is comparative literature as it ought to be done, not the superficial tracing of 'sources', but the organic study of a theme at a deep level. Giamatti asks where the image of the garden went, why modern man no longer conceives of happiness as a garden existence, no longer yearns for a lost Eden. He suggests that it is because man is diminished and 'in losing the Renaissance breadth of imagination, we have lost the earthly paradise once again, not simply as a state of joy, but also as an object of hope'. Another answer might be that true and false paradises depend on a conception of innocence which is no longer admired.

Chapter Twenty-six

ARTISTS AND THE SPIRIT OF THEIR AGE*

IN THE preface to this book, Hugh Trevor-Roper describes himself as a 'plain historian' but one who believes that art, like literature, is an expression of ideas and therefore an inseparable part of history. 'History which ignores art or literature is jejune history, just as a society without art or literature is a jejune society, and, conversely, art and literature which are studied in detachment from history are only half understood.' The words seem obviously true, though some literary and art critics are determined, on principle, to operate in a historical vacuum. The refreshing quality of Professor Trevor-Roper's book is that he makes his way through great periods of European art in the character of an immensely intelligent historian who can draw on a detailed range of information of a kind usually classed as 'art history' which he deploys as an integral part of history, or history of ideas.

The book is about four monarchs and their patronage of art. The four are the Emperor Charles V, King Philip II of Spain, the Emperor Rudolf II, the Archdukes Albert and Isabella. All were closely related Habsburgs. Their combined reigns cover perhaps the most momentous epoch in the whole of European history. The artists whom they patronized include some of the greatest names in the history of European art. Through study of the tastes

---

* Review of Hugh Trevor-Roper, *Princes and Artists: Patronage and Ideology at Four Habsburg Courts 1517-1633*, 1976, in *Times Higher Education Supplement*, 5 November 1976.

in art of these princes, as shown in their patronage and collections, the eye of the historian seeks to uncover the movement of ideas.

The story begins with the Emperor Charles V opening up glorious visions of universal empire. Titian was the artist who understood Charles, who alone was privileged to paint the portraits of the Emperor and who succeeded in expressing through those portraits the 'imperial idea' of Charles V. It was an idea Roman and commanding in its world-wide claims, yet also sensitive to religious duties and obligations. Charles was influenced by Erasmus. Many of his contemporaries hoped that there might be found, through the imperial office as wielded by such an emperor, an Erasmian and liberal solution of the religious problems of the age. The great Titian portraits of Charles V, beautifully reproduced and excellently placed, illustrate the theme of history through art in their expression of the 'imperial idea' of Charles V. The sculptor Leone Leoni was another who fully understood and expressed the idea. Charles was fortunate that there were artists of such quality in the world, but it was because of his Habsburg artistic taste that he recognized and employed them.

Professor Trevor-Roper emphasizes the decade of the 1550s as the terrible time when earlier hopes collapsed, and instead of reform came persecution and war. His remarkable power of rapid analysis and quick, and always vivid, presentation of a wide range of facts and ideas in a few words is well illustrated by his page on the 1550s.

> The 1550s were to prove a decisive decade in the century of the Reformation, the water-shed of the century. They marked the extinction in blood and fire of the humanist hope. . . In the 1550s a disillusioned generation turned from reform to persecution. . . These are the years of the fierce *Placards* against heresy in the Netherlands. They are also the years of the *Chambre Ardente* in Paris, the revived Inquisition in Rome, the Smithfield Fires in England, the burning of the Spanish Erasmians at Seville and Valladolid. After the fierce cautery of that terrible decade, the climate of Christendom could never be the same.

It was in the middle of the terrible decade that the Emperor Charles V abdicated, and his son Philip succeeded to part of his dominions as King of Spain.

Philip belonged to the new age – repression, persecution, war, must stamp out religious disunity throughout his realms. The Duke of Alva with his armies was sent to the Netherlands; the dreaded Spanish Inquisition set to work with zeal. And a vast building arose, the Escorial, for Philip both the mausoleum of his family and the symbol of the unyielding rigidity of Catholic reaction in its Spanish form. The building had to be decorated, and in describing Philip's dealings with artists, Professor Trevor-Roper seeks to bring out the trend of the new times.

Actually, Philip continued his father's patronage. Titian and Leoni were still the favoured artists but they did not come to Spain, preferring to keep at a safe distance from the gloomy and dangerous world of the Spanish court. Closest to Philip of all his artistic advisers was the architect, Herrera, highly favoured by the King, constantly in his company, and in his deepest confidence concerning the decoration of the Escorial and other matters.

The change of temper in the new age is illustrated through comparison of a statue by Leoni of Charles V in a heroic pose, dominating a monster, and a coloured wooden image of the Duke of Alva in the same pose, dominating a monster one of whose heads is a parody of Queen Elizabeth I. The comparison brings out the frightful character of the experience through which Europe passed when the 'imperial idea' of Charles V turned into the dark death-wish of Philip's religious policies as carried out by Alva.

The plan of treating four Habsburg monarchs in succession brings us next to the Emperor Rudolf II, Philip's uncle, ruling over the German half of what had been the empire of Charles V, plus the kingdoms of Hungary and Bohemia. Rudolf moved the imperial court from Vienna to Prague, capital of an ancient kingdom which had been associated with Hussite heresy long before the Reformation. The change indicated Rudolf's heterodox views as compared with the rigid orthodoxy of the Spanish branch. In the great Prague palace he assembled vast collections, which reflected his interest in nature, in the arts and sciences, and a philosophy and outlook strongly tinged with Renaissance occultism. To Prague came artists, scientists, occultists from all over Europe. Tycho Brahe, the Danish astronomer, Giordano Bruno, the Hermetic philosopher, John Dee and his associate Edward Kelley. The collections and the art of Rudolf's court are illustrated, and as the reader turns the pages of the book, he comes to Prague and the Rudolfine world, after gazing at the Escorial in Philip's Madrid. Professor Trevor-Roper compares the Escorial with the Hradschin in Prague, both palaces inhabited by peculiar

Habsburgs; in one, the fanatical Philip lived in gloomy seclusion surrounded by his monks; in the other, Rudolf hid himself amongst his alchemists, occultists, Lullists, Cabalists in what was perhaps a desperate effort to escape from the bigotry of the hated Spanish branch of his family. Rudolfine occultism became a symbol of liberalism and religious tolerance; its influence spread to the Protestant courts of Germany; the Elizabethans were very much aware of it.

Though the contrast between Madrid and Prague brings out the rift between the Spanish and the German Habsburgs, yet it appears from an article (which seems to have escaped Professor Trevor-Roper's notice) by René Taylor in *Essays in the History of Architecture presented to Rudolf Wittkower* (1967) that the Escorial may have been a 'magical' building, its design influenced by a recent reconstruction of the Temple of Solomon, and that its occupant was secretly involved in the Hermetic trends of the age. Both Philip and his intimate friend and adviser, the architect Herrera, were ardent Lullists. Herrera owned two copies of Dee's *Monas hieroglyphica*, a copy of one of Bruno's works on magic mnemonics, and a whole range of other examples of Renaissance Hermetic literature. Herrera's mathematical, mechanical, and probably magical interests have suggested to Taylor a comparison between Herrera and Dee. One wonders whether the esoteric interests evidently rife in the Escorial and unmentioned by Philip's contemporary Spanish biographer may have had anything to do with the King's passion for the strange pictures of Hieronymus Bosch.

As the last of his four Habsburg courts, Professor Trevor-Roper chooses that of the Archdukes Albert and Isabella, installed as rulers of the Catholic Netherlands by Philip II just before his death. This chapter is the most brilliant in the book, with its evocation of a society broken by incessant war and catastrophe, struggling to heal its wounds and to recapture civilized values. Much that is not well known to English readers is made clear in this chapter and its illustrations, particularly the importance of Justus Lipsius and his formulation of Christian stoicism as the philosophy which enabled sufferers to endure the devastation and to find ways of evading the religious impasse. Lipsian stoicism is seen as the Erasmian spirit adapted to the new age. Rubens was formed in the circle of Lipsius, and in that atmosphere of conciliation, the Counter Reformation influences fostered by the rule of the Archdukes became acceptable, or were accepted for the sake of peace.

Yet Rubens's acceptance of it was not uncritical, as Professor Trevor-Roper points out. In a recent article, Elizabeth McGrath has shown that Rubens introduced into his designs for the entry of the new Habsburg ruler into Antwerp in 1635 a lament for the past glories of the city and for the loss of its prosperity under Spanish rule.[1] The old Burgundian spirit still lived in this great artist.

The brilliantly original plan of comparing the art of four Habsburg courts opens new vistas of historical understanding, particularly through its integration of Rubens, a somewhat isolated artist, into the great world of the empire of Charles V in its disintegration. Turning the last pages of the book, we now see the tremendous figures of Rubens, overwhelming in their power and vitality, and we see them in the final stage of a journey which has taken us from the Netherlands of Charles V, to the Spain of Philip II, the Prague of Rudolf II, and back again to the Netherlands of the Archdukes. The text is beautifully and excitingly written; the illustrations excellently chosen and placed. To live in this book will be a revealing experience for all students of European culture.

Chapter Twenty-seven

IMPERIAL MYSTERIES*

STUDENTS OF the history and culture of Europe in the last decades of the sixteenth century and the first of the seventeenth know that there is a vast no-man's-land in the middle of this vital period. The character, the court, the interests, the influence of the Emperor Rudolf II have never been adequately studied. There has been much specialist literature in German and in Central European languages but no book of any weight or authority on the Emperor in English. So Rudolf, immured in self-chosen isolation in his palace in Prague, surrounded by the 'wonder rooms' which housed his immense collection of artistic treasures and curiosities, remains a mysterious figure of legend. Was he mad, as many have supposed? And if not mad, what was the nature of that life of secret contemplation, what the motive springs of that vast curiosity, of that patronage which attracted to Prague alchemists, occultists, scientists, artists from all over Europe? And what did the imperial figure who encouraged all this rich and varied activity stand for in that confused age? What were his political aims, his religion, the 'secret' of his search for hidden wisdom?

Robert Evans has written a remarkable book, full of information of a kind accessible nowhere else. Only a scholar with the rare type of equipment which he possesses could have written such a book. Evans combines knowledge of the culture and languages of

---

* Review of R. J. W. Evans, *Rudolf II and his World: A Study in Intellectual History 1576-1612*, Oxford, 1973, in *New Statesman*, 18 May 1973.

Eastern Europe, and of the Eastern European Renaissance, so little known in the West, with knowledge of the Renaissance as a whole and of modern scholarship concerning those Hermetic disciplines and outlook which characterized the recluse of Prague and his circle. Though the Emperor himself remains withdrawn, Evans's method of approach has immensely enriched our understanding of him. The method is to range over the whole Rudolfine world, giving detailed information about hosts of little-known figures, and some well-known ones, and so to build up through study of his entourage the hidden figure behind it. I can only give an impression here of the extraordinary richness of the book.

Evans divides Rudolf and his world into chapters and then seeks the unity behind the various aspects. First of all, there is the basic importance to Rudolf of the imperial idea, his consciousness of ancestors, particularly Charles V, even though the Empire by that time was a still-powerful symbol rather than a power in any real sense. And deeply important for Rudolf's almost instinctive reaction to contemporary issues was his suspicion and dread of the Spanish branch of his house, of the extremist and active Counter-Reformation policies with which the Spanish Habsburgs were identified. Rudolf represented the Austrian Habsburgs and the more tolerant ways of his father Maximilian II. He was not unconscious of the reforming and religious side of the imperial inheritance, though he interpreted this in a secretive and apparently negative way. Much of Rudolf's policy of inanition was a policy of blocking and evading the Jesuit and Counter-Reformation pressures from Rome and Madrid. His own religious attitude remained nebulous and undefined; certainly he was against confessional extremists, whether Catholic or Protestant, inclining towards the liberalism of earlier Renaissance attitudes. Here, his favourite physician and his favourite confessor are indicators; about both of these key figures Evans has new things to say. The physician, Johannes Crato, belonged to conciliatory and eirenic groups, to the so-called 'crypto-Calvinism', the cryptic side of which inclined not towards extremes of Calvinist doctrine but rather quite the reverse, towards eirenic or mystical solutions of religious problems. Crato numbered among his friends Hubert Languet, the friend of Philip Sidney, and Sidney himself, and he was in touch with the 'Family of Love' groups around Plantin and Ortelius in the Netherlands. The favourite confessor was Johannes Pistorius, Cabalist, and editor of a noted collection of Cabalist texts. It was Pistorius, and not the more strictly orthodox

religious advisers in his entourage, who helped Rudolf through
the near-breakdown which he experienced around 1600. Turning
next to Rudolf's patronage of learning and letters, Evans examines
a curiously neglected field and has much to tell about the emblema-
tist Sambucus and his library (he is invaluable on libraries, so
important as an index of cultural range), about Jessenius,
immersed in Neoplatonism and *prisca theologia*, about Hajek,
astronomer-astrologer and friend of Kepler, and many others. He
next surveys Rudolf and the fine arts, Rudolf as patron and collector; this is the side of him which has been the least neglected,
though it has not been assimilated into his world-view as a whole,
as in Evans's study.

Then comes the central preoccupation which draws all the
aspects of the Emperor's complex personality together – Rudolf
and the occult arts. Rudolf's occultism was not that of an isolated
crank but was rooted in the magical universe of the Renaissance,
in which everything is linked with everything else by magical
correspondences and the adept believes it possible to penetrate to
hidden divine powers. As Evans interprets him, Rudolf emerges
as really rather like the two magi who were amongst those who
came to Prague – Giordano Bruno and John Dee. As Bruno
sought to include the whole universe in the images of his magic
memory systems, so Rudolf used the innumerable objects in his
'wonder rooms' for contemplative efforts to grasp the whole. As
Dee sought to summon spiritual powers from which to learn the
secrets of the universe, so Rudolf's 'spiritualism' was not of the
kind suggested by modern uses of this word, but fitted into the
world-view associated with the magical and animated universe.
And as both Bruno and Dee nourished schemes of some universal
reform, connected with their manipulations of the magical universe, so the Emperor, weighed down and obsessed with the world
responsibility of his sacred imperial office, brooded in the recesses
of his Prague palace over unifications of the cosmos, collections
symbolizing all its contents, meditating with astronomers, astrolo-
gers, alchemists, occultists, artists, over ways of penetrating to
the one mystery behind nature of which the Empire was the one
symbol in the political sphere.

Mad, you may say. Yet what is madness in one world-view
may not be madness in another. Within that world of people
which Evans re-creates for us, the Emperor was not mad. The
members of the great noble families of Bohemia and all the characters whom most English readers will meet for the first time in this

book lived in similar mental worlds. The art, the learning, the science, rested upon similar presuppositions about the magical universe. And, moreover, this late survival of Renaissance mentality in its most extreme form was not a hardened reaction. It was alive and it was liberal. Within its own strange frame of reference it represented an 'open society'. Its dreaded enemy was the modern hardening of intolerance in both its extreme Counter-Reformation Catholic and extreme Protestant forms. It feared the loss of the old tolerance, the liberal search for middle ways of conciliation, the open-minded welcoming of new possibilities which the modern doctrinaire extremists would meet with persecution and repression.

Against this background, the famous visit of John Dee and Edward Kelley to Bohemia in 1583-9 stands out in a new light. Dee's strange accounts of communications with the spirit world, his schemes for universal reform 'when set against the contemporary mood . . . grow much more comprehensible'. His wide European reputation gains in meaning as belonging to universalist hopes and plans familiar in the context of Rudolfine occultism and imperialism. Evans provides more evidence than has hitherto been available about the nature of Dee's mission in Bohemia. He quotes the words of a Lutheran leader who knew Dee personally:

> A learned and renowned Englishman whose name was Doctor
> Dee came to Prague to see the Emperor Rudolf II and was
> at first well received by him; he predicted that a miraculous
> reformation would presently come about in the Christian world
> and would prove the ruin not only of the city of
> Constantinople but of Rome also. These predictions he did
> not cease to spread among the populace.

According to this same Lutheran source, Rudolf's later dismissal of Dee was due to the papal nuncio having stirred up the Emperor against him.

After leaving Prague, Dee found a refuge on the estate of a member of the Rožmberk family, and here Evans's knowledge of the Rožmberks, their circle and interests, fills in the background of the stay of Dee and Kelley in Bohemia. They were but two individuals among the large clientèle of alchemists and occultists patronized by this powerful Bohemian family, a group with wide European connections and representing a liberal middle way, a search for salvation in a menacing world through appeal to Hermetic, Cabalist, alchemical influences.

In a book published last year, Peter French studied John Dee as 'the Elizabethan Magus'. Dee's life and career in Elizabethan England seem more than sufficient as a life-work for one man. Yet he had another life in his many contacts with foreign scholars, his trips abroad, of which the visit to Bohemia was the last and most important. For Evans, the most significant period of Dee's life was the years spent in Bohemia. His mission to Prague

> was conceived on a grand scale; Dee sought a world reform by harnessing ancient spiritual powers and working through occult and magical forces. The legends surrounding him and Kelley are muddled and far-fetched, but they contain a grain of truth. . . Irrationality, even superstition, was not merely a cover for action or a cloudiness of perception: it formed a vital component of contemporary intellectual activity. The very worst misunderstanding – of Dee and Kelley no less than of Rudolf – consists in under-rating its role.

Thus, in the context of the world of Rudolf, Dee appears as a figure whose missionary activities are understandable in relation to that world. 'Dee made himself reprehensible to orthodox Catholicism precisely because his message was both *relevant* and *meaningful* to his Prague audience.'

About the other famous magus, present in Prague at the same time as Dee and Kelley, Evans also has illuminating new material to present. Giordano Bruno and his works were known in Bohemia. That interesting character, Johann Wacker, who knew Philip Sidney, possessed a copy of the *Spaccio della bestia trionfante*. Hans von Nostitz, a member of the Bohemian aristocracy, a Lullist and a poet (the kind of person about whom only Evans would be full of information), had attended Bruno's lectures in Paris, took notes on them, and incorporated Brunian notions in his obscure works on mnemonics. The extreme importance of the Prague atmosphere for the understanding of the 'mission' of late Renaissance seers like Bruno and Dee is borne in on the reader of Evans's book. Bruno's mission ended with his death at the stake in Rome in 1600. Dee's mission would appear to have to come to an end when he returned to England.

Evans does not take the history of the ideas with which he has been concerned later than 1612, the year in which Rudolf died.

The seeds which Dee sowed were to have a tremendous after-growth in the Rosicrucian movement. Evans's picture of Dee preaching a universal reformation in Prague, announced by signs and portents, fits remarkably with the universal reformation announced in Germany, some years after Rudolf's death, in the Rosicrucian manifestos, which definitely associate their message with Dee through quotation from one of his most significant works.

In its massive scholarship, Evans's book must be hailed as a major work, another milestone on the road to the new approach to the history of thought through critical and historical study of areas once regarded as out of bounds for serious historians. The great reservoir of Hermetic influences (to use this word as an inclusive term) represented by Rudolfine Prague has been opened up and made accessible by this amazingly detailed and informative study. Evans's strength lies in the actual presentation and analysis of a large range of material. He is less strong on interpreting his evidence; the discussions of 'mannerism' and 'baroque', for example, represent a temporary lapse into rather second-hand generalizations after the splendidly high levels of his original scholarship. He is, however, very perceptive on religious history. His careful analyses of the impact of Counter-Reformation influences on Bohemia are most illuminating.

What is now coming more and more to the fore in the treatment of the history of ideas in Europe in the significant years immediately before the emergence of the modern period is the way in which the inhabitants of the magical universe were turning towards the world of nature in a spirit of investigation which prefigures, and leads up to, the scientific revolution. Francis Bacon reflects the Rosicrucian manifestos; Isaac Newton copies out the works of Michael Maier, an alchemist-physician who had formed one of Rudolf's circle in Prague. Yet, as Evans points out, for an observer living within the magical universe the exact study of natural forms involves a kind of magical identification with such forms, rather than objective analysis. Even such a subject as mechanics, the fascination with clocks or mechanical contrivances, presupposes, for those still within the magical universe, a preoccupation with mechanism as a living, a talismanic, attracter of forces. A great problem for the future is to elucidate the steps by which the magical universe lost its magic and gave way to the mechanical universe. And here the world of Rudolf II must contain many of the major clues. It was, after all, the world which Kepler chose to work in.

Chapter Twenty-eight

THE GREAT ERASMUS*

THIS BOOK is fascinating reading now. How the *Colloquies* must have been devoured when first-rate journalism was a thing as yet unknown, a thing only just made possible by the then new-born art of printing. For a women's page on how to manage your husband read 'Marriage'. Or for an exposé of conditions in students' hostels in Paris, read 'A Fish Diet'. Or, for an up-to-date coverage of a pilgrimage to the shrine of St Thomas of Canterbury just before the Reformation, read 'A Pilgrimage for Religion's Sake'. What treasure of gold and silver and gems as big as eggs glitter in this dimly lighted shrine; what constant unhygienic kissing of unsavoury relics; what comic patter by the guides; what sharp little vignettes – for instance, the crowd of old men from an almshouse rushing at the pilgrim on the narrow part of the road with St Thomas's shoe to be kissed. The mystery of medieval Canterbury recedes as we make the pilgrimage with this most amusing man, who is as germ-conscious as any modern tourist in backward countries.

But the brilliant writer, making a first use of the opportunity provided by the new medium to reflect critically and to influence profoundly the life of his times, is only one aspect of the complex phenomenon which is summed up under the name Erasmus. The classical scholar, the fervent believer in 'good letters', good Latin-

---

* Review of *The Colloquies of Erasmus*, translated by Craig R. Thompson, Chicago, 1965, in *New York Review of Books*, 1 July 1965.

ity, in a literary culture based exclusively on classical authors as the only basis of true education – in short, Erasmus the humanist is present on every page of the *Colloquies*. This it was which made his every utterance so impressive. Here was a man steeped in the New Learning, who wielded the new Latin with infinite flexibility and skill, who could draw on inexhaustible funds of apt learned allusion. How fashionable was this new style of Erasmus's and how intensively it was to be imitated.

Beneath all these enormous attractions lay the vein of religious seriousness, giving weight and timeliness to these fascinating writings. Beginning with Erasmus's curiously modern physical sensitivity which made him unable to support the stink of rotten salt fish, the dialogue between a fishmonger and a butcher in 'A Fish Diet' passes on to the theme of spiritual liberty, where for a blind following of man-made ordinances, such as the rules for fasting, he calls for the substitution of a true effort to follow the Gospel teachings. The kindly and gentle evangelical religion is supported by a classical nurture which interprets its favourite ancient authors as Christians before Christianity, as in the famous invocation to Saint Socrates in the charming colloquy called 'The Godly Feast'. In this essay, friends meet in a beautiful garden for a banquet; their talk passes easily and happily from witty classical allusion to devout examination of Scriptural texts. This feast of learning and piety sums up Erasmus's panacea for the times, the return to pure Gospel teaching as found in the Book, and the return to pure good letters as found in those hardly less sacred books, the classics.

Erasmus is, or so it seems to me, one of whom the often misapplied term of 'Christian humanist' can be used with perfect accuracy. Born in Rotterdam in 1466, he was a true humanist in the precise sense of the term of one concerned with a philological and literary approach to classical texts. And he associated this culture with a Christian programme. In his earlier and more hopeful years he believed that a golden age would come when there had arrived an international society of politely learned people, communicating easily with one another in an international language of good Latin. His remedy for the religious disorders was that of a humanist scholar with an intense belief in the sovereign importance of a well-edited text. The remedy was to use the new invention of printing to make available the basic texts of Christianity. Hence the primary labours of his life devoted to the publication and annotation of the New Testament and of the Greek and Latin Fathers of the Church. The secondary activity was the pouring forth of writings like the *Colloquies* which diffused the Erasmian spirit, critical and kindly, classical and evangelical, the spirit of a Christian man whose culture was purely literary.

The *Colloquies* began as dialogues on bright and interesting topics designed for use in teaching boys the Latin language; they were expanded in edition after edition to include all the themes most dear to Erasmus, forming a marvellous mirror of the times as seen by a humanist scholar and an evangelical Christian. This genesis of the *Colloquies* is in a sense illuminating for the Erasmian humanism as a whole. As they developed out of 'grammar', so did Erasmian humanism develop to include his whole religious outlook. Belief in the power of the book, in a good and critically established text, and in the diffusion of such books through printing, is the mainspring of the huge labours of the life of Erasmus, which was passed in close association with the printing press.

Erasmian humanism, though it derived of course from Italian humanism, particularly as developed by Lorenzo Valla, was different from it in that it included the new Christian pietistic spirit of the *devotio moderna*, diffused in Erasmus's native country of Holland. Though Erasmus himself never broke with the Catholic Church and was shocked by much in early Protestantism, yet Erasmian humanism was the direct ancestor of Protestant humanism. Probably nowhere did the Erasmian influence take so strong a hold as in England. As the author of this new translation of the *Colloquies* reminds us, English translations of some of them appeared at the time of the Dissolution of the Monasteries to encourage the process by disseminating Erasmus's satires. The Tudor Church was permeated with Erasmian influences; and the substitution of a philological and literary classical culture for the old philosophical culture was to persist as the normal education of a 'parson' right through the main periods of English history. The trace of this was stamped on English life, letters, and religion, and, reading the *Colloquies*, one senses the genesis of so much that is attractive in the 'humane' piety of the generations, and also, at times, of the spirit of donnishness.

Now that classical culture is dead, now that the printed book has lost its prestige, we may look back and ask ourselves the question which Huizinga asked. Were Erasmus and his fellow-workers as leaders of civilization on a wrong track? In spite of the gentleness and tolerance which make Erasmianism an oasis for the spirit amidst the religious conflicts of the sixteenth century, in spite of the beautiful fruits of human character brought forth in the long tradition of pious literary classicism, did Erasmianism, in fact, introduce a fatal crack in the cultural tradition by its isolation of literature and religion from philosophy and science? The Neoplatonists were perhaps working along an ultimately more hopeful line with their attempts at comparative religion. They were certainly much nearer to the trends eventually leading to the emergence of seventeenth-century science, which humanism of the Erasmian type was to drive into an opposite camp.

The new English translation of the *Colloquies* by Craig R. Thompson, the first complete translation to be published since 1725, renders them in a lively and 'colloquial' style which gives that impression of immediate and urgent contact with the reader which was one of Erasmus's great gifts. In a lucid Introduction, Professor Thompson indicates the main problems in Erasmus scholarship, including the hardest one of all: Erasmus and Luther, Erasmus and the Reformation. 'Printing alone', he says, 'does not explain Erasmus, any more than it explains Luther, who enjoyed the same advantage and exploited it just as successfully.' Though these two men were both concerned with attacking abuses and corruptions in the Church, through the same medium, the fundamental difference in temper between them – through which Luther initiated the schism which Erasmus never intended – is one of the great imponderables of history. When the Reformation got under way, Erasmus found himself in the inevitable position of the tolerant person. Hated by the conservatives for having laid the egg which Luther hatched, execrated by the revolutionaries for his lack of 'commitment' amidst the burning issues of the day, what did Erasmus himself think in those last years after the outbreak of the storm? The advocate of Christian tolerance and unity saw the beginnings of the great schism. The pacifist and hater of war watched the growth of a situation which would lead to the most cruel wars that Europe had ever known, the wars of religion of the sixteenth century. The Erasmian dream of the polite Europe bound together in unity under its Christian princes was most painfully shattered by the march of events beyond the control of the scholar in his study. Delicately ironical as he was, how did that scholar react to the coarse bludgeoning of the terrible irony of history? One has the impression that he was too old and ill and tired to face it.

In addition to his general Introduction, Professor Thompson prefaces each colloquy with a note which leads into the subject of the dialogue and suggests bibliography for following it up. These notes open up routes into a very wide range of subjects; some are better than others, and the best ones are very good indeed; but even for subjects in which the translator seems less at home (Erasmus and Reuchlin, for example) some useful help is given. Professor Thompson promises to provide a further volume of more detailed commentary, and his modest hope that the translation 'may be of interest to the reader of general literature, if that old-fashioned character still exists, and useful to students whose special province is the social, literary, and religious history of the Renaissance' is certainly justified.

The research student looking for 'sources' will find them staring him in the face, as colloquy after colloquy reminds him of plays or novels. This was one of the most widely read books, not only in the Renaissance but long after; no student of English literature can ignore it. It is immensely rich for students of social history. Erasmus was sympathetic and enlightened in his attitude to women; the learned lady who pleads for advanced education with the reactionary abbot may be Thomas More's daughter, Margaret Roper. He takes an unusual interest in such subjects as the organization (or lack of organization) of the fish and meat trades. He is horribly fascinated by diseases, particularly syphilis and the plague, and has a shrewd idea that one might catch things in the stove-heated rooms of German inns, which from his description of them seems more than likely. How he hated dirt and stinks! It would be interesting to know whether he was the first to have this highly developed longing for sanitation.

And for the student of human nature, this book is the revelation of a most extraordinary character. In spite of the solemn question which I have asked as to the rightness of the direction which Erasmus took, there can be no doubt that he is himself a wonderful example of the development of a richly humane personality out of Christian humanism. Irritable through overwork and through an oversensitive physical organization he often was, but the *Colloquies* give one a sense of someone moving in an environment full of friends and of enemies, too; Erasmus reacted quickly to human contact and never forgot a friend. And then what shall one say of the humour? Very few writers can really make one laugh, even those with a reputation for wit. But Erasmus can.

This book makes accessible in a readable and attractive translation a great feast of learning and humanity. And the godly aspect of the feast raises questions which have been of infinite significance to the religious history of Europe.

Chapter Twenty-nine

THE HERMETIC TRADITION IN
RENAISSANCE SCIENCE*

'IF THERE is any characteristic by which the Renaissance can be recognised it is, I believe, in the changing conception of Man's relation to the Cosmos.'[1] That is a quotation from a fairly recent book on *Science and the Renaissance*, the writer of which proceeds to inquire where we should look for the origins of a change in the climate of opinion in western Europe which could have produced this changed relation to the cosmos. He looks, naturally, first of all in the movement known as 'Renaissance Neoplatonism', originating in the renewed study of Plato and the Platonists in the Florentine circle of Marsilio Ficino, but he dismisses this movement as useless for his search. There is no evidence, he thinks, that the Florentine academicians had any but an incidental interest in the problem of knowledge of the external world or of the structure of the cosmos.[2] Yet the movement loosely known as 'Renaissance Neoplatonism' is the movement which – coming in time between the Middle Ages and the seventeenth century – ought to be the originator of the changed climate of opinion, the change in man's attitude to the cosmos, which was to be fraught with such momentous consequences. The difficulty has been, perhaps, that historians of philosophy may have somewhat misled us as to the nature of that movement. When treated as straight philosophy, Renaissance Neoplatonism may dissolve into a rather

---

* Published in *Art, Science and History in the Renaissance*, edited by Charles S. Singleton, Baltimore, 1967.

vague eclecticism. But the new work done in recent years on Marsilio Ficino and his sources has demonstrated that the core of the movement was Hermetic, involving a view of the cosmos as a network of magical forces with which man can operate. The Renaissance magus had his roots in the Hermetic core of Renaissance Neoplatonism, and it is the Renaissance magus, I believe, who exemplifies that changed attitude of man to the cosmos which was the necessary preliminary to the rise of science.

The word 'Hermetic' has many connotations; it can be vaguely used as a generic term for all kinds of occult practices, or it can be used more particularly of alchemy, usually thought of as the Hermetic science *par excellence*. This loose use of the word has tended to obscure its historical meaning – and it is in the historical sense alone that I use it. I am not an occultist, nor an alchemist, nor any kind of sorceress. I am only a humble historian whose favourite pursuit is reading. In the course of this reading and reading, I came to be immensely struck by the phenomenon – to which scholars in Italy, in the United States, and in my own environment in the Warburg Institute had been drawing attention, namely the diffusion of Hermetic texts in the Renaissance.[3]

I must very briefly remind you that the first work which Ficino translated into Latin at the behest of Cosimo de' Medici was not a work of Plato's but the *Corpus Hermeticum*, the collection of treatises going under the name of 'Hermes Trismegistus'. And I must also remind you that Ficino and his contemporaries believed that 'Hermes Trismegistus' was a real person, an Egyptian priest, almost contemporary with Moses, a Gentile prophet of Christianity, and the source – or one of the sources with other *prisci theologi* – of the stream of ancient wisdom which had eventually reached Plato and the Platonists. It was mainly, I believe, in the Hermetic texts that the Renaissance found its new, or new-old, conception of man's relation to the cosmos. I illustrate this very briefly from two of the Hermetic texts.

The 'Pimander',[4] the first treatise of the *Corpus Hermeticum*, gives an account of creation which, although it seems to recall Genesis, with which Ficino of course compared it,[5] differs radically from Genesis in its account of the creation of man. The second creative act of the Word in the 'Pimander', after the creation of light and the elements of nature, is the creation of the heavens, or more particularly of the Seven Governors or seven planets on which the lower elemental world was believed to depend. Then followed the creation of man who 'when he saw the creation which the demiurge had fashioned . . . wished also to produce a work, and permission to do this was given him by the Father. Having thus entered into the demiurgic sphere in which he had full power, the Governors fell in love with man, and each gave to him a part of their rule . . .'

Contrast this Hermetic Adam with the Mosaic Adam, formed out of the dust of the earth. It is true that God gave him dominion over the creatures, but when he sought to know the secrets of the divine power, to eat of the tree of knowledge, this was the sin of disobedience for which he was expelled from the Garden of Eden. The Hermetic man in the 'Pimander' also falls and can also be regenerated. But the regenerated Hermetic man regains the dominion over nature which he had in his divine origin. When he is regenerated, brought back into communion with the ruler of 'the all' through magico-religious communion with the cosmos, it is the regeneration of a being who regains his divinity. One might say that the 'Pimander' describes the creation, fall and redemption not of a man but of a magus – a being who has within him the powers of the Seven Governors and hence is in immediate and most powerful contact with elemental nature.

Here – in the Hermetic core of Ficinian Neoplatonism – there was indeed a vast change in the conception of man's relation to the cosmos. And in the Hermetic *Asclepius*,[6] the work which had been known all through the Middle Ages but which became most potently influential at the Renaissance through the respect accorded to the Egyptian Hermes Trismegistus and all his works, the magus man is shown in operation. The Egyptian priests who are the heroes of the *Asclepius* are presented as knowing how to capture the effluxes of the stars and through this magical knowledge to animate the statues of their gods. However strange his operations may seem to us, it is man the operator who is glorified in the *Asclepius*. As is now well known, it was upon the magical passages in the *Asclepius* that Ficino based the magical practices which he describes in his *De vita coelitus comparanda*.[7] And it was with a quotation from the *Asclepius* on man as a great miracle that Pico della Mirandola opened his *Oration on the Dignity of Man*. With that oration, man as magus has arrived, man with powers of operating on the cosmos through magia and through the numerical conjurations of Cabala.[8]

I believe that the tradition which has seen in Pico della Mirandola's oration and in his nine hundred theses a great turning-point in European history has not been wrong, though sometimes wrongly interpreted. It is not as the advocate of 'humanism' in the sense of the revival of classical studies that he should be chiefly regarded but as the spokesman for the new attitude to man in his relation to the cosmos, man as the great miracle with powers of acting on the cosmos. From the new approach to them, Ficino and Pico emerge not primarily as 'humanists', nor even primarily, I would say, as philosophers, but as magi. Ficino's operations were timid and cautious; Pico came out more boldly with the ideal of man as magus. And if, as I believe, the Renaissance magus was the immediate ancestor of the seventeenth-century scientist, then it is true that 'Neoplatonism' as interpreted by Ficino and Pico was indeed the body of thought which, intervening between the Middle Ages and the seventeenth century, prepared the way for the emergence of science.

While we may be beginning to see the outlines of a new approach to the history of science through Renaissance magic, it must be emphasized that there are enormous gaps in this history as yet – gaps waiting to be filled in by organized research. One of the most urgent needs is a modern edition of the works of Pico della Mirandola, an edition which should not be merely a reprint but which would trace the sources of, for example, the nine hundred theses. Though laborious, this would not be an impossible task, and until it is done, the historian of thought lacks the foundation from which to assess one of its most vital turning-points.

It is convenient to consult the practical compendium for a would-be magus compiled by Henry Cornelius Agrippa as a guide to the classifications of Renaissance magic.[9] Based on Ficino and the *Asclepius*, and also making use of one of Ficino's manuscript sources, the *Picatrix*,[10] and based on Pico and Reuchlin for Cabalist magic, Agrippa distributes the different types of magic under the three worlds of the Cabalists. The lowest or elemental world is the realm of natural magic, the manipulation of forces in the elemental world through the manipulation of the occult sympathies running through it. To the middle celestial world of the stars belongs what Agrippa calls mathematical magic. When a magician follows natural philosophy and mathematics and knows the middle sciences which come from them – arithmetic, music, geometry, optics, astronomy, mechanics – he can do marvellous things. There follow chapters on Pythagorean numerology and on world harmony, and on the making of talismans. To the highest or supercelestial world belongs religious magic, and here Agrippa treats of magical rituals and of the conjuring of angels.

The magical world-view here expounded includes an operative use of number and regards mechanics as a branch of mathematical magic. The Hermetic movement thus encouraged some of the genuine applied sciences, including mechanics, which Campanella was later to classify as 'real artificial magic'.[11] Many examples could be given of the prevalent confusion of thought between magic and mechanics. John Dee, for example, branded as the 'great conjuror' for his angel-summoning magic, was equally suspect on account of the mechanical Scarabaeus which he constructed for a play at Trinity College, Cambridge.[12] In his preface to Henry Billingsley's translation of Euclid, Dee bitterly protests against the reputation for conjuring which his skill in mechanics has brought him:

And for . . . marueilous Actes and Feates, Naturally,
Mathematically, and Mechanically wrought and contriued,
ought any honest Student and Modest Christian Philosopher,
be counted & called a Coniuror?[13]

Yet there is no doubt that for Dee his mechanical operations, wrought by number in the lower world, belonged to the same world-view as his attempted conjuring of angels by Cabalist numerology. The latter was for him the highest and most religious use of number, the operating with number in the supercelestial world.

Thus the strange mental framework outlined in Agrippa's *De occulta philosophia* encouraged within its purview the growth of those mathematical and mechanical sciences which were to triumph in the seventeenth century. Of course it was through the recovery of ancient scientific texts, and particularly of Archimedes, that the advance was fostered, but even here the Hermetic outlook may have played a part which has not yet been examined. Egypt was believed to have been the home of mathematical and mechanical sciences. The cult of Egypt, and of its great soothsayer, Hermes Trismegistus, may have helped to direct enthusiastic attention toward newly recovered scientific texts. I can only give one example of this.

In 1589 there was published in Venice a large volume by Fabio Paolini entitled *Hebdomades*. D. P. Walker has said of this work that it contains 'not only the theory of Ficino's magic but also the whole complex of theories of which it is a part: the Neo-Platonic cosmology and astrology on which magic is based, the *prisca theologia* and *magia*'[14] and so on. It represents the importation of the Florentine movement into Venice and into the discussions of the Venetian academies. The movement has not yet been adequately studied in its Venetian phase, in which it underwent new developments. When speaking of the magical statues of the Hermetic *Asclepius*, Paolini makes this remark: 'we may refer these to the mechanical art and to those machines which the Greeks call *automata*, of which Hero has written.'[15] Paolini is here speaking in the same breath of the statues described by Hermes Trismegistus in the *Asclepius*, which the Egyptian magicians knew how to animate, and of the work on automata by Hero of Alexandria which expounds mechanical or pneumatic devices for making statues move and speak in theatres or temples. Nor is he intending to debunk the magic statues of the *Asclepius* by showing them up as mere mechanisms, for he goes on to speak with respect of how the Egyptians, as described by Trismegistus, knew how to compound their statues out of certain world materials and to draw into them the souls of demons. There is a basic confusion in his mind between mechanics as magic and magic as mechanics, which leads him to a fascinated interest in the technology of Hero of Alexandria. Such associations may also account for passages in the *Hebdomades*, to which Walker has drawn attention, in which Paolini states that the production of motion in hard recalcitrant materials is not done without the help of the *anima mundi*, to which he attributes, for example, the invention of clocks.[16] Thus even the clock, which was to become the supreme symbol of the mechanistic universe established in the first phase of the scientific revolution, had been integrated into the animistic universe of the Renaissance, with its magical interpretations of mechanics.

Among the great figures of the Renaissance who have been hailed as initiators of modern science, one of the greatest is Leonardo da Vinci. We are all familiar with the traditional reputation of Leonardo as a precursor, throwing off the authority both of the schools and of rhetorical humanism, to which he opposed concrete experiment integrated with mathematics. In two essays on Leonardo, Professor Eugenio Garin argues, with his usual subtlety, that Vasari's presentation of the great artist as a magus, a 'divine' man, may be nearer the truth.[17] Garin points to Leonardo's citation of 'Hermes the philosopher' and to his definition of force as a spiritual essence. According to Garin, Leonardo's conception of spiritual force 'has little to do with rational mechanics but has a very close relationship to the Ficinian-Hermetic theme of universal life and animation'.[18] If, as Garin seems to suggest, it is after all within the Renaissance Hermetic tradition that Leonardo should be placed, if he is a 'divine' artist whose strong technical bent is not unmixed with magic and theurgy, whose mechanics and mathematics have behind them the animist conception of the universe, this would in no way diminish his stature as a man of genius. We have to get rid of the idea that the detection of Hermetic influences in a great Renaissance figure is derogatory to the figure. Leonardo's extraordinary achievements would be, on the hypothesis put forward by Garin, one more proof of the potency of the Hermetic impulses toward a new vision of the world, one more demonstration that the Hermetic core of Renaissance Neoplatonism was the generator of a movement of which the great Renaissance magi represent the first stage.

In the case of John Dee, we do not have to get rid of a reputation for enlightened scientific advance, built up by nineteenth-century admirers, in order to detect the Hermetic philosopher behind the scientist. Dee's reputation has not been at all of a kind to attract the enlightened. The publication in 1659 of Dee's spiritual diaries, with their strange accounts of conferences with the spirits supposedly raised by Dee and Kelley in their conjuring operations, ensured that it was as a conjuror, necromancer, or deluded charlatan of the most horrific kind that Dee's reputation should go down to posterity. Throughout the nineteenth century this image of Dee prevailed, and it warned off those in search of precursors of scientific enlightenment from examining Dee's other works. Though Dee's reputation as a genuine scientist and mathematician has been gradually growing during the present century, some survival of the traditional prejudice against him may still account for the extraordinary fact that Dee's preface to Billingsley's translation of Euclid (1570), in which he fervently urges the extension and encouragement of mathematical studies, was not reprinted until 1975. While I suppose that practically every educated person either possesses one of the many modern editions of Francis Bacon's *Advancement of Learning* or has had easy access to them in some library, Dee's mathematical preface could, until then, be read only in the rare early editions of the Euclid. Yet Dee's preface is in English, like Bacon's *Advancement*, and in a nervous and original kind of English; and as a manifesto for the advancement of science it is greatly superior to Bacon's work. For Dee most strongly emphasizes the central importance of mathematics, while the neglect or relative depreciation of mathematics is, as we all know, the fatal blind spot in Bacon's outlook and the chief reason why his inductive method did not lead to scientifically valuable results.

It is not for me here to go through the mathematics of the preface nor to discuss Dee's work as a genuine scientist and mathematician, consulted by technicians and navigators. The work done on these matters by E. G. R. Taylor[19] and F. R. Johnson[20] is well known, and there is a remarkable thesis on Dee by I. R. F. Calder[21] which is unfortunately still unpublished. My object is solely to emphasize the context of Dee's mathematical studies within the Renaissance tradition which we are studying. That Dee goes back to the great Florentine movement for his inspiration is suggested by the fact that he appeals, in his plea for mathematics, to the 'noble Earle of Mirandula' and quotes from Pico's nine hundred theses the statement in the eleventh mathematical conclusion that 'by numbers, a way is to be had to the searching out and understanding of euery thyng, hable to be knowen'.[22] And it was certainly from Agrippa's compilation with its classification of magical practices under the three worlds that he drew the discussion of number in the three worlds with which the preface opens. It may be noticed, too, that it is with those mathematical sciences which Agrippa classifies as belonging to the middle celestial world that the preface chiefly deals,[23] though there are many other influences in the preface, particularly an important influence of Vitruvius. This may raise in our minds the curious thought that it was *because*, unlike Francis Bacon, he was an astrologer and a conjuror, attempting to put into practice the full Renaissance tradition of Magia and Cabala as expounded by Agrippa, that Dee, unlike Bacon, was imbued with the importance of mathematics.

I should like to try to persuade sensible people and sensible historians to use the word *Rosicrucian*. This word has bad associations owing to the uncritical assertions of occultists concerning the existence of a secret society or sect calling themselves Rosicrucians, the history and membership of which they claim to establish. Though it is important that the arguments for and against the existence of a Rosicrucian society should be carefully and critically sifted, I should like to be able to use the word here without raising the secret-society question at all. The word *baroque* is used, rather vaguely, of a certain style of sensibility and expression in art without in the least implying that there were secret societies of baroquists, secretly propagating baroque attitudes. In a similar way the word *Rosicrucian* could, I suggest, be used of a certain style of thinking which is historically recognizable without raising the question of whether a Rosicrucian style of thinker belonged to a secret society.

It would be valuable if the word could be used in this way, as it might then come to designate a phase in the history of the Hermetic tradition in relation to science. A very generalized attempt to define two such phases might run somewhat on the following lines. The Renaissance magus is very closely in touch with artistic expression; the talisman borders in this period on painting and sculpture; the incantation is allied to poetry and music. The Rosicrucian type, though not out of touch with such attitudes, tends to develop more in the direction of science, mixed with magic. Thus though the Rosicrucian type comes straight out of the Renaissance Hermetic tradition, like the earlier magi, he may orientate it in slightly different directions or put the emphasis rather differently. The influx of Paracelsan alchemy and medicine, itself originally stimulated by Ficinian influences, is important for the latter or Rosicrucian type, who is often, perhaps always, strongly influenced by Paracelsus. The tradition in its later or Rosicrucian phase begins to become imbued with philanthropic aims, possibly as a result of Paracelsan influence. Finally, the situation of the Rosicrucian in society is worse and more dangerous than that of the earlier magi. There were always dangers, which Ficino timidly tried to avoid and from which Pico della Mirandola did not escape. But as a result of the worsening political and religious situation in Europe, and of the strong reactions against magic in both Catholic and Protestant countries, the Rosicrucian seems a more hunted being than the earlier magi, some of whom seem able to expand quite happily in the atmosphere of the early Renaissance Neoplatonism, feeling themselves in tune with the age. The artist Leonardo or the poet Ronsard might be examples of such relatively happy expansion of great figures who are not untinctured with the Hermetic core of Neoplatonism. The Rosicrucian, on the other hand, tends to have persecution mania. Though usually of an intensely religious temper, he avoids identifying himself with any of the religious parties and hence is suspected as an atheist by them all, while his reputation as a magician inspires fear and hatred. Whether or not he belongs to a secret society, the Rosicrucian is a secretive type, and has to be.

His experience of life has confirmed him in the Hermetic belief that the deepest truths cannot be revealed to the multitude.

John Dee seems obviously placeable historically as a Renaissance magus of the later Rosicrucian type. Paracelsist and alchemist, a practical scientist who wished to develop applied mathematics for the advantage of his countrymen, full of schemes for the advancement of learning, branded in the public eye as conjuror and atheist, Dee felt himself to be an innocent and a persecuted man. 'O unthankfull Countrey men,' he cries in the preface to the Euclid, 'O Brainsicke, Rashe, Spitefull, and Disdainfull Countrey men. Why oppresse you me, thus violently, with your slaundering of me. . .' And he goes on to compare himself, significantly, with 'Ioannes Picus, Earle of Mirandula', who also suffered from the 'raging slander of the Malicious ignorant against him'.[24]

In the so-called Rosicrucian manifesto published in Germany in 1614 in the name of the Fraternity of the Rosy Cross,[25] the characteristics of what I have called the Rosicrucian type of thinking are perceptible. The brethren are said to possess the books of Paracelsus, and the activity to which they are said to bind themselves is the philanthropic one of healing the sick, and that gratis. The manifesto states that the founder of the society based his views and activities on 'Magia and Cabala', a mode of thinking which he found agreeable to the harmony of the whole world. It expresses a wish for closer collaboration between magician-scientists. The learned of Fez, says the writer, communicated to one another new discoveries in mathematics, physics, and magic, and he wishes that the magicians, cabalists, physicians, and philosophers of Germany were equally co-operative. Thus whether or not this manifesto really emanates from a secret society, it sets forth a Rosicrucian type of programme, with its devotion to Magia and Cabala, its mixed scientific and magical studies, its Paracelsan medicine.

The utopias of the Renaissance show many traces of Hermetic influences, which can even be discerned, I believe, in Thomas More's foundation work. Campanella's *City of the Sun*, which he first wrote in prison in Naples in the early years of the seventeenth century, is a utopian city governed by priests skilled in astral magic who know how to keep the population in health and happiness through their understanding of how to draw down beneficent astral influences.[26] This is after all a philanthropic use of magical science, though somewhat arbitrarily applied. And the Solarians were in general greatly interested in applied magic and science; they encouraged scientific inventions, all inventions to be used in the service of the community. They were also healthy and well skilled in medicine, that is in astral medicine of the Ficinian or Paracelsan type. I would classify the *City of the Sun* as belonging to the later or Rosicrucian phase of the Hermetic movement.

The Rosicrucian flavour is also clearly discernible in a less well-known work, the description of the ideal city of Christianopolis by Johann Valentin Andreae, published at Strasbourg in 1619.[27] Andreae's Christianopolis is heavily influenced by Campanella's City of the Sun. Its inhabitants, like Campanella's Solarians, are practisers of astral magic and at the same time are deeply interested in every kind of scientific research. Christianopolis is busy with the activity of scientists who are applying their knowledge in inventions which are to improve the happiness and well-being of the people.

When, after a course of reading of this type, one returns once again to the so much more famous *New Atlantis* of Francis Bacon (written in 1624), it is impossible not to recognize in it something of the same atmosphere. The New Atlantis is ruled by mysterious sages who keep the citizens in tune with the cosmos; and in this later utopia the wisdom tradition is turning ever more and more in the direction of scientific research and collaboration for the betterment of man's estate. Yet there are significant differences as compared with the earlier Rosicrucian utopias which I have mentioned; the priests of the New Atlantis do not practise astral magic and are not exactly magi; its scientific institutions are drawing closer to some future Royal Society. But to me it seems obvious that the New Atlantis has its roots in the Hermetic-Cabalist tradition of the Renaissance, though this is becoming rationalized in a seventeenth-century direction. The magus had given place to the Rosicrucian, and the Rosicrucian is giving place to the scientist, but only very gradually.

Francis Bacon is, in my opinion, one of those figures who have been misunderstood and their place in history distorted by those historians of science and philosophy who have seen in them only precursors of the future without examining their roots in the past. The only modern book on Bacon which makes, or so it seems to me, the right historical approach is Paolo Rossi's *Francesco Bacone*, published in Italian in 1957.[28] The significant subtitle of Rossi's book is *Dalla magia alla scienza (From Magic to Science)*. Rossi begins by outlining the Renaissance Hermetic tradition,

pointing out that Bacon's emphasis on the importance of technology cannot be disentangled from the Renaissance Hermetic
tradition in which magic and technology are inextricably mingled.
He emphasizes those aspects of Bacon's philosophy which show
traces of Renaissance animism, and he argues that the two main
planks of the Baconian position – the conception of science as
power, as a force able to work on and modify nature, and the
conception of man as the being to whom has been entrusted the
capacity to develop this power – are both recognizably derivable
from the Renaissance ideal of the magus. While urging that the
approach to Bacon should take full cognizance of his roots in the
Renaissance Hermetic tradition, Rossi emphasizes that such an
approach does not diminish Bacon's great importance in the
history of thought but should enable the historian to analyse and
bring out his true position. In Rossi's opinion, Bacon's supreme
importance lies in his insistence on the co-operative nature of
scientific effort, on the fact that advance does not depend on
individual genius alone but in pooling the efforts of many workers.
He emphasizes, and this second point is related to the first one,
Bacon's polemic against the habit of secrecy which was so strongly
ingrained in the older tradition, his insistence that the scientific
worker must not veil his knowledge in inscrutable riddles but
communicate it openly to his fellow-workers. And finally he
draws attention to Bacon's dislike of illuminism and of the pretensions of a magus to knowledge of divine secrets, his insistence
that it is not through such proud claims but through humble
examination and experiment that nature is to be approached.

I believe that Rossi has indicated the right road for further
research on Bacon, who should be studied as a Rosicrucian type
but of a reformed and new kind, reformed on the lines indicated
by Rossi, through which the Rosicrucian type abandons his
secrecy and becomes a scientist openly co-operating with others
in the future Royal Society, and abandons also his pretensions to
illuminism, to being the 'divine' man admired in the Hermetic
tradition, with its glorification of the magus, for the attitude of a
humble observer and experimentalist. The interesting point
emerges here that the humble return to nature in observation and
experiment advocated by Bacon takes on a moral character, as an
attitude deliberately opposed to the sinful pride of a Renaissance
magus with his claims to divine insights and powers.

Yet Bacon's reactions against the magus type of philosopher
or scientist themselves belong to a curious context. Rossi has

emphasized that Bacon regarded his projected *instauratio magna* of the sciences as a return for man of that dominion over nature which Adam had before the Fall but which he lost through sin. Through the sin of pride, Aristotle and Greek philosophers generally lost immediate contact with natural truth, and in a significant passage Bacon emphasizes that this sin of pride has been repeated in recent times in the extravagances of Renaissance animist philosophers. The proud fantasies of the Renaissance magi represent for Bacon something like a second Fall through which man's contact with nature has become even more distorted than before. Only by the humble methods of observation and experiment in the Great Instauration will this newly repeated sin of pride be redeemed, and the reward will be a new redemption of man in his relation to nature.[29] Thus Bacon's very reaction against the magi in favour of what seems a more modern conception of the scientist contained within it curious undercurrents of cosmic mysticism. Though Bacon's attitude would seem to dethrone the Hermetic Adam, the divine man, his conception of the regenerated Mosaic Adam, who is to be in a new and more immediate and more powerful contact with nature after the Great Instauration of the sciences, seems to bring us back into an atmosphere which is after all not so different from that in which the magus lived and moved and had his being. In fact, Cornelius Agrippa repeatedly asserts that it is the power over nature which Adam lost by original sin that the purified soul of the illuminated magus will regain.[30] Bacon rejected Agrippa with contempt, yet the Baconian aim of power over nature and the Baconian Adamic mysticism were both present in the aspirations of the great magician – though for Bacon, the claim of the magus to illuminism would itself constitute a second Fall through pride.

Bacon's reaction against the animist philosophers as proud magi who have brought about a second Fall is extremely important for the understanding of his position as a reformed and humble scientific observer, and I would even go further than Rossi and suggest that some of Bacon's mistakes may have been influenced by his desire to rationalize and make respectable a tradition which was heavily suspected by its opponents, by the Aristotelians of the schools and by the humanists of the rhetorical tradition. Bacon's admirers have often been puzzled by his rejection of Copernican heliocentricity and of William Gilbert's work on the magnet. I would like to suggest, though there is hardly time to work this out in detail, that these notions might have seemed to Bacon heavily engaged in extreme forms of the magical and animist philosophy or like the proud and erroneous opinions of a magus.

In the sensational works published by Giordano Bruno during his visit to England, of which Bacon must have been well aware, Bruno had made use of heliocentricity in connection with the extreme form of religious and magical Hermetism which he preached in England. Bruno's Copernicanism was bound up with his magical view of nature; he associated heliocentricity with the Ficinian solar magic and based his arguments in favour of earth movement on a Hermetic text which states that the earth moves because it is alive.[31] He had thus associated Copernicanism with the animist philosophy of an extreme type of magus. When Bacon is deploring the sinful pride of those philosophers who have brought about the second Fall, who, believing themselves divinely inspired, invent new philosophical sects which they create out of their individual fantasy, imprinting their own image on the cosmos instead of humbly approaching nature in observation and experiment, he mentions Bruno by name as an example of such misguided *illuminati*, together with Patrizi, William Gilbert, and Campanella.[32] Is it possible that Bacon avoided heliocentricity because he associated it with the fantasies of an extreme Hermetic magus, like Bruno? And is it further possible that William Gilbert's studies on the magnet, and the magnetic philosophy of nature which he associated with it, also seemed to Bacon to emanate from the animistic philosophy of a magus, of the type which he deplored?

The magnet is always mentioned in textbooks of magic as an instance of the occult sympathies in action. Giovanni Baptista Porta, for example, in his chapters on the occult sympathies and how to use them in natural magic constantly mentions the loadstone.[33] The animist philosophers were equally fond of this illustration; Giordano Bruno when defending his animistic version of heliocentricity in the *Cena de le ceneri* brings in the magnet.[34] I think that it has not been sufficiently emphasized how close to Bruno's language in the *Cena de le ceneri* is Gilbert's defence of heliocentricity in the *De magnete*. Gilbert, like Bruno, actually brings in Hermes and other *prisci theologi* who have stated that there is a universal life in nature when he is defending earth movement.[35] There are passages in the *De magnete* which sound almost like direct quotations from Bruno's *Cena de le ceneri*. The magnetic philosophy which Gilbert extends to the whole universe is, it seems to me, most closely allied to Bruno's philosophy, and it is therefore not surprising that Bacon should list Gilbert with Bruno as one of the proud and fantastic animist philosophers[36] or that notions about heliocentricity or magnetism might seem to him dangerous fantasies of the *illuminati*, to be avoided by a humble experimentalist who distrusts such proud hypotheses.

Finally, there is the suggestion at which I hinted earlier. Is it possible that the reputation of John Dee, the conjuror, conjuring angels with number in the supercelestial world with a magus-like lack of humility of the kind which Bacon deplored, might have made the Lord Verulam suspicious also of too much operating with number in the lower worlds? Was mathematics, for Bacon, too much associated with magic and with the middle world of the stars, and was this one of the reasons why he did not emphasize it in his method? I am asking questions here, obviously somewhat at random, but they are questions which have never been asked before, and one object in raising them is to try to startle historians of science into new attitudes to that key figure, Francis Bacon. To see him as emerging from the Renaissance Hermetic tradition and as anxious to dissociate himself from what he thought were extreme and dangerous forms of that tradition may eventually lead to new adjustments in the treatment both of his own thought and of his attitude toward contemporaries. It would be valuable if careful comparisons could be organized between the works of Dee, Bacon, and Fludd. The extreme Rosicrucian types, Dee and Fludd, might come out of such an examination with better marks as scientists than Bacon. Dee certainly would, and even Fludd might do better than expected.

Nevertheless, all this does not do away with Bacon's great importance. As compared with Dee and Fludd, Bacon had unquestionably moved into another era in his conception of the role of the scientist and of the character of the scientist. Though Bacon descends from the magus in his conception of science as power and of man as the wielder of that power, he also banishes the old conception of the magus in favour of an outlook which can be recognized as modern, if the Adamic mysticism behind the Great Instauration is not emphasized. Bacon obviously qualifies as a member of the future Royal Society, though one with surviving affiliations with the occult tradition – as was the case with many early members of the Society. The figure of Bacon is a striking example of those subtle transformations through which the Renaissance tradition takes on, almost imperceptibly, a seventeenth-century temper and moves on into a new era.

I would thus urge that the history of science in this period, instead of being read solely forwards for its premonitions of what was to come, should also be read backwards, seeking its connections with what had gone before. A history of science may emerge from such efforts which will be exaggerated and partly wrong. But then the history of science from the solely forward-looking point of view has also been exaggerated and partly wrong, misinterpreting the old thinkers by picking out from the context of their thought as a whole only what seems to point in the direction of modern developments. Only in the perhaps fairly distant future will a proper balance be established in which the two types of inquiry, both of which are essential, will each contribute their quota to a new assessment. In the meantime, let us continue our investigations in which the detection of Hermetic influences in some great figure and acknowledged precursor should be a parallel process to the detection of genuine scientific importance in figures who have hitherto been disregarded as occultists and outsiders.

And we must constantly beware of giving an impression of debunking great figures when we expose in them unsuspected affiliations to the Hermetic tradition. Such discoveries do not make the great figures less great; but they demonstrate the importance of the Renaissance Hermetic tradition as the immediate antecedent of the emergence of science. The example of this which I made the subject of a book is Giordano Bruno. Long hailed as the philosopher of the Renaissance who burst the bonds of medievalism and broke out of the old world-view into Copernican heliocentricity and a vision of an infinitely expanded universe, Bruno has turned out to be an 'Egyptian' magus of a most extreme type, nourished on the Hermetic texts. Bruno's vision of an infinite universe ruled by the laws of magical animism with which the magus can operate is not a medieval or a reactionary vision. It is still the precursor of the seventeenth-century vision, though formulated within a Renaissance frame of reference. As I have tried to suggest in this paper, even the mathematical and mechanical progress which made possible the seventeenth-century advance may have been encouraged by Hermetic influences in the earlier movement. The emergence of modern science should perhaps be regarded as proceeding in two phases, the first being the Hermetic or magical phase of the Renaissance with its basis in an animist philosophy, the second being the development in the seventeenth century of the first or classical period of modern science. The two movements should, I suggest, be studied as interrelated; gradually the second phase sheds the first phase, a process which comes out through the double approach of detecting intimations of the second phase in the first and survivals of the first phase in the second. Even in Isaac Newton, as is now well known, there are such survivals, and if Professor Garin is right, even in Galileo,[37] while Kepler provides the obvious example of a great modern figure who still has one foot in the old world of universal harmony which sheltered the magus.

Renaissance and early seventeenth-century literature abounds in vast tomes which it is beyond the power of any one scholar to tackle unaided. They sleep undisturbed on library shelves or are only dipped into at random, while people turn to the easier and more lucrative occupation of writing little books about the Renaissance and seventeenth century, and the great names – Kepler, Newton, Galileo – run easily off all our pens. Yet do we really understand what happened? Has anyone really explained where Kepler, Newton, Galileo, came from? I wish that a concerted effort could be made, less on the published writings of the great in their modern and accessible editions than on the vast sleeping tomes. I think of two in particular with which I have often tried to struggle: Francesco Giorgi's *De harmonia mundi* and Marin Mersenne's *Harmonie universelle*. Giorgi's *Harmony of the World* is full of Hermetic and Cabalist influences; the Franciscan friar who wrote it was a direct disciple of Pico della Mirandola. This tome represents the Renaissance Hermetic-Cabalist tradition working on the ancient theme of world harmony. Mersenne is a seventeenth-century monk, friend of Descartes. And just as Bacon does in his sphere, Mersenne attacks and discards the old Renaissance world; his *Universal Harmony* will have nothing to do with the *anima mundi* and nothing to do with Francesco Giorgi, of whom he sternly disapproves. Mathematics replaces numerology in Mersenne's harmonic world; magic is banished; the seventeenth century has arrived. The emergence of Mersenne out of a banished Giorgi seems somehow a parallel phenomenon to the emergence of Bacon out of the magus. It is perhaps somehow in these transitions from Renaissance to seventeenth century that the secret might be surprised, the secret of how science happened. But to understand Mersenne and Mersenne's rejection of Giorgi, one must know where Giorgi came from. He came out of the Pythagoro-Platonic tradition plus Hermes Trismegistus and the Cabala.

In a review of my book on Bruno,[38] Allen G. Debus has suggest-

ed that I have over-emphasized the importance of the dating of
the Hermetic writings by Isaac Casaubon in 1614 as weakening
the influence of the Hermetic writings after that date. He points
out that 'the first half of the seventeenth century saw an increased
interest in the occult approach to nature which parallels the
contemporary rise of mechanical philosophy. The real collapse of
the Renaissance magical science only occurs in the period after
1660. Until then it remained a positive force stimulating some
scientists to a new observational approach to nature.'[39] I would
accept this criticism as valid; I think that I may have over-esti-
mated the importance of Casaubon's dating, which was totally
ignored by, for example, Fludd and Kircher, and I also believe,
as indeed I have suggested in this paper, that the late Renaissance
movement which I would like to label 'Rosicrucian' does continue
to exert a strong influence through the seventeenth century.
Nevertheless I still think that Casaubon's dating does, as it were,
mark a historical term which helps to define and delimit the
Hermetic movement. Though the importance of Ficino's propag-
ation of the Hermetic writings and his adoption of Hermetic
philosophy and practice must not be exaggerated to the exclusion
of the many other influences fostering the movement, yet it was
basic, and the Hermetic attitude toward the cosmos and towards
man's relation to the cosmos which Ficino and Pico adopted was,
I believe, the chief stimulus of that new turning toward the world
and operating on the world which, appearing first as Renaissance
magic, was to turn into seventeenth-century science. And it was
the sanction which the misdating of the *Hermetica* gave to these
writings that sanctioned procedures and attitudes which St Augustine had severely condemned and which were prohibited by the
Church. If, as Ficino believed, the *Hermetica* were all written
many centuries before Christ by a holy Egyptian who foresaw the
coming of Christ, this encouraged him and other Christian souls
to embark on the Hermetic magic. Casaubon's dating of the
Hermetica as written after Christ destroyed an illusion without
which the movement might not have gained its original
momentum, though it could not stop the movement after it had
gained such force and influence. That is perhaps a better way of
putting it.

It would be absurd, of course, to suggest that the Hermetic
texts and Ficino's interpretation of them were the only causes of
the movement. These were only factors, though important ones,
in disseminating a new climate of opinion through Europe which

was favourable to the acceptance of magico-religious and magico-scientific modes of thinking. Neoplatonism itself was favourable to this climate, and medieval traditions of the same type revived. If one includes in the tradition the revived Platonism with the accompanying Pythagoro-Platonic interest in number, the expansion of theories of harmony under the combined pressures of Pythagoro-Platonism, Hermetism, and Cabalism, the intensification of interest in astrology with which genuine astronomical research was bound up, and if one adds to all this complex stream of influences the expansion of alchemy in new forms, it is, I think, impossible to deny that these were the Renaissance forces which turned men's minds in the direction out of which the scientific revolution was to come. This was the tradition which broke down Aristotle in the name of a unified universe through which ran one law, the law of magical animism. This was the tradition which had to contend with the so much more prominent and successful disciplines of rhetorical and literary humanism. This was the tradition which prepared the way for the seventeenth-century triumph. But it must be emphasized that the detailed work, the great body of research, necessary for tracing this movement is not yet done. It lies in the future.

There is yet another way of regarding this strange history of the Renaissance Hermetic tradition in its relation to science. We may ask whether the seventeenth century discarded notions from the earlier tradition which may have been actually nearer to the views of the universe unfolded by the science of today than the movement which superseded it. Was the magically animated universe of Bruno, so close to the magnetic universe of Gilbert, a better guess about the nature of reality than those seemingly so much more rational universes of the mechanistic philosophers?

> It may be illuminating to view the scientific revolution as in two phases, the first phase consisting of an animistic universe operated by magic, the second phase of a mathematical universe operated by mechanics. An enquiry into both phases, and their interactions, may be a more fruitful line of approach to the problems raised by the science of to-day than the line which concentrates solely on the seventeenth-century triumph.

Professor Debus quotes these words of mine in his review,[40] adding, 'I heartily agree with this opinion, and in essence it is the approach which I have been taking in my own courses on Renaissance science.' It is most gratifying to me to learn that a point of view which I put forward in some fear and trembling is actually already the basis of teaching in the United States. I must, however, not come before you on false pretences, and I must emphasize that, just as I was careful to state in the beginning that I am no magician, so I must be even more careful to state at the end that I am no scientist. Though when I read in the *Observer* for 26 September 1965 that five hundred of the world's most expensive scientists, gathered at Oxford, were in a mood of breathless expectation because they believed that high-energy physics, burrowing ever deeper into matter, may be about to break into 'quite a new level of reality', it seemed to me that I had heard something like this before. In the Rosicrucian manifesto of 1614 it is announced that some great aurora is at hand in the light of which man is about 'to understand his own nobleness and worth, and why he is called Microcosmus, and how far his knowledge extendeth into nature'. Perhaps these words are not so much a prophecy of the limited vision of the seventeenth-century revolution as of yet another aurora. And perhaps the view of nature of a Rosicrucian like John Dee as a network of magical forces which can be dealt with by mathematics is nearer to the new aurora – notwithstanding his belief in talismans and in the conjuring of angels – than an ignorant person like myself can understand.

Chapter Thirty

SCIENCE, SALVATION AND
THE CABALA*

IN A BOOK published in Italian in 1957 and in English translation in 1968 (*Francis Bacon: From Magic to Science* – see above, pp. 60–6), Paolo Rossi drew attention to the millennial aspect of Bacon's philosophy. He showed by quotation that Bacon thought of his 'Great Instauration' of learning as an attempt to return to the pure state of Adam before the Fall, when, in close contact with God and nature, he had insight into all truth and power over the created world. This insight and this power were lost by man at the Fall, when sin clouded his perceptions.

This outlook gave a strongly religious tinge to Bacon's projected reform of the sciences. The primary object of the Great Instauration was 'to redeem man from original sin and to reinstate him in his prelapsarian power over created things'. When this salvation through science was achieved the millennium would be at hand. Bacon seems to have believed that the great reform could be brought about within a relatively short time and that its sequel, the End, might therefore be not far off. Rossi's extraction of millenarianism from Bacon's works came as a great surprise at a time when the older type of history of science was not as yet seriously challenged.

In his essay on 'Three Foreigners: The Philosophers of the Puritan

---

* Review of Charles Webster, *The Great Instauration: Science, Medicine, and Reform 1626-1660*, London and New York, 1975, in *New York Review of Books*, 27 May 1976.

Revolution' (1961, republished in enlarged form in *Religion, the Reformation, and Social Change*, 1967) Hugh Trevor-Roper demonstrated the importance of three foreigners, Samuel Hartlib from Germany, John Dury from Scotland, and John Amos Comenius the Czech, in forming the outlook of the English Puritans. All three might be described as 'millenarian Baconians', enthusiasts for the Baconian reform interpreted as a religious movement. The sufferings of the Protestants in the Thirty Years War, between 1618 and 1648, had intensified the apocalyptic side of the movement. The Puritans, led by Hartlib, Dury, and Comenius, combined their Baconian philosophy with their grave religious anxieties. 'Was it not a time to count the few remaining days of the world, to expect the conversion of the Jews, to listen for the last Trump?' The situation of the Jews was particularly a matter for anxiety; for the conversion of the Jews was expected to usher in the Last Days. In this intense atmosphere, Baconianism took on an increasingly strong millenarian tinge.

The researches of Christopher Hill have turned up an immense amount of material on the thought of the Puritans, particularly in his books *Antichrist in Seventeenth Century England* (1971) and *The World Turned Upside Down* (1972). He illustrates the importance of millenarian expectations in the excited imaginations of the Puritans and searches for indications of the growth of science within this movement.

To these trends of modern scholarship on the English Puritans, Charles Webster has now added the weighty volume under review. He makes Puritan eschatology the ideological framework of his study of 'science, medicine, and reform 1626–1660'. Obviously he is following in a track prepared by other scholars in underlining millenarianism as a basic factor in the Puritan outlook, but the originality of his book lies in the detailed way in which he relates the scientific effort of the period to this outlook. I can only give a few examples of how he works this out.

The Puritans laid great stress on reform and spread of education, following the Baconian programme as expanded by Hartlib and Comenius. The vital force behind this effort, according to Webster, was the Puritan insistence on the ruin of human abilities at the Fall, a ruin which needed to be restored in preparation for the millennium. With this interpretation of the spiritual motive force behind the intensive cult of education by the Puritans, Webster couples his detailed factual analysis of Puritan education, using writings on the subject, examination of practical efforts of educationalists, the chief of whom was Samuel Hartlib.

Medicine was of prime importance in the Puritan programme. Webster relates this interest to the effort to restore man's physical perfection, lost at the Fall. His intellectual perfection was to be restored by the new educational programme; his physical perfection by the new medicine. Hence the surge of influence of the doctor and alchemist Paracelsus; for notions of the kind congenial to Puritans were implicit in the Paracelsan medicine. Webster's detailed factual survey, compiled by a trained historian of medicine, is probably the fullest account of the subject hitherto available.

The Puritan attitudes to technology, and particularly to agriculture, developed in the context of the Garden of Eden, to which man would be restored when he had regained control over nature by the new science and technology. Research and practical efforts were directed toward increasing productivity, through which food and wealth would be available to all. This was very obviously to be interpreted as a move toward the millennium, or (as Blake might say) toward the building of Jerusalem in England's green and pleasant land. In connection with this vision, Webster gives what is probably the first full account of Puritan husbandry.

The book includes surveys of every aspect of Puritan science and will thus be indispensable to historians quite apart from its ideological argument. Most readers, confronted with the enormous range of detailed information, will feel convinced that science did advance in the period and that it was Puritanism which encouraged the advance. Another vexed question which the book solves is that of the actual influence of Bacon on the Puritans. It has been said that Puritan Baconianism might have been an abstract interest without practical results. Webster demonstrates that Puritans made a determined effort to give practical form to the Baconian programme.

But the remarkable new view which emerges from Webster's work is his argument that it was actually the Puritan eschatology that was the religious spur driving the Puritans to the cultivation of science. One would think that people who believed that the End was near would fold their hands and make no further effort. For the Puritans, the millennium had to be worked for with hard social effort, with intense application toward regaining for man the lofty position which he had lost at the Fall. The Puritan doctrine of work was applied to working for the restoration of all things (a Biblical phrase frequently used) – man and the world would be prepared, through increased knowledge and scientific advance, for a millennial restitution of the state of Adam before the Fall.

Thus the aspect of the Puritan religion and outlook which seems most remote from mundane reality, the eschatology, was actually, according to Webster, the driving force behind the Puritan scientific advance. This argument will not be welcomed by many historians of thought to whom it may well seem entirely unrealistic. They will, however, find it hard to demolish an argument supported by such a wealth of evidence. For my part, I believe Webster. It seems to me that he has made his case.

Where could such ideas as these have come from? It is all very well to trace them to Bacon, undoubtedly their immediate source, but how did Bacon himself arrive at them?

In spite of contemporary enthusiasm for 'interdisciplinary' studies, scholars can still be imprisoned within their 'special fields' and unaware of what has been going on beyond their hedges. The tremendous outburst of millennial excitement among English Puritans was contemporary with another religious movement which the great work of Gershom Scholem has revealed in recent years. This was the intensification throughout the seventeenth century of apocalyptic hopes of the imminent coming of the Messiah, working up in Jewish mystical, or Cabalist, tradition toward a climax when it was believed that the Messiah actually had come. Scholem's books, *Major Trends in Jewish Mysticism* (first English edition 1941) and his more recent volume, *Sabbatai Sevi: The Mystical Messiah* (English translation 1973), have made available knowledge about this movement which had been obscured or lost. Historians of thought have not yet fully grasped the significance of Scholem's work for their studies. One area in which comparison with developments in the Jewish Cabalist tradition is certainly long overdue is the English Puritan movement of the seventeenth century.

The important date to hold in mind is 1492, the date of the expulsion of the Jews from Spain. Before that date the Jewish mystical tradition as it developed in Spain is known as Spanish Cabala. After that date, the frightful experience of the expulsion altered the character of Cabala, concentrating it far more than earlier on apocalyptic hopes of the coming of a Messiah. A new school of Cabala developed, reflecting the new attitudes. It was centred at Safed in Palestine and its founder was Isaac Luria (1534-72), after whom it is called the Lurianic Cabala.

The new or Lurianic Cabala held that its chief task was to prepare for the coming of the Messiah. The task of man, says Scholem, was defined by Luria as the restitution of his primordial situation before the Fall. The Fall of Adam affected the whole cosmos, as well as man, and the prayers of the Cabalist must be for the restoration or redemption of all things. In a sense man himself, co-operating with God, is responsible for the restoration of all things. 'The task of man is seen to consist in the direction of his whole inner purpose toward the restoration of the original harmony which was disturbed by the original defect and by the powers of evil and sin.' Scholem compares the older version of the Messianic process, that man and the cosmos will not be restored until the Messiah comes, with this Cabalist view that the Messiah cannot come until the restoration has been effected, the work of the Cabalist being to effect this preliminary restoration through his spiritual efforts.

The similarity of this outlook to the Puritan aim, as elucidated by Webster, of working to make the millennium come is obvious. As Christians, the Puritans expect a Second Coming and a millennium, rather than a new Messiah. And as scientists they seem to give a somewhat materialist interpretation of the work they must do in preparation. Yet when we remember that their practical works had for them a spiritual or salvational meaning the parallel remains close. In fact, the very practicality of the Puritans has a certain Jewish ring about it.

The influence of the Lurianic Cabala from about 1630 onward was intense throughout Jewry. It fomented apocalyptic and messianic hopes 'and raised every Jew to the rank of protagonist in the great process of restitution.' And the Messiah came. A young man called Sabbatai Sevi announced in 1665 his Messianic mission. A tremendous mass movement spread among the Jews, 'already prepared for this event by the influence of the new Cabala'. And, almost immediately, came the tragic anticlimax. In 1666, the Messiah apostatized to Islam.

Look at the dates, the gathering strength of the movement from 1630 onward, the climax in 1665–6. Within these dates, the English Puritan movement ran its enthusiastic course. The Puritan movement was intensely philosemitic, Hebraic, and Biblical in all its modes of expression. Surely there can be no doubt that there must have been interaction of some kind between the two movements. Webster's analysis of the eschatology of English Puritanism and its influence on their scientific outlook should certainly be seen in the context of the contemporary messianic movement among the Jews.

There was also a European movement known as Christian Cabala, the history of which has not yet been written with the immense intellectual power and grasp such as Scholem has shown in his studies of Jewish Cabala. Christian Cabala was founded by Pico della Mirandola. It claimed to be able to convert the Jews by proving to them by their own Cabalistic methods that Jesus is the name of the Messiah. The conversion of the Jews was an important item in the Puritan millennial programme, though I do not think that there has been any study of Christian Cabala from this point of view. We know however that a Christianized version of Lurianic Cabala was known in the period, for example to Henry More.

In my book *The Rosicrucian Enlightenment* (1972) I attempted to make a critical historical study of the so-called Rosicrucian manifestos published in Germany in the early seventeenth century. Though wrapped in a fable about 'Christian Rosencreuz' – his travels; his foundation of a group of brethren devoted to mystical and scientific studies – this movement turned out to have affiliations with the scientific interests of Johann Valentin Andreae and his friends.

Since writing my book I have found it stated by Leibniz that he understood that the Rosicrucian manifesto known as the *Fama Fraternitatis* was written by Joachim Jungius (Leibniz, *Philosophische Schriften* I, edited by P. Ritter, 1930, p. 276). Jungius was a scientific thinker of first-class ability whose work and efforts to found scientific societies were frustrated by the Thirty Years War. His *Fama* announces a dawn of new knowledge and power for man before the approaching End. It describes the mythical travels of Christian Rosencreuz from Spain, where he is rejected, to the East. This story may contain a hint of the movement of Cabala after the Expulsion, though it is definitely stated that the revelation now announced is Christian. The author is Protestant in his interpretation of Antichrist.

I drew attention to the parallels between the Rosicrucian myth described in the *Fama* and the myth in which Bacon wraps his scientific programme in *The New Atlantis*, and suggested that the

German Rosicrucian movement should be seen as parallel to, or in some way connected with, the Baconian movement in England. It was a distinctively Cabalist method to present some truth or movement in the guise of a tale or fable. The Rosicrucian fable, as used by the two scientific thinkers, Joachim Jungius and Francis Bacon, suggests a current of Cabalist mysticism in both the German and the English movements.

It is important to notice what Bacon says about Cabala and the Jews in *The New Atlantis*. The visitor to this imaginary country is told that Solomon's House, or College, where all the sciences are cultivated, is based on the wisdom of the Hebrews. He meets a Jewish merchant, for the people of the country allow some Jews to dwell among them, who tells him that the laws of the country are based on those ordained by Moses 'by a secret Cabala' and that when the Messiah comes the king of that country shall sit at his feet. Bacon adds these words to his description of the Jew: 'But yet, setting aside these Jewish dreams, the man was a wise man and learned, and excellently seen in the laws and customs of that nation.' Surely we can now understand that the learned Jew expecting an imminent Messiah was a Lurianic Cabalist from whom the Christian learned much, including his belief that earnest preparation must be made for the coming of the Messiah. Transferred into Christian terms, this would mean earnest preparation for the coming of the millennium through the cultivation of the sciences, exactly the programme of the later Puritan Baconians as now elucidated by Webster.

One of the German Rosicrucian pamphlets describes an 'Invisible College', an imaginary institution of similar meaning to Bacon's College of Solomon. As is well known, the natural philosopher Robert Boyle referred in letters of 1646 and 1647 to an 'Invisible College' with which he was in contact, apparently a group of friends with wide scientific and philanthropic interests. This seems an obvious, half playful, reference to the Invisible College of the Rosicrucians. The expression was certainly known in England. Ben Jonson scoffed at the Invisible College of the Rosicrucians in a masque at court in 1624.

Webster produces an elaborate membership for Boyle's Invisible College, recruited from 'Anglo-Irish intellectuals associated with the Boyle family'. Though it sounds so factual, there does not seem to be any real evidence whatever for this detailed application of Boyle's vague words, and Webster's remark that Boyle's college 'was invisible not out of a desire for secrecy of the Rosicrucian type, but because its members were likely to be geographically separated' is highly unconvincing. Boyle was writing to a French Protestant who would have understood the Continental allusion. Webster wants to transfer to an English clique an allusion that seems obviously to refer to the Continental movement which Hartlib and his friends, refugees from the disasters of the Thirty Years War that had overwhelmed Andreae and the Invisible College, were trying to continue in England.

This refusal to admit a Continental derivation for the Invisible College is typical of Webster's approach, which tends to make the English scientific movement parochial. He says little about the environment abroad whence Hartlib came to England. He ignores the connections of the 'three foreigners' with the Queen of Bohemia and her circle, representative of the Protestant cause abroad. He mentions only once, and that in passing, the Queen of Bohemia's son, Charles Louis, Elector Palatine, so important a figure for Hartlib, the scientist Theodore Haak, and for the English Puritan sympathizers with the Palatinate cause.

I am convinced that Hartlib, Dury, and Comenius nourished the hope that Cromwell might be persuaded to name the Elector Charles as his successor, and that this was why it was so important to show Cromwell the book *Lux in tenebris*, containing the Kotter prophecies about the sacred destiny of the Palatinate house. Charles, Elector Palatine, as Charles II, King of England, might have supported the Puritan social, as well as scientific, revolution, for he was a great admirer of Hartlib. At any rate, Charles Louis makes a striking alternative to Charles Stuart. The prospect was not so impossible as it now seems. The principle of choosing a Protestant relative of the Queen of Bohemia as king in preference to a rightful, but Papist, Stuart heir was actually applied in the case of George I.

These questions affect Webster's main subject of Puritan science and they matter still more in any discussion of the origins of the Royal Society and the reasons why Thomas Sprat suppressed the evidence about the role of Haak – who was from the Palatinate – in the early meetings. The men of the Restoration and of the Royal Society had to suppress the memory of the Puritan revolution and its Continental connections. In suppressing the Invisible College from among the ancestry of the Royal Society and in forgetting the Palatinate and its history in relation to the Puritans (which the Puritans themselves never forgot) Webster is continuing the good work of Thomas Sprat, and without Sprat's political excuse for his obscurantism.

Thus one feels a certain narrowness in Webster's approach, a restriction to the 'special field' of English Puritan science. Nevertheless within his limits he has performed a valuable work in his exhaustive account of Puritan science, medicine, and reform between 1626 and 1660, which is, after all, the specific task which he set himself. And within his field he has dug deep, deep enough to uncover the spiritual motive force of Puritan science in its eschatology. This is an important discovery. And when Puritan millenarianism is compared, as I have tried to do in this review, with the contemporary Jewish messianic movement some remarkable vistas begin to emerge.

Protestants and Jews, experiencing similar agonies of persecution and exile, drew together in those years. The Puritan felt that the Jewish experience was not dissimilar to his own, and the climax of this rapprochement was reached when Oliver Cromwell received Manasseh Ben Israel and allowed the settlement of the Jews in England. Puritans expecting the Christian millennium and Jewish Cabalists expecting their Messiah had much in common in their intensive striving toward the restoration of all things and the restitution of man to his proud position before the Fall. The millennium did not come and the Messiah proved an illusion. But something came, the Royal Society, symbol of the arrival of science, through which man would indeed enlarge his knowledge and his powers, though it has not yet restored him to the Garden of Eden.

== Chapter Thirty-one ==

COPERNICUS*

IF YOU take in your hands the great work of Copernicus and open
it at the page with the amazing diagram which showed for the
first time the Sun at the centre and the Earth and the other
planets revolving round it, you will see, just after the diagram, the
following words (translated from the Latin):

> In the midst of all resides the Sun. For who could place this
> great light in any better position in this most beautiful temple
> [of the world] than that from whence it may illumine all at
> once? So that it is called by some the lamp of the world; by
> others the mind; by others the ruler. And Trismegistus calls
> it the visible god.

It is with a religious sense of awe and wonder that Copernicus
presents his epoch-making diagram, with the Sun at the centre.
He sees the world as a vast temple lighted by a great central lamp.
And he quotes, as an authority for this religious approach to the
Sun, Trismegistus, who has said that the Sun is the visible god.

Who is this Trismegistus cited by Copernicus as an authority
for giving an all-important position to the Sun? He is none other
than Hermes Trismegistus, the supposed author of the writings
known as the *Hermetica* which had such an enormous influence

* BBC Radio 3 talk, later broadcast also by the Australian Broadcasting Commission;
published in *The Listener*, 15 March 1973.

in the Renaissance. They date from about the second or third century A.D., but Renaissance scholars believed them to have been actually written in remote Antiquity by the 'Hermes Trismegistus' who is named in them, at a time which they supposed to be vaguely contemporary with Moses. They believed that Hermes Trismegistus had been an Egyptian priest who revealed in these writings something of the religion and philosophy of the Egyptians, and they were convinced that he had influenced Plato, who was supposed to have drunk at the well of this ancient wisdom. When the manuscripts of the newly recovered works of Plato were brought to Florence in the fifteenth century, a codex containing Hermetic writings was brought at about the same time. Marsilio Ficino was waiting to translate them all into Latin. The old, dying Cosimo de'Medici ordered Ficino to translate Hermes Trismegistus first, before beginning his translation of Plato. This story gives us an idea of the profound respect in which Hermes Trismegistus was held, as the supposed Ancient Egyptian author of the works bearing his name, works believed to be earlier than those of Plato and to have influenced Plato.

Modern scholars are divided as to what these Hermetic writings represent. They no doubt reflect various influences circulating in the late Antique period in which they were actually written. They contain Platonic and Stoic ideas derived from popularized versions of Greek philosophy. There is probably some Persian influence in them, and, still more probably, some Hebrew influence.

Everyone who reads the Hermetic account of Creation in the dialogue called *Pimander* is vaguely reminded of Genesis, an impression which helped the belief that Hermes Trismegistus should be dated at about the time of Moses, the supposed author of Genesis. It is by no means impossible that there may be some Egyptian influence in the *Hermetica*: the Egyptian temples were still functioning when they were written. Scholars take different views of this problem, some denying that there is any Egyptian influence – as does Festugière, the great French scholar who has edited the texts and translated them into French. Other scholars think that they do contain some traces of Egyptian influence. What can be said in a general way is that the *Hermetica* belong to the atmosphere and thought-background of late Antiquity – the time when Christianity was spreading in the midst of a world which was a melting-pot of many religions and philosophies. Ficino and the Renaissance scholars believed, as did some Fathers of the Church, that Hermes should be regarded as a prophet of

Christianity, and they tried to reconcile the Hermetic mysticism with Christianity.

For these Hermetic writings diffuse a very religious, mystical, magical atmosphere, and they teach a kind of cosmic religion in which the Sun is approached as a revelation of the divine. Even when read today, with all the critical apparatus of modern scholarship concerning them in mind, they make a considerable impression. When read, as Copernicus would have read them, as the writings of an Egyptian sage of immense antiquity, the impression may well have been overwhelming.

The words quoted by Copernicus come in the Hermetic treatise known as the *Asclepius*, so called because it is a dialogue between Hermes and a disciple named Asclepius, in the course of which Hermes says:

> The Sun illuminates the other stars not so much by the power
> of its light as by its divinity and holiness, and you should
> hold him [the Sun], O Asclepius, to be the second god,
> governing all things and spreading his light on all the living
> beings in the world, both those which have a soul and those
> which have not.

Copernicus quotes the statement that the Sun is a 'second god' as the Sun is the 'visible god'. Both statements have the same meaning, seeing the Sun as the second in a divine series, or as making visible a series descended from an uncreated light. Copernicus has not only quoted the statement of Hermes on the Sun, but his words reflect the whole atmosphere of the 'religion of the world', or of the approach to the divine through the world, which is characteristic of the Hermetic treatises, and which the Renaissance Neoplatonists tried to reconcile with both Platonism and Christianity.

The *Asclepius*, the dialogue from which Copernicus quotes, contains a remarkable description of what Renaissance readers believed to be Egyptian magic, or the ways in which Egyptian priests animated the statues of their gods. It also includes a remarkable lament for the passing of the holy Egyptian religion.

Marsilio Ficino, whose translations and other writings diffused the school of thought known as Renaissance Neoplatonism, was so profoundly imbued with respect for Hermes Trismegistus that he taught, in his works on the Sun, a Sun mysticism combined with Christian influences, and practised various techniques for attracting solar influences which amounted to a kind of white magic. His book *De vita coelitus comparanda* ('On drawing down the life of heaven') has been shown in a discovery made by a modern scholar to be based on the Hermetic *Asclepius* dialogue, with its emphasis on the Sun and its description of a kind of magic supposed by Ficino and his friends to be Egyptian.

In the time of Copernicus, Renaissance Neoplatonism – with its Hermetic core – was the new and fashionable philosophy which had superseded medieval scholasticism. Copernicus's quotation from 'Trismegistus', after his diagram of the Solar System, shows that he had absorbed the Hermetic Sun mysticism, combined with Neoplatonism, which was the characteristic philosophy of his time. It has long been recognized that Copernicus presents his discovery in a religious framework. Alexandre Koyré emphasized the importance for Copernicus of the Sun in a religious and mystical sense, and speaks of the influence on him of the Neoplatonic and Neo-Pythagorean Renaissance, mentioning Ficino in this connection. What has been less generally recognized, until recent years, is the importance of the Hermetic core in Neoplatonism in encouraging new attitudes to the Sun.

Now – let me make this quite clear – I am not saying that Copernicus made his great discovery through Hermetic mysticism and magic. He made it because he was a good mathematician and in the context of genuine science. What I am trying to convey is the *atmosphere* in which he made it. Why did Copernicus become interested in the Sun? What was the emotional or religious driving force which turned him towards his inquiry, and to his discovery that 'in the midst of all resides the Sun'?

One might say that the intense emphasis on the Sun in the new world-view of Hermetic Neoplatonism was the emotional driving force which induced Copernicus to undertake his mathematical calculations on the hypothesis that the Sun is indeed at the centre of the planetary system. Or one might say that he wished to make his discovery acceptable by presenting it within the framework of this new attitude. Perhaps both explanations would be true, or some of each. At any rate, Copernicus's discovery came out with the blessing of Hermes Trismegistus upon its head, with a quotation from that famous work in which Hermes describes the Sun-worship of the Egyptians in their magical religion.

This is a fact which historians of thought must take into account, however they may interpret it. To me, it is one among many facts which indicate that the scientific revolution did not burst straight out of the Middle Ages. There was an intermediary stage – Renaissance Neoplatonism with its magical core, the true nature of which is now beginning to be understood as a driving force in turning man towards the investigation of the world.

In the century after Copernicus, a famous Italian philosopher made the Copernican heliocentricity a fundamental point in his teaching. This was Giordano Bruno, who, in dialogues published in England in 1584, boldly proclaimed, amid what he describes as reactionary opposition from benighted doctors of Oxford, that the Sun was at the centre. Seven years later, Bruno returned to Italy, where he was thrown into the prisons of the Inquisition and burned as a heretic in 1600. If Copernicus is a hero of modern science, Bruno used to be proclaimed as a martyr for modern science, burned for his belief in the Copernican theory. Now, just as people have only fairly recently realized that Copernicus quotes Hermes on the Sun, they have also only fairly recently realized that what Bruno believed in and propagated was an extremely Hermetic interpretation of Copernican heliocentricity. In one of the dialogues written in England, he quotes at length from the Hermetic *Asclepius* and proclaims that the magical religion there described is the true religion. He also quotes from the *Asclepius* the moving lament for the disappearance of the old and true religion of the world. In this lament, it is foreseen that the true religion of the world, which men have abandoned, will return. Bruno quotes the words of the *Asclepius*, which have something of the fervour of Hebrew prophecy in them: God 'will bring back the world to its first beauty, so that the world may again be worthy of reverence and admiration, and that God also, creator and restorer of so great a work, may be glorified by the men who live then in continual praises and benedictions'. And it is clear from what Bruno says of Copernican heliocentricity that he regards this as a kind of presage or prophecy of the return of this true ancient religion. Copernicus, says Bruno, was 'only a mathematician' who did not penetrate to the inner meaning of his discovery which placed the Sun at the centre. Bruno sees Copernicus as a man divinely ordained to appear 'at the dawn which was to precede the full sunrise of the ancient and true philosophy' – the ancient and true philosophy being the Hermetic religious philosophy. Thus Bruno's defence of Copernicus and of heliocentricity had meanings other than those perceived by the nineteenth-century scholars who admired him as the martyr for modern science.

The misunderstandings about Bruno can be further studied through what is now known about his argument with the Oxford doctors. According to himself, he was expounding the Copernican theory to the doctors when one of them cried that he was making a mistake. The book of Copernicus was fetched, the diagram examined, and Bruno (according to himself) proved right. But another description of this argument has recently been discovered, told from the side of the Oxford doctors. Bruno is declaiming a passionate speech about the Sun. One of the doctors thinks that he has read something like this somewhere. He fetches a book, in which he proves that Bruno's whole argument is to be found. The book is Ficino's *De vita coelitus comparanda*, the description of his Hermetic solar magic.

Bruno's argument with the Oxford doctors, defending the Copernican theory, was the main text for the legend that he died as a martyr for the Copernican theory in the scientific sense. The Oxford doctors were evidently fully aware of the Hermetic meanings which he read into Copernicus on the centrality of the Sun. In fact, one now wonders whether the real point of the whole argument was not the word 'Trismegistus', after the diagram, and whether Bruno did not take this word as confirmation of his Hermetic, Sun-centred religious mission, propagating the doctrine throughout Europe as a way of ending religious differences through a return to a true and ancient magical religion.

Bruno's extraordinary writings are a remarkable example of how the philosophic and scientific imagination was stimulated by the Hermetic influences hidden in Renaissance Neoplatonism. And his wild interpretation of Copernicus had at least some justification in that curious footnote by Copernicus after the diagram: 'Trismegistus calls the Sun the visible god.'

Chapter Thirty-two

THE MAGIC CHRISTIAN*

AGRIPPA OF NETTESHEIM (1486–*circa* 1535), German occultist and mystic, played an important part in the Renaissance by popularizing in the North those magical practices and attitudes inherent in the Neoplatonic movement that was initiated in Florence by Marsilio Ficino and Pico della Mirandola. The Renaissance ideal of the magus, the 'divine' man with powers of operating on the cosmos and achieving universal knowledge and power – adumbrated in Pico's famous *Oration on the Dignity of Man* – found its theorist in Agrippa, who wrote a textbook on how to become a magus. His *De occulta philosophia* was the best-known manual of Renaissance magic, incorporating both the Ficinian magic deriving from the Hermetic revival, and the Cabalist magic indicated by Pico and further developed by Reuchlin and the hosts of Renaissance Cabalists. A few years before the publication of the final version of the *De occulta philosophia* (1583), Agrippa published his *De vanitate scientiarum* in which he attacked all sciences as vain and useless, including the occult sciences which he was about to expound enthusiastically in his next book. Which of these two sensational works represents the true mind of Agrippa, the one which teaches the techniques of Renaissance magic and promises to lead the student to Pisgah heights of illumination, or the one

---

* Review of Charles G. Nauert, Jr., *Agrippa and the Crisis of Renaissance Thought*, Urbana, Illinois, 1966; and Joseph Anthony Mazzeo, *Renaissance and Revolution*, New York, 1966, in *New York Review of Books*, 3 March 1966.

which casts doubts on those techniques, and indeed on all human hope of valid knowledge of any kind?

The reversal of mood from visions of power and 'knowledge infinite' to total doubt is believed by Nauert to represent a 'crisis' in Renaissance thought. The great Faust figures of literature, both Marlowe's and Goethe's, repeat the Agrippan pattern of confidence alternating with despair. Nauert examines the argument that doubt is inherent in magic through its reliance on the irrational, and from his analysis of the *De vanitate* he concludes that Agrippa's scepticism may derive, not so much from ancient scepticism and the contemporary revival of Sextus Empiricus, as from the mystical tradition, from the 'negative theology' of Pseudo-Dionysius, Cusanus and others. His use of the ass as the symbol of total 'unknowing' has mystical implications, and his insistence that faith in Gospel truth is the only refuge from the uncertainty of human knowledge suggests that Agrippa's spiritual oscillations might represent the hesitations of a Christian conscience disturbed about the legitimacy of the occult philosophy as much as a swing from credulity to scepticism. One undoubted fact in the confused situation is that Agrippa never abandoned his intensive study of the occult sciences either before, during, or after his attack on their vanity. Coupled with the fact that he published his attack on these sciences *before* he published his textbook on them this suggests a simpler explanation of the two books. When accused as a magician on account of the occult philosophy he could usefully point to what he had said of the vanity of magic in the other book. The life of a Renaissance magus was not a safe one. Ficino was always afraid; Pico got into bad trouble; and Giordano Bruno was burned at the stake. I am not entirely convinced by Nauert's interesting arguments that the *Vanity* was not, at least in part, a safety device.

Magic was important in medieval culture, and even more important in Renaissance culture. That fact in itself necessitates careful, unblushing study of magic as a historical phenomenon in its own right, whether or not it led western mankind toward the great scientific advances of the seventeenth and later centuries. Forgetting that medieval and Renaissance magic involved not just witchcraft and sorcerers' pacts with devils, but also a whole concept of the world and of the relation of man to the world, those historians of thought who have not judged magic solely as the threshold of modern science have engaged in a virtual conspiracy of silence about

its existence. It is as if the religious taboos which frightened
most medieval and Renaissance men away from open
consideration of magic still weighed on the consciences of
present-day historians.

Nauert is quoting from Eugenio Garin's epoch-making book,
Medioevo e Rinascimento (1954). And in relation to the Two Faces
of Agrippa to which he devotes so much thought, Nauert remarks
that

> Agrippa the Doubter, the destructive critic of his age, has
> found a deservedly important place in the works of modern
> intellectual historians, for the categories of modern intellectual
> history offer a respectable, established, even dignified
> position to those who carped at the remnants of medieval
> culture. But Agrippa the Credulous, whom Jean Bodin
> dubbed the 'master Sorcerer,' and the hostile Jesuit, Martin
> Del Rio, called the 'Arch-Magician,' what honorable place
> does the history of modern European thought have for him?

To this it may be added that if Agrippa's *De occulta philosophia*
is beyond the pale, then Marsilio Ficino and Pico della Mirandola
ought also to be hushed up, or at least should no longer appear
as they are, vaguely and inaccurately labelled as 'Renaissance
humanists' in textbooks on the Renaissance. For it is Pico's
conception of the Dignity of Man as Magus which Agrippa sets
out to codify; and it is from Ficino's *De vita coelitus comparanda*,
with its veiled allusions to the Hermetic *Asclepius*, that he
constantly quotes.

In his analysis of the *De occulta philosophia* Nauert has made full
use of D. P. Walker's fundamental studies of Renaissance magic
and of its reliance on pseudo-antique texts of which the *Hermetica*,
attributed to 'Hermes Trismegistus', were the most important. He
incorporates Walker's distinction between 'spiritual' magic based
on attracting the 'spiritus' of the stars, and 'demonic' magic aimed
at attracting intellectual beings; and he adopts Walker's analysis
of the Agrippan magic as much bolder and more 'demonic' than
that of Ficino. Where Nauert is defective is in the vagueness of
his allusions to Agrippa's sources. He does not specify what actual
treatises of the *Corpus Hermeticum* Agrippa is quoting; a generic
reference to *Pimander* is not enough, since Ficino included twelve

treatises under this title. Nor does he describe their contents or discuss how they were interpreted in the Renaissance. In fact he gives the curious impression of not having really studied the Hermetic literature or thought about its problems and its history. For this and other reasons one cannot regard his book as the final treatment of Agrippa, valuable though it is. The works of 'Hermes Trismegistus' carried with them, for the Renaissance, Christian overtones owing to the supposed role of Hermes as a prophet of Christianity. It was associations such as these which enabled the Renaissance to build up in its cult of Hermes what amounted to a revival of gnosticism, and Agrippa's work cannot be studied in isolation from the Renaissance Hermetic tradition as a whole, nor without more detailed attention to the contents of the Hermetic treatises. It is even possible that yet another interpretation of the Agrippa 'problem' might be that Agrippa in his reading of the *Corpus Hermeticum* had imbibed both 'optimist' and 'pessimist' types of gnosis, both of which are represented in different treatises of the *Corpus*.

The biographical chapters of Nauert's book are most scholarly and detailed, and extremely valuable, particularly in establishing Agrippa's religious position. Agrippa's birthplace was Cologne, where he was educated at the university, then a centre of Thomism, though there was also a rival faction which followed the teachings of that famous native of Cologne, Albertus Magnus. It seems probable that Agrippa imbibed an interest in natural philosophy and the occult from his early study of Albertus. The teachings of the Renaissance magi thus fell on already well-prepared German medieval soil, and it would seem that Agrippa was early in possession of the general principles of Renaissance 'Magia and Cabala' as laid down by Ficino and Pico. He became a great wanderer in many countries of Europe, where he was everywhere welcomed by groups of friends or adherents to his views. Paola Zambelli, whose learned articles are basic for the student of Agrippa and who is at work on other publications bearing on this theme, believes that he was the propagator of a secret society; Nauert thinks that there is not enough evidence to prove this. Agrippa had many contacts in Lyon, that focal point for the spread of the Renaissance to France; in 1510 he was in London, studying the Epistles of St Paul with John Colet; probably about 1511 he went to Italy, where he spent seven years, eagerly collecting books, conferring with groups of occultists, and deepening his knowledge of Cabala.

He then returned to the North, a move which took him 'from the exciting and vital culture of Renaissance Italy into the very different but also exciting and vital culture of northern Europe on the very eve of the Reformation.' In Metz, Cologne, Geneva, Agrippa was in touch with scholars in sympathy with the new evangelical teachings (reflected in the evangelical tone of the *Vanity*) and who were following the Lutheran movement at first with interest and sympathy though later with alarm and distrust. Some of Agrippa's associates became Lutherans – and it has even been suggested that Agrippa's group in Geneva was the centre of a disturbed atmosphere out of which Calvinism later developed – but Agrippa himself lived and died a Catholic, though a Catholic 'evangelical' who was also a gnostic magician! A mixture so strange as this is not normally taken into account in histories of sixteenth-century religious movements, though the extraordinary spiritual excitements generated in the Hermetic-Cabalist ferment may have relevance to the religious history of Europe in ways which have hardly yet been investigated.

As a Renaissance magus, Agrippa offers to man the power over nature, and the intimate communion with nature, which Adam possessed before the Fall but which was lost through sin. The illuminated magus, operating his magics in the three worlds – the elemental world, the celestial world, and the supercelestial world – is presented as a being of immense dignity and power, who through his manipulations of astral magic escapes from astrological determinism. Renaissance magic promised, as Garin has said in words quoted by Nauert, 'the new way which will open to man the rule over nature.' And, again following Garin, Nauert compares the claims of the Renaissance magus with those formulated by Francis Bacon for his new science through which men will become 'masters and possessors of nature'. It is a pity that Nauert, who is well read in modern Italian scholarship on these themes, happened to miss Paolo Rossi's book *Francesco Bacone* (1957), which explores those connections between the magical revolution and the scientific revolution about which Nauert reflects in several passages of his book. Rossi stresses that Bacon promises that the Great Instauration of the sciences will restore to man the power over nature which Adam had before the Fall! And he argues that Bacon emerges straight out of Renaissance magic and the Renaissance idea of the magus, which, however, he consciously modifies and turns in new directions. Pointing to passages in Bacon's works against Renaissance animism and magic, Rossi evolves the interesting theory that Bacon's insistence on a humble approach to nature in observation and experiment is a conscious reaction from the proud claims of the Renaissance magi. It is, as it were, a programme for a reformed and humbled magus through which he turns into a humble scientific experimentalist and observer, yet is still offered the promise that he shall be lord and possessor of nature.

The other book under review is of a very different character, being not a detailed research monograph but a series of essays on Machiavelli, Castiglione, Bacon and Hobbes, with an introductory chapter on 'Renaissance and Humanism' and a concluding chapter on 'The Idea of Progress'. I imagine that Mazzeo's book is intended for students who need to have explained to them at some length what the ancients meant by rhetoric or the difference between a cyclic view of history and 'the idea of progress'. Nevertheless this is not an unoriginal book, though its references (except in the case of Machiavelli) are almost entirely to secondary sources. Its originality lies in the strange choice of the four main figures, which seems to have been dictated by the author's purpose, as stated on the dust-jacket, of clarifying 'what in the Renaissance was of new and enduring importance.' Machiavelli stands for his famous realism about man and statecraft; Castiglione for 'the artistic creation of the self'; Bacon is the prophet of technology and of co-operation in scientific research; Hobbes represents the scientific organization of society and of the state. Thus the reader will learn something about Machiavelli, Castiglione, Bacon, and Hobbes (and find references in the notes for further reading), and will at the same time be led to reflect on the organized society, dominated by technology, in which he lives, and on the opportunity, or lack of opportunity, which it provides for the artistic creation of the self. Inevitably, the last chapter touches on the not unfamiliar problem of the divorce between science and the humanities. This is in its way a thoughtful book; the discussions are interesting and sometimes rather brilliantly expressed. The liveliest chapter, though it may not appeal to all specialists, is the one on Machiavelli, for whom the author has a passionate admiration. The worst chapter is the one on Castiglione, which dissolves for pages into a rapprochement of this stylized courtier with Montaigne, whose ideas on the investigation of the self seem (to me at least) to be of a quite different order.

Mazzeo's book may cause one to reflect that some branches of Renaissance studies are better established and have been put on a sounder historical footing than others. Through the work of a series of brilliant scholars, Renaissance historiography and political theory are established as deriving from humanistic interest in history plus the practical observation of Italian history and the evolution of the Italian city state. We understand pretty well where Machiavelli came from. But whence came Francis Bacon with his revolutionary statements that science is power, that man can and should gain dominion over nature? So long as Renaissance 'Neoplatonism' passes solely as a vaguely eclectic Platonic philosophy, so long as Ficino and Pico are classed as 'Renaissance humanists', so long as a revolutionary figure like Agrippa is banned from the polite society of Renaissance scholars, the historical origins of the forces which eventually turned into the scientific revolution will remain obscure.

Chapter Thirty-three

DID NEWTON CONNECT HIS MATHS
AND ALCHEMY?*

THE WORK which has been done in recent years on Isaac Newton's unpublished manuscripts has not affected his stature as the brilliant mathematical thinker of the *Principia* and the *Opticks*. But it has altered the context in which we now see Newton, for it appears from the unpublished papers that this major figure in the scientific revolution of the seventeenth century was still deeply involved in ideas which we have supposed typical of the Renaissance.

In their revolutionary article on 'Newton and the Pipes of Pan' published in the *Notes and Queries of the Royal Society* in 1966, J. E. McGuire and P. M. Rattansi quoted from the unpublished manuscripts words which showed that Newton believed that in discovering the law of gravity and the world-system associated with it, he was rediscovering an ancient truth, known to Pythagoras, and hidden in the myth of Apollo with his seven-stringed lyre.

With this profoundly Renaissance faith in ancient truth hidden in myth was associated Newton's trust in 'Hermes Trismegistus' as an ancient Egyptian sage; Newton ignored Isaac Casaubon's late dating of the *Hermetica*.

In my own book, *Giordano Bruno and the Hermetic Tradition* (1964), I suggested that Bruno's Hermetic universe turned into 'something like the mechanical universe of Isaac Newton'. It now

---

* Published in *Times Higher Education Supplement*, 18 March 1977, to commemorate the two-hundred-and-fiftieth anniversary of Newton's death.

appears that, after study of the unpublished papers, scholars are inclining to the view that Newton's mechanics are affected by Hermeticism, so that Newton, too, is in a sense a Hermetic philosopher.

The most startling revelation from the unpublished papers is the fact that Newton was not merely interested in alchemy (as has always been known), but that'he devoted more time and energy to this Hermetic pursuit than he did to his mathematical studies. He collected books on alchemy, endeavoured to unravel the scientific processes which he believed to be hidden in alchemical myth, and laboured incessantly to test by experiment with furnaces in a laboratory the recipes which he believed that he had deciphered from the mysterious language of the alchemists.

This was in no sense a vulgar pursuit of gold-making, but a religious scientist's endeavour to uncover the divine plan in matter. Newton's alchemical studies were complementary to his mathematical studies. They were rigorously controlled by experiment and exact calculation in a method as carefully scientific as that used in the works for which he is famous, as has been emphasized in B. J. T. Dobbs's recent study, *The Foundations of Newton's Alchemy* (Cambridge, 1975).

Other lines of investigation were pursued by this extraordinary man with equal passion. He was, for example, determined to unravel the exact plan and proportions of the Temple of Solomon. This was another Renaissance interest; the plan of the temple, laid down by God himself, was believed to reflect the divine plan of the universe.

For Renaissance scholars, the theory of classical architecture was believed to derive from the Temple and, like it, to reflect world and human proportions. One would expect to find Newton compelling architectural theory and temple-measurement to yield scientific results as exact and important in his eyes as those derived from his mathematical and alchemical studies. (Newton's plan of the Temple of Solomon has been published by F. Manuel in his book *Isaac Newton, Historian*, Cambridge, 1963.)

Newton was also intensely interested in the chronology of world history and in prophecy. He worked out chronological systems based on the prophetic books of the Old Testament, hoping that here also, by more rigidly accurate organization of such materials, he would be able to gain a better grasp both of past history and of prophetic insight into the future. In these apocalyptic calculations, Newton's Protestant bias comes out powerfully.

Where in the history of thought, religion, or science can one find a cluster of ideas at all comparable to the amazing content of the mind of Isaac Newton? Though this question cannot be answered as yet with complete confidence, there are certain fairly obvious clues which demand investigation.

Among the large number of alchemical writers studied by Newton, one of his favourites was Michael Maier, whose works were copied by him again and again. Maier belonged to the early seventeenth-century German Rosicrucian movement; he made a particular study of alchemical thought hidden in myth, and his own alchemical writings are close in spirit to those of John Dee, whose philosophy underlies the Rosicrucian manifestos.

Dee's mysterious *Monas hieroglyphica* is probably alluded to in one of Maier's alchemical emblems. Dee's *monas* was a symbol which seemed, for him, to unite mathematical and alchemical thought in such a way as to achieve insight into 'one truth' behind nature.

Another alchemical volume which Newton studied deeply and copied was Elias Ashmole's *Theatrum chemicum*, a collection of alchemical texts among which is a short description in verse of Dee's *monas*. In a commentary on the volume, Ashmole quotes from a Rosicrucian manifesto, alludes to Michael Maier, and gives a long account of John Dee and of his work as a mathematician, which he praises highly.

It seems not unreasonable to ask whether part of Newton's interest in these texts might have been because he sought in them possible connections between alchemical and mathematical thought – his own dominant interests – which Dee would seem to have found significant ways of combining. At any rate, he must have read about Dee in the *Theatrum chemicum*, and heard of his mathematics through the alchemical volume to which he attached such importance.

Among those probably connected with the antecedents of the German Rosicrucian movement was Simon Studion, whose unpublished treatise, written in 1604, has the title *Naometria* (temple-measurement). It is a most elaborate account of measurements of the Temple of Solomon, combined with theories of world-history, significant historical dates, and apocalyptic prophecy, all in a strongly anti-papal vein.

Studion's outpourings belong to a class of literature which

Newton knew, and used in his own unpublished manuscripts on such themes. I have suggested, in *The Rosicrucian Enlightenment* (1972), that Studion's prophecy that the year 1620 would see the downfall of Antichrist (the Papacy) may have encouraged Frederick of the Palatinate in his mad enterprise against the Habsburg powers. This suggestion cannot, of course, be proved; but a reading of Studion is certainly evocative of the atmosphere of those times.

Following Maier as a clue has led into a cluster of ideas relating to alchemy, mathematics, prophecy and apocalypse similar to those which preoccupied Newton. They belong to the period of the politico-religious movement which failed so disastrously in 1620, a failure which almost overwhelmed the cause of Protestantism in Europe.

Ideas from those times would have reached Newton through the Protestant tradition, of which he so strongly approved. Those who believed intensely in Protestant principles viewed with passion the collapse of Protestantism in Europe; some of this passion may have gone into Newton's intense search for God in mathematics, alchemy, and Biblical prophecy.

If the movements outlined here seem possible as the historical preparation for Newton, the problem still remains of explaining the change from a later Renaissance type of outlook and personality – such as that of John Dee – into the personality and outlook of the seventeenth-century scientist, Newton.

And yet there was a Hermetic core to the seventeenth-century scientist; Newton the mathematician was doubled by Newton the alchemist. Do the two interests overlap, even in the *Principia* and the *Opticks*, as some contemporary scholars now think? If so, should one not look for his antecedents in the early seventeenth-century alchemical movements which, as yet, have been only superficially explored?

AUTOBIOGRAPHICAL

FRAGMENTS

PREFACE
by
J. N. Hillgarth

The first part of the fragments published here, going as far as 1914, was revised by Frances Yates and is printed as she left it. To distinguish it from what follows it has been given the title 'Early Life'. It was not intended to stand alone. It was to be the first chapter of a book which would have traced her intellectual development from its beginnings in her family circle through her growing interest in Renaissance themes and then shown how that interest was deepened and changed by her meeting with the scholars of the Warburg Institute when that institution was re-established in England in the 1930s after its forced migration from Hitler's Germany. The book would necessarily have included a discussion of the genesis of the Warburg and of its impact on scholarship in England. Unfortunately for all of us, this book was never written. Most of it was not even sketched out. There remain a number of separate groups of notes on Frances's family and her life after 1914. These were apparently written after the 'Early Life'. The sections published here consist of a short note on her family's move in 1925 from Worthing to what proved to be their permanent home, the New House in Claygate (one of the last things she wrote; it is dated June 1981), and more substantial notes on her writings. Most of these are dated 1980 or 1981. These notes include the two pages on 'The genesis of Astraea'. The brief notes on the later books, from *The Valois Tapestries* onwards, were written in 1975 and exist in a more telegraphic form than the later notes. The decision to publish some of these notes (while omitting others) was made because it seemed unjust to deprive readers interested in Frances Yates's work of the light that only her own comments on it can give (the only books for which we have no comments by her are her last two publications, *Shakespeare's Last Plays: A New Approach*, 1975, and *The Occult Philosophy in the Elizabethan Age*, 1979). It should, however, be clearly understood that the post-1914 notes were left in an incomplete state and were not revised by their author. Some editorial changes were necessary; they have been kept to a minimum and were mainly directed at eliminating repetitions. My aim in editing these notes has been not to lose their personal tone.

Among Frances Yates's papers there is a journal which she kept from 24 April 1916 to 4 March 1917, when she was aged sixteen to seventeen and at school in Birkenhead. In general these pages are, I suppose, fairly typical of journals written by intelligent girls of that age at that time. There are, of course, references to the war, but more space is given to the author's family, her friends, her school, and the books she was reading. The journal contains some notes on 'my past life'. After describing the period up to the outbreak of the First World War (covered in greater detail and more vividly in her 'Early Life', published here), she refers briefly to her brother James's death 'on the 8th of October 1915, whilst leading a bayonet attack'. This deliberate restraint does not convey the impression James's death made on her, an impression which lasted all her life. In notes written in 1975, when she revisited Llandrindod Wells (the scene of her father's almost mortal illness in 1912, described in the 'Early Life'), Frances said of her brother's death: 'The 1914–18 war broke our family; as a teenager I lived among the ruins.' In its turn this should not be taken to mean that the other members of her family were not central to her life. Her two elder sisters, Hannah, a teacher and distinguished novelist, and Ruby, who, after working for many years as a teacher of coloured girls in South Africa, retired in 1949 to look after Frances, were both remarkable people and were very important indeed to her. The vital encouragement of her parents is apparent in the fragmentary memoirs printed here.

Her family set high standards for her. At the beginning of the 1916–17 journal proper there is a passage which seems worth quoting: 'The other day I wrote two poems. They might be called quite clever for a girl of my age, or really not bad in places, but they are not good. I want to write something great and splendid, something which will make my name famous, not only a "not so bad" poem. My brother wrote poems, my sister writes novels, my other sister paints pictures, and I, I must and *will* [her italics] do something. I am not much good at painting, I am no good at all at music, so there is only writing left. So I will write. But in order to write you must have read and I am reading like fury. During the last two months I have read Rossetti's poems, Boswell's *Life of Johnson*, Landor's *Imaginary Conversations*, a life of Lorenzo de' Medici, Keats's poems, a life and criticism of Shakespeare, four of Shakespeare's plays, Hazlitt's criticism of them, not to mention several novels.' The connection between several of the books listed (especially the Shakespeare and the Medici life) and Frances's later writings is evident. What is perhaps more surprising is that this passage, written at the age of sixteen, reveals the same critical sense and refusal to be content with the second-best, the same determination to succeed in what she thought worth doing, which appear throughout her life.

In the same journal of 1916 Frances records discussing with her elder sister Hannah the possibility of going to Oxford to read history. It is clear that the idea appealed to her very much. However, her education was to continue to follow the unorthodox course which she describes in her 'Early Life', and one can perhaps extend to her general 'escape from regular education' her comment on her earlier years that 'it was a marvellous good fortune'. While she earned an external First London B.A. and later an internal M.A., she was, as she says, 'largely left to my own devices'. This perhaps enabled her to absorb new ideas, whether they came from her own reading or, later, from scholars trained outside the conventional English lines. At the same time the absence of a secure English academic base for much of her life created problems for her which might not have confronted someone who had in fact been to Oxford. That she triumphed over these obstacles was due not only to the power of her original vision but also to the strength of a remarkable will which kept her going through all difficulties and enabled her, as Professor Hugh Trevor-Roper remarked in the *Sunday Times*, in the end to 'create her own discipline'.

AUTOBIOGRAPHICAL FRAGMENTS

I

EARLY LIFE

I WAS BORN on Tuesday, 28 November 1899, at a house called Fairfax in Victoria Road North, Southsea, Hants. According to my father's notes on this arrival of his fourth child, I was born at 9.18 a.m.; the nurse's name was Mrs Harrison; and the doctor was Dr F. Lord of Landport Terrace, Southsea. I was, says my father, a fine baby with a nice head of hair.[1]

My father at the time was Chief Constructor at Portsmouth Dockyard, in charge of the naval construction programme then in progress in the Dockyard. The British Empire was at the height of its power and glory, the British Navy second to none in the world, though it was my father's task to keep ahead of the German Navy and its ambitious naval construction programme. Yet the first cracks in the magnificent edifice had begun to appear. The South African War was in progress: I was born on the day of the battle of Modder River, a disastrous defeat for the British Army.

We were only temporarily at the house Fairfax, for my mother's confinement. The present home of the family was actually at Number One The Terrace, Portsmouth Dockyard, the official residence of the Chief Constructor. I remember nothing of the Fairfax period, though my father records that I was taken out of doors for the first time on 31 December 1899. My sister Ruby remembers holding me at the window to see snow, and that a paper shop opposite constantly displayed posters with bad news of the South African War. So ended my first month in the last month of the nineteenth century, having my first outing on the last day of the century, in an atmosphere of bad news.

We must have returned to the Dockyard early in 1900. A Victorian naval dockyard (the old Queen was still alive) was an impressive place, and Portsmouth was the premier dockyard. Surrounded by walls and entered through guarded gates, the Dockyard was a world apart. The officers and their families were housed in a very handsome Georgian terrace; all the dockyard buildings had a kind of sombre dignity; by day it resounded to the clang of hammering on iron, as the great ships were hammered out; on Sundays there was an unearthly silence save for services in the Dockyard chapel. It was a world somewhat cut off from the outside world, yet also at the centre of history. In those days Nelson's *Victory* was not in dry-dock within the dockyard, as now, but floated in the harbour.

I was christened in the Dockyard chapel on 24 February 1900. The Dockyard chaplain, the Rev. W. Law, officiated, my uncle Jim was godfather, and my parents and sisters and brother – Nannie, Ruby and Jimmy – were present. I wore an ancient robe worn on similar occasions by Mamma, Nannie, Ruby, and Jimmy, and I was awake and very good (source of these details, my father).

My eldest sister, Hannah (Nannie), was fifteen in the year of my birth; and my second sister, Ruby, was thirteen. They were schoolgirls at the Portsmouth High School, winning the handsomely bound prizes which I used afterwards to admire in the drawing-room bookcase. My brother Jimmy was eleven, attending the Portsmouth Grammar School and also winning prizes. I was thus a late-comer to an established late Victorian family which had already had a highly satisfactory family history, centred on dockyards – Ruby was born in Chatham Dockyard, Jimmy at Devonport – before my arrival. Only Hannah, the eldest, was not born in a dockyard: she was a Cockney, born within the sound of Bow Bells, when my father was working at the Thames Ironworks, supervising the building of the early Ironclads. I appeared at a time when my father's career was at its height. The splendours surrounding my earliest years were not characteristic of the family history as a whole. Nevertheless, they were splendours. I had a rather wonderful entry into life, welcomed not only by kind parents moving successfully in an atmosphere fraught with history, but also by kind and brilliant elder sisters and brother who received me enthusiastically as a fascinating new addition to their circle. I have no really distinct memory of those earliest Portsmouth years but whatever unconscious trace of them I may carry would be of a hopeful and confident nature – fortunately, since unconscious confidence would certainly be a help in the years ahead.

On 18 January 1901, Queen Victoria died. The coffin was brought from the Isle of Wight to Gosport between lines of warships. My sister Ruby remembers seeing the tremendous sight. Presumably the dockyard hammering would have been silenced on that most solemn day.

In 1902 my father was transferred to Chatham Dockyard, where he continued the work of supervising the production of Dread-noughts at record speed which he had been doing at Portsmouth, in accordance with Admiral Fisher's programme. The correct official residence on The Terrace in Chatham Dockyard was not yet available, so a house was taken in Rochester: Hawthornden, 217 Maidstone Road, whence my father bicycled into Chatham. With the Rochester house, my memories begin.

It was one of those houses in which from the front door you look straight through the hall to the garden at the back. The family was rather fascinated; a private house in a cathedral city was a change from a dockyard residence, which, however imposing, had an official severity and was in the midst of the anxieties of competitive naval construction. I think that it was hoped that life might now be more meditative, with possibly spiritual possibilities opening up for religious temperaments. We were not there long enough to sink deep roots, nor did we belong to the Cathedral set. Perhaps it was the dockyard influence, or perhaps it was something in the family temperament, but there seemed always a certain classlessness and isolation about our social position. But Rochester was certainly an influence. I began to be taken to the Cathedral services, at first only in the nave, though I demanded to be taken to 'more church' in the choir. I began to hear the language of the Old Testament, read by powerful bearded canons with splendid voices, who had probably had two mutton chops for breakfast and who looked round fiercely, from the fierce lectern eagle, as they shut the Book: 'Here endeth the first lesson.' It was frightening and thrilling. One heard how Balaam's ass prevented Balaam from cursing the People, and how Noah built the Ark. No affectations or Oxford accents; such things are marks of insecurity. When the social and religious position is firm, and it is clear that God really made His promises to the British People, the tremendous stories can be told forth in clarion tones. I had been given my first book, *Alice in Wonderland,* but I could not read: my mother believed in keeping children back from reading too soon so that their active little brains should not be prematurely tired. I do not know how much I understood of the stories; they had probably been previously explained to me. I certainly understood something, and I was certainly affected by the language and how it rolled round and round the Cathedral, the words cannoning into one another in the echoes in an utterly mysterious way. A child can take in something of that magic, which is of course completely lost when the sacred language is turned into the language of every day.

I had my first religious experience in Rochester, though one could hardly call it that; more like a theological experience.

I was standing in the garden. It had rained; a rainbow shone out; and the story of Noah's Ark came into my mind, in a clear logical sequence which I remember absolutely distinctly. It says in the Bible that God put His bow in the sky: it has rained and there is the bow; therefore the Bible is true. Evidently I had already had Doubts. And evidently I have changed very little since the age of five, only acquiring a little more experience and learning, for those are the kind of thoughts which I always think and I suppose shall think to the end.

My brother began, during the Rochester period, to go to the King's School, Canterbury; he was developing as a very interesting personality. My sisters' minds were active; they put themselves through the London Matriculation; Hannah took singing lessons and Ruby sketched. My mother sat in a window of evenings, when the birds were flying round before returning to roost in the way birds used to do, carving an intricate pattern on a table which we still have; the red may and the lilacs flowered in the garden into a brilliance of colouring only achievable in Kent. And in due course, the people in the official residence in Chatham Dockyard moved out and we moved in. Dockyard life began again.

The family had lived twice before on The Terrace in Chatham Dockyard, once at Number One in 1887, where Ruby was born, once at Number Three, where Hannah had her first serious illness. I had not been present on those occasions, being not yet born. It always seemed surprising that so much of the family life happened before my arrival, though I know it so well by hearsay and could often correct them on details of what they did before I was born. The dockyard life and the names of the people on the various terraces on which they lived were intensely familiar to me in later years through their reminiscences, but there was only one of the dockyard episodes which I could myself remember, and that was 'Chatham Third Time'. We moved out of the Rochester house and into Number Six at Chatham in 1905.

'The Terrace' in Chatham Dockyard is one of the most magnificent Georgian terraces in the country, though not familiar to the public because of the inexorable rule that no photographs may be taken inside a dockyard. Forty or more years later when I was working on the editing of the *Journal of the Warburg and Courtauld Institutes* with Rudolf Wittkower he showed me a set of photographs which he had obtained through his prestige as an art historian. They were photographs of Chatham Dockyard, including The Terrace. I was struck dumb with amazement that a dockyard terrace should have become Art History, and stupefied also by the thought of how impossible is the task of the historian. If one had actually been there, as I actually was in Number Six when it was a living part of history, it looked and felt so entirely different when seen as a historical monument. So might a *valet de chambre* who had been in attendance on Louis XIV grow baffled at a lecture on Versailles. The actual feel and taste of history as it passes, passes away with history and drains from the solid monuments themselves as they turn into museum pieces.

The Terrace, lofty in itself, gains an added impression of height because it is actually on a terrace: from it the ground slopes downwards to the Dockyard and the Medway. The entrances to the houses are on different levels: from the Terrace side you enter large basement rooms, and from these you must go upstairs to reach the front entrance from the road outside the Dockyard which skirts The Terrace. Our garden was on the other side of this road; to reach it one had to cross the road from the house and enter a door in a wall. Long and narrow, this garden sloped upward from the road, and it was rather an event to be conducted there to play in it. On the Terrace side, all was safe for children, since no traffic was allowed through the Dockyard Gate, guarded by its policemen. The Terrace was wide: each house had its columned portico, peaceful for sitting in on summer evenings. And on Sundays there was the curious Dockyard sabbath quiet, when the hum ceased, the hum of the riveters riveting the iron plates on to the ships for the Navy.

These magnificent terraces in the dockyards date from the days of the glory of the wooden navy, when England's walls were built of wood. My father actually remembered seeing, as a boy in Portsmouth Dockyard, trunks of great trees steaming hot, ready for shaping into the wooden walls. As a boy apprentice he had been taught the elements of wooden naval architecture, just about to be superseded. He himself belonged to the first generation of experts in iron ships. Thus history loomed over The Terrace: the past history of the wooden navy, and the present history of the iron navy now building up in preparation for the Great War.

Within, the terrace-house was roomy and complicated. The marvellous 'drawing-room', lighted by the tall windows on the first floor, had great dignity and classical elegance, fully appreciated by my mother in her furnishing of it. The walls were papered brown with a white frieze: golden brown chenille curtains framed the windows, and the 'drawing-room bookcase' here appeared for the first time, receptacle of the family's prizes in those elegant calf bindings which prizes used to have. I suppose that that room was, in a way, the apogee of our family history, deeply appreciated not for vulgar reasons of display but for its initiation into the classical elegance of a great house, an initiation to which our actual position in life did not entitle us. Afterwards, in other houses, the chenille curtains and the drawing-room bookcase, and my mother's escritoire, would appear in far less glorious settings. I remember the Christmas play of that year, written by Hannah and acted by the family. It was the only Christmas play in which I took part, as I was either not yet born or too young for the others, and Chatham was the last of the series. My brother as the hero was making an affecting speech and I was waiting in the wings, or rather on the stairs, to run in as his long-lost child. I failed to appear, and was found weeping outside, overcome by the pathos of the situation.

In that vast house, my brother would chase me up the back staircase and down the front staircase and through the huge apartment known as the 'laundry', where no laundering was ever done. It was large enough to do washing in for a whole ship's crew and aroused speculation as to what manner of use the Terrace houses had been put in days gone by. There were great, empty attics with mysterious wooden lockers fitted to the walls. I preferred not to go up there after dark, and indeed a dockyard house, with all its grandeur, had a forbidding side. I had insomnia, which I never had in after-life, and my long-suffering elder sisters would lie on the bed trying to induce me to sleep. Hannah would sing to me

> Gaily the troubadour
> Touched his guitar
> As he was hastening
> Home from the war . . .

On Sundays, the Terrace families attended Divine Service in the Dockyard chapel, occupying pews strictly in the order of the head of the family's rank in the Dockyard: the gallery was reserved for the Marines. The service was neither High Church nor Low Church, though definitely Church of England. The chapel was considered rather ugly and uninteresting, and I was surprised, when I saw it again a few years ago, for the first time since 1905, to find how light and pure it is, somewhat after the manner of Inigo Jones's St Paul's, Covent Garden. The Dockyard chapel, and perhaps its religion, must have been of the same date as the Terrace.

Sometimes, after church, some of the congregation went outside the Gate to watch the Marines form up and march off with their band. Now that mechanical music fills the ear from morn to night it must be difficult to realize the effect of a live band striking up. That ancient scene outside the Gate, as we stood in our Sunday clothes to watch the Marines, seems infinitely remote in time and history, more strange and far away than the Elizabethan age, yet I remember it absolutely distinctly, and remember the feel of that world. The images of the dockyard religion were slow in fading from my infant mind. Afterwards in Glasgow, when singing at children's services the hymn 'Around the throne of God a band', I would feel vaguely confused by the following line, 'Of glorious angels ever stand', since the band around the throne of God must surely be the band of the Royal Marines.

Early in 1906 we moved out of the Chatham Dockyard house, for my father had a new appointment. Constant moves were a feature of the profession, and my mother, I believe, almost enjoyed them. Once she had to move out of a house on the terrace in Devonport Dockyard into the one next door, because my father had been promoted. Now the move was not into another dockyard but into something quite new and strange. He had been made superintendent of shipbuilding for the government in private ship-yards on the Clyde, and we were all to live in Glasgow.

I am a little confused about this move. The parents went up to Glasgow to arrange about the house. Jimmy went back to school. Ruby and Hannah were in charge of me and with them I stayed at Apsley House in Southsea, a boarding house kept by a certain Miss Knight for girls attending the Portsmouth High School. Ruby and Hannah had stayed there before and Miss Knight was a well-known feature of the family landscape. She was a remarkable character and, I believe, an aunt of Wilson Knight, the Shakespearean scholar. I remember clearly the time at Apsley House, and a friendship with a little girl whose parents were in India; and here I was at last being taught to read by Ruby, out of a manuscript primer written and illustrated especially for me by herself: 'Little Nan dropped her fan in the pan', with a drawing of little Nan dropping her fan. Hannah must have drawn for me some of her celebrated (in the family) little men taking part in long stories, since one of these drawings is extant on Apsley House paper, very clever and lively.

I think we must have had the hymn 'There is a green hill far away' at prayers at Apsley House, for the image of the hill so far away where there was a sadness beyond my ken, where the dear Lord was crucified, merges somehow into a kind of Biblical transformation of Southsea Common. These were the last memories and impressions of those early days before our migration to the north.

The vans containing our furniture were unable to get through a tunnel on the railway, which meant a long delay in its delivery at our empty house in Glasgow – 9 Bellshaugh Road, Kelvinside. I suppose this was why we spent some time in gloomy lodgings in Burnbank Gardens, where I was woken out of sleep one evening to be shown an immense snowball which boys were rolling in the street, as my first introduction to the wonders of the north. We used to walk every day to the house in Bellshaugh Road to see if the furniture had come, but it hadn't. It came at last, and then began one of the best-remembered epochs of the family life.

The house was well-built and comfortable in a quiet suburb; it had absolutely no garden, save a patch of grass in the front, but the grounds and classical façade of Kelvinside Academy, immediately opposite, gave a feeling of space. There were no dockyard noises here, no hum of riveting: my father left on his bicycle every morning to superintend from his office in Partick the progress of naval construction on the Clyde. As at Rochester, we appeared here more as a normal family, with a normal social life, rather than a family insulated from the outer world by dockyard walls. We went to Glasgow in 1906 and left in 1911. During those years the main and most important part of the family grew up and entered upon adult fields of activity. In 1907 Hannah went to Girton College, where she stayed until 1910, taking an honours degree in classics and history. Ruby attended the Glasgow School of Art (the new building by Mackintosh). Jimmy left the King's School, Canterbury, and entered Hertford College, Oxford, in 1908, taking an honours degree in classics in 1912.

We lived in a good house and employed a cook and housemaid. Evidently we belonged to the educated middle classes. No one could doubt it. Yet this position had been won for us by my father's untiring efforts. He had no money of his own. He had taken the opportunity offered to a penniless boy by the dockyard career: he had spent practically nothing on himself and everything on giving his family the kind of advantages which he had not had. Yet he never mentioned this aspect of things: never, never did one hear such a remark as 'Remember what I have done for you.' He used to say a short grace before meals: 'For what we are about to receive, may the Lord make us truly thankful.' If anyone was to be thanked for what we received, it was the Lord and not my father.

Looking back, it seems positively miraculous what he achieved. I believe that his salary in the Glasgow period was around £1,000 a year, perhaps a little more. (Such things were not loudly proclaimed in those days: it was considered vulgar to talk about money.) Even allowing for the enormous increase in the cost of living, what he managed to provide on that salary seems astounding. We had good holidays too, sometimes foreign holidays. Books were bought: there were plenty of books in the house. Some toys were bought, though carefully: I had a most handsome dolls' perambulator. But no money was spent casually. I never had any pocket money, nor did I miss it, nor think I ought to have it. A very small sum was provided at Christmas out of which one bought Christmas presents with extreme care. It was reported of Hannah that on being given a penny as a small child, she said 'Ugly thing' and threw it into the fire. Another, less pleasing, story was told of me: asked what I would put into the church collection, I replied: 'The usual: someone else's penny.'

I believe, though this seems hardly credible, that my father did not have a bank account, perhaps for reasons of economy, or from general innocence of high finance. Certainly my mother did not have one. She paid the tradesmen in cash, making regular visits to the shops for this purpose. Presumably, my father handed her the housekeeping money in cash at regular intervals, though this transaction was not publicized. My mother undoubtedly helped very greatly towards the extraordinary results which they produced on their income. She had an air of munificence about her which made a little go a long way: when serving the pudding at meals she would appear to be giving it all to each person, yet there was always more. Yet behind this appearance of splendour she took very honourable care not to waste the household money.

There was, for example, the matter of counting the sacks of coal in, which I was sometimes called in to assist. A coalman entering with a sack of coal looks very much the same when entering a second time with another sack, and this holds good for the third and fourth time, and so on up to the total number of sacks ordered. You could count him on your fingers if you liked, but more than ten sacks were usually ordered and you could easily get into a muddle. Is that the fourteenth sack or the fifteenth? It was anxious work, and of course I caught the anxiety from my mother. This was a part of the careful supervision which she exercised over the whole domestic economy. This it was which made it possible to send a son to Oxford and a daughter to Cambridge and to maintain a house in which nothing was wanting for civilized life.

And if you were to imagine that the cooks and housemaids suffered from this care you would be wrong. They had exactly the same food as we had ourselves; they were spoken to in exactly the same tone of voice and with the same courtesy as ladies entering by the front door to leave cards. I cannot believe that any of my mother's cooks and housemaids really disliked her and many of them loved her. That nurse Emma of the early days whom I never saw was always spoken of as a dear friend.

I hear in my mind's ear the mutterings of an angry reader. These oppressed grimy coalmen and patronized cooks and housemaids were the products of the bad system. I was living, growls this reader, in a little island of bourgeois snobbery in one of the worst periods, and one of the worst areas, for the capitalist exploitation of the poor. We were not oblivious of the Glasgow slums: on the contrary, they haunted us. My mother knew something about them: she did what used to be called 'district visiting', in connection with the church. She had been up the filthy staircases and spoken to the inhabitants. I am quite sure that she didn't talk to them about religion, because she never did talk about it. She would have chatted in a friendly manner as human being to human being and with humour – an ingredient in social intercourse which can play no small part in alleviating the miseries of the human lot and which seems to have gradually died out. What became of the Cockney humour, for example?

I am not saying that the system was not bad. It was bad: I am only trying to write an account, as honest as I can make it, of a family living in times which I can remember.

My father could certainly not be accused of being a capitalist. I believe he thought that he was entitled to the salary for which he over-worked but to nothing more. Even his pension he used to worry about in extreme old age, wondering whether by living so long he had become what used to be called in Victorian times 'one of the Queen's bad bargains'. He did not take out a patent for a lamp to be used by gunners, the light of which was invisible to the enemy and which was much used in war-time, because he viewed the invention as belonging not to himself but to the government. His views on corruption were extreme, even to fanaticism; witness the episode of the sugar cake.

This sugar cake arrived one day in a parcel addressed, I believe, to me. It was one of those creations in which Glasgow confectioners specialized, a shortbread covered by an elaborate design of flowers in sugar. It had just been unpacked and was being examined with some interest when my father came in, asked where it came from, flew into a towering passion and ordered it to be sent back at once. I asked no questions about this mysterious scene but the memory image of it was stored and in much later years one guessed the meaning. The private shipbuilding firms on the Clyde were anxious to obtain government orders. A present to the government representative's little girl was innocent enough but, if accepted, might lead to other proposals. I think this may have been the reason for my father's passion. Such heroic intransigence may have done him no good in some quarters.

And what became of little Frances's education in the Glasgow years, the late arrival, always nearly a generation behind the others, petted and spoiled, still a child when the others were grown up? I was six when we went to Glasgow, eleven when we left. Ruby claims that she taught me to read by her method in three months, so that, since the lessons began in Apsley House,

I must have been reading by about April 1906. I remember one bedtime when Hannah asked me if there was anything in particular that I wished to pray for. I put up a petition that I might soon be able to read a whole book. The Lord must have attended fairly promptly to this request, for soon I was reading long books by myself. Ruby remembers me looking up from *Westward Ho!* and asking 'What does excommunication mean? Quick now.'

My religious and theological education continued under Hannah. I was rather bothered by the Trinity, and also by Eternity. Ruby remembers me standing on the bed in my nightgown chanting 'For *ever*, and for *ever*, and for *ever*. Doesn't it make you feel tired?'

At some point, I am not sure when, my mother began giving me lessons in the mornings; perhaps when Hannah and Ruby became otherwise occupied at Girton and at the Glasgow School of Art. I do not think that she exhausted herself in elaborate preparation for this educational work. Her approach to life and letters was rather in the expansive and leisured eighteenth-century manner which she had perhaps imbibed at Mrs Withers's school than in the modern and earnestly efficient methods which her elder daughters had acquired in the new era of the Girls' Public Day School Trust. Yet she was in her way brilliant, a great believer in the expansion and enrichment of the mind through observation and reading. And she admired a good style, or what she thought was a good style, for which she depended on no one's judgement but her own. She therefore set the child to copy out what she considered fine passages from good authors. One of her choices was the description in *Vanity Fair* of how they heard in Brussels the guns of Waterloo:

All that day, from morning until past sunset, the cannon never ceased to roar. It was dark when the cannonading stopped all of a sudden.

I had to copy from there up to the end of the chapter:

No more firing was heard in Brussels – the pursuit rolled miles away. Darkness came down on the field and city; and Amelia was praying for George, who was lying on his face, dead, with a bullet through his heart.

It is to be hoped that my style improved, and it was fortunate that we did not have the gift of prophecy.

I was now nine and I had been to no school, kindergarten, nor any place of instruction outside the bosom of my family. I had, however, had a liberal education within that bosom. I had lived in a highly civilized atmosphere: I had learned to read books in a natural way, because I was interested in them, unpressed, unhurried, with intense enjoyment. I had had a remarkable range of private tutors in the members of the family with whom I was constantly engaged in lively discussions. It was a wonderful world in which to have had one's first impressions and I was, in a manner of speaking, already formed along the lines of life which I would afterwards follow, before I went to my first school.

This was Laurel Bank School, Glasgow, which I began to attend in 1909, a private school founded a few years previously by Miss Hannan Watson and Miss Janet Spens, afterwards well known as an Oxford tutor and author of one of the best books on Spenser. Miss Watson and Miss Spens had, however, parted company some time before I entered Laurel Bank. This legendary lady in Oxford I was to meet many, many years later and to find as distinguished and noble as her legend.

The education at Laurel Bank was not severely academic and did not interfere with the even tenor of my way or press me towards examination proficiency. In those calm days, competitive examinations for children of eleven and under were not yet invented. What I intensely enjoyed and threw myself into was the society of little girls of my own age. Everyone in the form gave a party at Christmas or the New Year and this glorious round of social pleasure was an excitement and delight. I had other little friends, too, among the neighbours, and altogether, at that age, I was a social being.

There were marvellous holidays, too, the most memorable of all being 1910, the never-to-be-forgotten summer when the family inhabited a farm-house on the island of Colonsay in the Hebrides. This house stood on a brae near the sea: there was no other house within three miles in any direction. Three great bays of the sea, strewn with fascinating rocks to play round, with sea-pinks growing near the shores, with cowrie shells thrown up by the Gulf Stream to be collected after every tide – were ours alone. No other people were to be seen except our family. My brother and I fetched water from a well near which grew the Grass of

Parnassus, flower of ecstasy with its green-veined whiteness. The experience of Colonsay lives for ever in memory.

The family attended in Glasgow the Scottish Episcopal Church of St Mary, where influences rather different from the dockyard religion made themselves felt, more High Church perhaps, yet with a slightly different Scottish Episcopal mystique which, I believe, had distant French origins. Church on Sundays blended with literature, because my father decreed that no novels should be read on Sundays, but poetry was allowed. He himself would read *Paradise Lost*, Shakespeare, or Browning on Sunday after-noons, not with a view to a Ph.D. in Eng. Lit., unheard of, but for – so to speak – spiritual enjoyment.

Public events of those days might be impressive but were not alarming. Edward VII died. Motor cars (as they were then called, not cars) were not unknown sights but rare. The usual sound of traffic would be the distant clip-clop of a horse and cart, coming nearer and passing. No one noticed that there was no noise: this was natural, the natural background of thought and activity.

It seems to me now the Golden Age, in which the security and stability of the Victorian era were still intact and seemed the natural state of affairs which would continue for ever (though in a less severe and easier form). It was not, of course, a golden age for all, but for me it was a time of perfect safety and happiness when I first put down roots of experience and inquiry in a world which made sense.

Like all times, that time came to an end. My father retired in 1911, not quite entirely, but we left the house. There had been a rumour that he would be appointed to a new dockyard in Canada, but this fell through. There was no new dockyard created in Canada, perhaps with unfortunate results for naval preparedness. This uncertainty about the future probably affected my parents' plans on leaving Glasgow.

I remember well the day when my mother and I left Bellshaugh Road for the last time. We are walking up Kirklees Road and I am in an agony of grief which I am determined that she shall not see. Never again, no, never any more, something is over which will never come again. In my agony I am clutching in my hands boxes of matches, several boxes of matches. These matches, indub-itably present in the memory image, were probably due to our having been round the house for the last time. My mother had a phobia about fire, and would remove all inflammable matter. I had been ordered to collect all the match-boxes and was clutching them as we walked up Kirklees Road. Never again. How right I was in my agony.

My father was still doing some work in Glasgow and lived in lodgings in Bearsden with Ruby. All this meant that the parents deferred the problem of where to settle in retirement. They decided not to take another house immediately, to wait until my father's work was finished and his future settled, and in the meantime to store the furniture. The summer was coming on: a long summer holiday could be taken without the expense of maintaining a house at the same time: perhaps later there might be travel abroad. One can see the various reasons for this otherwise rather curious migratory period in the family life. The uncertainty about the Canada appointment was no doubt the main cause of the lack of decision to settle: the years in the north had interrupted some of their friendships and relationships: the mobility of dockyard life had meant that no strong roots had been laid down in any particular area: they were accustomed to being told where to live and not used to deciding this for themselves. Altogether, it seemed best to defer, to look around and move around.

As it turned out, and owing to unforeseen circumstances, the moving around went on for longer than they had intended. One result of the migratory period was that I did not go to school for two years, from the age of eleven to the age of thirteen. I do not know whether they even thought about this aspect of their problem. Probably they thought that I would continue to receive tuition from the gifted members of my family, and my mother, with her Grand-Tourish ideas, no doubt took the view that seeing the world would be an education in itself.

Thus it came about that I continued to escape regular education, and this almost accidentally. It was a marvellous good fortune such as can befall no child today.

The summer of 1911 was very hot: day after day of blazing sunshine. We had an unusually long summer holiday, really the first phase of the migratory period. They took rooms near to the sea at Whitby. A routine was established, going down on the sands, putting up the tent – a red-striped umbrella with awning attached – bathing, paddling, making sandcastles and watching the incoming tide demolish them. It went on and on, a long, long summer holiday in the Victorian tradition. We were all there, the parents, Nannie, Ruby, Jimmy and Frances. A family periodical was written called *The Heat Wave*, with contributions from Nannie, Ruby, Jimmy and Frances. The others got slightly bored with it but I went on and on producing instalments of a serial story. Some excursions were made into the interior. A little Glasgow friend of mine was staying with her family nearby at Kettleness. St Hilda's Abbey on the cliff made an impression.

The rooms had windows looking over the sea. One day some Glasgow friends (the Bottomleys) came to lunch. Pleasant social gathering, but someone looking out of the window espied ships at sea, rapidly passing. 'Destroyers,' said my father, 'and not British ones.' It was a detachment of the German Navy steaming by. This demonstration had something to do with the Fashoda Incident of 1911, when war came very near. Behind the long hot summer, a word used to appear in the papers, repeated by the adults – mobilization, mobilization – thunderous word.

In those days of family holidays, in families of widely differing ages, age-group segregation was unknown. An amiable grown-up brother would assist his little sister with her sandcastles. Intimations of adult thoughts floated down to the younger. One day I paddled with my father for what seemed miles and miles, paddling where the waves broke on the sand, my father discoursing on the theory of wave-mechanics, which he said was a beautiful theory, and I saw in a dim way how beautiful it was that there were all those circles inside the waves.

They intended to spend the winter in Harrogate, but the rooms they liked were not available until October, so the month of September was spent in Ripon, a beautiful autumn with the hips and haws scarlet along the path beside the river where I walked with Hannah. There was a long room with windows on the street in the house where we stayed: in the evening I played bezique with Jimmy, a serial game in which the scores reached hundreds of thousands. What a carefree life at nearly twelve! The only book I remember reading at Ripon is *Lorna Doone*, which was bought at a book shop near the Cathedral (recognized in a memory image on a visit to Ripon sixty-five years later). I think I did drawings with Ruby.

The winter at Harrogate yields no very notable memories. I was passionately keen at this time on a magazine called *Little Folks*, sending entries for its competitions. This was encouraged as being, I suppose, educational. It was discovered with alarm that I had some decay in my teeth (due, it was thought, to the soft Glasgow water when they were forming). There were visits to a dentist at Leeds, and walks on the Stray, and a visit to Fountains Abbey in winter quiet. This made an impression. Also the general 'feel' of the North of England, after the 'feel' of Scotland. Different.

Our next migration, I think in the very early spring, was to a farm-house at Ingleton, Yorkshire, where we stayed for several months. My mother and I were there the whole time, the others came intermittently. My father, with Ruby, was still in the Bearsden lodgings and still working. Nannie was at a training college in Leeds. Jimmy was still at Oxford. I believe that Ruby, or someone, looked up the set books for the Junior Cambridge examination that year and got them, or some of them, for me, with the general idea that my education would thereby be vaguely continuing. I think that this is why I was making an elaborate study of Macaulay's *Lays of Ancient Rome*, sitting by myself in the farm-house parlour, drawing maps of Italy and tracing the places in the poems with intense delight, or passionately declaiming

> Lars Porsena of Clusium
> By the nine gods he swore

to a lamb in the field opposite. I have a snapshot of that lamb standing quite alone in the distance beside a Yorkshire stone wall and looking slightly worried. I never took the Junior Cambridge: I do not think that any development as precise as that was really envisaged.

Ingleton was, I suppose, in the summer a beauty spot frequented by visitors from northern towns, but in the late winter and early spring months of our visit it was perfectly quiet. One of our favourite walks had an entrance labelled 'Scenery: sixpence', but it was untended and one could walk 'up scenery', as we called it, without producing sixpences and without seeing a living soul. And, truly, it was scenery. The path mounted gradually beside a rushing stream, the rocks in which one could reach by leaps and be alone in the midst of waters. Near the top was a waterfall which one could get behind and look out through the falling curtain, as at Niagara. Or in other directions there were stony moors, patterned with stone walls and mysterious with the danger of pot-holes. Or there was the golf course.

The golf course was merely a piece of Yorkshire, roughly laid out in holes, and with a hut for a club-house. I was allowed to accompany my brother there and to follow him round the course, carrying the clubs, even proffering advice as to which should be used, and looking for lost balls. From time to time we would observe Nature in Solitude (for there never seemed to be any other players about). I remember a primrose, newly opened, exquisitely pale and slender. My brother said 'Look', so we looked at it. He was a poet, though his published work was to consist only of one slim, unread volume of *War Lyrics*. I have had the experience of looking at a primrose with a poet in an utterly unpolluted world. That primrose always comes to me with Vaughan's line 'They are all gone into the world of light'.

I am anxious not to read a knowledge of what was to come into these early memories and yet I do not think that I am lying when I say that there were intimations of something looming, a darkness vaguely sensed as one watched him on a putting green in the twilight. Yet there was also marvellous happiness in that as yet untouched world. Bicycling home from the golf course, following Jimmy on my ancient fixed-wheel model (going down hill one simply took one's feet off the pedals and let them whizz round), moments of supreme ecstasy were reached. I never had a new bicycle of my own, only old ones handed down, nor did I ever think of this as a grievance. Nor have I ever in the whole of my long life through the materialistic age owned a car, and this really because I have never wanted one. Surely people could have kept the whole thing at bay, or within bounds, if they had refused to *want* the stuff.

The Ingleton period is clearly dated within the history of the twentieth century as early 1912, for one evening my father arrived with a newspaper. We stood outside near the gate into the lamb's field whilst he told us about the *Titanic* disaster. In view of the kind of news which we were soon to hear and would continue to hear in unbroken crescendo throughout life, the loss of the *Titanic* might seem relatively unimportant, and yet it retains its impressiveness because it was the first piece of Frightful News, the first revelation that the whole rich world of 'modern civiliz- ation' was not so safe as it seemed, that things could go badly wrong. (I have probably read something like this last phrase in histories and memoirs, which I may be repeating, yet it is true. That news did make that impression.) I believe that I realized this, even at the age of twelve, and it fitted with the Intimations. In our family, news about a ship had always a specialist slant. My father explained about the bulkheads, or the lack of bulkheads, in the *Titanic*.

The other thing that happened near the gate into the lamb's

field was that I remember standing there and excitedly telling my mother and Jimmy all about *My Schools and Schoolmasters* by Hugh Miller. I have never seen that book before or since and can only suppose that I found it in the farm parlour. Hugh Miller, so the book said, was a poor Scottish boy, who taught himself to read and write and studied in every moment he could steal from his labouring life, and learned from the Rocks and from Nature. He was his own schools and schoolmasters. Why did I have to read every word in that book with such extraordinary passion? I did not know.

Ingleton must altogether have been some kind of dim and dumb turning-point: the other places at which we subsequently stayed for shorter times, before going to France in the summer, were not so significant.

Why were we wandering about in this curious way? I was too young to be in the family councils; I took everything as it came. But as I write this account the whole thing begins to seem rather extraordinary. I believe that the confusion and apparent aimlessness of the family at this time should be put down to the appointment in Canada which my father did not get. He was, I believe, actually offered it, and had accepted, before we left Glasgow. It was not to start immediately but in about a year's time. I believe that the lease of the Glasgow house came to an end, and rather than renew it for three years when they would be leaving in a year (so they thought) for Canada, my father went into the Bearsden lodgings whilst he finished his Glasgow work, the furniture was stored and we wandered about. Some of us were more stationary – Ruby stayed in Glasgow with Father to finish her art course; Nannie was at her training college; Jimmy was in his last year at Oxford. Mother and I wandered, and where we were was the family centre which the others joined in vacations. I think that my father must have finally learned that he was *not* going to get the Canada appointment some time in the summer of 1912, but decided to go on with the plan of taking a holiday in France before settling somewhere in retirement. This confusion in the family plans (not really their fault) must have been made more disturbing by the imminence of the war, about which my father, in his position, must surely have known.

There had been numerous family holidays in France before, several before I was born and two after I was born. My father was fond of France. He could speak a correct French with an English accent to waiters and when he could afford it he bought a French book. His illustrated Molière is the copy I have always used. So there was nothing unusual in a French family holiday, though this was to be the last one. It was at St Valéry-en-Caux. Jimmy was already there, staying with a French family. The rest of us were in a hotel, though Ruby and I frequently visited the French family to improve our French. There were numerous young German students in the pension. It was a very wet summer, with constant downpours rushing through the cobbled streets. The family persisted in sea-bathing, undeterred by the cold. I suppose that these were the last of the family bathes in the Victorian tradition, which had been the central feature of family summer holidays. I was in a phase of intensive nature study and was keeping an illustrated nature journal. Ruby sketched. One of her watercolours of a French road receding into the distance has considerable atmosphere, evocative of a quiet, empty road, waiting for the next wars.

After St Valéry, the whole family removed to Paris, to a rather dark hotel in the rue des Pyramides. This was to have been the beginning of an educational tour, largely for my benefit. I was to be shown works of art in the Louvre to enlarge my mind, and later we were to go on to Tours, where I would be shown the châteaux of the Loire. Part of this plan was carried out. The *Winged Victory* was seen, and not forgotten, and Ruby and I spent much time in the galleries, passionately and industriously. I wanted intensely to know about Isabella d'Este. The others all saw Fontainebleau, without me. To console me for this deprivation, my father took me to a circus, where an immensely funny clown wrote letters with a fountain pen six feet high. At the end of, I suppose, about a fortnight, Nannie and Jimmy left to go to their first teaching jobs, Nannie to a school in Warwick, Jimmy to St Bees' School, Cumberland. The parents, Ruby and I remained in Paris, but the next part of the educational tour was destined never to take place, for disaster struck the family and I was not to see the châteaux of the Loire until many years later.

The drinking water in Paris was reputed to be bad in those days. My mother, always nervous about such things, wanted us to avoid it, but my father, who was in rather an excited and irritable state that summer (probably retirement, aggravated by the Canada disappointment), insisted on drinking it and urging us to do so. There were some (almost) scenes, and in the end my father was the only one who drank the water. My mother always firmly believed that this was the cause of his illness. At any rate, he began to be ill: at first it was hoped it would pass, but he got rapidly worse. I remember all these things both because I was there and because they were often repeated later in the family saga; but until now, as I write it down, it has not fully struck me what an astonishing story it is. Didn't they have a thermometer with them? Why was it out of the question to call in a French doctor? No, the one idea was to get back to England. I don't know who made the arrangements, Ruby probably, but there we are on the Newhaven boat with a man with a raging temperature, and nowhere to go when we get to England, no house, no home. This was what the migratory life had led to. He was really too ill to make a decision, but at last he said that we should go to Llandrindod Wells. Why Llandrindod Wells of all places? Because, said he, that was where they had spent their honeymoon. My mother, thankful for any decision, closed with that. A terrible night was spent in Newhaven, a terrible journey next day to London, across London, to Llandrindod Wells, a terrible night in an unknown hotel in an unknown town. Finally and at last, Ruby was sent out into the town to find a doctor. A kindly Providence must have been watching over the Yates family, for the doctor she found was to save us.

The doctor was Scottish, with a reassuring Scottish accent. He found lodgings for us and sent for nurses, 'hospital nurses', and this brought home the gravity of the situation. I am amazed, as I write this, that, apparently, no one thought of sending my father to a hospital. If the doctor suggested such an idea, no doubt my mother would have scouted it. Illness in the family in those days meant nursing the patient at home. If the illness was severe, 'hospital nurses' were sent for, but hospitalization was a remote and forbidding thought, and to be avoided. So, eventually, the whole of the house containing the lodgings was rented: the kind Welsh lady who normally let it as several sets of 'apartments' stayed to help; the nurses and patient were installed on one floor.

My father had typhoid fever. There were no antibiotics in those days: the treatment depended mainly on keeping the patient's strength up with constant liquid nourishment. My father nearly died three times. The anxiety was terrible, and I felt it, though I was not told everything. I did not know about the financial situation. On retirement my father had been offered the choice of a lump sum or a pension. After anxious deliberation, they chose the pension. Had he died then, in 1912, the pension would have ceased, and there would have been very little indeed for the support of the family. However, he did not die. His great strength told, though the convalescence was long.

Among the other problems of the period must have been the recurrent one of my education. That this weighed on my mother is shown by the fact that she sent me to a small dame school in Llandrindod Wells, which I attended for part of the time of my father's illness. There were only about seven or eight scholars of widely varying ages in the school. All subjects were taught by one hard-worked lady. We switched from, say, astronomy to English literature by picking up different exercise books. The one hard-worked lady was not stupid, though probably quite unqualified. It was for her that I wrote my first published work, an essay which was printed in the *Glasgow Herald* [in March 1913] through 'influence' (Ruby knew someone on the staff).

My father having recovered, the question of where to settle could no longer be delayed. Never, never again must the family be without a house. Hannah, always clear-headed, suggested a solution. She was teaching (classics) at Birkenhead High School. She had noted that there were numbers of houses available at moderate rents near the school. She found one that she thought might do. Here was a good house, a good school for Frances. It seemed the answer to 'where to settle', at least for a time. Early in 1913, the Yates family moved into 4 Kingsmead Road South, Oxton, Cheshire. A cook and housemaid were engaged, and a period of apparent Victorian-style stability seemed about to set in again, after the migratory period and its anxieties.

I was thirteen and threw myself with deep delight into going to school, having regular lessons, doing homework, and above all, making school friends. Life was expanding, becoming more normal. The pleasant house and garden could accommodate visitors. Oxford friends of Jimmy's, Girton friends of Hannah's, Ruby's Glasgow School of Art friends came to stay. We were an interesting and rising young family, with an assured place in the world and hopeful prospects.

Jimmy had developed into a very remarkable personality. Though his interests were not primarily academic, he had an excellent mind, and wonderful powers of sympathetic understanding of people, people of all kinds. There was a strong poetic strain, blended with religious temperament (as in my father) and great gifts of wit and humour (as in my mother). Yet the outlook on life was profoundly serious and responsible. How can one describe a personality like this? Impossible. When Jimmy was there the world lighted up. When he was gone, a light went out for ever.

One of the wonderful things about the Birkenhead era was the proximity of Wales. Mysterious Welsh mountains were visible from Bidston Hill, not far from our house. Frequent trips were made into Wales. On one of these, in 1913, Cilan was purchased, the little Welsh terrier, named after a promontory on the Lleyn peninsula, who became a valued member of the family. In the summer of the following year, my mother decided to take me for a short Welsh holiday, near a quiet seaside place to which my school friend was going with her family. Some sea-bathing would be good for me. With the zest and insouciance which seemed to characterize the Yates family in those days, we set off for Nevin in North Wales – at the beginning of August 1914.

There was, of course, no wireless or television then, but we read the newspapers. My mother was a great newspaper-reader. Surely rumours must have reached her. Yet the confidence of that confident age was not easily destroyed. We arrived happily at the seaside lodgings: I think we had one bathe. I found a book on the shelves in the sitting-room which looked interesting: *Trilby* by George du Maurier. I had to leave it, unfinished, in the seaside sitting-room – a terrible thing. I never see *Trilby* and its illustrations without remembering – that surge of wild excitement as of a huge wave breaking over the world. War! The newspapers had come to Nevin. We were at war! 'Jimmy will have to go,' said my mother in agony, and I knew that she was right.

We had to get home at once. The seaside station was in a confused state and would give no definite information about trains. Unthinkable to hire a 'motor car' in those days. Moreover, she appeared to have very little money. We hastened along the shore in search of my school friend and her family. They were out at sea – fishing. We signalled and cried desperately but they were too far out on the beautiful summer-holiday sea to heed us. Anguish, horrible excitement and grim foreboding overwhelmed my soul.

I was not able quite to understand this memory until I read recently in R. H. Mottram, *The Twentieth Century*, that on the outbreak of war the banks closed for two days. That was it. The bank was closed. That was why she could not pay for the lodgings until after we had reached home. I suppose she had hoped to borrow money from my friend's father.

How small and trivial an anecdote! Yet significant. The summer holiday, already so reduced as compared with the Victorian tradition, collapses in nervous agony. When the banks reopened, says Mottram, the gold sovereign had disappeared, never to be seen again. Many other things belonging to past golden ages would never be seen again.

II

1925: Claygate

1925, summer I suppose. Father and I were looking for a house near London. In Norwood we found a nice roomy house but it was a dull suburb. We had various other depressing experiences in other suburbs. Christine Ealand (a pious Worthing friend) had told me that there were some nice little places on the Guildford line. So one day Father and I came to Claygate and walked about in a pretty old-world village, saw an empty house in a field near a road, walked down a path near it on to a common, past a pond and a very old house. We got the keys from the builder, named Mitchell, and stood about in the house. We liked the feel of it and of Claygate, the price seemed possible (£1,750, I think), but the house seemed small for our furniture. We went several times and eventually Father took the house. It was Father and I who visited it and Father took it in agreement with me. Mother did not see it until we moved in, Hannah not until the beginning of the Christmas holidays. She was teaching at Ware and came home to the house in snow down Foley Road, saw it amongst the trees, fields and hedges, and thought it was sublime. Ruby was in Africa and did not see the house till 1930.

So it is my father's house, a Yates house: he planted the *cedrus atlanticus*, and he and I moved the pink horse-chestnut tree. With frantic enthusiasm he and I first mowed the lawn with an inadequate machine. The house had been empty for a year, waiting for the Yates family. Only Yateses have lived in it and I have written all my books in it.

Soon after we moved in, Father had one of his feverish attacks. Mother and I were alone in the raw new house and Father very ill. I went to a nearby garage and asked for the name of a doctor, and so made future fast friends, Edwards' Garage and Dr Crabb. There was a feel of ancient history still lingering. Mr Brown who sold toys was a character of the rural past. In Kingston there was a riverside restaurant, served by very ancient waiters, once a centre for boating youths from London. In January there was a fall of snow and the house and its hedges became the immemorial country in winter. It was a delight to us to be in such a place. Down one side of the garden there was an ancient hawthorn hedge – the remains of it are still there – the last field hedge in Claygate. One day there was a fog and we were hidden from the outside world. Ancient country ancestors who lived near Petersfield seemed at hand, people never seen but known from Mother's tales. Here was a place with roots and we put down roots, living very quietly, with no car but within easy reach of London and libraries by the electric trains to Waterloo. I had already become a reader at the British Museum (now the British Library) when working at my thesis in Worthing, but from Claygate it was much easier to get there.

It was my ideal, this, to live protected in some quiet place, free to follow my own thoughts and reading.

I had achieved the London B.A. in Worthing, working on my own, helped in reading by a correspondence course, and going as an external student two days a week to University College. I had also embarked in Worthing on an M.A. thesis on 'The French Social Drama in the Sixteenth Century', working now as an internal student at University College, supervised (but also left to my own devices) by Professors L. M. Brandin and F. Y. Eccles. I finished the thesis in Claygate.

The garden of New House, or 5 Coverts Road, is very beautiful on this June evening of 1981. Throughout all the years since 1925 – years of horror and destruction – it has remained unscathed, possessing something of the immemorial peace of an English garden. There is the garden house, there the weeping willow tree, there the many living greens of leafage, there the little path goes round the house as it has always done. The trains of thought started and nurtured here have drawn unconsciously upon the garden; it has preserved memories, and communicated the strength and stay upholding all creation. I bless and thank it. It has been an essential part of my spiritual history.

1925: English actors

'English Actors in Paris during the Lifetime of Shakespeare', *Review of English Studies*, I, 1925.[2]

This was my first publication (except for the childhood essay in the *Glasgow Herald*). In working for my M.A. thesis I came across a reference to English actors brawling in Paris in 1603. One of them rushed out of a tavern gnawing a leg of mutton. The article achieved the incredible fame of about ten words in the *Times Literary Supplement*, which at that time used to review journal articles. I was said to have thrown 'new and lively light' on the subject.

The family was thrilled at this first venture into high and deep scholarship, signalized by publication in so learned a journal. Hannah and I went specially to London to gaze at the number of the *Review* displayed in the shop window in Museum Street. Mother called the new house into which we had just moved in Claygate 'New House'. People naturally thought that the house was so called because it was in fact new, but that was not the real reason. 'New and lively': my mother thought that exactly fitted me. New and lively things would be done in the new house, standing amidst the fields and hedgerows of the old Claygate.

With such innocence, love, buoyancy, and enthusiasm, I was first floated into the world of scholarship. Fifty-five years later, I am still living in the same New House, in which I have written all my books. My family contributed most, but the old Claygate contributed something to the spurt which started me off. My family are all dead: the old Claygate is now Outer London.

My father, who was a devoted Shakespearean, was interested in this article on actors, which reflects a deep-seated family theatrical inheritance. My father was descended from Shakespearean actors. An engraved portrait of his grandmother as Lady Macbeth, in a small frame made by Father, is on the mantelpiece in the New House dining-room. This engraving is reproduced in the autobiography of the Australian actress Nellie Stewart. Nellie's mother was Theodosia Yates, my grandfather's sister.[3]

1927: French drama and contemporary history

'Some new light on *L'Écossaise* of Antoine de Montchrétien', *Modern Language Review*, XXII, 1927.[4]

Discusses Montchrétien's play on the execution of Mary, Queen of Scots, which gives Elizabeth's point of view in the first two acts and that of Mary and her supporters in the last three. The article uses new material from the State Papers found in the course of preparing my M.A. thesis. It is my first attack on the theme of allusion to contemporary history in Renaissance drama and relates *L'Écossaise* to Pierre Matthieu's *Histoire des derniers troubles de France* (1597). The use of historical sources for literary problems and themes of the French Renaissance is first touched on here.

1929: Florio

'John Florio at the French Embassy', *Modern Language Review*, XXIV, 1929.

Discusses Florio as a modern-language teacher and publishes for the first time documents proving that he was employed at the French Embassy in London. It was the documents I discovered in the Public Record Office which gave me the idea of writing a book on Florio. The article is thus a beginning of the work on Florio which had such important results for my work and life. Florio met Bruno at the French Embassy in London and, through Florio, I too met Bruno.

The article is important for the history of my work but need not be reprinted. All the new documentary material is fully dealt with in *John Florio*; the passages on Bruno are very immature. Unlike the pre-*Bruno* articles on Bruno, there is nothing in this pre-*Florio* article which is not in the book.

1931: John Eliot

'The Importance of John Eliot's *Ortho-epia Gallica*', *Review of English Studies*, VII, 1931.[5]

Discusses the manuals for modern-language teaching published in Elizabethan England by refugee language teachers, particularly Florio, and the satire on them by John Eliot, whose French-English manual borrows from Florio, Hollyband, and others.

This study of the language manuals and of Eliot's satire on them was quite new at the time. The subject was connected with John Florio, the book on whom was already started, and with the problem of whether Shakespeare satirized Florio as the pedantic teacher, Holofernes, in *Love's Labour's Lost*. This problem would be explored in *A Study of Love's Labour's Lost*, to be published in 1936, two years after *John Florio*. These two articles represent work preparatory to these two books, though only one aspect of Florio was dealt with, his activity as a language teacher. Both articles were written at a time when I was myself teaching French, so this interest in modern-language teaching had relevance to my life at the time.

I was much attracted by Eliot's attacks on pedantry, which appealed to the outlook of my sister Hannah and myself. I did not mention, and had no understanding of, Eliot's mentions of

Hermes Trismegistus, Cabala, etc., and of his use of Rabelaisian drinking as a metaphor for Enthusiasm.

Like all students at this time, I had no knowledge of Renaissance thought.

1934: *John Florio*[6]

The work on Florio was begun soon after completing the M.A. thesis (1926) and after we had moved to Claygate, whence easy and cheap journeys to London for work in libraries and in the Public Record Office were possible. There were, however, many social interruptions (visit to Antwerp with my father for naval architecture outings, etc., tennis and badminton playing, young friends in Claygate and so on). After the death of Aunt Minnie in 1930 pure research was funded from a small income (about £150 a year) inherited from her which paid for my journeys, London Library subscription, very small expenses on working visits to London and so on.

I was isolated academically. I had taken my first London degree as an external student, using a correspondence course, and attending a few classes at University College where I was something of an unknown quantity, not a proper internal student, and not fully participating in the life of the college. For the M.A. I was, however, an internal student. Meanwhile I lived at home in these years, first in Worthing whence I journeyed to London for day visits, and then in Claygate. I finished the M.A. in 1926, after we had moved to Claygate.

With the usual Yates intense preoccupation with family cares and the family culture, I did not greatly feel my academic isolation. Professor Louis M. Brandin and Professor F. Y. Eccles took an interest in me and I attended some language courses by J. W. Jeaffreson. But in all this time I did not really have a normal student life, or feel the impress of any academic institution as of importance to me. My ideal was a life of civilized leisure with opportunity for research and thought, for meditation and prayer, for movement towards some unidentifiable goal of creative achievement, perhaps poetic, perhaps some epic poem in which the sense of history and of religion would play a major part. Yet what about earning a living? We were not really well off, living on my father's pension. I was receiving no sort of academic grant; the First Class honours in the B.A. examination which I had achieved – in my external and unattached way – did not automatically bring with it a grant. I worried from time to time about these things and applied for jobs which I did not get. Brandin and Eccles always wrote me very kind testimonials but I suppose that prospective employers took note of the curious gaps in my academic career.

When I received the Honorary Degree of Edinburgh University in July 1969, the speaker of the witty laureation address emphasized kindly what he considered the great originality of my writing and drew attention, firmly, to the gaps. 'The idea that Miss Yates has received an education is difficult to accept. All the evidence tells against it . . . She has played no very conspicuous part in the educational machine . . . Unblushingly, she confesses that from 1926 to 1939 she spent most of her time on private study and writing . . . The record is deplorable . . .' I suppose that Edinburgh professor is saying the kind of thing that Hannah expressed in her dryly humorous way when she said that what had mattered to me were the jobs that I didn't get. Owing to the curious set of circumstances whereby I missed the career bus in early life, I escaped any kind of normal educational formation, had no school tie, was free to follow wherever the lines of my research led me. This outsider position, which left me free, had also the disadvantage of making me for many years rather diffident, unsure of my position – for I had no position until Florio led me to Bruno and Bruno led me to the Warburg Institute.

John Florio had always attracted interest as the teacher of Italian to the Elizabethans, as probably known to Shakespeare, and possibly satirized as Holofernes in *Love's Labour's Lost*. Such studies of Florio as existed were rather slight and fanciful. I set out to discover all that I could about him and to write a new biography, based, largely, on new findings. The life of his father, Michelangelo Florio, a Protestant refugee who taught Italian to Lady Jane Grey and moved in the circle of Edward VI, turned out to be important. New facts were discovered about him, and a journey (with my parents and Hannah) traced his footsteps through the Grisons and through research in Swiss libraries. It was discovered that his son, John, had probably never been in Italy but had returned to England, probably via German Protestant circles, to inherit his father's Protestant patrons, particularly the Earl of Leicester. Florio's teaching methods in his manuals were studied. His interest in words in his dictionary gave a new slant on his translation of Montaigne. New documentary evidence was used to trace Florio's employment at the French Embassy in London.

At the French Embassy Florio met Bruno; this meant a first attempt at investigating Bruno. Florio's later years and other aspects of his career were looked at again and the result was a biography which established Florio's position in England on new lines with much new material.

It also established me on new lines. The book was very widely reviewed. All my friends, and myself, were deeply impressed at the book's having two columns devoted to it by Desmond McCarthy in the *Sunday Times*. David Garnett enjoyed it, J. Dover Wilson greatly approved of it. A. W. Pollard read the manuscript for the Press and wrote to me kindly about it. Altogether it had a great *succès d'estime* both among the educated general public of those times and among specialist English scholars. It was recognized in Italy, with a long review by Mario Praz in *La Stampa*.

Looking through old papers it is interesting to trace the stages by which I emerged from total obscurity in Claygate into the author of a well-known book. G. B. Harrison, it appears, kindly offered to read the manuscript. I cannot remember how I got in touch with Harrison, who, as the well-known author of the *Elizabethan Journals*, would have been quite out of my reach. C. J. Sisson appears also to have been interested in the manuscript; perhaps I knew him slightly through my articles in the *Modern Language Review*. Although Harrison kept the manuscript for nearly a year (I must have finished it by about 1932–3) he ultimately proved the book's best friend. He recommended me to send it to the Cambridge University Press and also advised me about the grant towards publication which the Press demanded.

The tortuous negotiations with the Press are fully documented. I made not a penny from the book. (One did not expect to make money from such books in those days.) The grant was paid off, and the scrupulously rendered accounts, paying me nothing, ceased. A curious sequel to the business side of the book was that the Cambridge Press made over *Florio* to the Octagon Press without consulting me. What upset me chiefly about this was that I had been collecting further information to add in a second edition if this became possible. However, the publication of the book made me known and the British Academy awarded the book the Rose Mary Crawshay Prize. And *Florio* was fundamental for my life and work, for Fritz Saxl of the Warburg Institute read it, and it was through *John Florio* that I eventually joined the Institute.

John Florio has stood up well to the passage of time and is still (in 1980) the standard biography. It is a competent factual biography, using much new material. It belongs to the time in which it was written in the sense that it represents the English scholarship of an age when literary history was often not much interested in the history of ideas, or in a European approach to literature. Yet the book escapes from insularity owing to its Italian subject. The early chapters on Michelangelo Florio break new ground in the history of Italian Protestantism, using something like the methods of Delio Cantimori, then quite unknown to me, whose *Eretici d'Italia* was not yet published. The history of Italian Protestantism, as exemplified by the Florios, father and son, runs through the book and so relates the Elizabethan age – and John Florio's teaching methods in that age – to basic European currents.

I had made a surface acquaintanceship with historical situations and problems with which I have been concerned ever since: the Elizabethan age, what in fact was it? What were the Italian influences on it? What was Giordano Bruno's relationship to the French Embassy? What was the contemporary situation in France? Much of my subsequent work has been concerned with such problems, treated in different ways and at different levels.[7]

1936: *Love's Labour's Lost*

I had hinted in *John Florio* that a new study of Florio and Shakespeare was required. Several of the reviewers took this up and expressed eagerness to read my forthcoming book on this subject. I had therefore to attempt something. I wrote *A Study of Love's Labour's Lost* fairly quickly and sent it to the Cambridge University Press, whose reaction was favourable, but who demanded some revisions. Parts of the book were thought to repeat *John Florio* too closely and an introduction on the history of the text of the play was required.

I produced the textual introduction (which bored me rather and seemed a boring beginning to the book) as necessary for a Shakespeare problem. My chapters of the book were printed more or less as I wrote them, though with some omissions and alterations. One alteration was that the book began with 'Florio' instead of with 'Eliot' as in my manuscript. This seemed rather a pity, since one of the chief points in the book was to introduce John Eliot and his satire on the language teachers as a new ingredient for 'topical allusion' in the play, to be added to Florio, Harvey–Nashe, Chapman and other ingredients.

The original manuscript of my book began as follows:

John Eliot was an Elizabethan, a man of some slight notoriety among a certain set for a short time and then soon completely forgotten. He was born somewhere in Warwickshire, two years before Shakespeare, was educated at Brasenose College, Oxford, and travelled extensively abroad where, being naturally a good linguist, he picked up a knowledge of the tongues as well as much curious information and experience. He had seen the Escorial at Madrid, a palace enriched with great gardens, closes and orchards, and with the rarest fruits that a man can wish. He had seen some Japanese, then very rare visitors to Europe, passing through the streets of Rome on a visit to the Pope in the year 1585, and had overheard their speech, princely, thundering, proud and glorious. His stories were worth listening to, for he was a witty talker and, although not a deep scholar, a well read man in several languages. He had a hearty and heartening enthusiasm for fine writing, fine poetry, fine oratory, being of the opinion that the glory and majesty of man appears in nothing more than his speech, because thereby he shows his reason, the light of his soul and body. Among the classics he venerates Homer who has penned things so profound and admirable, whose verses are flowing, full of art, and reveal infinite graces the more we consider them; Plato, a spirit marvellously pure and profound; Cicero, the quickness and vivacity of whose mind is truly ravishing; Virgil, whose words are so proper, his epithets so fit, his metaphors and figures bestowed so well in their places. Among the moderns, he admires John Bocace, who is so much loved by worldlings; Francis Petrarke, who has invented many trim words and enriched his verses with pretty devices taken out of other authors; Lodovico Ariosto, whose poem called *Mad-Rowland* is so constantly quoted; Torquato Tasso, a fine scholar, who – when Eliot was in Italy – fell mad for love of an Italian lass descended of a great house; Guevara who was secretary to the Spanish Emperor; Clement Marot, the French King's fool; Peter Ronsard, rich in the spoils garnered from Greek and Latin authors, and many others. But his favourite was undoubtedly Francis Rabelais, 'that merry Grig', whose wit he was never tired of quoting. Being naturally rather fond of taverns and company, the cheerful Rabelaisian gospel suited him admirably and he loved to emphasize the importance of frequent libations in the development of a poet's inspiration.

This was cut. I did not protest at this and other alterations, being still in awe of the great. Yet it was the right opening for the book in its lively and humorous use of dialogues intended to be used for teaching French (the'French was in parallel columns to the English) and set the tone for the argument that Eliot, Florio and the refugee language teachers generally figure in some way or are in some way reflected in the jokes about languages and schoolmasters in *Love's Labour's Lost*. Moreover, it illustrates the extremely interesting Rabelaisian side of Eliot's humour. To open a book thus could initiate a theme of inspired language and Rabelaisian wit compared with the uninspired language of pedants. This was the theme that I thought central to the play – that it is about language, and the difference between poets and pedants in their use of language, the songs of Apollo and the words of Mercury, which are harsh after the songs of Apollo. You this way; we that way. This theme became obscured in the detail of the book. For the present-day reader (myself today), it also suffers from deep gaps in knowledge. The author (myself in those days) has little knowledge of what Giordano Bruno is talking about, and seems never to have heard of Hermes Trismegistus.

The best part of the book is at the end, with its daring suggestion that this silly play about four girls and four young men might have some secret bearing on different religious attitudes, different complexions of religious thought. Berowne's love is black, of a dark complexion. The book touches here on something deep.

The reviewers on the whole were pleased with the book. They were trained by Shakespearean scholarship of a certain type to hunt for topical allusions, and the book seemed to afford much sport of that kind. Like its author, they did not know what Bruno was talking about and so were not worried by the gaps.

I regard this book as the worst of my efforts. It failed to develop forcibly and clearly the good points which it glimpsed and it was lamentably ignorant of Renaissance thought and Renaissance magic. This was a serious drawback for tackling the so-called 'School of Night', about which Miss Bradbrook was also writing at the same time.[8]

During these years, when we were so busy looking for topical allusions in Shakespeare, the news was rapidly growing worse and worse. I had seen Mussolini's Blackshirts marching in Florence in

1931 when I was chasing Michelangelo Florio. Now all our lives were punctuated by the severe shocks of Hitler's actions. The years were moving on rapidly towards the Second World War. Refugees were on the move, refugees from Hitler's Germany. In 1937 I was to meet for the first time members of the Warburg Institute, and under their influence my scholarship and publications would take a new turn.

III

The translation of the *Cena*

After *Love's Labour's Lost* was published in 1936, or perhaps even before it was published, I began to make an English translation of Giordano Bruno's *Cena de le ceneri*. Bruno had seemed to me important for the understanding of that play and the issues which it raised. There existed no English translation of *The Ash Wednesday Supper*, with its defence of the Copernican theory. I thought that I could easily make a translation of the book and a neat introduction to it, outlining the history of the Copernican theory, and of its bold defence by Bruno, marking the emergence of 'modern science' from the darkness of the Middle Ages.

The translation was unfinished, the introduction was unpublishable, and I have spent the greater part of my life since in trying to solve the problems raised by these peculiar dialogues between courtiers and pedants in Elizabethan London, illuminated by a Copernican sun.

On 4 July 1936 I took the most unusual course (for me) of writing to the *Times Literary Supplement* stating that I was working on a translation of Bruno's *Cena*. This produced a letter from Dorothea Waley Singer, wife of the well-known historian of science, Charles Singer, who said that she was working on a translation of Bruno's *De l'infinito* and suggested that we should meet in Oxford.[9] We were to meet outside Elliston's, a draper's shop. One day I set out excitedly for this momentous meeting – momentous for my whole life and work.

My family spent part of the summer in a house in Seaford, very near the sea, and there I continued work on the translation of the *Cena*, using Florio's Italian–English dictionary, which I had bought for working on Florio. It was a rough summer; the wind blew, the sea roared, and I became more and more baffled by Giordano Bruno and the *Cena*. The weird text did not seem at all what one would expect from a philosopher bursting out of the

Middle Ages with his enlightened acceptance of Copernicus. Whilst we were at Seaford an invitation arrived from Dorothea Singer to spend a week-end at her house at Par in Cornwall in November. One wondered whether this might be an answer to prayer; Singer, the historian of science, might help.

I went excitedly to Par. There turned out to be a small house party: a professor and his wife, whose names I do not remember, a sad young man, whose name I also do not remember, and Edgar Wind of the Warburg Institute. I had never heard of the Warburg Institute. Edgar Wind seemed to have heard of me, which was very gratifying to an unknown and nervous outsider. He had read *Florio*, and he flatteringly held in his hand one evening a copy of *A Study of Love's Labour's Lost*, which he appeared to be studying.

I suppose I told him about my labours on the Bruno translation, for he invited me to use the library of the Warburg Institute, then in its first home in England, in Thames House. I eagerly availed myself of the opportunity and thenceforth was in touch with the Institute. The Institute's library is designed to present the history of culture as a whole – the history of thought, science, religion, art – and to include in this the history of imagery and symbolism. The library works in association with the photographic collection, which is arranged iconographically. All this was entirely new in this country.

The unpublished Introduction to the *Cena* is a long and peculiar work, partly entirely wrong but with some right instincts, and it introduces themes which I was later to develop into *Giordano Bruno and the Hermetic Tradition* and other works. However, at that time I knew absolutely nothing whatever about the Hermetic tradition and precious little about the Renaissance. I must have written the Introduction before I had begun to learn anything from the Warburg Institute. The main influence upon this Introduction is Duhem's *Système du monde*, which I had studied intensively and from which I derived the general idea that science was medieval and the Renaissance and humanism impeded rather than helped it. The theme of my Introduction to the *Cena* is that the work is directed against the Oxford Protestant academics of the time (called Pedants by Bruno) and constitutes a defence of the Oxford medieval Catholic tradition, represented especially by Roger Bacon. There is a certain truth in this and it was a startling reversal of the then generally accepted idea that Bruno was modern in his Copernicanism, breaking away from the Middle Ages. But the argument is very crude in its equation of Bruno with medieval

'Catholicism'. I had no idea of his Renaissance side. I had glim-
merings of the complexity of the Brunian argument, which I
expressed in the rather crude form of 'Codes', suggesting that he
uses a philosophical code (the Copernican sun, etc.), a political
code (Henri III of France), and a poetic code, to express one and
the same mystical truth. With more knowledge of Renaissance
philosophy and magic, *Giordano Bruno and the Hermetic Tradition* tries to hammer out these things, still, probably, not with
complete success.

When the Cambridge University Press rejected the manuscript,
Edgar Wind poured balm into the wound in a letter in which he
said that he was not surprised, because my approach was too
unfamiliar, as yet, to be understood. This was kind, since he
certainly knew how naive I was. But he evidently thought that
some of the Introduction was worth salvaging, for, with his
advice, I produced for the *Journal* of the Institute 'Giordano
Bruno's Conflict with Oxford' (what the Introduction calls the
'philosophical code'), and later 'The Religious Policy of Giordano
Bruno' (the 'political code', hinted at in the Introduction), and
finally 'The Emblematic Conceit in Giordano Bruno', which
works out the message in terms of poetic imagery.[10]

Thus the Introduction to *La cena de le ceneri* is highly seminal
for my work as a whole, but it is unprintable and unpublishable
because of its crude generalizations and wrong-headed fanaticism.
The early Bruno articles, developed out of the Introduction, are
used in *Giordano Bruno and the Hermetic Tradition*; they also
contain material which is not in the book. But they lack the fuller
understanding, the unifying tone with which the book is able to
bind them together through understanding Bruno and the
Hermetic tradition. Bruno the magus I had not arrived at in these
early studies.

'International Relations in the Sixteenth Century'

Lecture delivered to the British Federation of University Women,
Friday, 5 March 1943.[11]

The British Federation of University Women had awarded me
a small grant towards the expenses of my research, the Marion
Reilly Award mentioned in the Preface to *The French Academies*.
Theirs was the only financial assistance I received in these years,
all applications for research fellowships having failed. I had not
yet officially joined the staff of the Warburg Institute.

1943 was a pretty bad year. One remembers the dreariness of

rigid blackout and rationing, constant danger from bombing (I think that our land-mine in Claygate was this year, though I am not sure); fire-watching and ambulance duties were constant. We had by no means yet won the war; anxious listening to news was a major preoccupation. The question I raised in this lecture was: how will history be written if the Germans win this war? It was a pressing question then.

The talk was a plea for a return to history based on the main European tradition rather than on hysterical nationalism. The screams of Hitler were still reaching us from across the Channel. I quoted from a book published in 1907 (translated from the French) to show that the idea of a return to mythical paganism was already rampant in the early twentieth-century nationalism, out of which Hitler's German variant developed. I quoted Christopher Dawson's view that we ought to be writing new history textbooks now, during the war, so as to be ready for the non-nationalist teaching of history which could begin after the war was over.[12]

I indicated that my own research was moving in this direction and quoted from my recently published articles on Bruno to show how nationalist misunderstanding had distorted the nature of his impact in England. I had in mind *The French Academies of the Sixteenth Century*, then in progress; the work had been begun in the lectures given to the Warburg Institute in 1940.

The lecture on 'International Relations' reflects my own state of mind in 1943. Before it and after, I kept my mind fixed on the *French Academies*, as an expression of the kind of historical writing which I hoped would develop after the war – history in the round, encyclopedic history, the history of symbolism and imagery integrated with general history – in short *Warburgian history* as I had picked it up through informal contacts with the Warburg Institute in the years since 1937.

1947: *The French Academies of the Sixteenth Century*

The genesis of this book was in that rather inferior second book, *A Study of Love's Labour's Lost:*

> Our court shall be a little academe,
> Still and contemplative in living art.

In these words, in that apparently rather ridiculous play, the King urges his courtiers to establish a contemplative academy. The names of the King and courtiers are French. Were there any French mystical academies at the time? Better find out, because the problems of this play were far from being solved. So I started off trying to find out about sixteenth-century French academies. The rather poor book on *Love's Labour's Lost* was germinal for the next stage of my work, and that stage led on to other stages.

There was one book on French academies of the sixteenth century, Fremy, *L'Académie des derniers Valois* (1887), and that I used, looking up every reference. I was now in touch with the Warburg Institute and I had absorbed at least one of its ideas, the encyclopedic idea, that in the Renaissance all subjects connected with one another and were not departmentalized into English literature, French literature, etc. I read Pontus de Tyard, the philosopher of the French Academy of the sixteenth century. His mystical encyclopedism obviously connected with what I had been hearing about Renaissance thought in lectures at the Warburg Institute. I talked to Edgar Wind about Pontus de Tyard and he suggested that I should give four lectures at the Institute on 'The French Academies of the Sixteenth Century'. Immensely stimulated and flattered, I set earnestly to work.

The war had started and Wind had departed for the United States. But in that winter of 1939–40 nothing had as yet happened here. The war was still a 'phoney' war, full of blackouts and restrictions but no bombs. I was to give my four lectures at the Institute in January 1940. The day of the first lecture there was a terrific frost, all electricity broke down, no trains or buses. I managed somehow or other to make my way to the Institute but severe problems of transport had affected the potential audience. It consisted of Gertrud Bing, Fritz Saxl and Enriqueta Frankfort, and perhaps two other people, but it was enough. Saxl asked me to write a book on the French academies, which the Institute would publish.

There followed the war years, the blitz over London, which passed over Claygate every night for weeks, ambulance work, fire-watching, but I was determined that Hitler should not prevent me from writing that book. I went on working at it whenever possible. The Warburg Institute was evacuated to a house called The Lea near Uxbridge. Towards the end of the war I joined the staff and used to spend two nights a week at The Lea, working on the early numbers of the Institute's *Journal* with Rudolf Wittkower. *The French Academies* was progressing and I used to take instalments of it to The Lea to be read by Saxl. After the war the Institute moved back to its then premises in South Kensington,

where I was very hard at work on the *Journal* and other work for
the Institute, and on *The French Academies*. I had to do all the
work on the actual publishing of the book myself. The war had
left us all pretty exhausted. My father had died in 1941, in the
middle of one of the worst raids. Saxl died in 1948, in the midst
of restarting the Institute after the war. *The French Academies of
the Sixteenth Century* was a book which entered the world under
very hard circumstances. I look back to the time of its inception
and writing, notwithstanding all these dangers and difficulties, as
a fortunate time, for I was working and thinking and talking in
close contact with Saxl and Bing and learning something of the
European tradition, living in a wider world of scholarship than I
had known, adding great new riches to my own family traditions
of thought and effort, which remained always with me as the basic
driving force, but were now expanded in a way which suited them
and which I could never have learned in more normal academic
channels in England.

I learned hard. There was at that time, owing to war difficulties,
only one copy available of Jean Seznec's *La Survivance des dieux
antiques*. I was allowed to borrow the one copy, and learned
from it the Warburg approach to mythology and its history – an
absolutely new world to an English-educated person at that time.
I began to learn the use of mythological manuals and to try to
follow the expression of these themes in art. Saxl was writing his
Ruthwell Cross article, which I was allowed to see as it progressed.
Wittkower was writing his Palladio articles in the *Journal*, which
afterwards became his book *Architectural Principles in the Age of
Humanism*. I was consulted and shown such current work by
original and profoundly learned members of the Institute, both
out of kindness, because of my deep interest, and also because I
was supposed to know English and in those days their English
was still pretty German and they needed help in writing in English.
I was not at all good at helping. They used an English vocabulary
far larger than my own, in which they were saying things entirely
new to me, using approaches unfamiliar to an English mind. The
trouble was that, though they used an enormous vocabulary and
were grammatically correct, somehow what they wrote was often
not English – but how to explain why not? Of course my ignorance of German prevented me from being able to help as I should
have done.

In all this effort and exciting intellectual experience, *The French
Academies* went on. As some French reviewers would point out,
it was not a properly organized book on a subject belonging to

French literature. It began with a subject which properly belonged to musicology (then not the kind of discipline that it is today), but it could not be reviewed as musicology, for it went on from poetry and music leading to early opera to discuss speeches in the Academy on moral and philosophical themes and the images which the speakers used, bringing in mythological imagery (already present in the discussion of the musical themes). *The French Academies* was interested in the religious side of the Academies, in the processions and the religious enthusiasm which they fostered. One long chapter was devoted to the expression of the academic ethos in a great French court entertainment of the period, how its musical techniques, imagery and production used all the arts and sciences of the encyclopedia. Another long chapter was on the funeral of Ronsard and the imagery used in the sermon. The philosophical and mystical works of Pontus de Tyard were elaborately expounded as keys to the mentality of the age. Finally the book went on to argue that the Renaissance French academies, which contained the whole encyclopedia and knew how to express it in music, art, rhetoric, or what you will, were broken down in the seventeenth century into specialist academies of literature, art, and so on, thus illustrating the break-up of the European mind into separate disciplines.

The book was an ambitious effort to apply Warburgian modes of work, to use art, music, philosophy, religion for the elucidation of one phenomenon, the French academies of the sixteenth century. I had tried to place this phenomenon against its social background, showing how it was expressed through festival processions and how it was relevant to the religious issues of the time and to the French wars of religion. The book had a number of good reviews, but reviewers on the whole tended to be baffled by the way the book moved round apparently disparate centres of inquiry. The basic theme, that the union of poetry and music was intended to have an effect comparable to that of ancient music, and to solve the problems of the age by uniting Catholics and Protestants in a new harmony, was not fully understood, and nor was the idea that the whole encyclopedia itself constituted a harmony of arts and sciences.

I do not know whether *The French Academies* is a good book. It is a book in the writing of which I myself learned how to try to use a new kind of historical scholarship. I still think that it may be a useful book from which to learn this.

The harsh war-time atmosphere in which it was conceived may have influenced the insistence on the theme of harmony – harmony through the effects of music and through a syncretist religious approach to the harmonizing of religions, and through the harmonizing of all the arts and sciences in the encyclopedia. I lived at one time in the rather absurd expectation that this might come about.

As I said, I had to deal with all the business of the publication of the book. It appeared as Number 15 in the *Studies of the Warburg Institute*, edited by Fritz Saxl. I understand from an old note that the production costs were about £1,000, and that the price was £2 10s. I believe that the edition was very small, perhaps 600 or 800 copies. It was fairly soon sold out and, according to the custom of the Institute, there was no second edition. I had no contract and expected none. I thought that the writing of the book was merely part of my duties, and I esteemed it a great favour to be published under these auspices, as it undoubtedly was. However, I think that it was a pity that the Institute did not reprint its publications. This restricted their diffusion. *The French Academies* has been much used and studied by those who have had access to it, but it is among the least known of my books. There was a reprint by Kraus in 1968. The work was never translated into French.

1959: *The Valois Tapestries*

This book, devoted to the great series of tapestries in the Uffizi Gallery at Florence which depict festivals at the French court, represents the same interest in France and the French Renaissance as *The French Academies*. Both books are largely concerned with the reign of Henri III of France, a reign which had attracted me since the time I was working on the Introduction to Bruno's *La cena* in the 1930s. The deciphering of the meaning of the tapestries was a complicated problem and the book has been likened to a detective story, but it is a story which involves the interpretation of a moment in history through understanding of the tapestries.

1964: *Giordano Bruno and the Hermetic Tradition*

The career of Giordano Bruno, linking Italy, France and England in the Renaissance, remained an ever-present problem to me, and his philosophy, presented in the then standard works about him as that of a modern, or rather a nineteenth-century rationalist breaking out of medieval trammels, was in part incomprehensible. The discovery that one of its sources was to be found in the works attributed to Hermes Trismegistus – seen as an Egyptian sage by Renaissance Neoplatonists – transformed Bruno into a magus, and his mysterious career became that of a missionary of Hermetic reform and philosophy. At the time my book was published this seemed astonishing and incredible, but today when it has become fashionable to look for Hermetic and magical influences in the thought of scientific figures of the Renaissance, it excites no wonder. For me the Bruno problem was transformed and much that had seemed inexplicable in my earlier studies fell into place. I began to see the whole Renaissance in a new light.

1966: *The Art of Memory* and related books

Another field, though related to all my other interests, was the art of memory. In classical times a kind of memory-training was used by Roman orators, using images memorized on places. This method passed through the Middle Ages and the Renaissance – much medieval and Renaissance imagery can be explained through it – and in the seventeenth century it developed into a kind of scientific method. My book on the art of memory drew on Bruno's works and on studies of the Art of the thirteenth-century philosopher, Ramon Lull, which had appeared in 1954 and 1960.[13] By also dealing with 'memory theatres' in sixteenth-century Italy and seventeenth-century England, *The Art of Memory* pointed to the *Theatre of the World* (1969), where Robert Fludd's art of memory is used in greater detail. But the *Theatre of the World* is perhaps more concerned with the Elizabethan magus and mathematician John Dee; his preface to the English translation of Euclid is studied and its possible bearing on the theatre architecture in the age of Elizabeth shown. The interest in Dee carried on into my book *The Rosicrucian Enlightenment* (1972), a study of the German Rosicrucian movement of the early seventeenth century, influenced by Dee, and representing a late stage of the traditions of Renaissance magic. This book has nothing whatever to do with modern occultist movements calling themselves Rosicrucian. It is a purely historical study of a historical movement, a critical attempt to locate it as a phase of transition between the earlier Renaissance and the seventeenth century.

The genesis of *Astraea*

In the nineteen-thirties and forties I belonged to a little literary society called the Elizabethan Literary Society, run by Professor F. S. Boas. Always very kind to me in my early days, Professor Boas asked me to give the Elizabeth Howland Lecture on some aspect of Queen Elizabeth and the poetry of her time. The Elizabeth Howland Lecture had an interesting history. It was founded by Elizabeth Howland, a great admirer of Queen Elizabeth from the religious point of view, and the endowment was originally used to endow a sermon to be preached annually in her honour. The sermon idea had to be discontinued and the very small endowment was taken over by the Elizabethan Literary Society to be used for an annual lecture in honour of Queen Elizabeth, from a literary point of view.

I gave the Elizabeth Howland Lecture on 17 November 1945, at Streatham, for it was under the auspices of both the Elizabethan Literary Society and the Streatham Antiquarian Society. The remuneration provided from the endowment was, I think, £2 10s. The hall was still suffering from the war and tattered blackout. My sister Hannah came, and a then friend of ours called Mary Manton, and of course the members of the Elizabethan Literary Society. I said that I wanted to use slides, which caused some consternation, for it was an absolutely unheard-of thing in those days to use pictures in connection with a talk on poetry (poetic imagery having then absolutely no connection with pictures in the minds of the literary). There was no screen, and the pictures, pale and dim from insufficient darkening of the hall, were reflected on the wall behind my back.

The lecture fell absolutely flat, naturally. It was my first attempt, arrived at with intense excitement, at using a Warburgian visual approach to English literature. I believe that I showed the device of Charles V amongst the slides, with depressing results.

This lecture eventually became, with much more work, the *Journal* article on 'Queen Elizabeth as Astraea'.[14] The *Journal* was very little known amongst English literature students at the time (1947), so the influence of the article in that direction was almost nil. I was not asked to lecture on the theme at the Warburg Institute but when I was asked to give a set of lectures in London University (in 1952) the Astraea theme formed one of them. There was a set of four lectures, beginning with Charles V and the idea of the Empire, followed by the Elizabethan imperial theme, and then a lecture on French monarchy and the imperial idea. These lectures attracted some attention. I used their themes afterwards in seminars with students at the Warburg Institute, and they form roughly the structure of *Astraea: The Imperial Theme in the Sixteenth Century* (1975), a collection of essays, revised and with new material added. The book is concerned with my original interests in Elizabethan England and sixteenth-century France, combined and compared. Or rather, it is concerned with the idea of the monarch in England and France, with the symbolism in which this idea was expressed and with the history of the imperial theme in Europe. 'Queen Elizabeth I as Astraea' dates back to my early initiation into the visual methods of the Warburg Institute; visual imagery used of the Queen is studied in connection with the imagery of the poets, Spenser, Sidney, Shakespeare. Similarly, in the French half of the book the poets of the Pléiade are seen in relation to the imagery of French monarchy. Festivals come to the fore again, English Accession Day tilts, magnificence of chivalry in French court festivals. The volume might even be classified, in the old manner, as English Literature and French Literature, but returned to anew after forty years of immersion in the European Renaissance.

LIST OF THE WRITINGS

OF FRANCES A. YATES

LIST OF THE WRITINGS OF
FRANCES A. YATES

JW(C)I   *Journal of the Warburg (and Courtauld) Institute(s)*
TLS   *Times Literary Supplement*
NYRB   *New York Review of Books*

1913

'Snowpine Country', in *Glasgow Weekly Herald*, 15 March.

1925

'English Actors in Paris during the Lifetime of Shakespeare', in *Review of English Studies*, 1, 392–403.

1927

'Some new Light on "l'Écossaise" of Antoine de Montchrétien', in *Modern Language Review*, 22, 285–97.

1929

'John Florio at the French Embassy', in *Modern Language Review*, 24, 16–36, 328.

1931

'The Importance of John Eliot's *Ortho-epia Gallica*', in *Review of English Studies*, 7, 419–30.

1934

John Florio. The Life of an Italian in Shakespeare's England, Cambridge, 364 pp. (Reprinted, New York, 1968).

'Swithin Wells' [Letter], in *TLS*, 1 November.

1936

A Study of Love's Labour's Lost, Cambridge, vii, 224 pp. (Reprinted, Folcroft, Pa., 1973; Norwood, Pa., 1975; Philadelphia, 1976).

'A Study of Love's Labour's Lost. The Marriage of the 9th Earl of Northumberland', in *Notes & Queries*, 171,31.

[Review]: *Godes peace & the Queenes*, by N. J. O'Conor, in *Review of English Studies*, 12, 86–87.

'Donne & Giordano Bruno' [Letter], in *TLS*, 4 July.

'Harriot & the "School of Night"' [Letter], in *TLS*, 7 November.

1937

'Italian Teachers in Elizabethan England', in *JWI*, 1, 103–16.

'Fulke Greville' [Letter], in *TLS*, 7 August.

1938

[Review]: *Civiltà italiana e civiltà inglese*, by Piero Rebora, in *Italian Studies*, 1, 143–45.

1938/39

'Giordano Bruno's Conflict with Oxford', in *JWI*, 2, 227–42.

1939/40

'The religious Policy of Giordano Bruno', in *JWCI*, 3, 181–207.

1942

'Shakespeare and the Platonic Tradition', in *University of Edinburgh Journal*, 12, 2–11.

1943

'The emblematic Conceit in Giordano Bruno's *De gli eroici furori* and in the Elizabethan sonnet Sequences', in *JWCI*, 6,

101–21. (Reprinted in *England and the Mediterranean Tradition*, Oxford [1945], 81–101.)
'An Italian in Restoration England' [Giovanni Torriano], in *JWCI*, 6, 216–20.
[Review]: *Scots abroad in the fifteenth Century*, by Annie I. Dunlop, in *University Women's Review*, 33, 20.

1944
'Paolo Sarpi's *History of the Council of Trent*', in *JWCI*, 7, 123–43.

1947
The French Academies of the sixteenth Century (Studies of the Warburg Institute, 15*)*, London, xii, 376 pp. (Reprinted, Nendeln, 1968.)
'Queen Elizabeth as Astraea', in *JWCI*, 10, 27–82.

1950
'Le Warburg Institute et les études humanistes', in *Pensée humaniste et tradition chrétienne aux XVe et XVIe siècles*, Paris, 343–47.

1951
'Transformations of Dante's Ugolino', in *JWCI*, 14, 92–117.
'Antoine Caron's Paintings for triumphal Arches', in *JWCI*, 14, 132–34.
'Giordano Bruno: some new Documents', in *Revue internationale de philosophie*, 5, 174–99.
[Review]: *The symbolic Persons in the Masques of Ben Jonson*, by Allan H. Gilbert, in *Review of English Studies*, n.s. 2, 177–79.

1952
Allegorical Portraits of Queen Elizabeth I at Hatfield (Hatfield House Booklet, I), London, 8 pp.

1953
[Review]: *English Miscellany. A Symposium of History, Literature and the Arts*, ed. Mario Praz, 3, in *Comparative Literature*, 5, 282–84.

1954

'The Art of Ramon Lull', in *JWCI*, 17, 115–73.

'Dramatic religious Processions in Paris in the late sixteenth Century', in *Annales musicologiques*, 2, 215–70.

'Poésie et musique dans les "Magnificences" au mariage du Duc de Joyeuse, Paris, 1581', in *Musique et poésie au XVIᵉ siècle*, 241–64. (*Colloques internationaux du Centre national de la recherche scientifique. Sciences humaines*, 5.)

'Considérations de Bruno et de Campanella sur la monarchie française', in *L'art et la pensée de Léonard de Vinci. Communications du Congrès international*, Paris-Algiers, 409–22.

1955

'The Ciceronian Art of Memory', in *Medioevo e Rinascimento. Studi in onore di Bruno Nardi*, Florence, 875–903.

[Review]: 'Michelangelo Florio e le sue "Regole de la lingua thoscana" ', by G. Pellegrini. (Estratto da *Studi di Filologia italiana*, 12), in *Italian Studies*, 10, 78–81.

[Review]: *Italian Scholarship in Renaissance England*, by R. C. Simonini, Jr, in *Comparative Literature*, 7, 281–83.

1956

'Poètes et artistes dans les entrées de Charles IX et de sa reine à Paris en 1571', in *Les Fêtes de la Renaissance*, 1, Paris, 61–84.

[Review]: *La cena de le ceneri*, by Giordano Bruno, ed. G. Aquilecchia, in *Italian Studies*, 11, 146–47.

1957

'Elizabethan Chivalry: the Romance of the Accession Day Tilts', in *JWCI*, 20, 4–25.

1958

[Review]: *L'Illustration de la poésie et du roman français au XVIIᵉ siècle*, by Diane Canivet, in *The Book Collector*, 7, 306–10.

1959

The Valois Tapestries (Studies of the Warburg Institute, 23), London. xx, 150 pp. (2nd ed.: London, 1975).

'Boissard's Costume-Book and two Portraits', in *JWCI*, 22, 365–66.

[Review]: *The Oxford Companion to French Literature*, ed. Sir P. Harvey and J. E. Heseltine, in *The Listener*, 26 February.

1960

'Ramon Lull and John Scotus Erigena', in *JWCI*, 23, 1–44.

'Charles Quint et l'idée d'empire', in *Les Fêtes de la Renaissance*, 2, Paris, 57–97.

'La Teoría Luliana de los elementos', in *Estudios Lulianos*, 3, 237–50; 4, 45–62 and 151–66.

1961

[Review]: *The royal funeral Ceremony in Renaissance France*, by Ralph E. Giesey, in *English Historical Review*, 76, 705–7.

[Review]: *The Quenes Maiesties Passage through the Citie of London to Westminster the day before her Coronation*, ed. James M. Osborn, in *English Historical Review*, 76, 714.

1962

'Ramón Llull y Johannes Scotus Eriugena', in *Estudios Lulianos*, 6, 71–81.

'Religious History in the Valois Tapestries', in *Proceedings of the Huguenot Society of London*, 20, 324–40.

[Review]: *John Florio e il 'Basilikon Doron' di James VI*, by G. Pellegrini, in *Italian Studies*, 17, 68–69.

1964

Giordano Bruno and the Hermetic Tradition, London and Chicago, xiv, 466 pp. (Reprinted in hardback, London, 1977; in paperback, New York, 1969; London, 1971 and 1978; Chicago, 1979; and as *Giordano Bruno e la tradizione ermetica*, Bari, 1969 and 1981.)

'No Man's Land' [Review]: *Eight Philosophers of the Italian Renaissance*, by P. O. Kristeller, in *NYRB*, 19 November.

[Review]: *Engraving in England in the sixteenth and seventeenth Centuries . . .* , 3, by A. M. Hind, Margery Corbett and Michael Norton, in *The Book Collector*, 13, 514–18.

1965

'Giovanni Pico della Mirandola and Magic', in *L'opera e il pensiero di Giovanni Pico della Mirandola nella storia dell'umanesimo, Convegno internazionale, Mirandola, 1963*, Florence, 1, 159–203. (Also distributed at the Congress as a separate publication, 1963. Substantially chap. 5 of *Giordano Bruno and the Hermetic Tradition*.)

'The History of History' [Review]: *Machiavelli and Guicciardini*, by Felix Gilbert; and *Maxims and Reflections of a Renaissance Statesman*, by Francesco Guicciardini, trans. Mario Domandi, in *NYRB*, 25 February.

'The great Erasmus' [Review]: *The Colloquies of Erasmus*, trans. Craig R. Thompson, in *NYRB*, 1 July.

'Renaissance Man' [Review]: *The heroic Frenzies*, by Giordano Bruno, trans. P. E. Memmo, in *NYRB*, 23 December.

[Review]: *The Expulsion of the triumphant Beast*, by Giordano Bruno, trans. with introduction and notes by Arthur D. Imerti; and *The heroic Frenzies*, trans. P. E. Memmo, in *Renaissance News*, 18, 330–33.

[Review]: *Lotta politica e pace religiosa in Francia fra Cinque e Seicento*, by Corrado Vivanti, in *History*, 50, 223–24.

[Review]: *Sermo de passione Domini*, by Flavius Mithridates, ed. and trans. Chaim Wirszubski, in *Journal of Theological Studies*, 16, 534–37.

1966

The Art of Memory, London and Chicago, xv, 400 pp. (Also published in paperback, Harmondsworth, 1969, and Chicago, 1974; and as *L'arte della memoria*, Turin, 1972; *El arte de la memoria*, Madrid, 1974; *L'Art de la mémoire*, Paris, 1975; *Sztuka Pamięci*, Warsaw, 1977).

'New Light on the Globe Theater', in *NYRB*, 26 May (based on a chapter in *The Art of Memory*).

'The magic Christian' [Review]: *Agrippa and the Crisis of Renaissance Thought*, by Charles G. Nauert, Jr; and *Renaissance and Revolution*, by J. A. Mazzeo, in *NYRB*, 3 March.

'Foxe as Propagandist' [Review]: *Foxe's Book of Martyrs*, ed. G. A. Williamson, in *Encounter*, 27, October, 78–86.

[Review]: *Leicester's Triumph*, by R. C. Strong and J. A. van Dorsten, in *English Historical Review*, 81, 387–88.

1967

'The Stage in Robert Fludd's Memory System', in *Shakespeare Studies*, 3, 138–66.

'The allegorical Portraits of Sir John Luttrell', in *Essays in the History of Art presented to Rudolf Wittkower*, London, 149–59.

'Raymond Lull, Bl.', in *New Catholic Encyclopedia*, 8, 1074–76.

'Bruno, Giordano', and 'Hermeticism', in *Encyclopedia of Philosophy*, New York, 405–8 and 489–90.

'The Hermetic Tradition in Renaissance Science', in *Art, Science and History in the Renaissance*, ed. C. S. Singleton, Baltimore, 255–74.

'Paradox and Paradise' [Review]: *The Race of Time*, by Herschel Baker; *Paradoxia epidemica: the Renaissance Tradition of Paradox*, by Rosalie L. Colie; and *The earthly Paradise and the Renaissance Epic*, by A. Bartlett Giamatti, in *NYRB*, 23 February.

'Not a Machiavellian' [Review]: *Machiavelli*, by Giuseppe Prezzolini, trans. G. Savini, in *NYRB*, 15 June.

'Vicissitudes' [Review]: *The Life and Works of Louis Le Roy*, by Werner L. Gundersheimer, in *NYRB*, 24 August.

1968

'Architecture and the Art of Memory', in *Architectural Design*, December, 537–78.

'Bacon's Magic' [Review]: *Francis Bacon: from Magic to Science*, by Paolo Rossi, trans. S. Rabinovitch, in *NYRB*, 29 February.

1969

Theatre of the World, London and Chicago, xiv, 218 pp. (Also published in paperback, Chicago, 1971; and in Japanese, Tokyo, 1978.)

'Bacon and the Menace of English Lit.' [Review]: *Francis Bacon and Renaissance Prose*, by Brian Vickers; and *The eloquent 'I': Style and Self in seventeenth-century Prose*, by Joan Webber, in *NYRB*, 27 March.

'The last Laugh' [Review]: *Rabelais and his World*, by Mikhail Bakhtin, trans. Helene Iswolsky, in *NYRB*, 9 October.

1970

'The old new History' [Review]: *The Idea of perfect History*, by George Huppert, in *NYRB*, 22 October.

1972

The Rosicrucian Enlightenment, London and Boston, xv, 269 pp. (Also published in paperback, St Albans, 1975, and Boulder, 1978; and as *Aufklärung im Zeichen des Rosenkreuzes*, Stuttgart, 1975; *L'illuminismo dei Rosa-Croce*, Turin, 1976; *La Lumière des Rose-Croix*, 1978.)

'Ramón Lull and the Ars Combinatoria' [Review]: *Ramon Lull and Lullism in fourteenth-century France*, by J. N. Hillgarth; and *Quattuor libri principiorum*, by Raymundus Lullus, reprint with introductory note by R. D. F. Pring-Mill, in *TLS*, 2 June.

[Review]: *Religion and the Decline of Magic: Studies in popular Beliefs in sixteenth and seventeenth century England*, by Keith Thomas, in *British Journal for the History of Science*, 6, 213–14.

1973

Introduction to [facsimile] *Recueil de la joyeuse . . . entrée de Charles IX en . . . Paris, 1572*, by Simon Bouquet, Amsterdam and New York.

'Copernicus', in *The Listener*, 15 March.

'The Theatre as moral Emblem', in *Sociology of Literature and Drama*, ed. Elizabeth and Tom Burns, Harmondsworth, 296–303 (from *Theatre of the World*, 162–68).

'Science in its Context' [Review]: *Science, Medicine and Society in the Renaissance. Essays to Honor Walter Pagel*, ed. Allen G. Debus, in *History of Science*, 11, 286–91.

'A great Magus' [Review]: *John Dee: the World of an Elizabethan Magus*, by Peter J. French; 'John Dee e il suo sapere', by Furio Jesi (in *Comunità*, 166); and *The occult Sciences in the Renaissance: A Study in intellectual Patterns*, by Wayne Shumaker, in *NYRB*, 25 January.

'Imperial Mysteries' [Review]: *Rudolf II and his World: a Study in intellectual History 1576–1612*, by R. J. W. Evans, in *New Statesman*, 18 May.

'Underground Routes' [Review]: *The ancient Theology*, by D. P. Walker, in *NYRB*, 4 October.

1974

'Broken Images' [Review]: *The Reformation of Images: Destruction of Art in England, 1535–1660*, by John Phillips, in *NYRB*, 30 May.

'The Idea of universal Empire' [Review]: *The Coronation of Charlemagne*, by Robert Folz, trans. J. E. Anderson, in *TLS*, 1 November.

'Mito e Scienza' [Appreciation]: *Storia d'Italia*, pub. Einaudi, in *Libri Nuovi*, 14.

1975

Astraea. The imperial Theme in the sixteenth Century, London, xvi, 233 pp. (Also published in paperback, Harmondsworth, 1978; as *Astrea. L'idea di Impero nel Cinquecento*, Turin, 1978; and in Japanese, Tokyo, 1982.)

Shakespeare's last Plays: a new Approach, London, xi, 139 pp. (Also published as, in USA, *Majesty and Magic in Shakespeare's last Plays*, Boulder, 1978; *Gli ultimi drammi di Shakespeare*, Turin, 1979; and in Japanese, Tokyo, 1980.)

'Magic in Shakespeare's last Plays', in *Encounter*, 44, April, 14–22 (chapter 4 of *Shakespeare's last Plays*).

[Review]: *Istoria del concilio tridentino* di Paolo Sarpi, seguita dalla *Vita del Padre Paolo* di Fulgenzio Micanzio, ed. Corrado Vivanti, in *Rivista storica italiana*, 87, 575–79.

1976

'Lodovico da Pirano's Memory Treatise', in *Cultural Aspects of the Italian Renaissance. Essays in Honour of Paul Oskar Kristeller*, Manchester and New York, 111–22.

'Magia e scienza nel Rinascimento', in *Magia e scienza nella civiltà umanistica*, ed. C. Vasoli, Bologna, 215–37 (chapters 8 and 9 of the Italian translation of *Giordano Bruno and the Hermetic Tradition*).

'Science, Salvation and the Cabala' [Review]: *The great Instauration: Science, Medicine and Reform 1626-1660*, by Charles Webster, in *NYRB*, 27 May.

'Chivalric Lady' [Review]: *The Order of the Rose: the Life and Ideas of Christine de Pizan*, by Enid McLeod, in *The Listener*, 29 July.

[Reviews]: *The five Senses: Studies in a literary Tradition*, by

Louise Vinge; and *Les Fêtes de la Renaissance*, 3, ed. Jean Jacquot and Elie Konigson, in *Modern Language Review*, 71, 870–73.

'The Mystery of Jean Bodin' [Review]: *Colloquium of the Seven about Secrets of the Sublime (Colloquium heptaplomeres de rerum sublimium arcanis abditis)*, by Jean Bodin, trans. M. L. D. Kuntz, in *NYRB*, 14 October. (Also letter from Frances A. Yates about Professor Kuntz's reply to her review, in *NYRB*, 3 March 1977.)

'Artists and the Spirit of their Age' [Review]: *Princes and Artists: Patronage and Ideology at four Habsburg Courts 1517–1633*, by Hugh Trevor-Roper, in *Times Higher Education Supplement*, 5 November.

'Revivalist' [Review]: *The living Monument: Shakespeare and the Theatre of his Time*, by M. C. Bradbrook, in *New Statesman*, 17 December.

1977

Elizabethan Neoplatonism reconsidered: Spenser and Francesco Giorgi (Society for Renaissance Studies, Occasional Papers, 4), London, 18 pp.

'Did Newton connect his Maths and Alchemy?', in *Times Higher Education Supplement*, 18 March.

'The Image and the Idea' [Review]: *Allegory and the Migration of Symbols*, by Rudolf Wittkower, in *TLS*, 18 March.

'The solar System of Tolerance' [Review]: *The Ash Wednesday Supper (La cena de le ceneri)*, by Giordano Bruno, ed. and trans. E. A. Gosselin and L. S. Lerner, in *TLS*, 3 June.

1978

'The Spirit of Chivalry' [Review]: *The Triumph of Honour*, by Gordon Kipling, in *TLS*, 23 June.

1979

The occult Philosophy in the Elizabethan Age, London, x, 217 pp. (Also published as *Cabbala e occultismo nell'età elisabettiana*, Turin, 1982; and in Spanish and Japanese.)

'Print Culture: the Renaissance' [Review]: *The printing Press as an Agent of Change: Communications and cultural Transformations in early modern Europe*, by Elizabeth L. Eisenstein; and

Man and Nature in the Renaissance, by Allen G. Debus, in *Encounter*, 52, April, 59–64.

'The Fear of the Occult' [Review]: *Symphorien Champier and the Reception of the occultist Tradition in Renaissance France*, by Brian P. Copenhaver, in *NYRB*, 22 November.

[Review]: *The printing Press as an Agent of Change* by Elizabeth L. Eisenstein, in *TLS*, 23 November.

1980

'Architecture and the Art of Memory', in *Architectural Association Quarterly*, 12, 4–13.

'Oracle to the Cock of France' [Review]: *The Prophecies and Enigmas of Nostradamus*, by Michael Nostradamus, trans. and ed. Liberté E. LeVert, in *TLS*, 14 March.

'The new Rabelais' [Review]: *Rabelais*, by M. A. Screech, in *The Guardian*, 14 February.

'A magical Critic' [Review]: *Form and Meaning: Essays on the Renaissance and modern Art*, by Robert Klein, in *NYRB*, 21 February.

'A new Erasmus' [Review]: *Ecstasy and the Praise of Folly*, by M. A. Screech, in *The Guardian*, 7 August.

'Dante's Temple' [Review]: *Dante the Maker*, by William Anderson, in *The Guardian*, 4 December.

1981

'Chapman and Dürer on inspired Melancholy', in *University of Rochester Library Bulletin*, 34, 25–44.

'Renaissance Philosophers in Elizabethan England: John Dee and Giordano Bruno', in *History and Imagination. Essays in Honour of H. R. Trevor-Roper*, London, 104–14.

'Architectural Themes', in *AA Files. Annals of the Architectural Association*, 1, 29–53.

'The Hermetic Tradition in Renaissance Science', in *Natuurwetenschappen van Renaissance tot Darwin*, ed. H. A. M. Snelders and K. van Berkel, The Hague, 55–74. (Reprinted from *Art, Science and History in the Renaissance*.)

[Review]: *The royal Tour of France by Charles IX and Catherine de' Medici: Festivals and Entries 1564–1566*, by Victor E. Graham and W. McAllister Johnson, in *Journal of the Society of Architectural Historians*, 40, 1.

[Review]: *Thomas More 1477–1977* (Colloque international tenu en novembre 1977, Bruxelles), in *Bibliothèque d'Humanisme et Renaissance*, 43, 195–97.

'Learning from the great Architect' [Review]: *The first Moderns. Architects of the eighteenth Century*, by Joseph Rykwert, in *TLS*, 16 January.

'In the Cards' [Review]: *The Game of Tarot from Ferrara to Salt Lake City;* and *Twelve Tarot Games*, both by Michael Dummett, in *NYRB*, 19 February.

'An alchemical Lear' [Review]: *The chemical Theatre*, by Charles Nicholl, in *NYRB*, 19 November.

1982

Collected Essays, I: *Lull and Bruno*, London, xii, 279 pp.

'The occult Philosophy in the Elizabethan Age', in *Humanities in Review: Volume I*, ed. R. Dworkin, K. Miller and R. Sennett, Cambridge, 201–17.

1983

Collected Essays, II: *Renaissance and Reform*, London, xii, 273 pp.

1984

Collected Essays, III: *Ideas and Ideals in the North European Renaissance*, London, xii, 356 pp.

NOTES

Occasional footnotes have been added by the editors, but in general the apparatus has been left as Dame Frances left it. In all footnotes, books in English and French should be understood to have been published in London and Paris respectively, unless contrary indications are given. Details of original place of publication are given at the foot of the first page of each essay.

1 THE ALLEGORICAL PORTRAITS OF SIR JOHN LUTTRELL

1 This well-known picture has frequently been seen at Royal Academy exhibitions; *British Art*, 1934 (*Commemorative Catalogue*, No. 19); *Works of Holbein and other Masters*, 1950–1, catalogue No. 56; *British Portraits*, 1956–7, catalogue No. 18. The picture is discussed in its relation to the Luttrell family in H. C. Maxwell Lyte, *History of Dunster*, 1909, I, pp. 156 ff.
2 Maxwell Lyte, I, p. 159.
3 *Ibid.*, I, p. 166.
4 Information from the Courtauld Institute.
5 See above, pp. 22–30. The Director of the Courtauld Institute kindly allowed his Institute's picture to spend several weeks at the Warburg Institute while I was working on the allegories.
6 On Somerset and his policies, see A. F. Pollard, *England under Protector Somerset* 1900.

7 W. Patten, 'The Expedition into Scotland in 1547', in *Tudor Tracts*, ed. A. F. Pollard, 1903.

8 These movements can be studied in Patten's diary, *Tudor Tracts*, pp. 91 ff. See also J. A. Froude, *History of England*, 1856–70, V, pp. 49 ff.; article Clinton in the *Dictionary of National Biography*.

9 *Tudor Tracts*, p. 121.

10 Thomas Fuller, *Worthies*, ed. Nuttall, 1840, II, p. 277.

11 Maxwell Lyte, *History of Dunster*, I, pp. 142 ff.

12 *Ibid.*, I, p. 155.

13 For an account of the French attack on Boulogne, see the preface to *Calendar of State Papers Foreign, 1547–53*, pp. viii–ix; Froude, *History of England*, V, pp. 220 ff.

14 The text of the Treaty of Boulogne is printed in T. Rymer, *Foedera*, 1713, XV, pp. 211–17.

15 These commissioners are all named in the treaty.

16 R. Grafton, *Chronicle; or History of England*, ed. 1809, II, p. 524.

17 See Paget's letters in *Cal. S.P. Foreign*, vol. cited, pp. 40–5.

18 Rymer, vol. cited, pp. 211–12.

19 P.R.O., E.30/1060 (*Lists and Indexes*, XLIX, p. 92); Rymer, vol. cited, pp. 228–9.

20 Sir Leonard Beckwith.

21 *Acts of the Privy Council*, N.S., III, p. 24.

22 'De officio Magni Admiralli', October 1549, printed in Rymer, vol. cited, pp. 194–200.

23 *Acts of the Privy Council*, vol. cited, p. 29.

24 The description of the visit of the French ambassadors comes from the report about it sent by the Privy Council to Sir John Mason, ambassador in France (briefly calendared in *Cal. S.P. Foreign*, vol. cited, p. 48). There is a copy of the letter in Sir John Mason's letter-book (S.P. 68, 9A, fols. 1–10). Most of it is printed in P. T. Tytler, *England under the reigns of Edward VI and Mary ... illustrated in a series of original letters*, 1839, I, pp. 284–8. See also *Acts of the Privy Council*, vol. cited, pp. 30 ff.

25 F. Saxl and R. Wittkower, *British Art and the Mediterranean*, Oxford, 1948, p. 39.

26 See P. Valeriano, *Hieroglyphica*, ed. Cologne, 1614, p. 44.

27 P.R.O., E.30/1110 and E.30/1111; see *Catalogue of Manuscripts and other objects in the Museum of the Public Record Office*, 1948, p. 13.

28 The Dunster copyist not only left out the crescent on this lady's head; he added a squirrel in her hair! How he could possibly have misunderstood the coils of hair in the original as a squirrel remains a mystery.

29 P.R.O., E.30/1054.

30 P.R.O., E.30/1058.

31 The fact that the allegory is unfinished might support his suggestion; if the artist was connected with the embassy he might have had to leave with it before he had quite finished his painting on the Luttrell portrait. The Three Graces are only roughly sketched in and there are other figures at the back too indistinct to discuss or identify – the apparently flying figure above France and the face above Minerva's shield.

32 See *100 Things to See in the Victoria and Albert Museum*, No. 85; H. Clifford Smith, *Jewellery*, 1908, p. 249 (the Jewel is reproduced in colour in the frontispiece of this book); Peter Stone, 'Baroque Pearls', *Apollo*, LXIX, February 1959, p. 33. There is a companion jewel of a mermaid which is reproduced in Peter Stone's article.

33 Judges 15:14–16.

34 Judges 14:5–6.

35 Many examples could be cited. A notable one is the bronze in the Boston Museum in which Samson rides on the lion, rends its jaws with one hand, and holds the jawbone in the other. See H. Swarzenski, *Monuments of Romanesque Art*, 1954, Pl. 236.

36 Since nothing whatever is known of the origin and early history of the Canning Jewel, anything is possible and nothing could be proved. Could it have been made by a foreign jeweller in England and have belonged to an atmosphere and field of reference similar to that of the Luttrell portrait? The face of the Triton of the Jewel is remarkably like the portrait of Admiral Clinton in the National Portrait Gallery. Suppose that it was made for Clinton, fell later into the clutches of Queen Elizabeth, who used it as a diplomatic gift to an oriental potentate, and after long sojourn in the east was eventually found in India by Canning. It is as good a guess as any other in a field where everything would have to be guesswork. But the companion jewel of a mermaid (illustrated in Peter Stone's article) would have to be taken into account in guesswork about this problem. I wish to thank Miss Yvonne Hackenbroch, of the Metropolitan Museum of Art, New York, who is a specialist on Renaissance jewellery, for valuable consultations about the Jewel. See now her *Renaissance Jewellery*, London, New York, Munich, 1979, p. 240.

37 Maxwell Lyte's interpretation of the picture is worth quotation: 'It is not necessary to suppose that Sir John Luttrell ever suffered actual shipwreck. The year 1550 witnesses the wreck of the English cause in Scotland. Sir John Luttrell, one of its chief representatives, is a prisoner, denuded of all that he values most. He does not, however, give way to unseemly grief. No offer of lucre can turn him from his duty; no danger can break his lofty spirit. In a sea of misfortune he

stands erect. The rainbow of hope appears in the sky and the darkest cloud shows a silver lining. The goddess of peace takes him by the arm and holds forth a sprig of olive symbolical of the treaty concluded between England and Scotland. Behind her stand satellites, ready to restore to the hero all that he has recently lost' (*History of Dunster*, I, pp. 158–9). This may be not far from the truth, except for lack of understanding of the Peace allegory and of the allegorical meaning of Sir John's denudation.

38 In the Dunster version, the corpse in the sea has been turned into an allusion to a dead man in a coffin. George Luttrell may have meant this as an allusion to his own father, Thomas Luttrell, who served in the Scottish wars under his brother Sir John, died in 1571 and was buried at Dunster (see Maxwell Lyte, *History of Dunster*, I, pp. 166–71). Since the face in the coffin in the Dunster version floats just above the rock on which George Luttrell records that it was through Sir John's bequest to his brother (Thomas Luttrell) that the property has come to him, it seems likely that the face in the coffin refers to that brother. It was entirely for family reasons that George Luttrell had the portrait of Sir John Luttrell copied; for the same reasons he might also wish to record in his copy an allusion to Sir John's brother, his own father.

39 Exhibited at the Royal Academy, *Works of Holbein and other Masters*, 1950–1, catalogue No. 54; *British Portraits*, 1956–7, catalogue No. 17.

40 See Maxwell Lyte, *History of Dunster*, I, pp. 146 ff.; and on Wyndham's life and career the article in the *Dictionary of National Biography*.

41 Maxwell Lyte, I, p. 155.

42 *Ibid.*, pp. 161 ff.

43 Lionel Cust, 'The Lumley Inventories', *Walpole Society*, VI, 1918, pp. 23, 25.

44 Lionel Cust, 'The Painter HE, Hans Eworth', *Walpole Society*, II, 1912, p. 19.

45 Cust thought ('The Lumley Inventories', p. 24 note) that it was either the Dunster picture or the picture then at Badmondisfield Hall, now in the Courtauld Institute. The catalogue entry (No. 54) of the *Works of Holbein and other Masters* exhibition assumes that it was probably the Courtauld version that is mentioned in the Lumley Inventory.

It would now seem certain that it was the Courtauld version which was in the Lumley collection in 1590, since the Dunster version is a copy, not made until 1591. Did George Luttrell see the Courtauld version in the Lumley collection about 1590? The picture must have been accessible to his artist when the copy was made in 1591.

Any attempt to trace the later history of the Courtauld picture would presumably have to start with the Bromleys of Badmondisfield Hall, to whom it belonged when Lord Lee bought it in 1932, and work backwards. The ownership of Badmondisfield goes back from the Bromleys to a family called Warner who had inherited it from the Norths of Mildenhall (see A. Page, *History of Suffolk*, Ipswich, 1847, p. 904). The founder of the North family, Sir Edward North, had held important official posts in the time of Edward VI. It is thus possible that the North family might have been interested in acquiring from Lord Lumley the Courtauld picture with its historical associations. However, there is no reason to assume that the Courtauld picture necessarily descended with Badmondisfield Hall to its successive owners and so its history, after its appearance in the Lumley Inventory in 1590, really remains unknown. Since the picture was in such a bad state when Lord Lee acquired it, probably it had been little valued or understood by previous owners.

46 'The Painter HE, Hans Eworth', *Walpole Society*, II, 1912.

47 The three portraits are as follows:

> Of Mr. Edw. Shelley slayne at Mustleborough feilde, drawen by Haunce Eworth.
> Of Haward a Dutch Jueller, drawne for a Maisters prize by his brother Haunce Eworth.
> Of Mary, Duchesse of Northfolke, daughter to the last old Earle of Arundel doone by Haunce Eworth.

See L. Cust, 'The Lumley Inventories', *Walpole Society*, VI, pp. 24, 25, 26; 'The Painter HE', *Walpole Society*, II, pp. 3–4.

It is of course not impossible that Hans Eworth may come into the HE problem in some way, but not in the form of the sweeping statements of Cust.

48 By Roy C. Strong. For the results of this, available only after the present article was in the printer's hands in 1965, see Strong, 'Hans Eworth. A Tudor Artist and his Circle', in the Catalogue of the Hans Eworth exhibition at the City of Leicester Art Gallery and the National Portrait Gallery, London, November 1965 to January 1966; and see also Strong, 'Hans Eworth Reconsidered', *Burlington Magazine*, CVIII, 1966, pp. 225–33.

5 A GREAT MAGUS

1 The catalogue of Dee's library is at present being edited by Julian Roberts and Andrew G. Watson for publication by the Bibliographical Society.

10 ENGLISH ACTORS IN PARIS DURING THE LIFETIME OF SHAKESPEARE

1 *Les comédiens italiens à la cour de France*, 1882, pp. 101–2.
2 *Shakespeare en France sous l'ancien régime*, 1898, pp. 48–53.
3 E. K. Chambers, *The Elizabethan Stage*, Oxford, 1923, II, pp. 292–4.
4 *Recherches sur Molière et sur sa famille*, 1863, p. 153.
5 *Alexandre Hardy et le théâtre français*, 1889, pp. 105 ff.
6 *Journal de Jean Héroard*, ed. E. Soulié and Ed. de Barthélemy, 1868, I, pp. 88, 89, 91, 92.
7 It has been suggested that the head of this troupe of English performers was the Italian player Ganassa, and that his company consisted of Italians, English, and Spaniards – the Spanish players mentioned by L'Estoile in August 1604 being connected with it.
8 *Intermédiaire des chercheurs et des curieux*, I, 1864, p. 85.
9 *Ibid.*, II, 1865, cols. 105–6.
10 P.R.O., State Papers, Foreign, French 49.
11 Montmartre? There is probably a pun intended here on Saint Denis and 'père Denis', i.e. Dionysus.
12 P.R.O., *ibid.*
13 P.R.O., State Papers, Foreign, French 51.
14 *Ibid.*
15 *Op. cit.*, II, p. 280.
16 J. T. Murray, *English Dramatic Companies, 1558–1642*, 1910, I, p. 193; II, pp. 253, 359.

14 THE OLD NEW HISTORY

1 See above, 'Vicissitudes', pp. 134–80.
2 See above, 'Underground Routes', pp. 105–10.

15 THE FEAR OF THE OCCULT

1 See D. P. Walker, *Spiritual and Demonic Magic from Ficino to Campanella*, 1958, pp. 40-43.
2 See Jurgis Baltrušaitis, *Anamorphic Art*, 1977, pp. 61-70.

19 THE LAST LAUGH

1 Quotations from Rabelais in English are from the translation of Jacques Le Clercq.

22 SOME NEW LIGHT ON 'L'ÉCOSSAISE' OF ANTOINE DE MONTCHRÉTIEN

1 Sir Ralph Winwood, *Memorials of Affairs of State in the Reigns of Queen Elizabeth and King James I*, 1725, I, p. 398.
2 Published in the *Revue d'histoire littéraire de la France*, IV, 1897, pp. 89-91.
3 P.R.O., State Papers, Foreign, French 51.
4 E. Rigal, *Le théâtre français avant la période classique*, 1901, p. 50.
5 G. Lanson, 'Études sur les origines de la tragédie classique en France', *Revue d'histoire littéraire de la France*, X, 1903, pp. 177-231, 413-36.
6 *Documents concernant la Normandie* (extracts from *Le Mercure François*), ed. A. Héron, 1883, p. 188.
7 The passage in the *Mercure* was written by a political enemy of Montchrétien and is very likely to be unjust and unreliable. Théophile Funck-Brentano, in his introduction to Montchrétien's *Traicté de l'œconomie politique*, 1889, p. xii, note i, finds the story of the dedication of *L'Écossaise* to James I difficult to believe.
8 G. Lanson, 'Les sources historiques de la "Reine D'Escosse"', *Revue universitaire*, XIV, 1905, p. 395.
9 Ed. G. Michaut, 1905, ll. 389-91.
10 *Ed. cit.*, ll. 47-54.
11 Curiously enough this 'M. de Believre', sent by Henri III to remonstrate with Elizabeth on her treatment of the Queen of Scots, is the same Pompone de Bellièvre who later, as Chancellor, took proceedings against the players for the 'lewde Indiscretion' of performing *L'Écossaise*.
12 *Ed. cit.*, ll. 189-90.
13 *Ed. cit.*, ll. 1385-8.
14 Montchrétien uses a few details not given by Matthieu; he introduces,

for instance, the character of Davison who announces the death sentence to Mary at the beginning of Act III. Davison is not mentioned in the *Histoire des derniers troubles*. The latter was therefore Montchrétien's chief, but not quite his only source.

15 P.R.O., State Papers, Foreign, French 56. The Matthieu incident is related in the following (unpublished) letters: Salisbury to Edmondes, 16 October 1610 and 27 October 1610; Edmondes to Salisbury, 2 and 3 November 1610.

16 See E. K. Chambers, *The Elizabethan Stage*, Oxford, 1923, I, pp. 322–8.

17 *Ed. cit.*, ll. 1539–610.

18 *Ed. cit.*, ll. 1242–4.

19 P.-F. Godart de Beauchamps, *Recherches sur les théâtres de France*, 1735, II, pp. 10–11.

20 *Bibliothèque dramatique de M. de Soleinne*, Catalogue rédigé par P. L. Jacob, bibliophile (Paul Lacroix), 1843–5, No. 920.

26 ARTISTS AND THE SPIRIT OF THEIR AGE

1 'Rubens's *Arch of the Mint*', in *Journal of the Warburg and Courtauld Institutes*, XXXVII, 1974, pp. 191–217.

29 THE HERMETIC TRADITION IN RENAISSANCE SCIENCE

1 W. P. D. Wightman, *Science and the Renaissance*, Aberdeen, 1962, I, p. 16.

2 *Ibid.*, p. 34.

3 The fundamental bibliographical study of Ficino's translation of the *Corpus Hermeticum* and its diffusion is P. O. Kristeller's *Supplementum Ficinianum*, Florence, 1937, I, pp. lvii–lviii, cxxix–cxxxi; see also Kristeller's *Studies in Renaissance Thought and Letters*, Rome, 1956, pp. 221 ff. The Hermetic movement is studied by E. Garin in his *Medioevo e Rinascimento*, Bari, 1954, pp. 150 ff., and in his *La cultura filosofica del Rinascimento italiano*, Florence, 1961. The volume *Testi umanistici su l'ermetismo*, ed. by E. Garin, Rome, 1955, publishes some Renaissance texts containing Hermetic influence. The importance of the *prisca theologia* tradition in establishing Hermetic influence in the Renaissance is brought out by D. P. Walker in his article 'The *Prisca Theologia* in France', *Journal of the Warburg and Courtauld Institutes*, XVII, 1954, pp. 204–59, now reprinted in his

book *The Ancient Theology*, 1972. Walker's book *Spiritual and Demonic Magic from Ficino to Campanella*, 1958, analyses Renaissance magic particularly in relation to Ficino. In the first ten chapters of my book *Giordano Bruno and the Hermetic Tradition*, 1964, I have endeavoured to give an outline of the Hermetic tradition in the Renaissance before Bruno.

The best modern edition of the *Corpus Hermeticum* and the *Asclepius* is that by A. D. Nock and A.-J. Festugière, with French translation, Paris, 1945 and 1954.

4 *Corpus Hermeticum*, ed. Nock and Festugière, I, pp. 7–19. A précis of this work is given in my *Giordano Bruno and the Hermetic Tradition*, pp. 22–5.

5 In the *Argumentum* before his Latin translation of the *Corpus Hermeticum* (*Opera omnia*, Basel, 1576, pp. 1837–9). Ficino gave his translation the collective title of *Pimander*, though this is really the title of only the first treatise.

6 *Corpus Hermeticum*, ed. Nock and Festugière, II, pp. 296–355. Précis in Yates, *Giordano Bruno and the Hermetic Tradition*, pp. 35–40.

7 As demonstrated by Walker, *Spiritual and Demonic Magic*, pp. 40 ff.

8 On Pico's yoking together of Magia and Cabala, see Yates, *op. cit.*, pp. 84 ff.

9 H. C. Agrippa, *De occulta philosophia* (1533); see Yates, *op. cit.*, pp. 130 ff.

10 The *Picatrix* is a treatise on talismanic magic, originally written in Arabic, a Latin translation of which circulated in the Renaissance in manuscript.

11 Tommaso Campanella, *Magia e grazia*, ed. R. Amerio, Rome, 1957, p. 180; see Yates, *op. cit.*, pp. 147–8.

12 See Lily B. Campbell, *Scenes and Machines of the English Stage during the Renaissance*, Cambridge, 1923, p. 87.

13 H. Billingsley, *The Elements of Euclid*, London, 1570. Dee's preface, sig. Ai^v, now reprinted in facsimile with an introduction by Allen G. Debus, New York, 1975.

14 Walker, *Spiritual and Demonic Magic*, pp. 126–7.

15 Fabio Paolini, *Hebdomades*, Venice, 1589, p. 208. See also Agrippa's listing of the 'speaking statues of Mercurius' among mechanical marvels, quoted in Yates, *op. cit.*, p. 147; and Dee's citation of the works of Hero followed by mentions of the brazen head made by Albertus Magnus and of the 'Images of Mercurie' (preface to the Euclid, sigs. Ai^{r-v}).

16 Paolini, *Hebdomades*, p. 203, quoted in Walker, *Spiritual and Demonic Magic*, p. 135, n. 1.

17 Eugenio Garin, *Scienza e vita civile nel Rinascimento italiano*, Bari, 1965, pp. 57–108.

18 *Ibid.*, p. 71. See also Garin's *Cultura filosofica del Rinascimento italiano*, pp. 397 ff., for a similar approach to Leonardo.

19 *Late Tudor and Early Stuart Geography*, 1934, pp. 75 ff.

20 *Astronomical Thought in Renaissance England*, Baltimore, 1937, pp. 135 ff.

21 I. R. F. Calder, 'John Dee Studied as an English Neoplatonist' (Ph.D. thesis, University of London, 1952).

22 Dee's preface to the Euclid, sig. *i^v. See Yates, *op. cit.*, p. 148; also my note in *L'Opera e il pensiero di Giovanni Pico della Mirandola nella storia dell'umanesimo* (Convegno internazionale, Mirandola 15–18 settembre 1963), Istituto Nazionale di Studi sul Rinascimento, Florence, 1965, I, pp. 152–4.

23 'Thynges Mathematicall', he says in the preface (sig. *^{v}), are 'middle betwene thinges supernaturall and naturall.'

24 Dee's preface to the Euclid, sig. Aii^r.

25 *Fama Fraternitas, dess Löblichen Ordens des Rosencreutzes etc.*, Cassel, 1614. See Yates, *Giordano Bruno and the Hermetic Tradition*, pp. 410–11.

26 See Yates, *op. cit.*, pp. 370 ff.

27 J. V. Andreae, *Reipublicae christianopolitanae descriptio*, Strasbourg, 1619; English translation by F. E. Held, *Christianopolis, an Ideal State of the Seventeenth Century*, New York, 1916. Andreae was the author of the *Chemical Wedding of Christian Rosencreutz (Chymische Hochzeit Christiani Rosencreutz)*, Strasbourg, 1616.

28 English translation published by Routledge and Kegan Paul, London, 1968.

29 See F. Bacon, *Historia naturalis et experimentalis, quae est Instaurationis magnae pars tertia*, London, 1622, in the *Works*, ed. Spedding et al., 1857 edition, II, pp. 13–16. Bacon constantly repeats the statement that it was not his pure and direct knowledge of nature which caused Adam's fall, but his proud judging of good and evil: see *Advancement of Learning, ibid.*, III, pp. 264–5; *Instauratio magna, praefatio, ibid.*, I, p. 132, etc. See Rossi, *Francesco Bacone*, pp. 321 ff., 392 ff., etc.

30 See *De occulta philosophia*, III, p. 40; and see C. G. Nauert, *Agrippa and the Crisis of Renaissance Thought*, Urbana, Illinois, 1965, pp. 48, 284. Nauert in this book makes interesting comparisons between Agrippa's theory of the magus as possessing power through his magical knowledge and Bacon's promises that man will be lord and

master of nature; but he does not know of Rossi's book with its analysis of the difference between the outlook of the magus and that of Bacon.

31 See Yates, *Giordano Bruno and the Hermetic Tradition*, pp. 241–3.

32 *Historia naturalis; Works*, ed. Spedding et al., II, p. 13.

33 G. Porta, *Natural Magick*, ed. D. J. Price, New York, 1957 (reprint of the English translation of Porta's *Magia naturalis*), pp. 10, 14, etc. As is well known, this book was the source of a large part of Bacon's *Sylva sylvarum*.

34 G. Bruno, *Cena de le ceneri*, dialogue III; see G. Bruno, *Dialoghi italiani*, ed. G. Aquilecchia, Florence, 1957, p. 109.

35 Against the 'monstrous' opinion of Aristotle that the earth is dead and inanimate, Gilbert cites 'Hermes, Zoroaster, Orpheus', who recognize a universal life; see W. Gilbert, *On the Magnet*, ed. D. J. Price, New York, 1958, p. 209. E. Zilsel, 'The origins of William Gilbert's scientific method', *Journal of the History of Ideas*, II, 1941, pp. 4 ff., emphasizes that Gilbert's philosophy of magnetism is animistic and belongs to the same current as that of Bruno.

36 Marie Boas, 'Bacon and Gilbert', *Journal of the History of Ideas*, XII, 1951, pp. 466–7, has suggested that it was primarily Gilbert's expansion of his work on the magnet into a magnetic philosophy of nature to which Bacon took exception, having studied these ideas, not only in *De magnete*, but perhaps primarily in Gilbert's posthumous work, *De mundo nostro sublunari philosophia nova*.

37 On survivals in Newton, see J. E. McGuire and P. M. Rattansi, 'Newton and the Pipes of Pan', *Notes and Records of the Royal Society of London*, XXI, 1966, pp. 108–43; on survivals in Galileo, see Garin, *Scienza e vita civile nel Rinascimento*, p. 157.

38 In *Isis*, LV, 1964, pp. 389–91.

39 See also the many observations in Allen G. Debus's book *The English Paracelsians*, 1965, confirming the connections between Renaissance magic and Neoplatonism and the rise of science.

40 In *Isis*, LV, p. 390, quoting *Giordano Bruno and the Hermetic Tradition*, p. 452.

AUTOBIOGRAPHICAL FRAGMENTS

1 Frances Yates's father, James Alfred Yates (12 July 1852–4 May 1941) married Hannah Eliza Malpas in 1884. He served successively as Constructor at Chatham, Acting Chief Constructor at Devonport, Chief Constructor at Chatham, then at Portsmouth (1895–1902), Civil Assistant to the Admiral Superintendent at Chatham (1902–6),

and Senior Constructive Officer on the Clyde and at Barrow (1906–12). He retired at the age of sixty in 1912 but was recalled to the Admiralty for special duties in 1916–18. His key role in relation to Admiral Sir John Fisher's shipbuilding programme comes out in the article (which incorporates some of his memoirs) edited by his daughter Ruby W. Yates, 'From Wooden Walls to Dreadnoughts in a Lifetime', *The Mariner's Mirror*, XLVIII, 1962, pp. 291–303.

2 Reprinted in this volume.

3 From notes left by Frances and Ruby Yates it appears that their great-grandfather, Thomas Yates, an actor, married (in 1802) Mary Ann Croshaw and that Mrs Yates had a fairly successful career on the stage. The couple had three children, two daughters and one son, James, Frances Yates's grandfather. James joined the Royal Navy but never rose above the rank of warrant officer. After his retirement he settled in Portsmouth. His sisters went onto the stage. Theodosia was successful in Australia in many plays and operas. Her singing is mentioned in a novel about early life in Sydney, *A House is Built*, by M. Barnard Eldershaw, 1929. The book mentioned in the text is Nellie Stewart, *My Life's Story*, Sydney, 1923.

4 Reprinted in this volume.

5 Not reprinted, because, like the preceding article (1929), it is substantially incorporated in *John Florio*.

6 The next few pages, on *John Florio*, were headed by Frances Yates: 'July 18, 1980. Preliminary rough summing up of remembrances of past time in relation to the writing and publication of *John Florio*.'

7 The last paragraph is taken from some notes made by Frances Yates in 1975 on her books.

8 See Muriel Bradbrook, *The School of Night*, Cambridge, 1936.

9 This letter from Mrs Singer is dated 15 July 1936. Frances Yates visited Par in November of that year (see below).

10 These three articles, published between 1938 and 1943, are reprinted in *Collected Essays*, I, pp. 134–209.

11 Frances Yates adds: 'The miserable state of the manuscript of this lecture, crumpled and almost illegible, bears witness to the stress of the times in which it was delivered.'

12 The books referred to (as one can see from the manuscript of the lecture) are H. de Tourville, *The Growth of Modern Nations: a history of the particularist form of society*, 1907, and Christopher Dawson, *The Making of Europe*, 1932.

13 See *Collected Essays*, I, pp. 9–125.

14 *Journal of the Warburg and Courtauld Institutes*, X, 1947, pp. 27–82.

INDEX

Conduitt, John, 120
Confrérie de la Passion, 84–6
Constantine, Emperor, 30, 31, 33, 34, 37, 165
Conti, Natale, 96
Copenhaver, Brian P., 120–8
Copernicus, Nicolas, and Copernicanism, 50, 63, 127, 146, 239–40, 256–61; *see also* Bruno, Giordano
Corpus Hermeticum, see Hermetic texts
Counter-Reformation, 44, 212–13, 215, 217
Court entertainments, French, 99, 144, 318, 322
Cranmer, Thomas, 43
Crato, Johannes, 215
Cromwell, Oliver, 254
Cusanus, *see* Nicolas of Cusa

Dante, 31–2, 34, 186–7, 199, 208
Darwin, Charles, 127
Davison, William, 344 n. 14
Dawson, Christopher, 315, 348 n. 12
Debus, Allen, G., 185 n., 187, 191–2, 243–4, 347 n. 39
Dee, John, 49–57, 216–19, 320; and Agrippa and Pico, 51, 54, 56, 234, 236; compared with Bacon, 49, 54, 63–4, 233–4, 241; influence and reputation, 50–5, 56, 59, 77, 126, 212, 217–19, 241, 271, 272; magus, 50–1, 53, 54, 56, 126, 189, 216, 217–18, 231, 236, 241, 246, 271; mathematician and scientist, 49–51, 53, 54, 63, 231, 233–4, 236, 241, 246, 271; philosopher and scholar, 52, 53, 55–7, 218; in Prague, 57, 211, 216, 217–19; religion, 54, 56, 57, 217–19; *Monas hieroglyphica*, 53, 54,

56–7, 76, 192, 212, 271; Preface to Euclid, 49–51, 53, 55, 63–4, 231, 233, 236, 320, 345 n. 15; *Spiritual Diaries*, 50, 52, 59
Del Rio, Martin, 264
Descartes, 108, 110, 127, 243
Diderot, Denis, 119
Dolce, Ludovico, 196
Donne, John, 69, 71, 73, 76, 206
Drake, Francis, 33
Drama, French, 85, 95, 169–82
Druids, 116, 117, 118
Duhem, Pierre, 313
Dunster Castle, Luttrell portrait, 3–23, Plates 1, 3A
Dury, John, 248, 254

Eccles, F. Y., 303, 306, 307
Education, 248–9
Edward VI, King of England, 6, 8 ff., 38, 43
Effigies, 164–6
Egypt, Egyptians, 106–7, 114, 117, 118, 123, 127, 136, 229, 231, 232, 244, 257–9
Eisenstein, Elizabeth L., 185–9
Electors Palatine, *see* Charles Louis; Frederick V
Eliot, John, 305, 309–11
Eliot, T. S., 35
Elizabeth I, Queen of England, 29 ff., 38, 45, 52, 54, 139, 145, 174–8, 211; cult, 26, 33–4, 36–8, 45–6, 48, 55–6, 57, 80–2, 102, 116, 322
Elizabeth, Princess, *see* Elizabeth Stuart
Elizabeth Stuart, Queen of Bohemia, 80, 254
Elyot, Thomas, 202
Emblems, 100, 101
Encyclopedias, encyclopedism, 119, 120, 186, 316, 318–19
Erasmus, Erasmian influences, 155–8, 210, 212, 221–6; *Colloquies*,

158, 221–6; *Praise of Folly*, 155
Essex, Earl of, 79
Euclid, Dee's Preface, *see* Dee, John
Eusebius, 29, 31, 36, 37, 165, 203
Evangelical reform, 125, 155–8, 160, 222–3, 266
Evans, R. J. W., 214–19
Eworth, Hans, 20–1, 341 n. 47
Exemplarism, 202–4

Fall of Man, *see* Adam
Family of Love, 215
Fathers of the Church, 154, 222, 257
Faust, 191, 263
Febvre, Lucien, 156, 162
Fénelon, F. de Salignac de la Mothe, 110
Festivals, 24, 26, 81, 200, 322
Festugière, A.-J., 58, 106–7, 257
Ficino, Marsilio, 25, 133, 190, 227–30; astral medicine, 121, 124, 125, 235, 237; and Hermetic texts, 58, 196, 228–30, 244, 257, 258–9, 264, 344–5 n. 3, 345 n. 5; influence (*see also* Agrippa), 197, 198, 230, 231–2, 233, 244, 258, 261, 268; in France, 118, 122, 123, 135; and magic, 51, 58, 106, 108, 110, 121, 123, 188, 199, 228–30, 258–9; timidity, 124, 230, 235, 263; *De vita coelitus comparanda*, 229, 259, 261, 264
Fisher, John, 36
Florio, John, 205, 307–9, 311
Florio, Michelangelo, 307, 309, 311
Fludd, Robert, 57, 58, 64, 65, 71, 101, 126, 191, 244, 320
Fohi, 109
Fontainebleau, 87–8
Fontenelle, Bernard le Bovier de, 120–1
Foxe, John, 28–39, 203